# MIGRATION AND DEMOCRACY

# Migration and Democracy

## HOW REMITTANCES UNDERMINE DICTATORSHIPS

ABEL ESCRIBÀ-FOLCH

COVADONGA MESEGUER

JOSEPH WRIGHT

PRINCETON UNIVERSITY PRESS

PRINCETON AND OXFORD

Published by Princeton University Press
41 William Street, Princeton, New Jersey 08540
6 Oxford Street, Woodstock, Oxfordshire OX20 1TR

press.princeton.edu

Library of Congress Cataloging-in-Publication Data
Names: Escribá-Folch, Abel, author. | Meseguer Yebra, Covadonga, author. | Wright, Joseph (Joseph George), 1976– author.
Title: Migration and democracy : how remittances undermine dictatorships / Abel Escribá-Folch, Covadonga Meseguer, Joseph Wright.
Description: Princeton, New Jersey : Princeton University Press, 2022. | Includes bibliographical references and index.
Identifiers: LCCN 2021013537 (print) | LCCN 2021013538 (ebook) | ISBN 9780691199382 (hardback) | ISBN 9780691199375 (paperback) | ISBN 9780691223056 (ebook)
Subjects: LCSH: Emigration and immigration—Political aspects. | Emigration and immigration—Economic aspects. | Emigrant remittances—Political aspects. | Democratization—Economic aspects. | Dictatorship. | BISAC: POLITICAL SCIENCE / Public Policy / Immigration | POLITICAL SCIENCE / Comparative Politics
Classification: LCC JV6255 .E74 2021 (print) | LCC JV6255 (ebook) | DDC 332/.04246—dc23
LC record available at https://lccn.loc.gov/2021013537
LC ebook record available at https://lccn.loc.gov/2021013538

British Library Cataloging-in-Publication Data is available

Editorial: Bridget Flannery-McCoy and Alena Chekanov
Production Editorial: Natalie Baan
Cover Design: Karl Spurzem
Production: Erin Suydam
Publicity: Kate Hensley and Kathryn Stevens
Copyeditor: Francis Eaves

This book has been composed in Arno

10 9 8 7 6 5 4 3 2 1

# CONTENTS

*List of Illustrations and Tables*   ix

*Preface*   xi

*Acknowledgements*   xv

1  Introduction                                                                        1
  1.1  *Globalization, Migration, and Political Change*                     7
    1.1.1  Existing Theories: Migration and Democracy            9
    1.1.2  Foreign Income Inflows and Autocratic Rule            13
    1.1.3  Remittances in the Global South                       17
  1.2  *Previewing the Argument*                                            18
  1.3  *Plan of the Book*                                                   23

2  Migration and Repertoires of Contention: How Remittances
   Undermine Dictatorship                                              26
  2.1  *Citizens as Agents of Change*                                       29
  2.2  *Global Forces and Democratization*                                  33
    2.2.1  How International Forces Shape
        Authoritarian Survival                                   35
    2.2.2  Remittances as a Global Force for Bottom-Up
        Democratization                                         37
  2.3  *Remittances and Democratization: What Comes*
     *after Exit?*                                                  38
    2.3.1  Remittances Sustain Dictatorship: Repression,
        Patronage, and Grievance                                 42
    2.3.2  How Exit Funds Voice and Weakens Loyalty              45
  2.4  *Refining the Theoretical Mechanisms: Political*
     *Preferences and Poverty*                                      56
    2.4.1  Protest                                                57
    2.4.2  Voting                                                 59

v

|  | 2.4.3 | Political Context and Political Behavior | 62 |
| 2.5 | | *Conclusion* | 64 |

3 Remittances, Revenue, and Government Spending
in Dictatorships — 66
| 3.1 | | *Remittances, State Resources, and Authoritarian Stability* | 71 |
| | 3.1.1 | The Revenue Effect | 72 |
| | 3.1.2 | The Substitution Effect | 73 |
| | 3.1.3 | Taxation and the Demand for Democracy | 77 |
| 3.2 | | *Do Remittances Increase Government Revenue in Dictatorships?* | 78 |
| 3.3 | | *Remittances and Government Spending* | 81 |
| | 3.3.1 | Government Health Spending and Military Spending | 83 |
| | 3.3.2 | Do Remittances Boost Petrol Subsidies? | 85 |
| 3.4 | | *Remittances and Repression* | 88 |
| | 3.4.1 | Do Remittances Enhance Violent Repression in Dictatorships? | 90 |
| | 3.4.2 | Do Remittances Harm Civil Liberties and Political Rights? | 92 |
| 3.5 | | *Conclusion* | 95 |

4 Remittances Fund Opponents — 97
| 4.1 | | *Remitted Income and the Global Rise in Protest* | 100 |
| | 4.1.1 | Anti-Government Protest | 100 |
| | 4.1.2 | Pro-Government Mobilization | 104 |
| 4.2 | | *How Remittances Boost Protests* | 108 |
| | 4.2.1 | Capturing Political Preferences: Opposition and Regime Strongholds | 113 |
| | 4.2.2 | Testing the Micro-Logic Linking Remittances to Protest | 119 |
| | 4.2.3 | Remittances, Poverty, and Protest | 126 |
| 4.3 | | *Conclusion* | 130 |
| 4.4 | | *Appendix: Measuring Pro-Government Areas* | 131 |
| | 4.4.1 | Vote Choice and Non-Response | 132 |
| | 4.4.2 | External Validity | 134 |

5 Remittances Demobilize Supporters — 136
| 5.1 | | *Remittances and the Electoral Fate of Ruling Parties* | 138 |
| | 5.1.1 | Ruling Party Vote Share | 142 |
| | 5.1.2 | The Turnout Contest | 144 |

5.2   How Remittances Cut Clientelistic Ties to the Ruling Party   149
      5.2.1   Testing the Micro-Logic of Remittances
              and Turnout                                           153
      5.2.2   Remittances, Poverty and Turnout                      156
      5.2.3   Remittances, Political Preferences, and Turnout
              in Swing Districts                                    157
      5.2.4   An Alternative Measure of Government
              Support                                               159
5.3   Conclusion                                                    160

6   Remittances and Democratization                                162
    6.1   Closing the Resource Gap                                  164
    6.2   Remittances, Voting, and Protests in Senegal and Cambodia 167
          6.2.1   Senegal                                           168
          6.2.2   Cambodia                                          172
          6.2.3   Conclusion                                        176
    6.3   Meso-Level Analysis: Remittances, Civil Society, and Opposition
          Party Strength                                            176
    6.4   Macro-Level Analysis: Remittances and Democratic
          Transitions                                               180
    6.5   Remittances and Democratic Transition in The Gambia       183
    6.6   Conclusion                                                185

7   Social Remittances and Financial Remittances                   187
    7.1   Social Remittances: Mechanisms and Evidence               189
    7.2   Political Remittances and Destination Regime Type          191
    7.3   Remittances from Migrants Residing in Democratic
          and Autocratic Countries                                  195
          7.3.1   Remittance Flows from Democratic and
                  Autocratic Origins                                197
          7.3.2   Revisiting the Macro-Evidence                     199
    7.4   Does Political Discussion Mediate or Moderate How
          Remittances Shape Behavior?                               202
          7.4.1   Political Discussion as a Mediator                205
          7.4.2   Political Discussion as an Amplifier              207
    7.5   Conclusion                                                209
    7.6   Appendix: Measuring Remittances by Origin                 209

8   Conclusion                                                      212
    8.1   Remittances and the Ethics of Migration Policy            215

| | | |
|---|---|---|
| | 8.1.1 Emigration | 216 |
| | 8.1.2 Immigration policy | 217 |
| 8.2 | *Immigration as Democracy Promotion* | 221 |
| 8.3 | *Do Remittances Fund Anti-Incumbent Politics?* | 224 |
| | 8.3.1 Intra-European Migration and the Rise of Populist Parties | 225 |
| | 8.3.2 Remittances and Democracy in India | 227 |
| 8.4 | *What Does This Mean for Globalization?* | 230 |
| | 8.4.1 How Migration Differs from Trade and Investment Liberalization | 230 |
| | 8.4.2 Political Implications for the Next Wave of Globalization | 233 |

*Notes*   237

*References*   257

*Index*   293

# ILLUSTRATIONS AND TABLES

## Figures

| 1.1 | Global remittances, 2010–18 | 14 |
| 1.2 | Remittances and democratization | 19 |
| 2.1 | How dictatorships collapse, by time period | 30 |
| 2.2 | Empirical predictions for remittance, protest, and turnout | 62 |
| 3.1 | Foreign income flowing to autocracies, 1988–2018 | 68 |
| 3.2 | Remittances and government revenue | 80 |
| 3.3 | Remittances and government spending | 83 |
| 3.4 | Remittances and high-intensity, state-led repression | 91 |
| 3.5 | Remittances and "soft" repression | 94 |
| 4.1 | Remittances and anti-government protest | 103 |
| 4.2 | Remittances and pro-government mobilization | 107 |
| 4.3 | Dictatorships and democracies in Africa, 2008. | 111 |
| 4.4 | Non-response rates for Afrobarometer survey questions | 116 |
| 4.5 | Remittances increase protest in opposition districts | 123 |
| 4.6 | Remittances, poverty, and protest | 129 |
| 4.7 | Predicting non-response rates for various outcomes | 132 |
| 4.8 | District-level government support and electoral support | 135 |
| 5.1 | Remittances and presidential vote share | 143 |
| 5.2 | Remittances and turnout in executive elections | 148 |
| 5.3 | Remittances and vote turnout, by district-level government support | 155 |
| 5.4 | Remittances and vote turnout, by poverty level | 157 |
| 5.5 | Remittances and turnout: alternative swing district measure | 160 |

6.1   Remittances and incumbent vote shares in Senegal
       and Cambodia                                                    169

6.2   Remittances strengthen opposition parties and civil
       society organizations                                           179

6.3   Remittances and democratic transitions                          182

7.1   Share of remittance inflows from democracies: estimates
       for 1990–2015                                                   198

7.2   Revisiting the macro-evidence                                    201

## Tables

4.1   African autocracies, 2008                                        110

4.2   Remittance estimates using an alternative measure of
       opposition district                                             125

4.3   Items in the *Progovernment* measure                            131

7.1   Remittances, political discussion, and behavior                  206

7.2   Remittances and behavior: heterogeneous effects                  208

By the end of the century, the number of people living in Africa will approach the number living in Asia, with each region home to between four and five billion people. Meanwhile, populations in Europe and the Americas are projected to stagnate, and even fall in some countries. Further, accelerating climate change is likely to prompt large-scale population movements as currently inhabited areas, particularly coastal and tropical regions, become uninhabitable. Together, the uneven distribution of future population growth and the unequal impact of climate change mean human migration will become the central global issue of the current century and beyond.

An emerging consensus argues that migration, especially emigration from low- and middle-income countries to high-income countries, is good for development. Migrants not only earn higher wages than they would without migrating, but they also send financial remittances directly to family members left behind, who invest these resources in human capital and public goods, a first-order benefit to individuals, households, and even their communities. Migration thus boosts well-being both for those who move and for the people they leave behind. Economists have also reached a consensus that the development of societies with open access to political and economic organizations that foster competition is the key to sustained well-being; and the most important socio-political institution to ensure open societies and sustain long-term well-being is democracy. This book builds on these insights—the micro-benefits of migration and the macro-benefits of democratic, open access societies—to explore how out-migration shapes democracy in low- and middle-income countries.

While the benefits of migration for the well-being of migrants are now widely understood, there is growing concern over whether migration undermines democracy in host countries by, for example, abetting the rise of nationalist governments, weakening democratic values, or hindering cooperation and public goods provision. Lost in this debate, however, is reflection on how migration influences democracy in migrant-sending countries. Indeed, policy discussion of migration focuses almost exclusively on how immigration influences democracy in rich countries—a view that neglects the reality of circular migration and the power of migrants to shape outcomes in their home countries.

This book highlights how migration fosters democracy in the Global South. We advance a theory of democratic migration that focuses on the foreign monetary resources, namely worker remittances, that flow directly to the agents of democratic change in autocracies, namely citizens. Remittances are not only the largest source of foreign income in most autocratic countries, but, in contrast to revenue from natural resource exports, foreign aid, and even international investment, remittances flow directly to citizens, largely circumventing autocratic governments. We show that remittance income in recipient autocracies increases political opposition resources and decreases government-dependence, two mechanisms that undermine dictatorships and foster democracy. These findings turn the debate about global migration on its head by focusing on the democratizing potential of emigration for the Global South.

Remittances reshape the internal balance of resources and power in autocratic countries because this large source of foreign income flows directly to citizens. First, remittances increase the resources available to political opponents for mobilizing dissent against the government. This argument contrasts with claims that remittances—because they are a counter-cyclical income source for recipients—reduce economic grievances towards, and therefore mobilization against, the government. At the micro-level, we show that remittance recipients are more likely to protest than citizens whose income is not supplemented by this external resource; and that, consistently with our theory that remittances fund political opponents, they mobilize resistance in opposition areas but not in regime-stronghold regions. Globally, we demonstrate that remittances boost anti-government protest mobilization in non-democracies. Popular mobilization against autocratic governments has become the most successful path to democracy in the past quarter century, and this book documents how global migration finances the political mobilization necessary for peaceful democratization.

Second, remittances undermine the electoral strategies that autocratic governments employ to retain power. Since the end of the Cold War, autocratic governments have come to rely on buying electoral support for their monopoly on power, a strategy often dubbed "electoral—or 'competitive'—authoritarianism." Autocratic governments win elections—even relatively fraud-free multiparty contests—by distributing patronage to voters and hence activating their constituencies through "turnout buying." In countries as diverse as Malaysia, Mexico, and Zimbabwe, autocratic governments' clientelistic networks target voters concentrated in stronghold regions. By decreasing voters' dependence on government patronage, income-boosting remittances sever the clientelistic ties between electoral autocracies and the low-income voters they mobilize. We use this observation to explore how remittances influence individual-level voter turnout, demonstrating that they decrease electoral turnout in incumbent stronghold regions but have little effect on turnout in opposition areas. Our global analysis further shows that remittances decrease vote shares for autocratic parties. In short, by boosting private income, migrant remittances undermine the electoral strategies that sustain authoritarian governments throughout the world.

Our theory of migration emphasizes the moral agency of individuals who bring about democratic change, namely the citizens of low- and middle-income countries who resist autocratic rule. This framework contrasts with the dominant macro-structural theories that emphasize the role of economic globalization and Western foreign policy in democratization, by changing government behavior. We demonstrate how the movement of people from dictatorships to higher-income countries furthers the development of open access societies in the Global South. Debate about migration policy in high-income countries, we argue, should therefore reflect the democratizing potential of migration as a powerful tool for fostering democracy.

# ACKNOWLEDGEMENTS

The authors thank Tobias Böhmelt, Katrina Burgess, Liz Carlson, Johannes Fedderke, Scott Gartner, Carl-Henrik Knutsen, Maria Koinova, Daniel Krcmaric, Tomila Lankina, Desiree Lim, Barry Maydom, Jørgen Møller, Yonatan Morse, Nonso Obikili, Berkay Özcan, Isik Özel, Toni Rodon, Paul Schuler, Svend-Erik Skaaning, Jakob Tolstrup, Vineeta Yadav, Kelly Zvogbo, and reviewers at Princeton University Press for helpful comments and suggestions. We also received useful feedback from participants at APSA (2016) and seminars and workshops at the Institut Barcelona d'Estudis Internacionals, IE University, the Instituto Juan March Carlos III de Madrid, King's College London, the London School of Economics, Manchester University, the University of Oxford, the Penn State School of International Affairs, Trinity College Dublin, Universitat Autònoma de Barcelona, the University of Arizona, University College London, the University of Southern California Center for International Studies, and the University of Essex.

We are grateful to Bridget Flannery-McCoy for supporting this project from the outset, and the production team at Princeton University Press for seeing it through to the end.

Covadonga acknowledges the support of a Mid-Career British Academy Fellowship and research assistance from Beatriz Jambrina-Canseco. Joe gratefully acknowledges support in residence from Economic Research Southern Africa (ERSA). The authors thank Seyed Soroosh Azizi for sharing data.

Abel dedicates this book to Tània (*el meu camí*) and Marta (*el meu Cutx*). Joe dedicates this book to Jaimie. Cova dedicates this book to her friends and family.

# MIGRATION AND DEMOCRACY

# 1

# Introduction

According to United Nations' estimates, there were nearly 272 million international migrants worldwide in 2019, representing 3.4 percent of the world's total population (United Nations 2019; International Organization for Migration 2020). This total had increased by 56 percent since 2000 and by 78 percent since 1990, when the number of migrants was 153 million. Human history has witnessed many waves of migration that have transformed the social and political landscape of regions and countries across the globe; but the current patterns present a number of distinctive traits. The most recent prior wave of mass migration, during the second half of the nineteenth century and the first decades of the twentieth century, saw mostly Europeans—perhaps as many as 55 million—leave their countries for the Americas and other territories under colonial control (Hatton and Williamson 1998; McKeown 2004).[1] Advances in transport and communications technology not only facilitate movements of people over long distances, but also provide better access to information about opportunities in other countries for those aspiring to emigrate, which helps to explain the large volume of migrants and its steady growth over the past few decades.

Most importantly, "the primary destinations of inflow and outflow are different" (Freeman 2006, 148). Today's migration patterns mostly entail migrants from the Global South trying to reach the Global North, particularly the relatively high-income countries in North America, Western Europe, and Australia. In 2019, high-income countries, mostly advanced democracies, hosted more than two-thirds of international migrants (United Nations 2019). As Czaika and de Haas (2014, 315) observe, over time "migrants from an increasingly diverse array of non-European-origin countries have been concentrating in a shrinking pool of prime destination countries." The prevalence of internal violence, poor governance, and poverty makes exit an attractive if not predominant survival strategy for many people in the Global South. But while migration brings with it enormous potential to transform sending societies (as this book shows), a narrative focusing on the negative consequences of immigration in host countries dominates academic studies and policy debates.

The key questions this book aims at answering are: Can migration foster democracy? And if so, where? And through which mechanisms? Many on the receiving end of migration streams would swiftly answer "No" to the first of these questions, since they have come to see increasing immigration as a challenge to democracy in host countries. Academics, commentators, and politicians in the West point to several potential mechanisms to suggest that migration weakens democracy (IDEA 2017). One view, often expressed in facile, even derogatory, language by politicians, emphasizes a lack of cultural fit between migrants from the Global South and citizens of countries in the Global North. Ex-US president Donald Trump, for example, reportedly once asked, "Why are we having all these people from shithole countries come here?"[2] The values and behaviors that migrants from some specific, supposedly dysfunctional, and problematic backgrounds would, according to this view, threaten the norms, culture, and security of host democratic communities (Dawsey 2018). Many voters, not only in the USA but also in Europe, share this sentiment with regard to migrants from Muslim countries. A more thoughtful version of the same argument suggests that migration erodes shared social values and identities, which in turn undermines trust in political institutions, hinders cooperation among citizens, and diminishes public support for social welfare provision (Sniderman and Hagendoorn 2007; Dancygier 2010; Collier 2013). According to this line of reasoning, migration, in the most extreme case, could even breed violent internal conflict.

A second view suggests that the greatest threat to democracy may not stem from migration itself, but rather from the political backlash it might trigger. Increasingly, politicians exploit and even foster anti-immigrant sentiment—as well as animosity towards other minority groups—which has altered the political landscape of many Western democracies, where public support for radical-right populist parties has grown (Inglehart and Norris 2017; Judis 2018). At the time of writing, populist anti-immigrant parties—some even openly sympathetic to racist platforms and neo-Nazi ideologies—control governments in Brazil, Hungary, and Poland; and similar parties have until recently held key positions in governing coalitions in Italy and Austria. Even where right-wing anti-immigrant parties have failed to win power—in

Germany, France, Spain, and Sweden, for example—their electoral support in national and subnational elections has steadily increased in the past decade and may continue to do so in the coming years. In the USA, even with Donald Trump's electoral defeat in 2020, nativism is unlikely to recede as a motivating force in the Republican Party.

The emergence and growth of right-wing, anti-immigrant political parties is not only a direct threat to democracy; it may also shape public opinion and thus political support for policies that undermine democratic norms, institutions, and government respect for human rights. Even some mainstream, traditional parties in government attempt to halt the rise of radical groups by embracing their political rhetoric and policies that chip away at the foundations of democracy. For example, President Trump's decision to build a wall at the US–Mexico border led to a government shutdown in the late 2018, and subsequently to Trump declaring the so-called "invasion" a national emergency and assuming additional executive powers allowing him to bypass the usual political process (Baker 2019). Earlier in 2018, the Trump administration implemented a policy of separating migrant parents from their children, prompting UN condemnation: this policy contravened both domestic and international law, constituting a government violation of human rights. More than prior US presidents, Trump deployed executive orders and proclamations to make and enforce immigration policy, "circumventing Congress and even members of his own administration" (Waslin 2020, 54).

In Europe, Italy's anti-immigrant interior minister Matteo Salvini dismantled migrant camps and reception centers, and refused humanitarian rescue ships entry to Italian ports. Under pressure from Salvini, the Italian parliament passed a law in 2018 to abolish humanitarian protection for those who are not eligible for refugee status but cannot be returned to their place of origin. A law of 2019 then set out to punish any citizen who used a boat to rescue refugees from the sea. When some of his policies were challenged in court, Salvini responded with threats against judges and called for a reform of the judicial system. In Spain, meanwhile, a decree passed by the Popular Party government in 2012 had denied undocumented immigrants access to the public healthcare system. In 2014, at least fifteen people died trying to reach Tarajal beach, which separates Spain and Morocco, when Spanish Guardia Civil officers fired rubber bullets to stop migrants from attempting to swim into Spanish territory. Hungary, under Viktor Orbán's government, closed its border with Croatia to all refugees in 2015, and in 2018 its parliament passed a law criminalizing "good-Samaritan" aid to immigrants and asylum seekers. Similar worrisome trends have crept into European Union policy. For example, European Commission President Ursula von der Leyen announced in September 2019 that Europe's migration policy would become the responsibility of a so-called "vice-president for protecting our European way of life," raising concerns that the EU will undermine its own commitment to the free movement of people.

In efforts to curb migration, some governments in the Global North undermine democracy and human rights not only within their own borders, but also in third countries, via their foreign policies, most notably migration management partnerships. Migration to rich democracies has prompted their governments to outsource migration policy enforcement to sending and transit countries, a process whereby democratic governments pay autocratic ones to repress migrants' rights in order to prevent them from reaching their borders. This migration management aid, in turn, funds *government* budgets in sending countries, thereby entrenching government power and weakening states' respect for human rights in these countries (Oette and Babiker 2017). For example, the EU created a partnership with Libya to strengthen its coastguard's ability to intercept migrants in the Mediterranean. These people were later detained in inhumane conditions in Libya and have been victims of racist attacks. The EU also pays millions of euros to Niger in exchange for increased military control of its northern borders, to combat smugglers and to reduce migrant flows to Libya (Penney 2018).

Moreover, in pursuit of this goal, other foreign policies, some officially aimed at fostering economic development, are being reshaped. For example, European foreign aid and other bilateral development assistance increasingly flow into border-control budgets, to contain migration and enforce readmission. Likewise, under the Trump administration, the US government used trade policy to force sending and conduit countries to detain and repress migrants hoping to reach the States. Democratic governments may see this as the most viable method of preventing the rise of nativist populist parties: as one observer notes, "If Mr. Trump's experience is anything like Europe's, he may find that persuading Mexico or Guatemala to detain refugees on the United States' behalf will drastically worsen conditions for refugees, but alleviate much of the backlash from Americans" (Fisher and Taub 2019b). This worrisome phenomenon may result in less migration to wealthy countries, but also entails a reduction in democracy and human rights in sending countries, insofar as democratic governments in the Global North provide economic benefits directly to non-democratic governments, rather than to the citizens who live in those countries.

Despite these costly efforts to protect and even militarize borders, international migration will likely continue to grow. The income gap between poor and rich countries has been widening for decades if not centuries, providing people with powerful incentives to seek a better standard of living by moving to another country (Pritchett 1997). And even in countries, such as China, where rapid economic growth over the past three decades has closed the average income gap with rich countries, much of the wealth produced by this growth has been captured by elites, leaving hundreds of millions of their citizens still much poorer than the average citizen in OECD countries (Milanovic 2016). As income disparities persist and even grow, the attractiveness of leaving one's own country increases, especially when poverty is accompanied by conflict, violence, gender inequality, and autocratic government. Furthermore, native-born population levels in Europe, the Americas, and wealthy countries in East Asia are stagnating, if not already starting to decline; and global warming will likely prompt mass population movements, as some areas become increasingly uninhabitable. Thus, despite the economic growth in some low- and middle-income countries during the wave of globalization over the past three decades, the incentives for migration from the Global South to the Global North are growing stronger.

Discussion of migration policy focuses almost exclusively on how immigration influences democracy, security, and social cohesion *in rich host countries*. Yet, this narrow view neglects the reality of circular migration and the power of migrants to shape outcomes in their home countries. Public debate over migration and its consequences has not only intensified but also polarized in the recent years, and a migration debate focused on host countries is often simplistic and, worse, prone to manipulation by opportunistic leaders. This makes it all the more important for researchers to examine carefully and empirically the many claims about the social, economic, and political consequences of migration. One element that tends to be lost in the debate is any reflection on and analysis of how emigration influences politics and democracy in migrant-sending countries. *Both* ends of the migration stream deserve attention. This book focuses on the sending end and, in particular, on the political effects of the money migrants send back home: that is, of remittances.

Technological changes not only facilitate the movement of people and information, but also increase migrants' capacity to send money back home. Indeed, the recent rise in migration has been accompanied by an even larger increase in the money migrants send to the relatives and friends they have left behind. In 2017, migrants totaling nearly one-quarter of a billion sent via formal transfer mechanisms over $600 billion in remittances back to their families, friends, and communities in their home countries, with over 75 percent of this money flowing to low- and middle-income countries (World Bank 2019a). According to most recent estimates, the equivalent figure neared $700 billion in 2018.[3]

This remitted income is vital for the survival and economic well-being of millions of households across the globe. For some, such inflows make it possible to escape poverty and weather domestic economic downturns and other shocks to family incomes. For others, remittances boost consumption of basic goods (such as food or clothes), durable goods (such as housing), and services (such as clean water), and allow them to make long-term investments in education, health, and businesses. Furthermore, many recipients pool these resources from abroad to fund the provision of local public goods, such as infrastructure, social services, and agricultural projects that benefit a wider community. The potential economic benefits of these private money transfers are so large that the United Nations considers them a vital pathway for reaching its Sustainable Development Goals. With the aim of boosting remittances' size and global impact, UN members set a target (Goal 10, target 10.c) to reduce remittance transaction costs to less than 3 percent, in doing so eliminating remittance corridors with costs higher than 5 percent, by 2030. Indeed, in 2018, the UN General Assembly proclaimed 16 June the International Day of Family Remittances to raise awareness of the importance of this type of cross-border flow.

The consequences of migration and the attendant remittances are not exclusively economic, however. As this book demonstrates, this massive inflow of money also directly transforms the balance of political power in recipient countries. Indeed, most of this income accrues to middle- and low-income societies, many of which are—or historically have been—governed by non-democratic governments. This book aims to reshape the debate about migration by demonstrating how emigration fosters democracy in the Global South. We advance a theory of democratic migration that focuses on the foreign monetary resources, namely worker remittances, which flow directly to the agents of democratic change in autocracies, that is, citizens. Our research shows that remitted income in recipient autocracies increases political opposition resources and decreases government-dependence, two mechanisms that undermine dictatorships and foster democratic transitions. Our investigation thus turns the debate about global migration on its head, focusing on the democratizing potential of emigration for developing countries.

While we explain how remittances enable citizens in the Global South to challenge their governments, the consequences of migration and remittances have larger political and economic implications. As Paul Collier points out, "[a]lthough migrants themselves do well from migration, it can only be truly significant in addressing hardcore global poverty if it accelerates transformation in countries of origin. In turn, that transformation is at base a political and social, rather than economic, process. So the potential for migration to affect the political process for those left behind really matters" (Collier 2013, 187). Our story of the power of migration to foster democracy in origin countries therefore has profound implications for human development in the Global South. If remittances sent from rich countries to poor ones help transform politics and institutions in the latter, the second-order effect of migration on global poverty—via democratic change in migrant-sending countries— is likely to be large. As ample research shows, open societies with democratic governments underpin sustained economic development (North et al. 2009; Acemoglu et al. 2019).

## 1.1. Globalization, Migration, and Political Change

Globalization entails reducing barriers to economic, cultural, and political exchanges resulting from rapid innovations in transport and communication technologies, and migration is one dimension of the accelerating transnational exchange and interconnection that characterizes globalization. It is in fact the most human aspect of globalization; but it is debate over the economic aspects of globalization that remains predominant. Many, focusing on international trade and financial flows, argue that economic globalization promotes democracy. Economic globalization entails not only cross-border exchanges of goods and services (i.e., international trade), but also the global movement of the two key factors of production, namely capital and labor. Most of the faith in the democratic benefits of economic globalization stems from the belief that financial liberalization and increased trade improve overall well-being and help create open, democratic societies. Because many policymakers believed in the economic and political benefits of globally integrated capital markets, most developed countries have liberalized their capital accounts, and in turn put pressure on developing countries to do the same (Williamson 1993). While capital and goods and services are increasingly mobile, free to move from one country to another, labor is not (Freeman 2006). On the contrary, as the migration policy developments highlighted above indicate, governments in Europe and North America seem to be tightening restrictions on the cross-border movement of people.

Advocates of financial globalization claim that free-flowing private capital not only enhances economic growth via investment and technology spillovers, but also that it catalyzes liberalizing political reforms. This optimistic view—embodied in the Washington Consensus—contends that foreign private investment undermines non-democratic states' control over the economy, spurs economic modernization, and empowers domestic and foreign private actors, which in turn alters the internal balance of power (Maxfield 1998; Spar 1998; Kwok and Tadesse 2006; Malesky 2009; Arriola 2013a). However, it is not possible to be so sanguine in light of the cross-national evidence for economic integration improving democracy (Rudra 2005; Eichengreen and Leblang 2008; Li and Reuveny 2009). Such optimism is unwarranted, in part it seems because non-democratic governments so often divert, control, and hence benefit from, foreign capital inflows. As Dillman (2002, 64) stresses, non-democratic governments, "by preserving their states as the necessary intermediary between international and domestic economic actors [. . .] construct and reshape patronage networks in such a manner as to maintain, if not reinforce, their own economic and political power." Financial reforms and foreign direct investement (FDI) inflows create opportunities for strengthening state-controlled sectors, rent-extraction, and the distribution of targeted benefits to regime insiders and other politically relevant groups. Indeed, recent comparative research demonstrates that both international trade and, especially, foreign capital flows are in fact associated with increased autocratic durability, thereby harming the prospects of democratization (Quinn 2002; Roberto and Rodrik 2005; Li and Reuveny 2009; Bak and Moon 2016; DiGiuseppe and Shea 2016; Powell and Chacha 2016; Escribà-Folch 2017).

This book contributes to the debate about globalization by arguing that human migration (i.e., labor) and the remittances that flow from it are global factors of production that, unlike capital flows (or trade), move across borders in ways that shift the balance of power towards citizens and away from governments in migrant-sending countries. This creates opportunities for bottom-up democratization. Despite tight restrictions upon, and even repression of, cross-border labor movement, migration continues apace. Developing countries received $706 billion in FDI in 2018, while remittances were projected to surpass $550 billion in 2019 (UNCTAD 2019; Ratha et al. 2019). For the least developed countries, remittances remain substantially higher than FDI.

And while the global pandemic of 2020 stopped migration in its tracks, the underlying forces that motivate it are unlikely to dissipate.

While commentators and policymakers often emphasize the benefits of foreign investment for promoting political change, debates in comparative political economy largely overlook migration and the political consequences of remittances. Social scientists have only recently begun to ask questions about how out-migration influences political change (Eckstein and Najam 2010; Kapur 2010; Moses 2011; Kapur 2014; Mosley and Singer 2015), but this key dimension of globalization deserves more scholarly attention (Collier 2013). By demonstrating the positive political consequences of migration, we aim to alter the narrative of migrants as mere input to multinational production chains or as threats to some nativist-tinged 'way of life' in rich countries. Instead, we argue, migrants are agents of political change. Debates about migration policy in high-income countries should thus reflect the democratizing potential of migration as a powerful foreign policy tool for democracy promotion and human development.

### 1.1.1.  Existing Theories: Migration and Democracy

How does emigration shape politics in home countries? Before outlining the mechanisms that we claim make emigration a net positive for political change in home countries, we discuss the main contending arguments proposed so far.[4]

The migration literature articulates several theories suggesting that *emigration* either negatively or positively shapes the prospects for democracy and political development. Perhaps the best known argument—building on the "exit, voice, and loyalty" framework developed by Hirschman (1970)—posits that when citizens "exit" (emigrate from) a polity, they necessarily forgo using "voice" to change the status quo. If exit and voice are mutually exclusive strategies for channeling political discontent, then emigration should undermine the politics of contention and citizen mobilization that demand and foster democratic political change. Emigration of the young and unemployed, according to this logic, constitutes an economic "safety valve," which, because young men may be the most likely to protest, translates into a political safety valve as well.[5] In other words, an economic brain drain can also be a political brain drain, whereby those most interested in political change and most capable of pursuing it, and who at the same time may be the most frustrated and aggrieved, leave instead of organizing for change at home (Pfaff

2006). When voice is costly because it entails the risk of repression, as is often the case in countries ruled by autocratic governments, the lower-cost stategy exit may prove much more attractive (Bratton 2008). Thus, emigration can relieve domestic pressure, in the form of social discontent and civil unrest. This opens the door to the strategic use of foreign movement policies by incumbent autocrats facing domestic discontent, as they have an incentive to encourage political dissenters to exit the country rather than voice their dissent at home.[6] An emigrant interviewed in a recent study of remittances and politics in Mexico describes this "safety valve" logic: "If money was not coming in from the United States, maybe, I don't know, people would have to find a way [to survive]. Do like they did in the past: start another revolution. This is why the government wants us to migrate. You look for a way to survive. It is between killing each other or leaving. And this is what people are doing, leaving the country" (Germano 2018, 55).

There are also significant arguments suggesting the opposite: that emigration fosters democracy in sending countries. One mechanism, drawing on the work of Tiebout (1956) and implications of the Hirschman model, contends that a credible pathway to emigration raises the outside options available to local residents, boosting the relative bargaining power of citizens and potential emigrant groups vis-à-vis incumbent elites. Similar to the exit and loyalty argument, the exit option, according to Tiebout's logic, need not be exercised; this option only needs to be credible to force incumbents to adopt policies preferred by the potential emigrants. As Hirschman (1970, 93) emphasizes, "the effectiveness of the voice mechanism is strengthened by the possibility of exit." Accordingly, Moses (2011, 50) argues that emigration amplifies voice: "individual residents are able to exert more influence over political authority because the threat to exit provides them with an effective tool for voicing dissatisfaction." Under such circumstances, citizens can better express their demands and preferences. At the same time, elites—especially those dependent on labor cooperation for tax revenue—have an incentive to respond to demands for political change by granting political concessions; if elites do not concede, constituents may simply decide to vote with their feet and leave for better (and foreign) states that meet their expectations.[7] This logic might also help explain why some dictatorships impose severe restrictions on foreign movement, to impede citizens' en-masse exit. North Korea's regime, for example, imposes perhaps the tightest controls on population movement and considers unauthorized emigrants to be traitors. Similarly, emigration in East Germany was criminalized, thousands of people being charged with attempted unlawful emigration (Horz and Marbach 2020).

A second mechanism directly linking emigration and democracy emphasizes so-called social or political remittances: migrants and migrant returnees, according to this argument, transmit ideas, norms, and beliefs acquired or learned in the host country about the value and practice of democracy, via transnational networks and long-distance interactions or face-to-face exchanges. "Social remittances," a term coined by sociologist Peggy Levitt, comprise "the ideas, behaviors, identities, and social capital that flow from receiving- to sending-country communities" (Levitt 1998, 927). Krawatzek and Müller-Funk (2020, 1,004) consider political remittances to be a subset of social remittances, defining the former as "the act of transferring political principles, vocabulary and practices between two or more places, which migrants and their descendants share a connection with." According to this logic, both emigrants and returning migrants transform the views, values, and even political practices of those who remain at home. The argument thus focuses on a non-material form of cross-border flow that results from migration. This, in turn, shapes political change by altering (political) preferences and enhancing recipients' political efficacy. Migrants, according to these theories, act as agents of democratic diffusion via the inter-personal and transnational transmission of new democratic values and attitudes (Pérez-Armendáriz and Crow 2010). This argument assumes that migrants settle in democratic host countries, acquire new values and learn new practices, and then communicate with people at home, (re-)socializing them.[8]

Another pathway links emigration to political development indirectly, via economic development. If emigration increases average incomes in sending countries, and if, as modernization theory claims, economic development breeds democracy, then emigration should advance democracy (Bearce and Park 2019). Emigration may raise incomes via two, related, mechanisms. First, as we discuss below, monetary remittances from emigrant labor increase family incomes for those left behind. Second, emigration can boost incomes in sending countries by making labor more scarce. Especially if emigrants are relatively low-skilled workers, this factor–price equalization mechanism may reshape the internal balance of power in favor of relatively low-income workers. That is, emigration should foster convergence of low-skilled real wages between sending and host countries, leading to rising incomes for the poor in sending countries (Hatton and Williamson 1998). Rising incomes, according to this logic, then set in motion internal economic transformations—a growing industrial sector, technological advances, a rising middle class—that, some posit, favor the emergence of democracy.

The evidence available for these theories is scarce due to the limitations of migration data; yet some studies suggest a positive relationship between migration and democracy in migrants' countries of origin. Alemán and Woods (2014), for example, find that freedom of movement is correlated with civil rights protection and democracy in a global sample of autocracies; and Miller and Peters (2020) qualify this finding to show that autocracies adopt freer emigration policies if citizens want to leave for economic reasons, but restrict exit if emigrants mostly move to democratic countries. Lending some support to the idea of a social remittance mechanism, Spilimbergo (2009) reports evidence that foreign education in democratic countries fosters citizens who promote democracy in their home countries; and a more general test of emigration, in Docquier et al. (2016), finds that total emigration is associated with better civil and political rights in developing countries. This study emphasizes, however, that the "result is fully driven by emigration to rich, highly democratic countries, suggesting that the effect of emigration on home-country institutional outcomes is destination-specific" (Docquier et al. 2016, 222). Finally, focusing on the state competition argument, Moses (2011) also shows a positive relationship between emigration and political development.

We propose a third mechanism linking emigration to democracy in home countries: namely, financial remittances. Existing approaches tend to view financial remittances as only *indirectly* shaping democracy. Since emigrants remit both money (financial remittances) and ideas (social remittances), one view interprets the latter as simply being the political parallel of the former. As a result, many assume that only social remittances can directly transform politics in home countries, while monetary transfers only impact local economic conditions (Moses 2011, 46–47). In this framework, remittances are merely one of many potential side-effects of emigration, alongside wage equalization and increased labor strength, that indirectly influence democratic political change via economic development. This argument thus connects monetary remittances to modernization theory to suggest that money transfers boost economic development, which, in turn, breeds the conditions necessary for democratic change. Money transfers, accordingly, not only increase the family incomes but also raise local wages through a multiplier effect on local economies and by funding the private provision of services and local public goods. Nonetheless, while remittances do appear to reduce poverty levels, there is no consensus about their effect on long-term economic growth

(Pradhan et al. 2008; Barajas et al. 2009; Catrinescu et al. 2009; Clemens and McKenzie 2018). One could also argue that remittances in themselves have no real causal effect in terms of democracy—or that they in fact stabilize non-democratic regimes by decreasing social discontent—because they simply reflect higher emigration levels, the key factor driving democracy.

Contrary to these arguments, we posit that money transfers from migrant workers also have powerful democratizing effects on the migrants' countries of origin, even after accounting for net migration and economic development. We claim, that is, that remittances have a *direct* effect on the political dynamics in migration-sending, developing countries. As we discuss in the next chapter, additional private income from remittance inflows both weaken ruling parties' ability to mobilize electoral support and strengthen the organizational capacity of opposition groups. Before previewing our theory, however, we first outline how remittances differ in important ways from other types of foreign income—namely foreign aid, oil revenue, and foreign investment—to which they have been often compared.

### 1.1.2. Foreign Income Inflows and Autocratic Rule

Our theory focuses on the direct political consequences of monetary remittances, which are money transfers from migrant workers to individuals—typically relatives and friends—and groups in their home countries. We argue that these flows transform the political landscape of migration-sending countries and, therefore, reshape the balance of power in remittance-receiving authoritarian countries. This transformative potential, as well as the arguments we articulate below, hinge on two key characteristics of global remittances that make them distinct from other foreign financial flows.

First, remittances are not only growing in volume but also remain relatively stable from year to year.[9] Although there is substantial cross-national variation, over the past two decades remittances have rapidly become the main source of foreign income for many developing countries. Inflows have steadily increased for decades (prior to the 2020 global pandemic), with their growth accelerating in the last two: in 2018, for example, remittances grew by nearly 10 percent relative to the prior year. Remittance inflows are now more than three times larger than official development assistance (ODA) flows from DAC (Development Assistance Committee) members. Put differently, migrants send substantially more money to their relatives back home than Western democracies send in aid to promote economic and political development.

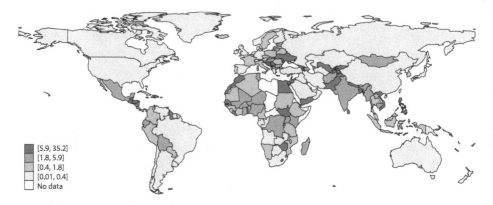

FIGURE 1.1. Global remittances, 2010–18

And although capital inflows (i.e., FDI plus portfolio investment) to developing countries remain larger in the aggregate, these resources are highly concentrated in a relatively small number of countries, mostly in Asia (UNCTAD 2019, 12).[10] In other words, more money flows to poor economies as a result of migrants wishing to help those left behind than as a result of foreign companies seeking to benefit from locational advantages.

Figure 1.1 illustrates the importance of remittances for many developing countries; the map shows the average remittances received as a percentage of GDP over the period 2010–18. For several countries located close to rich or emerging economies or in major migration corridors, remittances represent a substantial part of their economies, upon which many families depend. For example, between 2010 and 2018, remittances represented on average 35.2 percent of Tajikistan's GDP; 29.5 percent of Kyrgyzstan's; 25 percent of Haiti's; 18.2 percent of Lesotho's; 16.5 percent of Liberia's, 13.2 percent of Jordan's; and 11.9 percent of The Gambia's.

Along with their increasing volume, remittance inflows also display a great degree of stability over time, which further differentiates them from other, more volatile, forms of capital inflows such as FDI, portfolio investment, foreign aid, and oil revenue, the last of which tends to rise and fall with world oil prices (Ratha 2003; IMF 2005). And just as foreign aid, oil rents, and foreign investment have important economic as well as political consequences for recipient societies, remittances are also likely to influence politics in developing countries. The direction of that influence, especially compared to other inflows, is shaped by the second crucial feature of migrants' money transfers.

This second critical feature of remittances that distinguishes them from other foreign financial flows is the nature of the senders and the recipients: both are private citizens, not governments or firms. While remitted income comes from outside the receiving country and is thus an "external" or "foreign" source of income like oil revenue, foreign aid, and international investment, it does *not* flow directly to government coffers or state-aligned or state-owned firms. Rather, remittances flow to millions of individuals and families. The fact that remittances are indeed a foreign source of income has led some scholars to liken them to other revenue windfalls, such as foreign aid and oil rents, which, as substantial evidence shows, make autocracies more resilient.[11]

Theories linking foreign income to autocratic stability—and the dearth of democracy—presume that these foreign inflows accrue, directly or indirectly, totally or in part, to incumbent non-democratic governments and are diverted to their political allies. If governments generate substantial non-tax revenue from these external flows, they may forgo taxation and use the additional income to purchase political support and build up their repressive forces to suppress dissent. Foreign aid most often flows directly to governments in developing countries in the form of budget support, making it largely fungible; and when aid funds specific development projects, it may simply substitute for spending that recipient governments might have undertaken anyway, freeing up additional funds for purchasing support and improving security. Since the wave of oil and other natural-resource firm nationalizations in the 1970s, revenue from these resources has largely flowed to the state either directly or indirectly via state-owned firms. Finally, governments often play a key mediating role in agreements that bring in foreign investment, giving rulers ample room to capture part of these funds. For example, autocratic governments may require multinational corporations (MNCs) to make substantial payments—including bribes—to obtain licenses and permits, or may force foreign firms into joint ventures with local partners—often state-owned, parastatal, or politically aligned private firms. Thus, while most products of international financial flows accrue (directly or indirectly) to recipient governments, remittances differ inasmuch as they bypass governments and instead flow to individual citizens.

The nature of the sender's role is a significant feature of this relationship as well. In all cases of foreign income, the sender or donor is external to the recipient; that is, the sender is located outside the recipient country. Official government agencies in developed countries send bilateral aid and provide most of the funds that multilateral donors, such as the World Bank and the

United Nations, disburse.[12] Oil payments in the form of kickbacks and royalties are made by multinational oil companies and accrue to governments in the form of non-tax revenue, some of which is not captured in official revenue statistics. Fossil-fuel energy dependence and a strong interest in stabilizing oil markets has led many democracies and other international actors to prioritize keeping governments in oil exporting countries as cooperative allies. Even cash-crop export revenue often ends up in the hands of the government, via regulatory policies (Bates 1984).[13] Finally, FDI decisions are mostly in the hands of MNCs, whose main interest lies in accessing emerging markets to exploit locational advantages; as such they often prioritize policies that produce stable and favorable business environments in foreign countries, even when that conflicts with respect for human rights (Youngs 2004; Payne and Pereira 2016).[14]

Such incentives are absent in the case of remittances. First, remittances are private transfers made by individuals living and working abroad; migrants, not foreign governments or companies, are the senders, so the conflict typical of other types of donor, between their idealistic goals in terms of advancing democracy and other, more "realistic" foreign policy interests they might wish to pursue, is barely relevant. Migrants' primary motivation is to improve the living conditions of those left behind; indeed migration decisions are often central to families' strategies to smooth over income shocks and diversify income sources (Lucas and Stark 1985; Agarwal and Horowitz 2002; Azizi 2017). But remittances are also often involved in improving local institutions as well as providing local public goods and services (Chaudhry 1989; Adida and Girod 2011; Aparicio and Meseguer 2012; Mosley and Singer 2015). Further, an abundance of case studies shows that emigrants engage in the politics of their home countries via a wide array of transnational activities (Guarnizo et al. 2003; Østergaard-Nielsen 2003a; Fox 2007; Eckstein and Najam 2010; Kapur 2010; Danielson 2018). As importantly, remittance transfers, unlike natural-resource or cash-crop revenue, fungible aid, or even FDI, do not accrue to governments but instead flow directly to individuals, households, and even local civil society groups and organizations in migrant-sending countries. This boost to private income has great potential to transform remittance recipients' incentives and capacities for political action and to narrow the resource gap between the regime and the opposition. These differences between remittance inflows and other types of foreign income have crucial implications for the prospects of democracy, which we explore in this book.

### 1.1.3.  Remittances in the Global South

We focus on individual remittances, but also consider activities that are frequently financed by diaspora (collective) remittances. Individual remittances are private transfers from emigrants to their families and friends, while collective financial remittances are money raised by diaspora organizations. Evidence from various regions of the world shows that individual remittances are overwhelmingly devoted to financing recipient households' current consumption, alleviating poverty (Adams and Page 2005; World Bank 2006b,d; Adams 2007; Fajnzylber and López 2007; Chami et al. 2008). In countries as diverse as Guatemala, Kosovo, and Botswana, these resources are a lifeline for recipients as they cover basic needs and provide insurance against risks (Yang and Choi 2007). Frequently, remittances allow families to invest in their childrens' education, or pay for health coverage, utilities, appliances, or transportation. Remittances help improve housing and sanitation, can ease credit constraints, and help recipients start small businesses. Sometimes recipients choose to exit the job market as their reservation wage increases with remittance inflows (World Bank 2006d; Fajnzylber and López 2007; Posso 2012).

In addition to funding household consumption and investment that raise recipients' living standards, financial remittances allow migrants to invest privately in local public goods (Adida and Girod 2011). Among their other activities, diaspora organizations such as migrant clubs often fund development projects in their communities of origin (Iskander 2010; Aparicio and Meseguer 2012; Burgess 2012; Duquette-Rury 2019). Further, recipients' individual consumption and investments have multiplier effects, making an impact at the community level. Remittances often buy time and education, allowing recipients to engage in formal and informal political activities. Perhaps disenchanted with party politics, recipients turn instead to non-electoral political activities as a way to contribute to their communities.

Diaspora remittances also help strengthen local social capital. In comparison to the volume of individual remittances, remittances raised by migrant organizations represent a minor proportion,[15] but their importance should not be underestimated: collective remittances may represent sizable percentages of many communities' budgets in migrant-sending countries (Goldring 2002; Iskander 2010; Burgess 2012; Ambrosius 2019; Duquette-Rury 2019). For this reason, collective remittances are highly coveted resources. Alone or in partnership with local governments, migrant clubs finance the construction of public infrastructure such as schools, hospitals, electrification, paving projects, or recreation areas. As with individual remittances, the benefits of these partnerships are not only developmental: collective remittances empower emigrants and stayers in their dealings with local politicians. Migrant organizations often exercise close oversight of how their resources are spent, demanding greater accountability from local government and helping to curb corruption (Burgess 2012; Duquette-Rury 2019). Because co-production investments often require the existence of local groups that shadow migrants' organizations, as well as some transborder collective action, collective remittances are a factor that often contributes to strengthening local civil society vis-à-vis local government. As we show later, individual and diaspora remittances contribute to transferring social and organization capital that facilitates collective action and strengthens civil society (Burgess 2012; Germano 2018; Duquette-Rury 2019; Pérez-Armendáriz and Duquette-Rury 2021).

## 1.2. Previewing the Argument

How do remittances undermine autocratic rule and help promote democracy? We articulate theoretically how remittances change citizens' political behavior and think through the ways remittance flows shape macro-political outcomes in countries governed by non-democratic regimes. Figure 1.2 summarizes the logic of our argument. The starting point, using Hirschman's (1970) framework, is citizens' physical *exit* from their home country, that is, emigration. By Hirschman's account, such exit should stabilize sending societies, because exit constitutes a political safety-valve (Hirschman 1978).[16] According to this logic, potential dissidents who might mobilize against the government instead renounce their voice in favor of exit when they seek better opportunities abroad (Sellars 2019). However, modern migration often unleashes several transformative forces. Most importantly for our theory, exit in the form of emigration frequently results in migrants sending money back to their families and communities, that is, in monetary remittance flows. In contrast to some reformulations of Hirschman's model that focus on migrants as transnational political actors who directly exercise voice and loyalty from abroad after exit (Hoffmann 2010; Burgess 2012), we theorize how the remittances migrants send back after exit influence their family members' decisions about voice and loyalty. We agree with Hoffmann (2010, 68) that "it becomes necessary to rethink the meaning of the categories of exit, voice,

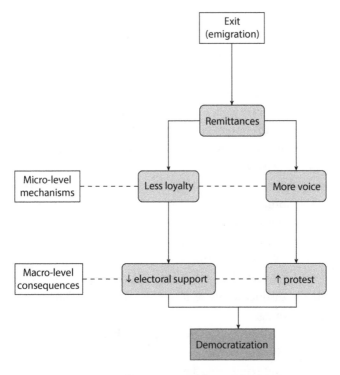

FIGURE 1.2. Remittances and democratization

and loyalty." We therefore build a theory that focuses on remittance recipients' behavior. Sending remittances, we posit, is simply a form of transnational activity through which migrants transform—either intentionally or unintentionally—the political dynamics of their home countries.

Let us first define and clarify the concepts we apply to those receiving remitted income. We focus on the political behavioral consequences of financial remittances in autocratic home countries of migrants, not the political behavior of migrants who remain abroad. That is to say, our theory does *not* speak to how migrants choose loyalty or exercise voice from abroad, aside from sending remittances home (often with political intentions). We simply take the large inflow of private income in the form of remittances as a starting point for theorizing about the impact of these upon the political dynamics of migrant-sending countries, given the ample empirical evidence that suggests remittances rank among the largest sources of foreign income in dictatorships.

The next step is to examine how these resources shape the political behavior of remittance recipients who, we posit, are the most likely agents of democratic change. Participation in almost any form of dissent—whether protesting in the streets, attending an opposition leader's rally, voting against the ruling party, or even expressing political grievances to friends and family—is potentially costly to individuals who pursue such activities; and these costs tend to be greater in autocratic contexts. Because remittances flow to individuals, families, and even organizations, we argue that this additional private income has the potential to help offset these costs.

As importantly, most autocracies now hold regular multiparty elections and are also increasingly vulnerable to anti-regime protests—patterns we document in the next chapter. Understanding how remittances influence autocratic elections, mass protest, opposition organizations' strength, and ultimately transitions from autocracy to democracy requires paying attention to the specific micro-mechanisms linking remittance receipt to individual-level behavior. We contend that remittances turn recipients into agents of democratic political change by altering their capacities and incentives for engaging in distinct forms of dissenting political behavior: specifically, protesting and voting.

This approach is especially useful for establishing a theoretical and empirical connection between macro-structural processes—such as globalization, migration, and remittance flows—and domestic political outcomes—namely, transitions to democracy. As Schwartzman (1998, 161) correctly notes, "The principal intellectual challenge is to link global processes with domestic ones and then to show how those domestic processes influence the daily experiences of both those who rule and those who are ruled." Because remittances largely flow to citizens and not to governments, as we show below, they do little to alter the behavior of those who rule; but, we propose, they do transform the resources, capacities, and incentives available to those who are ruled by non-democratic governments. Our task is therefore to establish a theoretical and empirical connection between individual-level political behaviors, such as protest and voting, that arise as a result of remittances and macro-political change, in the form of democratic political transitions.

The first mechanism linking remittances to macro-political change is *voice*. We argue that migrant remittances increase the ability of those left behind to raise their voice, a form of political dissent that is conceptually and empirically distinct from transnational political "voice" on the part of migrants themselves. Political participation is costly to individuals, especially in dictatorships where repression breeds fear and where opponents have a clear resource disadvantage. Drawing on the resource model of participation, we posit that remittances are a private income windfall that helps some recipients overcome resource constraints that prevent dissenting political action. Remitted money not only enhances individual—or household-level—resources that enable citizens to engage in contentious activities such as protest; diasporas also use these resources to finance directly opposition parties, groups, and civil society organizations. This should result in higher mobilizing and organizational capacity, especially among those opposing the regime who have fewer resources. A more autonomous partisan opposition and a more vibrant civil society emerge as a result. Remittances therefore *increase voice*.

The second mechanism linking remittances to democracy is *loyalty*. When households and communities receive remittances, their economic autonomy vis-à-vis the state increases by reducing their dependence on state-delivered transfers, goods, and services. Clientelistic exchanges targeting specific social groups are a crucial strategy upon which ruling parties rely to mobilize electoral support, made possible by the ruling party's monopoly on state resources: access to state-provided benefits, including gifts, local public goods and services, and even jobs, is conditional on showing up at the polls. Additional family income from remittances allows individuals, households, and even entire communities to acquire and provide for themselves a wide array of goods and services that substitute for those provided by ruling regimes. Ideological or material commitment to the ruling party erodes as a result; and individuals lacking a strong attachment might thus opt not to show support for the incumbents at election time. Remittances thus *weaken loyalty* to the regime, especially among poor and mild supporters in targeted districts—those whose electoral support for the rulers is most likely to be bought by the regime. If additional private income from remittances undermines clientelistic exchanges with ruling parties, entire social sectors or local communities may cease to vote for the ruling party at election time.

As importantly, increased voice and weaker loyalty that result from additional remitted income are more likely to apply to some groups of people than others. Hence, such micro-mechanisms are not mutually exclusive within a given national context. For some individuals and groups, remittances are likely to increase voice, thus mobilizing citizens; while for others, they are more likely to weaken loyalty and demobilize them. Crucially, both processes undermine authoritarian rule. Furthermore, these two mechanisms also have implications at the meso-level. The agents of political change include not only individuals whose behavior may be influenced by remittance receipts, but also opposition parties, grassroots associations, and civil society organizations that mobilize citizens, monitor governments, and demand democratic change. An extension of the two micro-mechanisms above has clear implications for organizations: diasporas can fund them from afar (Shain 1999; Østergaard-Nielsen 2003b; Lyons 2012; Betts and Jones 2016), thereby increasing their resources for mobilization as well as their autonomy vis-à-vis the regime. Remittances therefore make opposition groups and civil society organizations stronger.

We document these mechanisms using individual-level survey data from numerous dictatorships in Africa. The individual-level effects of remittances—namely increased voice and decreased loyalty—should, in turn, lead to observable aggregate macro-political change. That is to say, at the country-level, we expect remittances to increase anti-regime protests and also to reduce electoral support for autocratic incumbents. Our main contention is thus that remittances alter the balance of power between incumbent rulers and opposition groups, which in the context of non-democratic politics increases the possibility of democratization. Remittances do so by eroding both ends of the regime resource advantage and its strategic use aimed at punishing opponents and rewarding supporters. First, governments cannot capture remittance income, so these inflows do not increase the regime's resources; they accrue to individuals and organizations instead. Second, remittances provide those traditionally excluded, repressed, and deprived of economic and organizational resources with additional resources to overcome such constraints and increase their mobilizing capacity. Finally, remittances reduce the effectiveness of the vast resources the regime spends in rewarding and mobilizing support.

As Figure 1.2 (above) indicates, these challenges undermine autocratic rule, thus increasing the opportunity for democratic transitions to occur. Anti-government protest campaigns can weaken dictatorships, especially when security forces refuse to employ violent repression against them. Growing threats from a larger, better-organized opposition can force elites to make institutional concessions paving the way for democratic reforms. While it may be easily imagined, moreover, how opposition mobilization weakens dictatorships, we also show how political *de*mobilization can do likewise. Shrinking electoral support for incumbent authoritarian parties often leads to electoral defeat, bringing non-democratic regimes to an end; and even when ruling parties remain undefeated at the polls, decreasing electoral support pierces the image of regime invincibility, spurring elites to defect and opponents to invest more heavily. Finally, when ruling parties lose at the polls and either resort to fraud to alter the results or refuse to step down, this intransigence itself often mobilizes mass protests that then bring down the regime.

More broadly, our theory and evidence suggest that globalization can advance democracy in the Global South, but not necessarily through international trade or cross-border capital movements. Instead, we posit that cross-border movement of people and the booming transnational flow of money it generates provide resources to citizens as agents of political change to undermine dictatorships and further democracy.

## 1.3. Plan of the Book

In what follows, chapter 2 first of all presents our theoretical argument. We document how dictatorships fall, and explain how this process has changed in the last few decades to favor citizens as agents of democratic political change: coups are no longer the predominant way whereby dictatorships end; instead, elections and protest mobilization—the two mechanisms we posit to be closely linked to remittances—have become the most common ways for dictators to leave power. We then discuss the international dimensions of democratization, showing that most theories of democratization that posit an international cause focus on elite behavior. Our explanation, by contrast, points to *citizens* as the agents of democratic change, whereby *private* international financial flows in the form of remittances spur the individual-level behaviors that ultimately undermine dictatorship. We then articulate our theory in detail, documenting how and where we expect remittances to shape voice (i.e., protest) and loyalty (i.e., voting).

Nearly all arguments suggesting that remittances harm democracy and help sustain autocratic rule hinge on the assumption that autocratic governments capture some of the revenue from private remittance inflows and alter their spending behavior accordingly. In chapter 3 we therefore examine this assumption empirically by looking at how remittances influence government revenue collection. We then discuss how remittances, even if not captured directly by governments as revenue, might still allow autocratic governments to substitute one type of spending for another, freeing up their resources to buy additional political support or repress citizens. We examine how remittances in fact shape government spending practices and repressive behavior, finding that there is simply no empirical evidence in the relevant global data patterns consistent with the contention that remittances increase government revenue, alter government spending behavior, or increase political repression.

In chapter 4, we examine how remittances shape voice: that is, political protest. We posit that remittances increase the resources available to political opponents for mobilizing dissent against autocratic governments in two ways. First, additional private income from remittances eases material constraints upon political action. Second, remittances directly fund opposition parties and civil society organizations, making opposition protest more likely. Our argument therefore contrasts not only with the idea that emigration of unemployed young men should reduce protest, but also with claims that remittances reduce economic grievances towards, and therefore mobilization against, the government. We show that remittance recipients are more likely to protest than are citizens whose income is not supplemented by this external resource. Consistent with the theory positing that remittances fund political opponents, we demonstrate that remittances mobilize resistance in opposition areas but not in regime-stronghold regions. At a global level, meanwhile, we provide evidence that remittances boost anti-government protest mobilization in non-democracies.

Chapter 5 examines how remittances influence loyalty: that is, electoral outcomes. Worker remittances undermine autocratic ruling regimes, we argue, by reducing citizens' dependence on government transfers and public goods. By giving individuals and households an option to exit from government patronage networks, remittances sever the clientelistic links between voters and incumbent dictators, causing defections from their support coalition. Further, by increasing their resources, remittances boost the capacity of opposition parties to challenge the regime in elections. At the macro-level, we show that remittances are associated with lower voter turnout in elections and fewer votes for incumbent ruling parties. At the micro-level, we document precisely how remittances lower turnout: incumbents focus their turnout-buying strategies on poor voters in swing districts and thus it is among these voters in particular that we find evidence that remittance receipt reduces the likelihood of turning out to vote. By lowering turnout among those whose support is most easily purchased by incumbent ruling parties, remittances undermine electoral authoritarianism.

Chapter 6 brings together the various pieces of our story. We start with a discussion of two illustrative cases, Senegal and Cambodia, to show how the mechanisms we have described brought about political instability in both non-democratic countries. We then show that remittances have a meso-level impact. Particularly, they shape civil society organizations and enhance the strength of opposition parties by increasing their resources and autonomy.

These two intervening mechanisms, we posit, further contribute to linking the micro-level behavioral effects of remittances to the macro-outcome we ultimately care about: the prospects for democratic transition. Our tests reveal that remittances have a positive and significant effect on the likelihood of democratization.

In chapter 7, we examine the relationship between monetary and social remittances. Our theory posits that *financial* remittances alter the balance of power between citizens and governments in dictatorships by providing political opponents with additional resources and weakening loyalty among nominal supporters. However, whether using either aggregate measures of national-level remittance inflows or individual-level accounts of remittance receipt to test our theory, we cannot rule out the possibility that the social, rather than the financial or monetary, dimension of remittance transfers is the causal factor that shapes the individual behavior and macro-political outcomes of interest. The chapter therefore proposes several tests to allow us to adjudicate between these two competing mechanisms, social and monetary remittances.

The concluding chapter places our argument in context. We first discuss how our theory and evidence might simply be interpreted as an account of how migrant remittances finance anti-incumbent behavior. In autocratic contexts, anti-incumbent behavior undermines authoritarian rule and opens up the possibility of democratization. In other contexts, however, anti-incumbent behavior need not necessarily translate into democratic political change. Indeed there is a growing number of cases in which migration and consequent remittances may have fueled the rise of opposition parties that are not particularly democratic in a normative sense, but rather may seek to undermine democracy once in power. We then articulate the implications of our argument for several important political and economic debates: the merits of globalization, with an eye towards understanding how our theory might apply to future waves of globalization; the appropriateness of migration restrictions and border control policies; and finally, the understanding of migration as a tool for the promotion of democracy.

# 2

# Migration and Repertoires of Contention: How Remittances Undermine Dictatorship

Individuals and social groups use various forms of political engagement to oppose and resist autocratic rule. Tilly (2006) defined the set of strategies political actors employ to make claims in a given social context as "repertoires of contention." These repertoires, he stressed, vary across time and space, as do the political outcomes they generate. Globalization and international migration create new forms of contention and new types of (non-state) political actor that, as many scholars highlight, redefine the conceptual and territorial boundaries of political identity and action (Vertovec and Cohen 1999; Levitt 2001; Risse 2002; Tarrow 2005). A central tenet of this framework maintains that international migrants constitute a central and transformative part of homeland politics, and that the intensity and variety of their political activities has grown as the technological advances in communications and transportation that underpin globalization spread (Østergaard-Nielsen 2003b; Levitt and Jaworsky 2007).

At the same time, a growing strand of democratization studies offers new perspectives on the role that international factors play in this process. Until recently, however, the literatures on global migration and democratization have remained mostly separate. The former tends to focus on migrants and diasporas—on their complex identities, activities, and motivations for political engagement—and less on the political behavior of family members who remain at home. The democratization literature, meanwhile, has had a marked structuralist bias and often lacks clear conceptual categories for the many dimensions of the international forces that shape it. This obscures the causal mechanisms linking transnational actors and global processes to democratization. This book attempts to bridge the gap between these fields by exploring theoretically and testing empirically the specific mechanisms through which remittances shape democratic change in migrant-sending countries. It does so by examining how remittances influence the different repertoires of contention in which citizens in dictatorships engage.

This chapter explains how remittances shape autocratic survival, with a focus on the micro-mechanisms connecting global factors, such as migration and remittances, to citizens' repertoires of domestic political engagement. We proceed by several steps. First, we highlight the increasing importance of citizens as the key actors driving political change in autocratic polities. We show not only that elections and protests are the most common types of event leading to the collapse of dictatorships, but also that there exists a strong correlation between the way in which autocracies fall and the type of subsequent regime. Democratic transitions typically follow in those cases where dictatorships collapse as a result of bottom-up pressure in the form of protests or elections (and often both). This change in patterned pathways underscores the need to explore the political and economic transformations that empower the masses in the context of increased globalization: namely, migration and attendant remittance inflows. Remittances, we argue, by empowering citizens and narrowing the resource gap between the regime and the opposition, weaken autocratic rule. Moreover, crucially, by spurring protests and undermining electoral support for autocratic incumbents, remittances foster democratization. The literature documenting international explanations for democratization has largely ignored this key dimension of globalization. Many of the mechanisms suggested by comparative democracy studies remain untested; some neglect actors and agency, and others are not fully specified. Further, when this literature takes up the topic of remittances, it often treats them as a purely economic phenomenon, largely ignoring the political ramifications of one of the largest international inflows of foreign income in the developing world in the past three decades.

Second, we situate remittances within the broader debate about how international factors influence the prospects of democracy by outlining the specific micro-mechanisms through which this external income alters the internal balance of power in dictatorships. Rather than positing a structural explanation for democratization, or relying on assumptions about certain actors' preferences and behavior, we highlight how political actors' agency, fueled by remittances from abroad, shapes democratization trajectories. This is important, because the vast majority of autocratic breakdowns are the result of actions taken by domestic actors, either the elites or the masses; only a handful of dictatorships are defeated from the outside by foreign invasion. This means that, in general, to the extent that external forces advance democracy, they do so by changing the capabilities and/or incentives of domestic actors such as elites, the opposition, or the public. As we emphasized in our Introduction and document in the next chapter, remittances largely accrue directly to citizens, not to governments or even to elite domestic actors. Migrants' exit and the resulting remittances therefore alter the political behavior of those left behind, but do not boost state resources. In this way, we claim, they contribute to the undermining of autocratic rule by increasing citizens' ability to challenge the regime and by reducing their incentives to vote for incumbent ruling parties.

We then discuss the main arguments that, contrary to ours, claim remittances harm the prospects of democratization in recipient countries. One theory contends that remitted income stabilizes non-democracies by increasing, either directly or indirectly, the resources available to authoritarian governments as other windfall revenues have been shown to do. Such additional resources could then be used to reward loyalists, co-opt potential opponents, or repress the latter more effectively. Another argument suggests that because remittances provide a resource that boosts recipients' consumption of important welfare goods, this external income induces satisfaction with the status quo. If remittances boost consumption and reduce grievances, according to this logic, their effect should be to diminish citizens' incentives for voicing dissent.

Against this background, we propose two mechanisms that suggest migrants' remittances in fact advance democracy. The first posits that the additional resources from remittances increase the capacity and incentives of citizens to express their voice by taking to the streets in protest. Financial remittances can either provide additional income to households and individuals or directly fund opposition groups and organizations. The second mechanism suggests that remittances undermine a key strategy employed by autocratic regimes to retain loyalty: namely, buying voters' electoral support. By reducing citizens' dependence on regime-delivered goods, remittances sever the clientelistic ties to and reduce electoral support for incumbent ruling parties. Of importance is that we outline which types of citizen are theoretically most likely to be affected by each of these mechanisms. While remittances mobilize some recipients to voice dissent, they can simultaneously demobilize others, making them less likely to demonstrate loyalty. We focus on two factors, political preferences and socio-economic status, that explain who is mobilized and who is demobilized by remittances and that help to identify which theoretical mechanism better fits the expected empirical patterns.

## 2.1. Citizens as Agents of Change

The repertoires of resistance against dictatorships have changed dramatically over the past few decades. Historically, dictators' elite supporters were the greatest threat to the leader; and the main technique for ousting dictators was the military coup. Because the military are typically adept at acting collectively, one group could use them to oust another from power, replacing one dictatorship with another.[1] However, structural transformations related to globalization as well as normative and technological changes have altered the primary threats to authoritarian rule and thus the manner in which most dictatorships now collapse. The standard military coup that so often led to regime change during the Cold War period is rapidly giving way to situations in which the mass political behavior of large swathes of citizens—acting together in elections and popular uprisings—plays a central role in toppling dictatorships (Kendall-Taylor and Frantz 2014a;b).

Large, sustained anti-government protests precipitated the downfall of a number of autocracies in the recent decades (Zunes 1994; McFaul 2002; Chenoweth and Stephan 2011; Kim and Kroeger 2019), including the wave of protests that toppled Eastern European Communist regimes, the Color Revolutions in several post-Communist regimes, the Arab Spring in the Middle East and North Africa, and repeated waves of protest in sub-Saharan Africa. More recently, massive protests have been challenging autocratic governments in Venezuela and Nicaragua, while a series of demonstrations forced Omar al-Bashir and Abdelaziz Bouteflika from power in Sudan and Algeria respectively. In all of these cases, protesters did not simply call for dictators to step down, but sought additional democratic reforms.

Several other regimes lost at the ballot box and stepped down to pave the way for new political structures. In 2000 alone, opposition parties won executive elections in Mexico, Ghana, Taiwan, and Senegal, defeating long-lasting dominant parties. In 2002, the dominant Kenya African National Union lost presidential and parliamentary elections, ending four decades of one-party rule; and in 2018, the UMNO-led coalition Barisan Nasional (BN) suffered its first electoral defeat after more than six decades monopolizing power in Malaysia. A growing number of cases, meanwhile, involve protests toppling regimes after incumbents attempt to manipulate electoral results (Beaulieu 2014). In Serbia, for example, Slobodan Milošević resigned in the face of massive protests in the streets, sparked by his refusal to accept the results of the 2000 presidential election, which the opposition had won. In Belarus, an unprecedented wave of protests in 2020 followed the announcement of election results that gave President Lukashenko 80 percent of the vote.

Figure 2.1 illustrates how the manner in which dictatorships collapse has changed over time.[2] The chart shows the shares of regime-collapse events that fall into different categories, for three periods: the Cold War (1946–90), the post–Cold War era (1991–2010), and the 2000s.[3] During the Cold War, military coups were the predominant way in which dictatorships collapsed, comprising 44 percent of all regime-breakdown events. Regime collapse by election was half as likely as a military coup, while protest uprisings were just over a third as likely. Since 1990, by contrast, electoral defeats and popular protests have become the most common way for autocracies to collapse; indeed, in the 2000s, elections have accounted for 40 percent of regime-collapse events, and popular uprisings for another quarter; while military coups have meanwhile brought about only about 12 percent of collapses. In

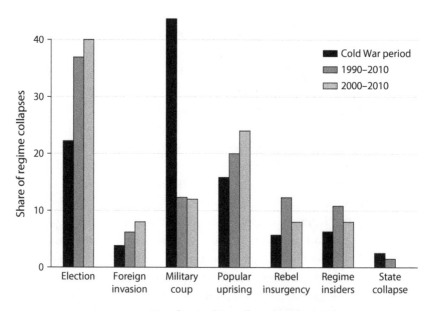

FIGURE 2.1. How dictatorships collapse, by time period

short, elections and protest campaigns have replaced military coups as the main means of political change in dictatorships. This means that large groups of dissenting citizens, organizing their collective behavior in elections and protests, are now the primary threat to authoritarian rule.

The way in which dictatorships collapse is not only relevant to an understanding of which key actors are involved, but also has implications in terms of the prospects for democracy. The manner in which an autocracy collapses often correlates with the type of regime that follows. When autocracies are forcefully or violently ousted, they tend to be followed by a further dictatorship (Hadenius and Teorell 2007; Rivera and Gleditsch 2013; Geddes et al. 2014a; Escribà-Folch and Wright 2015; Frantz 2018a). Use of violent force or the credible threat of violence to destabilize autocracies normally occurs in the context of competition for the control of power between rival elite groups. Indeed, over the entire period reviewed, roughly 90 percent of regimes that were overthrown in a coup gave way to a new autocracy; and this figure has not changed much since the end of the Cold War, remaining at 85 percent.[4] In contrast, overall, roughly 85 percent of regime breakdowns that have come on the heels of incumbents losing multiparty elections have given way to new democracies; and this total increases to nearly 95 percent for the post–Cold War period. Further, popular uprisings are more often than not followed by democratization (Rivera and Gleditsch 2013; Kim and Kroeger 2019).[5] Between 1946 and 2010, roughly 60 percent of revolts that managed to overthrow a dictatorship were followed by a transition to democracy. For the period since 1990, this figure stands at nearly 70 percent. These patterns suggest that when citizens drive political change in dictatorships, democracy is more likely to follow.

This marked change in the methods that political actors most commonly employ to bring down dictatorships is, in part, a response to several global political and technological transformations. First, the collapse of the Soviet Union and the consequent end of the Cold War brought about a profound change in the international geopolitical environment, as well as in the strategic priorities of Western democratic powers. It ended a period during which some democracies not only accepted but even encouraged and backed coups against unfriendly governments (though the post-1990 era of "democracy promotion" may now be coming to an end). Further, many members of the international community have increased their opposition to coups; indeed, some observers point to an evolving "anti-coup" norm as part of a broader commitment to democracy. Many regional organizations have institutionalized this norm and several democracies have made explicit commitments to condemn and impose sanctions upon regimes established by military coup by, for example, withdrawing aid (Shannon et al. 2015; Tansey 2017; 2018).

As coups have declined proportionally, so international promotion of multiparty elections has increased, broadening the opportunities for as well as the repertoires of contention citizens in dictatorships can exploit. Until the late 1980s and early 1990s, elections in dictatorships were mostly "contests" with only one party on the ballot; since 1990, however, most autocracies have permitted multiparty competition (Gandhi 2015; Geddes et al. 2018). Western countries and international organizations have promoted and rewarded the adoption of multiparty elections, even if they are flawed, with foreign aid and trade advantages (Miller 2020). International organizations have also become increasingly involved in assisting dictatorships in organizing—and even monitoring—elections.

The presence of pseudo-democratic institutions in dictatorships has become so common that almost all non-democracies now feature regular, multiparty elections. Yet elections can, at times, work to the dictators' advantage, aiding authoritarian resilience (Gandhi and Lust-Okar 2009; Knutsen et al. 2017). In fact, the growing number of elections alongside multiparty legislatures has been a critical analogue to the gradual decline in coups. Dictators may use these democratic-looking institutions to co-opt elites and opposition groups and, as importantly, to regularize access to power, which reduces the incentive for elites to mobilize against the dictator. Authoritarian regimes employ numerous strategies to tilt the electoral balance in their favor, including vote- or turnout-buying, opposition repression and intimidation, and outright fraud (Schedler 2013; Morse 2018). Despite substantial advantages for the incumbent, authoritarian elections often retain some degree of uncertainty about who will win and by how much, leaving plenty of room for mass political behavior to influence the outcome (Howard and Roessler 2006; Bunce and Wolchik 2010; Hyde and Marinov 2012; Knutsen et al. 2017). In the end, multiparty elections, and the emergence of opposition organizations that accompanies them, help coordinate citizens' behavior, lowering the costs of expressing discontent both in the voting booth and when demonstrating in the streets against unfair practices.

In parallel to these political transformations that have opened opportunities to coordinate mass dissent, rapid innovations in information and communications technologies (ICTs) have increased the capacity of citizens to engage in costlier forms of participation, contributing to a global rise of protest campaigns (Ruijgrok 2017).[6] The mechanisms behind this relationship are straightforward. For one, more channels for expressing grievances and an increased communication capacity reduce the collective action and coordination costs involved in mass action (Christensen and Garfias 2018). ICTs, according to this logic, enable political opponents to better estimate levels of dissatisfaction with the regime and to inform others rapidly about when and where to act (Little 2016). Further, citizens increasingly utilize communications technology to quickly spread information about events such as protests or acts of repression, both within and outside the country's borders, that encourages people to organize and join demonstrations (Christensen and Garfias 2018; Weidmann and Rød 2019).

Are there additional factors that empower citizens to undermine autocratic rule? We certainly think so; in particular, we argue that migration and especially the resulting remittance flows to migrant-sending countries are key components fueling the rise of popular action to challenge autocratic regimes. Remittances, we argue, provide additional resources to mobilize protests and erode incumbent electoral support—two complementary processes that undermine authoritarian rule. This underscores the influence of international factors, which the next section discusses.

## 2.2. Global Forces and Democratization

Migration and the monetary remittances that flow across borders are a key component of globalization. By studying the political consequences of these phenomena in non-democratic contexts, this book speaks to the literature that examines how international forces shape authoritarian stability and democratization.[7] After an initial focus on the domestic conditions for political change, a large body of scholarship now examines the role of international factors (e.g., Huntington 1991; Pridham 1994; Whitehead 1996; Pevehouse 2005; Levitsky and Way 2006).

External forces take several forms, including contextual events, such as the diffusion of protests across borders, and structural features of the international environment, such as the change from a bi-polar international order during the Cold War period to one with a sole superpower in the subsequent decades (Boix 2011; Gunitsky 2017). For example, the comparative-democratization literature identifies a pattern of spatial and temporal clustering of democracy that might be explained by the diffusion of protests and elections in neighboring countries (Starr 1991; Brinks and Coppedge 2006; Gleditsch and Ward 2006; Elkink 2011; Houle et al. 2016). A related argument suggests that membership of regional international organizations makes democratization more likely (Pevehouse 2005). Others point to structural changes that influence democratization prospects. For example, socioeconomic transformations brought about by economic globalization may shape the trajectory of democratization (Li and Reuveny 2009). Economic and cultural linkages to the West, meanwhile, combined with Western leverage over autocracies, may determine the prospects for democratization in a post–Cold War period characterized by competitive authoritarianism (Levitsky and Way 2010).

A second set of factors consists of deliberate foreign policies adopted by outside actors—mainly democratic governments and international organizations—who intend to promote liberalizing reforms in autocratic polities. Foreign actors promote democracy in differing ways that vary in their degree of coercion and effectiveness.[8] Some instruments, such as democracy assistance, electoral monitoring, and trade and investment agreements, attempt to persuade autocratic elites to reform or directly invest in internal pro-democratic actors (see, e.g., Finkel et al. 2007). Other policies, such as economic sanctions, military interventions, and conditional foreign aid, try to coerce non-democracies into pursuing democratic reforms (Escribà-Folch and Wright 2015).

Remittances can be mapped onto these conceptual categories, with some important caveats. For one, remittances are a facet of globalization driven by increasing linkages between countries. Indeed, Levitsky and Way (2010) point to migration as one of the cross-border ties that condition the degree of linkage between autocratic countries and the West. As noted earlier, high-income countries are the main destination for migrant workers, hosting about two-thirds of all international migrants (United Nations 2017). However, Levitsky and Way do not specify the mechanisms through which different types of linkages might influence the internal balance of power in dictatorships. Trade and investment, for example, establish different kinds of linkage from migration and remittances, the former presumably operating by influencing political and economic elite actors in autocracies, not mass behavior; and, while trade and investment flows are linkages that Western democracies have actively encouraged, migration is not.

On the other hand, remittances are not simply a passive force that shapes political outcomes devoid of agency and intentionality. Nor are they a specific foreign policy instrument that Western governments and international organizations deploy to promote democracy abroad. If anything, one might argue, governments in the Global North make periodic moves to curtail migration and, perhaps inadvertently, the remittance flows that follow from cross-border movements of people.[9] Migration and, specifically, the remittances that flow as a result are both relatively slow-moving structural features of globalization and an individually motivated cross-border flow that shapes contingent, actor-specific political behavior in migrant-sending countries.

### 2.2.1. How International Forces Shape Authoritarian Survival

Remittances or any other external force can only spur political change by altering the environment in which domestic actors operate and make political decisions. As illustrated earlier in this chapter, the vast majority of autocratic breakdowns result from actions by *domestic* actors: the individuals who execute coups, rebel, participate in elections, and join or repress protests nearly always reside in the targeted dictatorship.[10] With the exception of foreign invasion, external actors and forces can only influence autocratic regime stability through the behavior of domestic actors (Escribà-Folch and Wright 2015, 19,50).[11]

The extant literature on autocratic politics identifies two key domestic actors whose behavior largely explains stability and change in dictatorships: elites and the masses (Svolik 2012; Geddes et al. 2018). Elites are members of the ruling coalition who may decide to challenge the leader, either by defecting, pushing for democratic reforms, or staging a coup. The masses, meanwhile, largely stand outside the inner circle of the ruling coalition, but may manifest nominal support for the regime by either turning out at a pro-government rally or plumping for the ruling party at election time. Mirroring this distinction, an important part of the actor-centered democratization literature has been dominated by debates over whether transitions were primarily precipitated by elites' decisions or by the pressure exerted by non-elite social actors.

Both earlier and recent contributions to democratic transition theory favor elite-based explanations, claiming that regime breakdown and democratization result from intra-elite divisions and subsequent negotiations and, more recently, from conditions that reduce the risks associated with exiting from power and holding free elections (O'Donnell and Schmitter 1986; Przeworski 1991; Haggard and Kaufman 2016; Albertus and Menaldo 2018; Riedl et al.

2020). Alternatively, studies focusing on non-elite actors have tended to focus on discussions about which social class—the bourgeoisie or the working class—played a more prominent role (e.g., Moore 1966; Rueschemeyer et al. 1992; Bellin 2000), rather than on the repertoires employed to push for political reform. The role of bottom-up political change in contemporary regimes did not receive much empirical attention until the 1990s, when mass protests led to the collapse of much of the Communist bloc and to many dictatorships in sub-Saharan Africa, and later still with regard to other world regions (see, e.g., Bratton and van de Walle 1997; Chenoweth and Stephan 2011; Della Porta 2014; Pinckney 2020).

The recent wave of democratic change driven from below and the scholarly work investigating it highlighted several limitations of early studies. First, they underscored the higher effectiveness of nonviolent resistance campaigns as compared to violent revolutionary methods. Second, they reveal a broader role for protests in influencing democratization: protests can not only directly overthrow regimes, but they can also bring about splits in elites or coerce incumbent elites into conceding democratic reforms (Kim and Kroeger 2019; Riedl et al. 2020): pathways to democratization that scholars may had wrongly considered to be elite-driven.[12] Finally, the "third wave" of democratization also taught us that citizens taking to the streets in protest is not the sole mechanism of democratization, but that multiparty elections within autocracies—in many cases a response to foreign pressure—are a growing and crucial pathway towards it, furnishing citizens with opportunities to cease voting for ruling parties and even vote for the opposition instead (Howard and Roessler 2006; Bunce and Wolchik 2010; Schedler 2013).[13]

The behavior of both elites and the masses is undoubtedly shaped by external forces. Therefore, the study of the international dimension of democratization requires scholars to specify the causal mechanisms that link outside factors to changes in the incentives and capacities of domestic political actors (Escribà-Folch and Wright 2015, 50). In elite-based accounts of democratization, external forces, often accompanied by "carrots or sticks," either precipitate divisions within the regime's ruling coalition or alter elites' political preferences and incentives. For example, membership of regional international organizations may promote democratization by persuading, socializing, or pressuring autocratic elites into changing their beliefs and ultimately their behavior (Pevehouse 2005). A defeat in an international war or a global economic crisis may cause disagreements among elite factions about how best to address such situations. Democratic changes in neighboring countries, meanwhile, combined with stronger linkages to the West, may change the incentives of elites to pursue reform, by increasing the value of adopting democratic institutions, which come with the benefit of additional cooperation or increased economic exchange (Gleditsch and Ward 2006; Levitsky and Way 2010). Finally, instruments of foreign coercion—such as economic sanctions, human-rights shaming campaigns, and threats to prosecute repressive leaders—often undermine the regime's capacity to pursue its best survival strategy, whether it be co-opting elites or repressing the masses (Escribà-Folch and Wright 2015). The behavior of domestic political actors embedded in global historical transformations constitutes the key link between outside structural forces and domestic political change (Schwartzman 1998).

For domestic political opponents, including both large groups of loosely coordinated individuals and long-standing opposition parties, the impact of international factors remains under-studied. Previous research suggests that external forces operate by changing their incentives, beliefs, and preferences, but mostly by altering their capacity to challenge the regime. For example, external actors such as international non-governmental organizations (INGOs) and foreign governments may boost the capabilities of domestic opposition groups by providing material assistance as well as information, training, and tactical support to civil society organizations (Murdie and Bhasin 2011).[14] Further, international condemnation or economic sanctions may weaken the relative power of the government by emboldening anti-regime groups: signals of international disapproval when regimes repress their citizens might spur protests in response (Klotz 1995; Allen 2008; Escribà-Folch and Wright 2015). Similarly, citizens in one autocracy may mobilize against the government after witnessing protests in neighboring countries. Cross-border emulation, learning, and adaptation have aided several pro-democracy protest cascades throughout history (Hale 2013).[15] More generally, extensive linkages to the democratic West shape both preferences and capacities. Strong ties to the West increase "the number of domestic actors with a stake in adhering to regional or international democratic norms" and alter the internal balance of power in favor of pro-democratic actors by providing international support and, interestingly, additional resources (Levitsky and Way 2010, 47).

## 2.2.2. Remittances as a Global Force for Bottom-Up Democratization

Even when explicit causal links between outside forces and domestic actors are taken into account, however, elite-based explanations still dominate the study of international influences on regime transitions. In their recent book,

Haggard and Kaufman (2016, 142), for example, assert that these external pressures or influences "are complementary or secondary to the mobilization of mass protest." They further suggest that "[i]n elite-led transitions, by contrast, we would expect international inducements and constraints to play a larger role in the calculations of authoritarian incumbents." That might be true for some international factors but, as we shall argue in the following sections, not for the case of migrants' remittances.

The potential democratizing effect of remittances, we posit, works through citizens, not elites: placing our argument amongst bottom-up approaches to democratic change, broadly understood. Remittances both increase the resources available to political opponents for mobilizing dissent against the government and sever the clientelistic ties between electoral autocracies and the voters they traditionally mobilize. This external income thus alters the political behavior of the individuals and communities receiving it and, in turn, the internal balance of power in non-democratic, migrant-sending countries. As remittance flows have increased over time, so too have the macro-political phenomena that we postulate they shape: democratization resulting from protest and incumbent electoral defeat—two types of event that, as shown above, are increasingly associated with regime change.

Importantly, by investigating the liberalizing potential of remittances and the specific mechanisms through which this occurs, our theory and analysis moves from the micro- to the meso- and macro-levels. To explore the individual-level effects of remittances, we use survey data from several autocratic countries. In contrast to much of the research discussed above, this approach allows us to test the micro-mechanisms that connect external factors to changes in behavior of specific domestic political actors. We then examine whether global remittance flows shape the meso- and macro-political phenomena—protests, elections, oppositions' organizational strength, and ultimately democratic transitions—that we posit should result from aggregating the individual-level behaviors we identify.

## 2.3. Remittances and Democratization: What Comes after Exit?

The political impacts of migration have often been examined in terms of Hirschman's (1970) 'exit, voice, and loyalty' (henceforth EVL) model. This model explores alternative human behavioral choices when confronting discontent caused by deterioration in the quality of some organization's output.

In regard to relations between the state and its citizenry, Hirschman conceptualizes emigration as a form of exit, while voice involves the public expression of discontent. Thus voice is an attempt "to change rather than to escape from an objectionable state of affairs" (30), and comprises many behavioral responses, "all the way from faint grumbling to violent protest" (Hirschman 1970, 16). Importantly, this framework treats exit and voice as mutually exclusive strategies, whereby exit entails forgoing voice. Hirschman conceptualizes loyalty, meanwhile, less as a third, exclusive option and more as a factor that amplifies or conditions the choice between voice and exit. For example, strong affective ties to the state or an organization make exit less likely, which may instead lead citizens to opt for voice rather than exit, or make them more likely to remain silent when aggrieved. For those with strong attachments to the state or ruling regime, loyalty when discontented may simply be manifested as quiescence. However, many applications of the EVL framework to political contexts interpret loyalty, resulting from ideological or emotional attachments, rather as a third course of action that ranges from passive acquiescence to active support for an organization or institution.[16]

According to this approach, emigration makes political change less likely, because exit undermines voice. The resulting "exit as a safety-valve" analogy implies that "with exit available as an outlet for the disaffected, they were less likely to resort to voice" (Hirschman 1978, 102). States might tolerate or even encourage exit if emigration relieves social and political tensions that cause internal instability. If emigration weakens internal voices calling for democratization, a political "brain drain" may result (Moses 2011, 49). Open emigration policies, according to this logic, should reduce protests and other contentious activities in non-democracies, by allowing dissenters to leave (Alemán and Woods 2014; Barry et al. 2014).[17]

This framework, whereby voice and exit are alternative behavioral options, cannot account for migrants' transnational behavior once they have left, however, and in particular for their political engagement in home country politics from abroad. Many migrants are temporary laborers and engage in cycles of migration between home and host countries.[18] Even when migrants remain in host countries indefinitely, moreover, they still participate in politics in their home countries in a variety of ways. The standard EVL model, with mutually exclusive voice and exit options, cannot account for the real world experiences of transnational political activism and circular migration.

Recent work on migration has therefore adapted Hirschman's EVL framework to emphasize that exit and voice are not in fact mutually exclusive: the same actors, in this case migrants, may engage in voice *after* exit, and even after returning to their home country (Fox 2007; Hoffmann 2010; Burgess 2012). These adaptations of the EVL framework conceptualize remittances both as a strategy that migrants employ to exercise loyalty to their community of origin from abroad and as an instrument to exercise voice in home-country politics.

Our theory departs from these reinterpretations of the EVL framework, however, insofar as we focus less on migrants themselves—and how their exit, voice, and loyalty blend together—and instead theorize how remittance *recipients*—those left behind—change their political behavior and engage in home-country politics. Emigrant exit and the consequent remittance flows are a precondition or initial step for what comes next, irrespective of the individual-level political motivations of the migrants who send remittances. Our theory presented below focuses on the political behavior of remittance recipients in autocracies, and examines how their behavior differs from that of citizens who do not receive such external income; we then tease out the macro-political consequences of these behavioral differences. In the context of the EVL model, we argue that remittances shape how recipients exercise voice and loyalty, which alters the internal balance of power in authoritarian contexts and, in turn, increases the prospects for democratization.

That said, we can nevertheless map our proposed theoretical mechanisms linking remittances to democracy onto two extensions of the EVL model. First, Farrell (1983) proposes a two-dimensional framework for EVL: active vs. passive behavior, and destructive vs. constructive behavior. This model allows for "neglect," whereby citizens remain (i.e., do not exit) but also do not voice support for leadership. Neglect, or "destructive passivity" in Farrell's terms, maps closely onto our proposed mechanism whereby remittances reduce the effectiveness of the turnout-buying strategies that sustain electoral autocracies. Second, Fox (2007, ch. 10) conceptualizes a slightly different two-dimensional EVL framework in the context of migration, featuring voice vs. silence and stay vs. migrate. This model permits *exit with voice* (as opposed to exit without voice), which is consistent with our proposed mechanism suggesting that financial remittances fund political opposition to autocratic regimes at home.

In light of the various theoretical approaches stemming from the EVL framework and subsequent adaptations, we outline two sets of theories that yield opposite predictions about how remittances might influence political behavior and, ultimately, autocratic stability. A first view, which we call the *stabilization hypothesis*, suggests that remittances sustain autocracy by providing additional income and affecting behavior at two distinct levels. At the individual level, extra family resources reduce social grievances among recipients and weaken the motivation to oppose incumbent governments. At the state level, remittances may increase the resources available to authoritarian governments, which regimes would then deploy to reduce opportunities for expressing discontent, perhaps by increasing political repression or paying citizens to keep quiet. In terms of the EVL framework, but with a focus on remittance recipients, this process implies that those who receive remittances will have weaker incentives and opportunities for using dissenting voice: additional resources either increase loyalty, observable as manifest support, or alternatively, increase neglect, which is manifested as decreased interest and passive disengagement (Farrell 1983). This approach thus still conceptualizes exit as detrimental to voice, but rather than making exit and voice mutually exclusive options, it suggests mechanisms that entail migrant exit and consequent remittances increasing loyalty and decreasing voice among those left behind.

We propose instead a second view, the *destabilization hypothesis*, which claims that remittances in autocratic contexts increase voice among some recipients and reduce loyalty among others. For some, we argue, remittances lead to more voice, which, in autocratic contexts with limited institutional channels for expressing discontent, amounts to increasing manifest dissent in the form of protests. Remittances, according to this argument, provide economic resources that enable opponents to express their discontent in contexts where such activities tend to be quite costly and opposition groups lack sufficient strength. We anticipate that, in areas where loyalty to the regime is low, remittances will largely operate by channeling resources to the voicing of discontent among political opponents. Remittances can both provide lower-income citizens with additional resources necessary for costly participation and fund opposition organizations and social movements.

For others, receiving remittances weakens loyalty, by severing clientelistic ties between citizens and the regime. Weakened loyalty, we posit, should become manifest as reduced support—either at the polls or even in pro-government rallies—for incumbent rulers and parties. In autocratic settings, rulers sustain their power by mobilizing electoral support in exchange for handouts and other regime-delivered goods; and thus for many voters loyalty to the regime may not be particularly ideological, but arise rather from material benefits that result from turning out to vote for the regime. When remittances provide additional family income, recipients rely less on regime largesse, allowing them to escape from clientelistic networks. This turns them into unreliable voters, unlikely to turn out to support the incumbent party at election time. Because autocrats carefully target loyal or mildly opposed voters in an effort to maximize the electoral return on their material payments, exit from clientelistic networks should be most evident among poorer individuals who live in areas where ruling parties are most likely to concentrate their turnout-buying resources: namely, swing districts. While one might interpret this mechanism as detrimental to voice, because it leads to less voting and therefore disengagement from politics, in the context of electoral authoritarianism lower turnout for the ruling party erodes its hold on power.

In what follows, we discuss these approaches with a focus on the micro-mechanisms that underpin important macro-political outcomes, such as protest campaigns, electoral support for the regime, and ultimately democratization. Because most dictatorships collapse as a result of elections or popular uprisings, we concentrate on these two repertoires of contention, arguing that if remittances encourage protest and reduce turnout at the micro-level, they should be relatable to a higher probability of democratization at the macro-level. To explore the individual-level effects of remittances, we build on existing theories of political behavior to which, we think, remittances speak: the grievance theory and the resource model. We then theorize how moderating individual and contextual factors shape the political behaviors that we posit result from remittance receipt. In doing so, we identify the (sub-)groups of citizens who are most likely to mobilize (protest) in response to additional remittance income and those who, on the contrary, are most likely to be demobilized (abstain from voting).

### 2.3.1. Remittances Sustain Dictatorship: Repression, Patronage, and Grievance

Two main arguments suggest that remittances stabilize non-democratic regimes and incumbent governments more generally. Some specify individual citizens as the primary theoretical focus, while others emphasize state behavior, with the strong assumption that governments, either directly or indirectly, capture remittance income.

Individual-centered approaches focus on reduced motivation for individuals to use voice and act against the regime. Grievance-based approaches to the politics of contention posit that economic or political deprivation breeds discontent and resentment, and motivates dissent (Gurr 1970; Berkowitz 1972).

The basis for engaging in dissent activities, in this view, is thus motivation, and in particular motivation that emerges from the desire to transform a status quo deemed to be unfair to an individual or a social group.[19] Comparative evidence using cross-country data suggests that poor economic conditions and relative deprivation breed protests, especially in weak and non-democratic polities (Brancati 2014). Conclusions from evidence based in survey analysis are mixed. Using data on a wide cross-section of African countries, Bratton et al. (2005) find grievances to be only weakly related to protest, while Mueller (2018) finds that individuals are more likely to protest if they have low expectations of upward mobility, consider their economic conditions to have worsened over the past year, or they think their ethnic group is treated unfairly. Similarly, a large literature on economic voting finds that poor economic performance increases the probability that voters will punish the incumbent in the ballot box (e.g., Lewis-Beck and Stegmaier 2007).

Relying on grievance theory, then, a set of arguments postulates that remitted money insures recipients against local economic fluctuations and thus reduces economic and social grievances. If remittances boost family incomes, the argument goes, they should alleviate social discontent and democratizing pressure by discouraging protests and electoral turnout. In EVL terminology, remittances should undermine the exercise of voice and promote (perhaps passive) loyalty instead. A significant body of research indicates that remittances are an important source of income for households in many developing countries, resulting in more consumption, service provision, and investment (World Bank 2006c; Fajnzylber and López 2007; Chami et al. 2008; Adida and Girod 2011), as well as reducing poverty (Adams and Page 2005; World Bank 2006a; Acosta et al. 2008). What is more, remittance inflows are not only highly stable over time but, as Frankel (2011) highlights, also tend to increase when recipients' incomes decrease, providing insurance against local income shocks (Yang and Choi 2007; Combes and Ebeke 2011). Income transfers from migrants thus serve as transnational safety nets, which are increasingly important in an era of neo-liberal globalization that pressures governments into reducing spending on social insurance (Germano 2018, 11). Remitted money may thus have a compensation and insurance function that reduces pressure on governments. If remittances increase economic optimism and, in turn, satisfaction with the political status quo, they may cause recipients to disengage from local politics.

There is indeed some evidence—mostly from survey data from Latin American democracies—that remittance receipt may foster disengagement at the micro-level (see, e.g., Goodman and Hiskey 2008; Germano 2013; Ahmed 2017; Germano 2018), and may reduce the risk of rebellion during crises at the macro-level (Regan and Frank 2014). Similarly, others posit that remittances insulate recipients from local economic conditions, prompting a reduction in political participation aimed at holding decision-makers accountable and lower support for public goods provision (Goodman and Hiskey 2008; Bravo 2009; Ebeke and Yogo 2013), including, for example, lowering support for taxation and social welfare spending (Doyle 2015). Some even suggest that remittance recipients incorrectly attribute increased income from remittances to government policies at home, to the extent that additional remittances boost incumbent approval, and vice versa (Tertytchnaya et al. 2018).

A second set of arguments concentrates on how remittances may alter state behavior. These state-centered approaches contend that remittances stabilize incumbent regimes because governments capture some of this foreign income and adjust their spending policies accordingly. While it is almost universally acknowledged that remittances accrue directly to individuals and households and are quite difficult to tax, some claim that governments can still appropriate some of this income, albeit indirectly. First, because remittances boost household income, they also increase consumption, which the government then taxes (Singer 2012; Asatryan et al. 2017). Indeed, additional income and consumption may have a multiplier effect on local economies that further boosts economic activity, which the government can, in turn, tax. This argument posits that, by resulting in a rise in taxes on consumption, remittances augment governments' revenue, thereby increasing funds available to buy support and enhance the security apparatus. However, research is silent so far as to whether the revenue-collection mechanism yields resources for autocratic governments substantial enough to tilt the internal power balance in favor of the regime—a topic we take up in the next chapter.

Others claim that remittances increase the resources available to regimes even if they do not generate extra public revenue. Building on the individual arguments above, the suggestion is that additional household income and consumption stemming from this external resource permits governments to substitute patronage spending and repression for public goods spending (Abdih et al. 2012; Ahmed 2012; Tyburski 2014; Easton and Montinola 2017; Mina 2019). In other words, when remittances increase, governments divert public resources away from public goods and service provision—items such as subsidies, health care, or social protection— and use this money to buy political support (patronage) or spend more on repression. Additional patronage spending, in turn, should increase loyalty to the regime and more resources for repression should reduce opportunities for voicing dissent. By allowing autocratic governments to substitute patronage or repression spending for public goods spending, remittances, according to this logic, should stabilize autocracies.

The evidence for these state-centered arguments, however, is very limited. Several works suggest that, like natural resources, remittances may breed corruption, so test whether they are correlated with macro-measures of institutional quality, such as rule of law or government effectiveness (Abdih et al. 2012; Ahmed 2013; Tyburski 2014). Notably, however, these studies do not address autocratic stability (or failure). The only one that focuses on political stability combines remittances with foreign aid as the explanatory device, without any careful examination of the former (Ahmed 2012). As importantly, this research analyzes autocratic *leadership* turnover, conflating leaders with regimes;[20] but many changes of leader in fact "simply reshuffle the leadership atop a dictatorship without substantially altering the group which holds power" (Escribà-Folch and Wright 2015, 39). Indeed, institutionalizing leadership change in dictatorships is one way to make them more stable, lowering the likelihood of democratization.

### 2.3.2. How Exit Funds Voice and Weakens Loyalty

We propose an alternative view that argues that remittances undermine autocracies via two mechanisms: increased voice and weakened loyalty. Building on adaptations to Hirschman's EVL model, we posit that these mechanisms are not mutually exclusive, but rather complement one another: remittances both increase voice and weaken loyalty within the same country, but among different groups of citizens who live in distinct contexts. As we note throughout, most existing applications of the EVL logic to politics not only treat voice and loyalty as mutually exclusive options for individual decision-makers, but then move this individual-level logic up to another level of analysis, namely to that of nation-state political processes. This type of theorizing often leads to the fallacy whereby one applies the logic of individual choices to decisions made by larger groups and then tests this logic on aggregate outcomes. We circumvent this problem by allowing for remittances to shape voice for some citizens and work through loyalty for others, all of whom may face the same autocratic regime. We then test our expectations using both individual- and country-level data, which allows us to examine whether the behavioral patterns observed at the micro-level have observable aggregate effects at the macro-level.

The existing empirical literature examining the impact of remittances on political behavior is largely inconclusive: while some studies find that remittances increase political engagement, many others show the opposite to be the case (Goodman and Hiskey 2008; Bravo 2009; Pérez-Armendáriz and Crow 2010; Ebeke and Yogo 2013; Pfutze 2014; Danielson 2018; Germano 2018). These mixed results might be interpreted as contradictory if we assume that remittances shape all forms of political behavior, for all people, in the same way. However, remittances may encourage some forms of participation but discourage others (Easton and Montinola 2017). For example, they may both lower the propensity to turn out in an election (an electoral demobilization effect) while, for the same individual, increasing participation in local political projects (a local participation mobilization effect), such as providing local public goods (see, e.g., Adida and Girod 2011). Further, these seemingly contradictory effects may result from contextual factors as well as from different groups of individuals behaving distinctly, which means we need to theorize as to why some remittance recipients may respond by mobilization while others appear to disengage from politics.

Even while recognizing the differing impact of remittances between individuals and distinguishing between different types of political behavior, it is worth noting that most research relating migration and remittances to political behavior focuses on new democracies. For example, Kapur's (2012) influential discussion of migrants' post-exit voice and loyalty examines how migration influences the quality of new democracies, not dictatorships. The country that has recently received by far most recent empirical attention is Mexico, moreover, which transitioned to democracy in 2000 after the opposition won a competitive presidential election. Yet, the profound differences that exist between democratic and non-democratic polities may call into question the applicability of the theoretical models traditionally used to understand participation in democracies.

While most of the studies suggesting a demobilizing effect of remittances rely on *grievance* theories of participation, our theory of remittances' impact focuses on the *resource* model of political mobilization, which also figures prominently in explanations of both individual and social movement behavior, and on models of clientelism. In the end, remittances are an external flow of additional income and, hence, of economic resources. Research in democratic countries unambiguously demonstrates that resources—in the form of income, education, and social networks—increase individuals' propensity to participate in politics and boost the mobilization capacity of social groups. However, the way additional resources shape alternative forms of political engagement is likely *context*-dependent, and therefore remittance resources may to some extent work differently in autocratic and democratic contexts. The distinct dynamics of mobilization (and demobilization), opportunities and costs, and the political consequences of participation in autocracies differ from those in democracies. Most notably, in dictatorships, conventional channels of participation are limited and/or ineffective, elections are rarely free and fair, the ruling regime has an enormous resource advantage over opposition groups, and dissenters face a high risk of state repression—all of which increase the costs of contention. Yet, research on the determinants of the basic forms of political participation—protest and electoral turnout—in autocracies typically relies on data aggregated at the country level; so our empirical knowledge of how individuals respond to changes in resources (or grievances) is limited.

Consider first the case of voting. Research focused on autocracies contends that, contrary to patterns typically observed in democracies, resources reduce individuals' propensity to show up to the polls. For example, Blaydes (2010), using district-level data, shows that underclasses (i.e., illiterate citizens) turned out to vote at higher rates than did wealthy citizens during Mubarak's regime in Egypt. This pattern, she writes, largely results from the "underprivileged" being more susceptible to the threat of economic sanctions and, especially, to clientelism, than richer individuals. That is to say, in non-democracies, the instrumental underpinnings of many individuals' decision to vote have much more to do with clientelistic incentives and sanctions ("pocketbook" evaluations) than with the prospects of influencing policy outcomes (Lust-Okar 2006; Magaloni 2006). The expressive value of voting in autocracies is likely different too. Using individual data from Zimbabwe, Croke et al. (2016) find that better-educated individuals are less likely to vote, contact politicians, or attend community meetings than less educated citizens, even though those with more education demonstrate more support for democracy. Given that the implications of voting (or abstaining) are rather particular in dictatorships, the authors interpret these findings to suggest that "in the context of electoral authoritarianism, better-educated citizens are more likely to exercise [. . .] deliberate political disengagement" (Croke et al. 2016, 580).

Because high turnout and impressive electoral victories for ruling regimes can, by signaling regime strength, deter the opposition from making costly investments in winning elections, and can even boost regime legitimacy and international credibility, choosing *not* to vote (i.e., abstaining) can express disapproval and therefore acquires intrinsic meaning in autocracies. If we fail to think through how differing political contexts shape potential remittance responses, we may interpret incorrectly the political implications of observed demobilization. While the stabilization hypothesis outlined above emphasizes that remittances undermine the expression of voice that, in democracies, helps citizens hold governments accountable, in dictatorships, resource-driven demobilization may be the product not of fewer grievances, but rather of weakened loyalty. Demobilization in autocracies can thus work in practice as a mild form of "dissent," which, in the long run, may hold governments *more* accountable.[21]

Protesting in autocracies differs from protest in democracies, moreover, in several important ways. In the latter, protests are often routine and conventional forms of political activity; in dictatorships, by contrast, protesters incur much higher costs and face greater risk of repression.[22] The existing micro-evidence connecting resources to protest in dictatorships is not fully conclusive and rarely pays attention to income flows, but mostly finds that resources make citizens more likely to take to the streets. Some studies, relying on Afrobarometer and World Survey data (covering a variety of regime types), show that resources such as education and community networks facilitate protest participation (Bratton et al. 2005; Dalton et al. 2010; Mueller 2018). Others find that highly educated individuals facing adverse personal economic circumstances are more likely to protest (Campante and Chor 2014). Analysis of survey data from China suggests that while education may inhibit protest participation, income increases dissent in urban areas (Ong and Han 2019).

Theoretical models of protest in autocratic contexts often focus on how individuals evaluate the risks posed by repressive environments and limited political opportunities.[23] Based on this, some are skeptical that resources encourage protest, suggesting instead that even ample resources may not suffice to overcome the obstacles posed by repressive regimes that permit few political opportunities (Earl 2006). Further, more resources may mean that individuals have more to lose, especially among those with public sector jobs whose income largely depends on remaining loyal to the ruling regime (Chen 2013; Rosenfeld 2017). Nevertheless, despite the high risk of reprisal, and given that voting and other conventional forms of engagement in dictatorships are restricted and rarely produce responsive and accountable governments, protesting becomes a more meaningful strategy for expressing political demands in non-democracies (Kitschelt 1986; Machado et al.

2011). Moreover, the spread of multiparty elections alongside increasing access to new communication technologies and the emergence of local and transnational civil society groups has opened up new opportunities for political mobilization, thus increasing the relevance of resources (Almeida 2003; Meyer 2004; Schock 2014). In places where contentious politics is more costly and opponents tend to have modest means, additional outside resources are likely to have a strong marginal effect in boosting protest.

### 2.3.2.1. REMITTANCES INCREASE VOICE

One way in which remittances undermine autocratic rule, we argue, is by increasing citizens' exercise of voice. Additional private income spurs more political engagement in opposing the incumbent regime, observable, we posit, as a higher level of political protest. In our framework, more voice among remittance recipients results from someone else's exit (emigration) providing the external resources necessary to enable increased political participation. There are two mechanisms that potentially link remittances to protest: one emphasizes the capacity of would-be dissidents and the second focuses on the incentives for anti-government mobilization, each in relation to a different group of domestic actors.

The first mechanism builds on resource theories of political participation, which posit that because a politics of contention is costly—and more so in autocratic contexts than in democratic ones—additional income facilitates political engagement. Ample research establishes that citizens with greater resources are more likely to engage in contentious political action (e.g., Brady et al. 1995; Verba et al. 1995; Pattie et al. 2004; Dalton et al. 2010; Dalton 2017). Poverty, or deprivation, constrains political activity, especially in contexts that make it more costly; so additional resources that alleviate such deprivation enable costly political participation and reduce its opportunity costs. In contrast to the grievance approach discussed earlier, the resource model yields the prediction that remittances will mobilize citizens by increasing their ability to follow and get involved in politics. This logic thus points to citizens' *capacity* for engaging in some forms of participation. In other words, instead of being a discouraging factor that reduces motives for protesting, remittances can act as a stimulating or enabling factor for those motivated to engage in contentious actions but previously unable to do so.

First, prior exit by another party provides those left behind with additional private income above subsistence levels, enabling them to raise their voice and participate in dissent activities (Van Hear and Cohen 2017). Accordingly, remittances should increase the capacity for mobilizing against the regime among those individuals and groups who face the greatest resource constraints, namely low-income citizens in dictatorships. As Easton and Montinola (2017, 353) put it, "income from remittances reduces the cost of engaging in political activities and heightens recipients' stake in the community." Second, the flow of remittances can also help individuals to overcome the constraints imposed by various forms of economic and political repression aimed at raising the costs of participation and suppressing opposition activity, and that can result in the loss of income—such as the imposition of arbitrary taxes or fines, or restricting access to jobs and services among dissidents (Way and Levitsky 2006).[24] Third, when remittances are used collectively to fund local public goods and provide community services, they can spur attendance at community meetings, increasing group identity and cooperation and promoting the creation of associations; in turn, such activities foster the emergence of denser community networks that facilitate recruitment and collective action (Verba et al. 1995; Bratton et al. 2005; Dalton et al. 2010; Easton and Montinola 2017; Mueller 2018).

In addition, structural approaches to democratization, such as modernization theory, posit that increased income engenders social transformations that facilitate popular demands for political liberalization by, for example, increasing education levels and citizens' perception of political efficacy. Indeed, studies on the socio-economic effects of remittances at the household level show that such resources lead to higher education spending (Adams 2007). A remittance-driven boost to resources could thus increase political participation by fostering organizational capacity, coordination, self-perceived effectiveness, community involvement, and even by permitting time away from work for would-be protesters to mobilize (White et al. 2015).

The mobilizing effect of remittances may increase during elections. Both incumbent and opposition parties are aware that emigrants are a potential source of voters; knowing this, parties of all stripes attempt to organize diaspora voters and leverage the financial and organizational resources they possess (Lyons 2012; Kapur 2014; Pérez-Armendáriz 2014; Vari-Lavoisier 2016; Paarlberg 2017). By campaigning overseas and establishing diaspora engagement institutions (Gamlen 2014), parties seek migrants' resources and participation in shaping the political choices of those who remain at home. Most often, migrants' political influence over their relatives is subtle, and revolves around the recipients' dependence on emigrants' financial support (Lyons 2012; Kapur 2014; Pérez-Armendáriz 2014; Vari-Lavoisier

2016; Paarlberg 2017; Córdova and Hiskey 2019): recipients listen to their emigrant relatives and friends, and frequently mobilize support for candidates in line with relatives' preferences; seldom is any explicit "political conditionality" attached to remittances, though this is not unheard of. For instance, in a study of voting in El Salvador, Paarlberg (2017, 547) cites a party official of the Frente Farabundo Martí de Liberación Nacional (FMLN) who stated that Salvadoran migrants are known to include extra money in remittances to relatives before elections. In Senegal, recipients admitted that their vote for Macky Sall in the 2012 election followed the suggestion of emigrant friends, because emigrants bring gifts, clothes, and money for them and for their village (Vari-Lavoisier 2016, 27). In the case of The Gambia, some claim that Gambians abroad "even threatened to withhold their remittances from their families unless they voted for the opposition" in the crucial 2016 election (Zanker and Altrogge 2019, 171).

Remittances from abroad not only increase the capacity of citizens to mobilize, they also, at times, directly (or indirectly via dues or donations) fund opposition groups, such as political parties or civil society organizations. Similar to the resource model, but emphasizing social movements rather than individuals, resource mobilization theory acknowleges that groups and organizations also require resources, including monetary funds, to mobilize a wider population as well as to extend their network of influence and scope of activity (McCarthy and Zald 1977). Movement members' ability to acquire resources is central to their success. Financial autonomy enables organizations to overcome material constraints and escape state dependence and even political repression (Carothers 1999; Bellin 2000). Again, this argument emphasizes capacity, but at the organizational rather than the individual level. Additional external funding from remittances increases the opposition's organizational and mobilizing resources in contexts where regimes typically enjoy a resource advantage, which in turn boosts oppositions' ability to run more effective electoral campaigns, to recruit supporters, and to engage in anti-regime collective action (Burgess 2014).

These dynamics are most evident in the case of so-called "conflict-generated" diasporas, which, unlike development-oriented migrant organizations, coalesce around the political grievances that forced their departure, fleeing from war, autocratic rule, or persecution (Collier and Hoeffler 2004; Lyons 2007; 2012; Carment and Calleja 2018). These diasporas transfer funds to civil society organizations and support anti-incumbent protests and opposition parties, especially around elections (Koinova 2009; Lyons

2012; Betts and Jones 2016). For instance, Lyons describes (2006, 274) how Ethiopian emigrant groups, prior to the 2005 election, had a long tradition of "pushing for change in Ethiopia, including promoting human rights, press freedom, competitive elections, and other elements of good governance." He adds that "political leaders in the Ethiopian diaspora are particularly influential because they control political party finances and how political debates are framed and leadership ratified."

This organizational capacity mechanism assumes motivated political behavior on the part of (some) remittance-senders, who presumably intend to influence politics in their home countries (Guarnizo et al. 2003; Tarrow 2005; Kapur 2010).[25] O'Mahony (2013) and Nyblade and O'Mahony (2014), for example, demonstrate that emigrants from developing countries send more money home in election years, thereby channeling resources to their preferred candidates and parties to improve their chances in electoral contests. Maydom (2017) provides evidence of similar political-remittance cycles in subnational elections in Egypt and Jordan.[26] For example, in the wake of a 1980 coup d'état in Turkey, exiled citizens politicized existing migrant networks in Western countries, tapping their resources to support anti-regime mobilization (Adamson 2019b). And Edelbloude et al. (2016) document how a cyber-diaspora supported by migrant resources contributed to "cyber-dissidence" during the democratic revolution in Tunisia in 2011.

As the cases of Senegal and Cambodia discussed in chapter 6 below also illustrate, opposition parties and other civil society groups not only receive crucial financial support from migrant communities, closing the resource gap with the regime, but also engage in outreach activities to mobilize such support. Many organizations even create local branches in foreign countries hosting large diasporas for that purpose.[27]

A second mechanism linking remittances to increased voice draws on the contractarian or *asset protection model* of democratization (Ansell and Samuels 2010; 2014). This argument stresses the *incentives* of certain social groups to demand democracy; in particular, "politically disenfranchised yet rising economic groups" who struggle "to obtain credible commitments against expropriation of their income and assets by the autocratic governing elite" (Ansell and Samuels 2010, 1,544). Out-groups "will thus mobilize [for democracy], investing in protection against expropriation by the state" (1,549). The desire for income and asset protection, not redistribution, drives democracy demands. Democracy, in this model, is less a redistributive mechanism and more a credible contract preventing the arbitrary rent-extraction and expropriation that presumably characterize dictatorships. Important to note is that this argument assumes the poor to "lack the resources and organizational capacity to mobilize on their own behalf" (Ansell and Samuels 2014, 46).

Applying this logic to remittances, one group of scholars argues that remitted income boosts family resources such that recipients become members of the rising middle class, with a newly developed interest in protecting their growing income and assets (Bastiaens and Tirone 2019; Bearce and Park 2019). Income flows from migrants not only boost recipients' wealth but also, through the multiplier effect, encourage local economic production. Remittance recipients then become a "newly empowered and autonomous middle-class," with an incentive to push for democratization (Bastiaens and Tirone 2019, 2).[28] Note, however, that while Bearce and Park (2019) stress in their argument the incentives for asset protection, they acknowledge in passing that remittances may also provide the middle class with greater *means* to achieve their political goals (171).

Note that neither of the two approaches suggesting that remittances increase voice—the resource and the asset protection models—excludes the other, each stresses different underlying mechanisms and actors. Below we further specify the theoretical and empirical implications of these two approaches.

### 2.3.2.2. REMITTANCES WEAKEN LOYALTY

Our second key argument contends that remittances also undermine loyalty to dictatorships by severing clientelistic links between citizens and the ruling party, thereby decreasing mobilization and electoral support for incumbents (Pfutze 2012; 2014; Escribà-Folch et al. 2015). Political clientelism, or the distribution of material inducements to citizens in exchange for electoral support, is pervasive in electoral autocracies and even in several new democracies throughout the world (Stokes et al. 2013). Mobilization for many voters thus derives from material inducements provided by ruling-party agents and not from the chance to choose between alternative policy platforms. Autocratic governing parties use their control over the state to spend government funds on patronage goods that, in turn, give them an unfair electoral advantage (Magaloni 2006; Greene 2007; Croke 2017; Rosenfeld 2020).[29]

We argue that remittances weaken autocratic regimes by reducing citizens' dependence on clientelistic transfers and other state resources, and thus increase what McMann (2006, 28) calls "economic autonomy," or individuals' "ability to earn a living independent of the state." By increasing private income, remittances reduce the marginal utility of goods that characterize clientelistic relationships and enhance state dependence (Kitschelt and Wilkinson 2007): private goods—such as gifts and handouts—and club goods—providing benefits to certain groups of citizens—delivered by the ruling regime. Poorer voters are more easily trapped by clientelistic networks, since the marginal utility of such rewards is higher for them than for higher-income voters, which leads them to turn out to vote in larger proportions than do the richer or better educated (Blaydes 2010; Croke et al. 2016). In other words, lower incomes reduce the price the regime must pay in exchange for electoral support. By increasing income and thus the monetary value of transfers needed to buy support, remittances erode state clientelism, lowering the marginal utility of such gifts and other goods and potentially increasing the importance of ideological (and other) preferences in voting decisions.

This *weakened clientelism* argument builds on the stylized fact that remittances increase household consumption of goods and services, and thus represent a substitute for patronage goods and gifts that the regime or its local representatives would normally dole out especially during electoral campaigns. Ample research has found that recipient households use remittance income to finance private consumption, including basic necessities, as well as to make investments in education, health, agriculture, and businesses (Adams and Page 2005; World Bank 2006b;d; Adams 2007; Fajnzylber and López 2007; Chami et al. 2008). Via remittance-funded consumption, citizens can acquire with their own resources the types of gift—food, clothes, utensils, soap, and so on—that ruling-party intermediaries would traditionally distribute to induce them to vote. Moreover, remittances also enable citizens to obtain access to club goods—such as welfare, as well as local public goods and services—that substitute for government welfare and infrastructure expenditures (Sana and Hu 2006). For example, Adida and Girod (2011) find that some Mexican households use remittances to purchase access to basic services, such as sanitation and clean water, undermining the state monopoly on the provision of these goods. In Yemen during the 1970s, local cooperatives in rural areas used remittances to invest in local services and infrastructure. As Chaudhry (1989, 115) stresses, "apart from guaranteeing the financial independence of the private sector, remittances generate local resources that enable rural communities to suspend reliance on the state for the provision of basic infrastructure, such as roads, electricity, water, clinics and schools."

Similarly, in Senegal, migrant associations (*dahiras*) use remittances to fund projects and social services in their communities of origin "without having to rely on state intervention" (Diedhiou 2015, 6). These examples suggest that remittances provide households, individuals, and even communities with an alternative to the regime's provision of certain goods and services aimed at buying support and, thus, with an "escape" from its clientelistic network (Díaz-Cayeros et al. 2003; Pfutze 2012; 2014).

These arguments have implications for voting because, in the end, clientelism is an instrument aimed at mobilizing electoral support (Stokes 2007). In particular, remittances should turn out to be related to lower turnout for ruling parties in dictatorships (Pfutze 2014). According to this view, and contrary to the grievance model which interprets political disengagement as detrimental to political change, electoral demobilization can, in fact, be a mild form of dissent and, hence, a source of regime weakness (Croke et al. 2016). Incumbents in electoral non-democratic regimes are concerned with both the amount of support they receive and, especially if they win by large margins, with overall turnout levels. The latter often serve to legitimize electoral results, appease the international community, and signal the strength and mobilizing capacity of the ruling party (Magaloni and Kricheli 2010; Blaydes 2010). Failing to mobilize enough electoral support in elections reveals some degree of regime weakness and increases the risk of regime collapse via an electoral defeat.

The implications of this "weakened loyalty" argument for other forms of political participation, such as protest, are less clear. Some suggest that weakened loyalty might also spur more contentious activities, not simply reduce turnout at the polls. For example, Magaloni and Kricheli (2010, 128) contend that "[c]itizens with alternative sources of income can better afford to make 'ideological investments' in democratization and oppose the regime." Likewise, McMann (2006) posits that "economic autonomy" may enhance citizens' willingness to challenge local authorities instead of self-censoring their preferences. According to this second set of arguments, if remittances weaken dependence-based loyalty, then they could also increase mobilizing dissent in the form of protest. Yet this logic presumes that clientelist inducements target strong opponents to the ruling regime, in an attempt not only to entice their turnout but also to buy their ideological preferences. This sort of double persuasion is extremely costly for ruling parties, requiring substantial resources and sophisticated monitoring (Nichter 2008; Stokes et al. 2013; Gans-Morse et al. 2014). We therefore expect that the severing of clientelistic ties will have a stronger impact on political disengagement, namely failing to show up at the polls, and a weaker one (if any) on protest mobilization.

Similarly to the resource mechanism above, the 'weakened loyalty' argument can have implications at the meso-level as well. Particularly, it suggests that private, decentralized remittance flows can increase the autonomy of local political organizations, including opposition parties and civil society organizations. To be capable of and effective in monitoring government policies, enhancing accountability, advocating political reform, campaigning in elections, and challenging the regime in the streets, such groups need to be financially independent from the government (Carothers 1999; Bellin 2000). Otherwise, the civic space remains void or only partially occupied by co-opted or state-sponsored organizations. Under such circumstances, repression via harassment, material sanctions, legal restrictions, and inspections, among other means, also becomes more effective in discouraging the emergence of critical and voluntary associations (Buyse 2018). Remittances can thus have a powerful emancipatory effect and, as in the case of individuals, increase civil society's autonomy from the state (Duquette-Rury 2016).

## 2.4. Refining the Theoretical Mechanisms: Political Preferences and Poverty

The previous section introduced the theoretical mechanisms through which, in our view, remittances shape protest and voting in dictatorships. In this section, we first briefly summarize these mechanisms, and then discuss how some of them yield similar aggregate predictions but slightly different expectations for sub-populations. Digging deeper into two key factors, political preferences and poverty, that connect remittances to political behavior helps us to both adjudicate competing mechanisms and specify more precise scope conditions for the subsequent empirical analysis.

In short, the grievance model suggests the remittances reduce discontent and thus inhibit anti-regime participation. Conversely, the resource theory of mobilization posits that remittances increase the capacity to participate in contentious political behavior. Likewise, an implication of the asset protection argument suggests that remittances increase the incentive to demand democratization for a rising middle class. Finally, the weakened loyalty and clientelism argument suggests that remittances reduce individuals' reliance on state-delivered goods, which, in turn, saps electoral support for the incumbent.

Given these various approaches, extant research suggests that remittances both decrease mobilization and increase engagement, implying that they may be related to both political stability and change. Empirical predictions from this literature thus appear, at first sight, contradictory. These contradictions only hold, however, as mentioned earlier, if we assume that remittances have a homogeneous effect on political behavior across all individuals, or if we consider only one form of participation.

One crucial contribution that it is hoped emerges from this book is to clarify and demonstrate how these seemingly contradictory theoretical predictions are compatible once we allow remittances to have heterogeneous effects across individuals and different forms of political behavior. We show that remittances mobilize and demobilize different groups of recipients at the same time, because we consider two types of political behavior: protesting and voting. While we expect remittances to boost protest, we also expect remittances to decrease vote turnout. These predictions become clearer once we specify the circumstances within which these two mechanisms are most likely to operate. We expect the mobilization and demobilization mechanisms not only to be manifested in different behaviors, but also to be observable among different groups of individuals. This section thus explores the conditioning effects of remittances on political behavior, looking closely at two *moderating* factors: political preferences (pro-government or pro-opposition) that distinguish opposition areas from regime-stronghold areas;[30] and socio-economic status (or poverty) that distinguishes poor citizens from middle-class ones.

### 2.4.1. *Protest*

The resource theory postulates that additional remittance income augments individuals' and groups' capacity to mobilize. However, the model does not account for individuals' political preferences and does not distinguish between regime supporters and opponents. Additional resources might, by the standard resource model, increase mobilization among both groups alike (Chenoweth and Ulfelder 2017). However, as proponents of the resource model themselves stress (Brady et al. 1995), those who participate do so because they can and because they want to.[31] By incorporating a "willingness" dimension, the model provides a further theoretical refinement focusing on individuals' motivation and engagement, a factor conceptually distinct from resources. Consequently, individuals with existing anti-regime sentiments should be those most likely to increase protest participation once enabled by the additional resources send by migrants abroad (Escribà-Folch et al. 2018). Thus, if remittances undermine autocratic rule by spurring protests, we should observe this effect predominantly in areas of high dissatisfaction with incumbents: that is, in geographic units of low pro-government support.

The resource model posits that resources enhance the capacity to protest, which is a costly political behavior. A corollary is that it is amongst the resource-scarce that additional resources should have the most significant empowering effect. Extra private income from remittances should thus have the strongest mobilizing effect among low-income individuals, who could not otherwise afford to devote time and resources to protest, or who are more vulnerable than others to economic sanctions. In short, the greatest positive marginal impact of remittances on protests should be among poor recipients, declining as socio-economic status increases. Altogether, the resource mechanism predicts that remittances should increase protesting among poor recipients with anti-regime preferences, whom we identify as those living in opposition areas.

The asset protection argument also suggests that remittance recipients are more likely to engage in anti-regime protests than their counterparts who do not receive remittances. In the terms of this approach, political mobilization is a response to the fear that unaccountable governments will expropriate newly acquired assets of the rising middle class. The argument thus focuses on increased incentives for participation in contentious politics, rather than enhanced capacity. In contrast to the resource model, this theory predicts that remittances will increase protest among middle-class recipients, not the poorest. Thus, evidence that remittances increase protest behavior among middle-class recipients, rather than the poorest, would yield empirical support for the asset protection model. Upwardly mobile middle-class recipients should have stronger incentives to call for democracy, in order to protect their newly acquired wealth, and therefore will mobilize to demand an accountable government that will sustain the flow of remittances from abroad.

The asset protection model, however, is silent about the potential moderating effect of political preferences. It assumes that ascending social groups, irrespective of their pre-existing affinity or otherwise for incumbent ruling parties, all have the same incentive to oppose unaccountable authoritarian incumbents. Underlying political preferences play no explanatory role in the asset protection story, and if it is true we should observe no differences in the remittance effect between pro- and anti-government recipients. Further, the argument overlooks the fact that a significant section of what constitutes the middle class in authoritarian regimes is heavily state-dependent, as many members work in state administration and state-owned enterprises, making them less likely to join mobilizations and demand democratic change (Chen 2013; Rosenfeld 2017; 2020).

While grievance theory clearly predicts remittances will reduce protest, the resource and asset protection models both predict that remittances will increase it, on average. However, the resource and asset protection arguments yield divergent predictions for this positive effect as regards sub-groups of the remittance-receiving population. By the resource theory, low-income recipients and those in opposition areas should be the most likely to respond to remittances with more protest. In contrast, the asset protection theory predicts that remittances will increase protest most among middle-class recipients, and there should be no difference in this effect between pro- and anti-regime areas.

### 2.4.2. *Voting*

Our expectations for voting behavior draw on the weakened loyalty mechanism: additional private income from remittances should reduce voter turnout. This section drills down into this mechanism to specify the sub-populations for whom this prediction should be strongest by first identifying the groups that are most likely to be targeted by ruling-party clientelism. The extant literature on clientelism points to the same two moderating characteristics as those discussed in the previous section—income and political preferences—to identify these groups (Nichter 2008; Stokes et al. 2013; Gans-Morse et al. 2014).

Theories of clientelism stress that party machines tend to target poor voters (Stokes 2007). The prevailing account suggests that the marginal benefit of clientelistic goods is largest for low-income citizens and declines as income increases (Dixit and Londegran 1996; Stokes 2005; Robinson and Verdier 2013). Poverty breeds clientelism, according to these theories, because, in the context of party budget constraints, it lowers the price parties must pay for support, thereby increasing the electoral returns on clientelistic payments (Chubb 1983; Calvo and Murillo 2004; Blaydes 2010): a simple gift or handout may suffice.[32] The liberating, or demobilizing, effect of financial remittances should therefore be most clearly manifested among low-income recipients. An empirical pattern indicating that remittances lower electoral turnout more among poor voters than rich ones would thus provide additional evidence for the weakened clientelism mechanism.[33]

The theoretical and empirical debate about how citizens' political preferences shape party decisions about whom to target through clientelism is wide-ranging and still unsettled. Drawing on Gans-Morse et al. (2014), we begin with some conceptual clarification. Although clientelism often entails vote-buying, the term also describes additional electoral strategies, such as paying voters to abstain from voting, paying them to simply turn up at the polls, and even double persuasion, whereby parties pay citizens to both turn out and switch their vote choice. Each strategy targets different types of individuals. Parties direct vote-buying at citizens who are likely to vote irrespective of clientelism but who support another party; vote-buying by incumbent autocratic parties thus involves targeting known opposition (or neutral) voters, to encourage them to switch their vote. Turnout-buying, on the other hand, rewards supporters of the ruling party who are unlikely to vote, in an attempt to induce them to turn up at the polls. Abstention-buying seeks to convince would-be opposition voters to remain at home and not vote. And finally, double persuasion entails targeting indifferent or opposition-supporting individuals, to encourage them both to show up at the polls and to switch their vote to support the ruling party.

Existing models posit that, if vote-buying is a central goal of clientelistic efforts, parties should target marginal or swing voters in an effort to capture the vote they cast (Stokes 2007). These objects of vote-buying are either indifferent as between party platforms or are slightly opposed to the party concerned. Targeting voters who are too ideologically distant from the party is an expensive strategy, with uncertain electoral returns, making the opposition voters unlikely objects of clientelistic efforts.[34] At the same time, party largesse towards strong supporters would also be a waste, as these voters are likely to be loyal to the party anyway.

Although parties may combine several strategies, the empirical evidence most consistently points to turnout-buying. Particularly when ballots are secret, which hinders monitoring of vote choices, and when incumbent ruling parties have substantial resource advantages over the opposition as a result of state control, turnout-buying targeting un-mobilized supporters is the most effective strategy to ensure electoral victory and high turnout rates (Gans-Morse et al. 2014). By this argument, turnout-buying should indeed be observable in areas where the ruling party knows it has substantial, if latent, support.

The logic as to which citizens are most likely to be targeted by turnout-buying changes slightly, however, when parties require local brokers, or intermediaries, to implement it. Nearly all parties rely on some form of local agent to connect the party to potential voters (see, e.g., Blaydes 2006; Gingerich 2013; Koter 2013; Frye et al. 2014; Díaz-Cayeros et al. 2016). These brokers gather information and disseminate it to local groups, monitor behavior, and provide targeted benefits (Stokes et al. 2013). Local brokers act as agents of party elites: they know more about individual voters' preferences and behavior than the elites do, and are thus better able to monitor voting. This model yields the prediction that while local brokers have an incentive to mobilize non-voting loyalists—because they can better observe turnout than vote choice—party leaders, following standard swing-voter logic, will still have an incentive to target *marginal* districts. Thus ruling party clientelism should "flow disproportionately to 'swing' (electorally competitive) districts" but target "loyal individuals" within these districts (Stokes et al. 2013, 92).[35]

Incorporating income and political preferences (along with local vote-brokers) into the analysis allows for greater precision in explaining how and where remittances influence electoral behavior. If remittances do indeed erode clientelism, and ruling parties target un-mobilized individuals in swing districts, then it is in electoral swing districts that we should observe the strongest empirical link between remittances and turnout.[36]

In short, the theorized mechanisms predict that we will observe, at the micro-level, remittances reducing voting among poor recipients in swing districts, and at the macro-level, the consequent lower turnout translating into reduced electoral support for incumbents. The grievance model, on the other hand, does not yield clear implications for turnout. Increased economic satisfaction could demobilize poor opponents; yet one could also argue that if recipients mis-attribute responsibility for their improved conditions to the government, additional support for incumbent ruling parties could be mobilized among passive opponents who, without remittances, would have abstained or voted for the opposition (Germano 2013; Tertytchnaya et al. 2018).

Figure 2.2 summarizes the empirical expectations for how remittances influence protest and turnout in non-democracies, according to each theoretical approach. The axes show the two moderating variables, political preferences and income. The theoretical mechanisms appear in each cell, with our argument in bold. The resource model predicts that remittances will increase protest, or voice; and this should be strongest for low-income

Socio-economic status/income

| | | Low | Medium |
|---|---|---|---|
| Political preferences | Opposition | **resource model:**<br>↑ protest<br>grievance model:<br>↓ protest | asset protection<br>model: ↑ protest |
| | Swing | **weaker clientelism**<br>**model:** ↓ turnout | asset protection<br>model: ↑ protest |

FIGURE 2.2. Empirical predictions for remittance, protest, and turnout

citizens in opposition areas. The weakened-clientelism model suggests that remittances should reduce turnout among low-income supporters in swing districts. Figure 2.2 contrasts these expectations with predictions from the asset-protection and grievance models. The asset-protection argument suggests that remittances should increase protest among the rising middle class, but makes no prediction about how political preferences will shape this relationship; so we place this mechanism in both opposition and swing-district cells. Finally, the grievance model predicts that remittances will decrease protest among low-income citizens, particularly in opposition areas—the opposite of the resource-model prediction.[37]

### 2.4.3. Political Context and Political Behavior

Our theory of migration and remittances proposes that additional financial resources from migrant remittances both boost protest and reduce turnout in elections. In the chapters that follow, we test these propositions at both the macro-level (countries) and the micro-level (individual survey-respondents). At the macro-level, we examine a sample of dictatorships, because this group of regimes meets the scope condition of our theory, providing global evidence for our argument across multiple decades. The macro-analysis, however, cannot shed light on the specific mechanisms linking remittances to political behavior—mechanisms that we posit depend on the political context within countries. For example, we want to test whether remittances boost protest in opposition areas and whether they reduce electoral turnout in swing districts. We thus turn to micro-level analysis of individual survey-respondents to examine these contextual mechanisms.

Our theory, at its core, focuses on how additional resources alter individual incentives and opportunities to participate in politics. We posit that these individual incentives and opportunities change depending on the local political context. However, we also know that local political contexts may shape political behavior independently of any additional resources, including financial remittances. Indeed, it has long been noted that political opportunity structures, which may vary by local geographical context, shape protest and voting (see, e.g., Kitschelt 1986; Almeida 2003). For example, areas where the political opposition is strong may provide more opportunities for individuals to participate in protest. These opposition areas may also be the places that many migrants hail from, and thus are the areas most likely to receive substantial remittance income. If citizens in opposition areas receive more remittances, then a finding that remittances increase protest might be spurious, insofar as it could simply indicate that grievances drive emigration from (and hence remittances to) particular districts, as well as protest opportunity in those same districts.

There are many ways in which political context varies locally that may independently shape behavior. For example, there are likely to be geographical variations between the local histories of protest and mobilization efforts of opposition groups. Similarly, maltreatment by the government or, alternatively, provision of basic public services and government-sponsored get-out-the-vote campaigns may differ across local political contexts.

Because local political context firstly modifies how additional resources from remittances alter incentives for individual behavior, and secondly shapes behavior independently of remittances, we adopt a research design that compares individuals who receive remittances to those who do not *within the same local context*. Because the local political context alters behavior independently of remittances, we ensure that the micro-analysis adjusts for independent effects of differing local contexts that shape protest opportunity structure as well as voting opportunities. When we present the micro-analysis in chapter 4 (protest) and chapter 5 (electoral turnout), we specify in the course of our discussion how our research design accounts for location-based selection arguments.

Even with such a research design, however, there may still be individual-level selection effects that could account for an empirical relationship between remittances and political behavior. That is, unmodeled individual differences between recipients and non-recipients could explain why we observe a relationship between emigration (and hence remittances) and protest or voting. For example, individuals from more risk-accepting families may be more likely to emigrate (see, e.g., Katz and Stark 1986) and more likely to protest; and if risk-accepting families have one member who migrates abroad and another who protests, while another family has neither, then family-level risk-acceptance differences could yield a statistical relationship between remittances and protest at the individual level that has nothing to do with family resources. For this type of individual-level selection effect to account for our findings, however, the selection effect would have to operate more strongly in some contexts (e.g., opposition areas) than in others (e.g., pro-government areas).

Our micro-analysis cannot account for *all* of the possible individual-level differences that might lead to spurious identification of a relationship between remittances and political behavior. Throughout it, however, we account for demographic and economic differences between individuals, such as age, gender, educational attainment, employment status, and wealth. As importantly, we account for self-reported travel and cellphone access, as these individual characteristics are likely to alter political behavior and increase access to remittances.

A further approach to addressing individual-level selection is to match individuals who receive remittances to similar individuals who do not, and then compare their respective political behaviors. Escribà-Folch et al. (2018, Appendix), for example, use a matching approach that compares individuals with the same demographic and grievance profiles to examine their protest behavior, finding that remittance recipients are more likely to participate in protest than non-recipients—but only in opposition districts.[38]

Perhaps the best method of accounting for individual-level selection effects is to examine individual-level panel data, where the same person responds to survey questions on multiple occasions, including both before and after receiving remittances. However, individual panel surveys that ask questions about remittances as well as protest and voting behavior are not available for countries ruled by autocratic governments.[39] Another alternative, in theory, would be to randomly assign migrant remittances to families living in dictatorships. This approach, however, is not only unfeasible, but also unethical, because providing research funds to migrants on the condition they send this money back home—resources that may boost protest—may spur authoritarian governments to target families that receive foreign funds with repression.

## 2.5. Conclusion

While much attention has been paid to the alleged democratizing effects of the economic dimensions of globalization, such as trade and capital movements, the most human element of globalization, migration, remains not only subject to restrictions in practice, but also under-studied. Human migration is closely related to wider political and social transformations, some of the most important of which pertain to countries that migrants come from. This chapter has spelled out the mechanisms through which such transformations operate in the context of migration-sending, autocratic countries. We focus on one dimension (or outcome) of migration: the remittances migrant workers send back home.

Migration and, specifically, the remittances that flow as a result are both relatively slow-moving structural drivers of globalization and generate contingent, actor-specific political behavior in migrant-sending countries. Our main claim is that when such behavioral changes—concentrated among certain social groups—take place in autocratic contexts, they empower citizens and weaken incumbent regimes, thereby reshaping the internal balance of power and making democratization more likely.

We theorize how this now substantial flow of external, private income affects the choice of voice and loyalty for those left behind: that is, remittance recipients. By leaving their home countries to live and work abroad, migrants unleash a plethora of mostly (as yet) uninvestigated benefits for remittance recipients that enable them to become agents of democratic change. Key to understanding how remittances shape politics in autocratic contexts, we argue, is reconceptualization of these agents of change and the different forms their participation they can take: some recipients increase political engagement while others disengage from politics, yet both outcomes destabilize autocratic incumbents, as they translate into a higher propensity to protest and a lower likelihood of voting, respectively. Contentious politics, as Tilly noted (2006), takes many forms and varies from place to place and across time; and, as shown in this chapter, most autocratic regimes in the Global South collapse as a result of bottom-up efforts at transforming existing political structures. Remittances, we argue, contribute to these efforts. Both increased voice, manifested as more protest, and weaker loyalty, observed as lower turnout, undermine autocratic rule and should foster democracy.

# 3

# Remittances, Revenue, and Government Spending in Dictatorships

During the prior era of mass global migration, between Europe and the Americas roughly from 1850 to 1920, migrants had limited means to send money back home. In fact, for quite some time, sending money to families at home could only be done by physically carrying it back or by giving it to other family members or friends traveling home. With increased demand for such services, several institutions, mostly banks and mercantile houses, began gradually to provide them. Other transaction mechanisms, such as money orders and postal orders, became available soon after; and in the early twentieth century the telegraph became a new method to remit money across borders (Magee and Thompson 2006).

Currently emerging technologies for money transfer contrast sharply with those available in the past, being more secure, rapid, and less expensive. The *Financial Times*, for example, in a piece about the growing importance of remittances, recounts the story of a Ugandan lawyer living and working in London who sends money back to her family by simply pressing a button on her smartphone (Cocco et al. 2019). In the last thirty years, new technologies and services have largely digitized international money transfers, making them more accessible, reliable, and, as importantly, cheaper for customers. Migrants now employ several methods to remit funds back home, including money transfer operators such as Western Union and MoneyGram, bank services, in-cash transfers, shared debit cards, and, as the example above highlights, cell phones. Increasing numbers of migrants send money electronically via smartphone apps such as Circle, OFX, Abra, Wise, Pangea, Remitly, and

WorldRemit, thus making it possible to send money transfers overseas quickly at little cost.

These digital money-transfer tools have been instrumental in boosting the volume of cross-national income flows, thus enhancing their political consequences. The main impediment to remitting funds is not so much the reliability of available systems for sending them, but the fact that, despite declining costs, some of these systems remain quite expensive. Reducing these costs has thus become a priority for the United Nations and is now an official goal for the 2030 Sustainable Development Agenda. As mobile phone penetration increases access to these electronic transfer services, citizens in the Global South will continue to reap private transfers from abroad. For example, according to the Global System for Mobile Communications (GSMA), in 2018, 23 percent of sub-Saharan Africa's population (239 million people) were using the mobile internet on a regular basis and 44 percent of the region's population were unique mobile subscribers—an increase of 20 million users over the previous year. For the MENA (Middle East and North Africa) region, the equivalent figures are 40 percent and 64 percent respectively; in Latin America, 52 percent and 67 percent. By 2025, over 60 percent of the world's population is expected to be mobile internet subscribers (GSMA 2012).

The evolution of the mechanisms available to migrants for sending money back home has facilitated the mobility of this private capital, which, coupled with the growing number of migrants worldwide, explains the acceleration in global remittance flows in the last three decades. Figure 3.1 shows the size of different forms of foreign income in countries ruled by autocratic governments, as a share of the economy: oil, foreign aid, FDI, and remittances. Remittances, currently representing on average about 4 percent of GDP in these countries, are larger than all other forms of foreign income inflows, with the exception of oil rents, which only constitute a large share of the economy in a handful of autocracies.

Many scholars point to foreign economic windfalls as a leading cause of autocratic resilience and the dearth of democracy (e.g., Friedman 2006; Ross 2012; Morrison 2014). Foreign economic flows, according to these arguments, generate a "political resource curse", because the technologies of production and income generation associated with these international inflows are highly centralized, and thus the money accrues mostly to the state. During the 1960s and 1970s, a wave of nationalizations placed most oil and gas resources throughout the world under state control (Kobrin 1985).

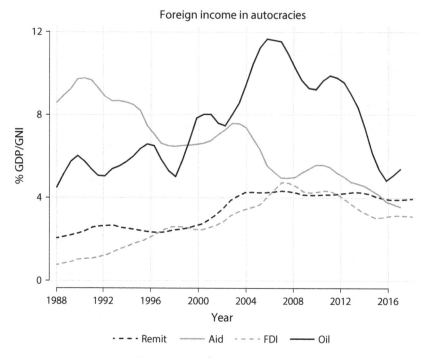

FIGURE 3.1. Foreign income flowing to autocracies, 1988–2018

Consequently, substantial oil and gas rents from sales operations of national oil companies accrue directly to authoritarian governments.

In other cases, oil revenues find their way into government coffers via taxes and royalties levied on foreign companies or the sale of concessions to exploit natural resource reserves. According to some estimates, "[s]tate-backed firms control around 80% of the world's oil," with the largest ones—the National Iranian Oil Company, Saudi Aramco, and Petróleos de Venezuela (PDVSA)—firmly under the control of autocratic governments (*The Economist* 2011). Autocratic governments also largely control other natural resource export income, including mineral and agricultural cash-crop revenue.[1]

Similarly, foreign aid accrues to authoritarian governments, either directly from donor country aid agencies or through multilateral institutions such as the World Bank. Donors traditionally use two delivery modes: budget support and project assistance. Budget support aims to strengthen national ownership and entails the direct transfer of funds to a country's budget, whereby the recipient government manages the additional funds autonomously. Project assistance entails donors funding specific projects with a well-defined purpose, often targeting specific sectors such as health-care or education. In response to mismanagement of aid funds by recipient governments, some donors increasingly bypass corrupt governments to deliver aid directly to non-state actors, such as NGOs, within the recipient country (Dietrich 2014). But even bypass aid relies on the consent and input of autocratic governments, who may steer aid projects to the locations that are most politically beneficial to themselves and claim credit for them (Jablonski 2014).

Dictators even manage to capture more decentralized private inflows such as foreign investment, an increasingly important source of external income for many countries with autocratic governments. While private capital flows may not be an obvious source of revenue for dictators, the state remains an unavoidable intermediary in facilitating these flows (Dillman 2002). Bak and Moon (2016, 2001–2002) note that "MNCs must negotiate the terms of investment with an authoritarian host government." As a result, the host government often imposes conditions—including direct tax payments, bribes, and kickbacks as well as forced joint ventures with local, often state-owned partners—on foreign investors. This creates ample opportunity for politically motivated distribution (Escribà-Folch 2017).

When foreign income flows to dictators, they use these funds to retain their grip on power. Most often, foreign income stabilizes autocracies by flowing directly to government coffers, thereby increasing government revenue without taxing the local population. And while FDI may not accrue directly to government budgets, it nonetheless generates rents and funds political allies, if not state-owned firms.

These external resources are not only useful in buying political loyalty, but also permit increased spending on the repressive apparatus, thus boosting the regime's capacity to quell internal dissent. Wright et al. (2015), for example, show that oil rents increase military expenditure in dictatorships. In Uzbekistan, under former leader Islam Karimov, the state-controlled cotton monopoly generated approximately one billion dollars in revenues, from which the regime inner circle profited immensely. These revenues were "syphoned into a special account, the Selkhozfond of the Ministry of Finance, a totally non-transparent entity accountable to only a narrow circle within the leadership" (Muradov and Ilkhamov 2014, 9). Importantly, key elites in the security sector were allowed to participate in the lucrative cotton export business. Rustam Inoyatov, chief of the National Security Service and the main official responsible for the 2005 Andijan massacre against protestors (Open

Source 2015), controlled one of the few state companies authorized to export cotton (EJF 2005, 15).

Foreign windfalls might also indirectly increase resources for autocratic governments by allowing them to substitute one type of government spending for another. It has been pointed out, for example, that foreign aid earmarked for specific programs, even if it bypasses the state and is delivered directly to NGOs, is highly fungible (Feyzioglu et al. 1998). This allows governments in recipient countries to divert aid money away from these programs and to other (more politically profitable) uses. For example, Kono and Montinola (2013, 615) note that "[a]lthough Uganda has received considerable foreign aid designated for health, its hospitals remain starved for resources. This is because foreign aid has allowed the government to cut its own health care spending." The liberated resources, as some research shows, have made it possible for autocracies to increase military spending, which, in these contexts, keeps military elites loyal and boosts the armed forces' ability to repress domestic opponents (Collier and Hoeffler 2007; Kono and Montinola 2013).

Do remittances likewise increase state resources? Do they boost autocratic resilience as a result? These are the central questions this chapter investigates. In contrast to natural resource revenue, foreign aid, and even foreign investment, remittance flows are much more decentralized, because they flow between family members on different sides of an international border. While these funds may tempt many revenue-starved governments, the direct taxation of inward remittances is uncommon, and quite difficult. This does not mean that governments do not try, of course: given the size of such resources, many governments devise strategies to try to tap into them (Eckstein 2010; Mohapatra et al. 2012). Lim and Morshed (2017, 148) provide the example of a (now abolished) Documentary Stamp Tax in the Philippines, for instance. Vietnam imposed a 5 percent tax on inward remittances, but removed it in 1997 (World Bank 2017). Other countries, such as Ethiopia and Venezuela, have at various points attempted to capture these inflows via the exchange rate, by requiring recipients to convert remittances to local currency at un-competitive official exchange rates (Mohapatra 2010). The Cuban government has also imposed a tax on income remitted as US dollars.

Despite these attempts, however, the World Bank has stated (2006d, 93) that "[m]ost remittance-receiving countries today do not impose taxes on incoming remittances"; and citing a 2005 World Bank study, Asatryan et al.

(2017) note that only five out of forty developing and transition countries in their sample imposed taxes on remittances. Indeed, many countries that have sought to subject remittances to taxes of one kind or another in the end remove them. In practice then, governments rarely tax remittances directly, because they are highly elastic in response: remitters can easily evade formal controls and rely on unregulated, informal channels (Eckstein 2010). Informal flows are estimated to be at least 50 percent larger than recorded flows. The World Bank, meanwhile, in various publications, insists that taxing remittances is a "bad idea" (World Bank 2017).

Hence, the consensus remains that remittances are largely non-taxable. However, even though remittances are difficult to tax and most governments decide not to tax them, this does not necessarily mean that they have no effect on government resources. Indeed some scholars and commentators suggest that remittances, despite the fact that they flow to private citizens, are a political curse, much in the way that natural resources or foreign aid can be (Chami et al. 2008; Amburn 2009; Abdih et al. 2012).

This chapter examines these state-centric arguments relating remittances to government revenue and spending, with implications for understanding how remittances might influence state-led repression and regime survival. Although our theory of how remittances undermine dictatorship focuses on citizens as agents of political change, we first examine how remitted income might alter government behavior. We review arguments that suggest remittances should enhance autocratic power by boosting government revenue—either from taxation or by substituting one type of spending for another. We then examine the empirical evidence in dictatorships. Our findings suggest that remittance inflows have no substantial effect on tax-revenue generation or various categories of government spending in autocracies, with predictable implications for whether remittances are likely to influence government repression. In sum, the evidence in this chapter provides little support for the revenue and substitution theories linking remittances to autocratic resilience.

## 3.1.  Remittances, State Resources, and Authoritarian Stability

We first articulate two related theories that link financial remittances to government revenue and spending behavior, and thus in turn, potentially, to the shaping of authoritarian regime stability and the trajectory of democratization.

### 3.1.1.  The Revenue Effect

A first argument suggests that because remittances are a large source of foreign income in dictatorships, they augment government revenue in recipient countries and thereby help sustain these governments in power. One way in which additional revenue boosts autocratic power is by enabling increased clientelistic payments to potential electoral supporters. Recall that one of the mechanisms through which remittances may undermine dictatorships is by weakening clientelistic ties: with additional external income, the marginal benefit to voters of state-provided transfers decreases, as does the government's capacity to influence voters' decisions. If remittances boost private income, this should raise the price of transfers the government must provide to retain their support (Pfutze 2014). If governments capture some of this remitted income, however, they will have greater resources to channel to voters to match this now higher price of a vote. The additional revenue would then allow the government to increase transfer payments to voters, canceling out the initial effect of remittances: with additional revenue to pay voters, the government can retain their support, and thus prevent defections from its electoral coalition.

A second mechanism linking additional revenue from remittances to autocratic power operates through spending on the repressive apparatus, including the military and internal security forces. Additional government resources spent on repressive forces can both keep these forces loyal and make them more capable, especially if the government calls upon these agents to harm its own citizens in an effort to quell or deter anti-regime mobilization. This argument parallels that regarding the mechanisms linking oil revenue (and foreign aid) to a dearth of democracy: more money for state-led repression suppresses the democratic agents and organizations who mobilize against the regime (Ross 2001; 2012). In summarizing the "first law of petrol politics", Friedman (2006) notes that oil revenue "allows governments to spend excessively on police, internal security, and intelligence forces that can be used to choke democratic movements." Indeed, Albertus and Menaldo (2012) show that a large, well-paid military keeps dictatorships in power by reducing the likelihood of a democratic transition. A massive, well-fed military, they posit, deters and quashes pro-democracy mobilization.

In a similar vein, additional government revenue from worker remittances may fund government patronage, which in turn could dampen demand for democracy. Morrison (2009), for example, builds on distributional theories of government to argue that foreign income funds more social spending in dictatorships, providing elites with resources to ameliorate the economic grievances of poor citizens that foment revolutionary mobilization. Ample pay and perks associated with government employment—all funded by revenue generated by oil exports—may keep citizens from demanding more say in government decisions.

These versions of the "spending" and "repression" mechanisms presume that autocratic governments collect additional revenues as remittances flow into their countries. Although the technology of sending remittances relies primarily on direct monetary transfers between family members on different sides of a border, the government may still capture some of this revenue through alternative taxation instruments. For example, autocratic regimes frequently collect revenue by value-added taxes (VAT), which yield it from the sale of goods and services at all stages of production in the domestic economy. Thus, if remittances increase household consumption of goods and services, which in turn spurs additional demand for domestically produced goods via a multiplier effect, governments may collect additional revenue not only from everyday final purchases, but from the entire domestic supply chain.[2]

In this scenario, remittances would generate extra government revenue; and indeed, this is exactly what several studies find (Ebeke 2014; Asatryan et al. 2017). While they posit that remittances primarily increase government tax revenue in developing countries via VAT, moreover, Singer (2012) finds that remittances also increase overall tax revenue, suggesting that the link between remittances and revenue may run through both value-added taxes and other revenue-generating mechanisms. In short, by boosting consumption, remittances may yield *additional* revenue for autocratic governments. These studies, rely, however, on global samples that include many developing democracies in addition to dictatorships. In the next section, we test the proposition for the specific case of dictatorships.

### 3.1.2.  *The Substitution Effect*

A second argument suggests that remittances may not necessarily boost overall tax-revenue collection but rather may allow governments in recipient countries to substitute one kind of government spending for another, a phenomenon known as "public moral hazard." If remittances fund citizens' consumption of private healthcare, for example, this may provide the government with an opportunity to shift public spending away from healthcare and towards other areas that are more helpful to the regime in retaining support. The shift in spending that results from increased remittance inflow might, for example, lead to more spending on the military, keeping them loyal to the regime. Or, the government may move health spending to off-the-books payments targeting key regime backers, again cementing its political support.

This idea was first formalized by Yasser Abdih and colleagues in a 2008 IMF working paper (Abdih et al. 2008) and later published as a journal article (Abdih et al. 2012). Their model makes three key assumptions that we highlight. First, they posit that remittances are purely private income and that the government cannot tax them.[3] This assumption is central to the idea of *substitution*: there is no additional tax revenue for the government to spend; instead, the government reacts to additional private income by adjusting its spending behavior. Given this assumption, the substitution mechanism implies that we might find no evidence that remittances increase overall tax revenue or even consumption tax revenue. That is to say, the substitution effect could still occur, even absent any change to the level of government revenue. For instance, Ambrosius (2019) finds that state governments in Mexico allocate funds away from municipalities with stronger remittance inflows, without changing overall outlays.

Second, the substitution theory assumes that the goods the government provides to citizens have a substitute in the private market, allowing citizens with more private income to purchase these goods when the government reduces the supply of them. This probably rules out the type of government spending for which there are no private market alternatives, such as building inter-city roads and ports, defense and public security spending, and arguably, public health programs aimed at disease prevention. However, if there is a private market for other services, such as primary healthcare, education, sanitation, and even some infrastructure, these types of goods might be good candidates for substitution, with the government shifting spending away from these areas when remittances increase private spending on them. In Mexico, for example, remittances often fund basic services, such as access to drainage and clean water (Adida and Girod 2011). Mexican immigrants in the USA also formed Hometown Associations, which are voluntary, philanthropic organizations through which migrants from the same town or region raise funds for projects at home, such as clinics and schools (Orozco and Lapointe 2004; Aparicio and Meseguer 2012). In Senegal, remittance-funded *dahiras* (migrant associations) provide ambulances, pay the salaries of ambulance staff, and establish medical centers (Diedhiou 2015); and in Ecuador, remittances are used to boost school enrollment and increase private health expenditure (Calero et al. 2009; Ponce et al. 2011).

Below, we examine whether remittances reduce an important component of public service spending, using data on government health spending that were collected specifically to assess whether foreign health assistance (i.e., foreign aid) reduces government health spending in recipient countries (Global Burden of Disease Health Financing Collaborator Network 2019). The researchers who collected these data wanted to test whether governments alter health-spending patterns in response to the availability of foreign unearned income, namely healthcare funding from foreign aid donors. Thus the data are well suited to test the substitution argument. Thus we use government healthcare spending to test the substitution argument (Ebeke 2012; Ahmed 2013; Easton and Montinola 2017).

Third, a central, but unstated, assumption of the substitution theory is that citizens must have good information about the level of government provision of the public good or service in order to adjust private consumption as government provision shifts. So while testing how remittances alter government healthcare spending offers some evidence of a possible substitution effect, this may not be the best test, because it is difficult for citizens to obtain accurate information regarding the level of government provision of healthcare. Healthcare—unlike say a haircut or mobile phone connectivity—is a service about which consumers may have poor information in terms of the individual-level quality of the service and even less information as regards government efficiency in its provision.

Therefore, in addition to assessing the substitution effect by examining government health spending data, we test another form of welfare expenditure, about which citizens have excellent information: petrol subsidies. Many governments throughout the world subsidize fuel consumption in an effort to buy social peace, as we discuss below. For now we simply note that these subsidies are closer to the ideal type of welfare good conceptualized in the substitution model, insofar as fuel subsidies are consumed by most citizens and the welfare good they provide—namely fuel—has a perfect private market substitute: whether the government or the citizens pay (or, more precisely, whatever their respective shares of the un-subsidized market price may be), the good is bought and consumed in the same way—either for transportation or for household energy. We therefore view the extent to which remittances shape government provision of fuel subsidies as a cleaner test of the substitution argument even than healthcare spending.

Finally, the substitution theory assumes that there is *no* political competition; instead the government simply maximizes rents (or an unspecified survival function) without having to contend with a challenger who might offer citizens welfare spending higher than its own. Desierto (2018) shows that once a minimal level of political competition is introduced into the basic substitution model, the incumbent government has little incentive to reduce welfare spending in response to increasing private income in the form of remittances. Instead, the government maintains welfare spending to thwart the efforts of a potential political challenger to enlist citizens' support. In equilibrium, according to Desierto's model, public good provision is independent of remittances.

It is to be noted that, in the past three decades, elections have become the new norm for most autocratic governments (Gandhi and Lust-Okar 2009; Levitsky and Way 2010; Gandhi 2015; Geddes et al. 2018). Miller (2020) shows, for example, that autocratic leaders adopted multiparty electoral competition for strategic reasons in countries that are more dependent on democracies for trade but where high poverty and inequality still allow them to control the outcome of elections via clientelism. In fact, most regimes in our sample are electoral autocracies with at least some semblance of multiparty electoral competition. In chapter 5 we analyze presidential elections in dictatorships and find that in roughly two-thirds of these contests, the ruling regime wins less than 75 percent of the vote. Thus not only do most remittance-receiving autocracies now embrace elections, but the top office is typically contested to some degree.

The substitution model faces yet another challenge in alleging a link between government spending substitution and autocratic survival. In its original formulation by Yasser Abdih and colleagues, the substitution mechanism leads to higher corruption, not incumbent survival (Abdih et al. 2008; 2012).[4] A link between substitution and autocratic survival is possible if reduced government welfare spending results in higher military or security spending, which would, in turn, increase the coercive capacity of the regime. However, diverting welfare spending in favor of patronage spending does not necessarily result in more stability, as this argument assumes that welfare spending plays no role in sustaining regimes in power. Rather, welfare spending is a concession from autocratic regimes aimed at buying support and, thus is necessary for their survival (Desai et al. 2009; Conrad 2011). When governments reduce this spending because individuals and communities provide these services for themselves, this should result in less dependence on the ruling regime and more defection from the electoral coalition—even if the government uses the resources gained to pay for more repression or increased benefits for remaining regime insiders.

If remittance inflows prompt governments to spend less on social welfare goods, this does not mean that the regime no longer needs political support from remittance recipients to survive in power. The regime could rely less on buying votes to sustain electoral support if remittance-funded private goods eliminate social grievances. But in this case, stability would not result from lower government spending, but rather from less societal pressure to change, because citizens (mistakenly) attribute the increased benefits of remittance-driven consumption to the government, not remittance senders.

### 3.1.3.  *Taxation and the Demand for Democracy*

These two theories—the revenue and substitution arguments—posit that inward remittance flows ultimately shape the spending behavior of a government. Whether this occurs via additional tax revenue or by substituting one type of spending for another, both mechanisms link remittances to authoritarian regime control and survival through alteration of government spending patterns. These mechanisms contrast with a key theory that links oil revenue to the dearth of democracy via reduced taxation of citizens. Building on the notion that government taxation of its citizens drives democratic revolution (see, e.g., Bates and Donald Lien 1985; Ross 2004), this argument suggests that external or foreign sources of revenue relieve governments of the need to tax their own citizens, thus dampening the "demand for democracy." (Residents in the US capital, Washington, DC, are continually reminded of this link, incidentally, as it is spelled out on their automobile license plates: "No taxation without representation.") Thus, in one key aspect, remittance income *must differ* from oil revenue or foreign economic (or military) aid: for governments to capture remittance income, they must tax it, which, given the technology of remittance transfers, means taxing citizens. Thus remittances cannot relieve a government of the need to tax its citizens in the first place.[5]

We can therefore rule out the possibility that remittances help autocracies survive by lowering need for these governments to tax citizens. By contrast, if we found that oil export revenue reduced taxes on citizens, we might interpret this as evidence of foreign income sustaining dictatorships by relieving them of the need to tax their citizens. As for remittances, however, it makes little sense to interpret a null or negative association between this *private* type of income and tax revenue as evidence that they help sustain dictatorship.

## 3.2. Do Remittances Increase Government Revenue in Dictatorships?

This section addresses the question of whether remittance flows increase government revenue in dictatorships. We examine both total non-resource revenue—which is revenue extracted from trade, income, and sales trans-actions but unrelated to the natural resource extraction and production sectors—and goods and services tax revenue. This latter category of taxes excludes trade and income taxes (including social contributions) as well as tax revenue from the resource sector. Importantly, this form of tax covers both final-point-of-sale tax revenue, which takes the form of direct taxes on individuals as they consume goods and services domestically, and taxes on transactions all along the domestic supply chain. Thus if remittance inflows increase demand for goods and services in the domestic economy, this will stimulate (presumably some domestic) supply, from which the government can potentially extract tax revenue.

We employ data on tax revenue in dictatorships updated from Prichard et al. (2014); data coverage extends from 1980 to 2017. These data were developed to test theories of the political resource curse (see, e.g Ross 2001) and thus address a number of shortcomings of earlier data sets constructed by the IMF and World Bank used in prior research (e.g., Morrison 2009; Singer 2012; Ebeke 2014; Escribà-Folch et al. 2015, Appendix).[6] Earlier data sets of government revenue and taxation suffered from "extensive missing data and gaps in coverage, especially for lower income countries" (Prichard et al. 2014, 9). For example, Prichard et al. (2018, 298) note that the nearly 70 percent of the ICTD (International Centre for Tax and Development) data on tax revenue in developing countries (from 1990 to 2012) is missing in the IMF series.[7] Further, the ICTD data address the issue of incomparability across countries, given varying revenue-data collection sources in different countries, and adopts a common GDP series for denominating the revenue figures (Prichard et al. 2014, 1). Finally, and perhaps most importantly, the ICTD data allow researchers to disentangle resource revenue (e.g., royalties from international oil firms, taxes on oil exports, and sales revenue from state-owned natural resource firms) from other forms of domestic tax revenue.

We test an error-correction model (ECM) that estimates both short- and long-run effects of explanatory variables. We focus on the long-run effect of remittances on revenue generation, because we want to know whether this form of "external" income boosts the revenue for autocratic governments that may then use this additional revenue to sustain their regimes.[8] To account for possible incomparability across countries arising from different domestic sources of the revenue data, we adjust for the baseline level of taxation in each country with country-fixed effects. Similarly, there is a positive common time trend in the revenue data, as domestic non-resource tax collection has improved in the past couple of decades (Prichard et al. 2014, 36). We account for this common time trend in the most flexible manner, with year effects.[9]

We draw our preferred specification from Singer (2012) and adjust for GDP per capita, trade openness, and capital-account openness—as measured by Chinn and Ito (2008). We also adjust for population size, net migration, and natural resource rents.[10] Adjusting for population accounts for changes in the pool of people transacting in the economy that may also correlate with remittance-receipt, because emigration (captured in the net migration variable) is a necessary determinant of remittance inflows. We include resource rents in the specification to allow comparison of the effects of this type of foreign income with the effect of remittances. Recall, however, that the tax revenue we model does *not* include resource revenue.[11]

The left panel of Figure 3.2 reports the results for total tax revenue. All the explanatory variables are standardized such that estimates reflect the marginal effect of a one-standard deviation change in the explanatory variable. The estimate for remittances is positive, but small and not statistically different from zero. As expected, trade volume increases total revenue because this figure includes trade taxes as well as income and sales taxes. Population size and GDP also boost tax take in the long run. The estimate for resource rents is negative—which is consistent with the political resource curse argument—but only marginally significant.

The right panel of Figure 3.2 reports the results for goods and services tax revenue, which, in addition to excluding resource revenue also omits import/export duties and income taxes.[12] The estimate for remittances is almost precisely zero, while net migration (i.e., emigration) reduces sales tax revenue and larger populations increase it. In contrast to total tax revenue, the

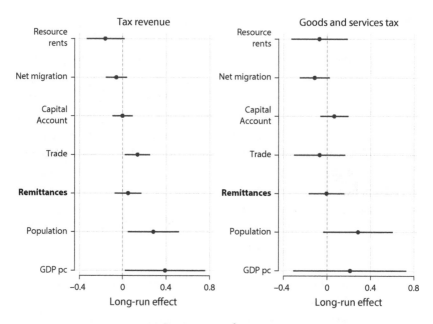

FIGURE 3.2. Remittances and government revenue

estimate for trade is negative, but small and not significant. Finally, resource rents appear to have little effect on goods and services tax revenue.

These findings suggest that remittance inflows have no substantial effect on tax-revenue generation—either total revenue or via sales taxes. In unreported results, we also examine data specifically on VAT, which is one revenue stream accounted for in the goods and services tax total. But this VAT sample suffers from severe bias due to missing data, as over half of the observations for which there are data on goods and services tax lack VAT data. Nonetheless, these tests for VAT also yield null results, again suggesting no strong long-term relationship between remittances and tax revenue.

To our knowledge, these tests are the most extensive to date to cover large panels of autocracies. For example, while Asatryan et al. (2017) find that remittances increase tax revenue via VAT—a test that most closely adheres to the idea that remittances increase revenue via direct consumption taxes—their analysis only examines data for fifty-seven countries, most of which are democracies, not autocracies. This suggests that neither prior studies nor our results should be interpreted as being conclusive, on account of the missing-data issues. That said, we find no empirical evidence that remittance inflows boost government revenue.

## 3.3.  Remittances and Government Spending

The findings in the last section suggest that remittances have no long-term impact on government revenue generation. If this finding is correct, then it rules out the possibility that remittances boost revenue that autocratic governments might use to sustain their rule. Further, the null finding linking remittances and revenue suggests there is little evidence that remittances somehow relieve the government of having to tax citizens in the first place, thereby reducing citizens' demand for accountability and representation. However, the revenue tests cannot rule out the possibility that remittances allow autocracies to shift spending away from universal welfare goods and towards payouts to groups whose support is necessary to sustain the regime. This section examines this substitution argument by examining whether remittances shape government spending behavior.

First, we test whether remittances alter overall government spending. While the substitution theory does not necessarily suggest that remittances boost overall government spending, some argue that remittance inflows may increase the size of government (Singer 2012). Because remittance inflows tend to be counter-cyclical—rising during periods of domestic economic contraction and returning to an equilibrium level in normal times—they buffer the domestic economy against consumption shortfalls that accompany domestic economic downturns. Thus, unlike other types of international financial flows that are pro-cyclical, such as FDI or trade, remittances allow the government to boost government spending to offset the consumption shortfall. This framework suggests that remittances—as a form or outcome of global economic integration—have a very different fiscal impact on recipient governments than other forms of economic integration, particularly trade and foreign investment, for which liberalization often entails reducing the size of the government. However, for our purposes, this argument simply suggests that remittances should increase government spending.

A second argument also suggests that remittances may pressure a government to increase public-goods spending because remittances boost political competition. In political systems that are more competitive (i.e., democracies), additional political pressure stemming from remittances provides the government with an incentive to increase spending (Easton and Montinola 2017). By contrast, if dictatorships are *not* competitive political systems, then increased political pressure from remittances inflows should boost repression spending: namely, government expenditure on the military.

Finally, in a manner similar to that envisaged by the substitution theory, private remittance flows may reduce the overall demand for government spending on social protection and redistribution because they insure against income shocks (Doyle 2015; Mina 2019). This argument suggests that as remittances increase, citizen demand for social spending reduces, which should *decrease* government size. Doyle (2015) tests this proposition in a sample composed of mostly Latin-American democracies.[13] If we extend this argument to autocracies, remittances should be associated with smaller government size in the long run, as citizens demand less redistribution as income insurance.

Thus our first step in assessing how remittances shape government spending patterns is to look at total government spending, using a data series from the World Development Indicators. The outcome in this analysis is government spending as a share of the economy (percentage of GDP).[14] We use an estimator similar to that used in the revenue analysis: an ECM with two-way fixed effects.[15] We drop resource rents from the specification because we do not have a theory linking this revenue to government spending, but we adjust for three additional factors: the age dependency ratio, urbanization, and election years. The age dependency ratio accounts for the fact that governments tend to spend more when a large share of the population is of non-working age (children and retirees). The age composition of society also tends to affect incentives to migrate and hence worker remittances. Urbanization may force governments to alter spending behavior: for example, by boosting spending to respond to the potential protest threat of increasingly urban population (Bates 1984; Wallace 2013); and urban migration is often the first step towards emigration across state borders (Hatton and Williamson 1998, 17). Finally, there may be an electoral spending cycle, whereby autocratic regimes boost government spending around elections to shore up their electoral support (Pepinsky 2007; Wright 2011); and remittances often increase during election periods (O'Mahony 2013).

The top left plot in Figure 3.3 shows the estimates for the long-run effect of the predictors. Remittances, according to this test, have no significant effect on long-run aggregate government spending in autocracies.[16] We find some evidence that the volume of trade increases government spending, which is consistent with a trade-compensation hypothesis suggesting that governments respond to adverse economic effects of trade liberalization in import-competing industries with additional government spending. There

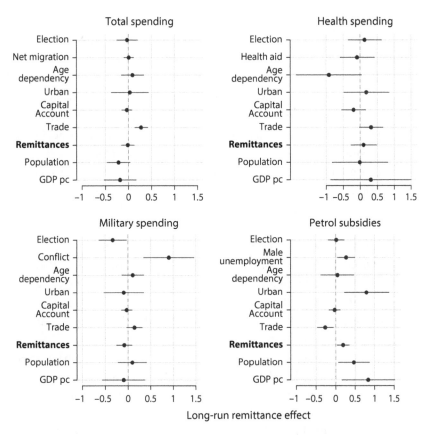

FIGURE 3.3. Remittances and government spending

is thus little evidence that remittances shift levels of aggregate government spending in autocracies.

### 3.3.1. Government Health Spending and Military Spending

Next we examine two components of aggregate government spending: health expenditure and military spending. Numerous scholars use public health expenditure as a proxy for government (i.e., public) welfare expenditure when testing the substitution argument (e.g., Ebeke 2012; Ahmed 2013; Easton and Montinola 2017). Ebeke (2012, 1010), for example, uses government health expenditure to test the argument that "remittances constitute a form of private subsidy, and therefore bad governments can easily reduce public subsidies in

these sectors." Mina (2019), meanwhile, uses social protection expenditure
for the same purpose. While some studies focus on human welfare outcomes
associated with health spending, such as immunization rates, access to clean
water, or infant mortality (see, e.g., Adida and Girod 2011; Zhunio et al.
2012; Ahmed 2013), assessing how remittances shape government spending
categories such as health expenditure, is a more direct test of the substitution argument than health outcomes, because the purchase of private health
services with remittance income influences health outcomes as well. Similarly, concerning military expenditures, we would not want to assess the
substitution argument by looking at success in conflicts or the absence of military coups—two political *outcomes* that may be shaped, in part, by military
spending.

We analyze data on government (i.e., public) health spending as a share
of GDP from the Global Burden of Disease Health Financing Collaborator
Network (2019). The data cover the two decades from 1995 (1996, given
lags) to 2016 and include an additional measure of health-sector aid provided to the government.[17] We adjust for health aid and election years in the
specification for health spending. We then examine military spending as a
share of GDP, with data from the World Bank (World Bank 2019b). Instead
of including health aid in the specification for military spending, we adjust
for conflict, which we operationalize as a binary indicator of high intensity
conflict (Gleditsch et al. 2002).

The upper right plot in Figure 3.3 (above) shows results for health spending. The explanatory variables are standardized so the estimates reflect the
marginal effect of a one-standard-deviation increase in the variable. The estimate for remittances is positive, but small and not statistically different from
zero. The estimate for trade is positive and significant, which is consistent with
a compensation argument.

The lower left plot in Figure 3.3 shows results for military spending as a percentage of GDP. Here the estimate for remittances is negative and marginally
significant, suggesting that remittances lower long-run levels of military
spending.[18] The estimates for other predictors of military spending are also
statistically significant: elections are associated with less military spending,
and conflicts with more. Both of these findings confirm intuition; and they
provide a comparison for interpreting the size of the remittance effect. The
remittance estimate suggests that a one-standard-deviation increase in remittances is associated with a 15 percent decrease in military spending, while
elections are associated with a 33 percent decrease. Finally, conflicts nearly

double military spending, increasing it by 97 percent. The remittance effect is therefore roughly half the size of the election effect and 15 percent of the size of the conflict effect.

The analysis of health and military spending provides no evidence consistent with the substitution argument, which implies that remittances should increase military spending and decrease public health spending. If anything we find the opposite.[19] We are reluctant to put much stock in the finding that remittances decrease military spending, because the finding is sensitive to the type of estimator we employ and the exact specification. In short, these tests provide little support for the substitution theory: remittances have almost no effect on public health expenditure, and if anything decrease military spending.

### 3.3.2.  Do Remittances Boost Petrol Subsidies?

In November 2019, amid a deepening economic crisis and massive budget deficits, the Iranian government decided to ration petrol and cut fuel subsidies, two policies that caused a rapid spike in the price of fuel: almost overnight Iranian citizens faced "a 50% increase on the price of the first 60 litres of petrol purchased each month, and a 300% increase on purchases above 60 litres" (*The Economist* 2019). To minimize the political backlash, the government announced the subsidy cut at midnight just before the start of the weekend; but this attempt to bury bad news failed, as the announcement was met with an immediate popular response. Massive protests spread rapidly across the country's main cities, at first voicing dissatisfaction with price hikes and economic mismanagement. The protestors' demands were soon turned against the government itself, however, calling for an end to the Ayatollahs' regime. The regime responded with violent and lethal force, leaving hundreds of protesters dead (Fassihi and Gladstone 2019).

As this example illustrates, fuel and other consumption subsidies are an instrument for buying social peace, especially in urban areas. Victor (2009, 8) sums up the logic of these dynamics:

> [T]he cheapest fuels are often provided by governments that do not face popular referenda. One reason for this paradox is that while these governments do not face elections they do confront other existential tests. In particular, they fear instability. And they believe that one way to reduce those dangers is to provide highly visible services at low cost. Once they

begin this process it is difficult to stop . . . [S]ubsidy is a readily available means of supplying visible goods and services to unrest-prone populations.

Petrol (gasoline) subsidies benefit all consumers—though more benefits accrue to higher-income citizens who consume more—either directly, when they purchase retail fuel, or indirectly, by lowering the production and transportation costs of consumption goods. This welfare expenditure is therefore a relatively pure public good, insofar as it is non-excludable. The subsidies are also largely non-rivalrous, because one citizen's consumption does not alter the availability of the subsidy for others.[20] Further, all consumers are likely to be aware of domestic retail fuel prices, even if they do not know the extent to which the government subsidizes them. However, all consumers are likely to know when retail prices change because the government alters the subsidy. For these reasons, government spending on petrol subsidies closely resembles the welfare good in the substitution model (Abdih et al. 2008). If petrol subsidies are a good proxy for a pure welfare good in the substitution model, then this argument would predict that remittance inflows will *decrease* subsidies: more private remittance income should relieve the government of the need to provide cheap fuel.

The measure of petrol subsidies is calculated from consumer gasoline subsidies using the price gap method that "compares the observed retail price in each country with a global benchmark price, which represent[s] the difference between the retail price and the international supply cost" (Ross et al. 2017, 2). Data are available for the period from 2004 to 2015 (with a one-year lag).[21]

Perhaps the largest determinant of the cost of petrol subsidies for governments is the world oil price. Not all countries are affected in the same way by changes in the world price of oil, however. Big oil-producers may benefit as they see revenues rise, and these governments often shield consumers from world price increases by refining and distributing domestically. However, many autocracies are net oil importers, and rising world prices simply increase the cost of subsidizing domestic fuel consumption.

To account for the myriad ways in which world oil prices shape domestic political economies, we adjust for the country-specific benchmark price of supplying consumer petrol. This allows for the differences between countries in how they can respond, given their domestic oil production and refining capacity, to changes in the world oil price. We also account for domestic male unemployment, with data from the World Development Indicators (World Bank 2019b). Male labor emigration (which results in remittance inflows) may lower unemployment, and governments may use fuel subsidies to mitigate the grievances that stem from male unemployment and can also drive anti-regime protest. Thus government welfare expenditure on fuel subsidies may respond to unemployment, which in turn shapes remittance inflows.

The lower right plot in Figure 3.3 (above) shows results for government welfare spending on petrol subsidies. The estimate for the long-term effect of remittances is positive and statistically significant at conventional levels. This suggests that, far from decreasing fuel subsidies, remittances may in fact increase them.[22] Other predictors are also associated with this welfare expenditure: male unemployment and urbanization—presumably both threats to social stability—increase petrol subsidies, while trade volume decreases them. The size of the estimate for remittances is roughly half that of the estimate for male unemployment, and one-fifth of that of the estimate for urbanization. In short, we find no evidence that remittances decrease spending on fuel subsidies, a universal and transparent item of public welfare expenditure. Thus, there is little evidence from this type of spending that is consistent with the substitution theory.

To recap, then: our analysis of remittances and various types of tax revenue and government spending yield very little evidence consistent with either the revenue or substitution mechanisms linking remittances to authoritarian survival. We interpret this evidence to suggest that remittances do not appreciably alter government revenues or spending patterns, and therefore do not enable authoritarian governments to spend more on the types of goods that enhance their repressive capacity or secure the loyalty of political elites.

The revenue and spending theories presume either that governments capture some remittance inflows via taxation, or that remittances sufficiently mitigate citizens' grievances deriving from loss of public welfare spending to enable the government to reduce that welfare spending while increasing expenditure on other items. We find little evidence for either hypothesis. Both mechanisms assume that remittance inflows ultimately alter government behavior and are therefore similar to other forms of global financial flow—especially oil export revenue—that influence domestic politics in authoritarian countries by providing governments with money to do "bad things." The key difference between remittances and other foreign resources is that remittances largely bypass governments and flow directly to citizens. In the chapters which follow, we examine the evidence for other pathways through which remittances may shape the balance of power in autocracies, by focusing on the behavior of the citizens who receive these remittance inflows.

In doing so, we articulate the mechanisms whereby remittances shift the balance of power away from governments and towards citizens as the primary agents of democratic political change in dictatorships.

## 3.4. Remittances and Repression

The previous section assessed the empirical support for the substitution theory by focusing on government spending and its composition. Indeed, this is the area in which substitution is most likely to be manifest in observed data. Nonetheless, it is possible that remittances allow governments to decrease spending in areas that we cannot readily observe or to increase other types of non-military spending that contribute to authoritarian survival. Recall that the substitution model in Abdih et al. (2012) yields the insight that remittances, at the margin, allow the government to decrease public-goods spending and divert it towards "its own consumption" (659), which Ahmed (2012) interprets as their contributing to an unspecified government survival function. While it is unclear whether an increase in patronage increases the chances of regime survival if remittances fund opponents and weaken clientelism, another survival strategy the government might pursue more robustly when remittances allow this diversion is state-led repression (Ahmed 2012, 164). This section therefore examines whether remittances increase government repression.

There are multiple mechanisms through which substitution could enhance government repression, other than simply by increased military spending. First, although the previous section examining whether remittances boost military spending in autocracies found that they do not, military spending data may not capture government spending on the domestic internal security forces that are mainly responsible for repressing domestic opposition in most dictatorships. As Croissant et al. (2018, 174) note, "most dictators rely on non-military agencies of internal security for day-to-day repression of the political opposition."

These agencies include internal police or military units, secret police forces, paramilitary and praetorian units, pro-government militias, and even intelligence agencies. For example, military spending totals for China do not cover spending on the People's Armed Police (PAP) (Greitens 2017, 5), which is the primary security force tasked with preserving social stability in the post-Deng era (Guo 2012, 221). Further, much of the low-level, everyday domestic repression in China is carried out by local security forces funded from provincial and county budgets (Xu 2021). In Uzbekistan, long-term president Islam Karimov relied "most heavily on the security services—the ministry of internal affairs (MIA) and the National Security Service (SNB)—to retain power" (International Crisis Group 2007, 3). Indeed, some reports hold the SNB responsible for the Andijan massacre in 2005 that put down a brief anti-regime uprising (Open Source 2015). Parallel and specialized units are often better paid, equipped, and trained than regular army units.

While the military may be called into action to repress opposition forces when the regime is on the brink of collapse (Svolik 2012), as occurred in China in 1989 and Egypt in 2011, this strategy is not optimal, because its success depends, in the end, on the loyalty of key commanders in the military, who are often trained to fight foreign, not domestic, opponents, and thus develop norms that promote defending—not killing—the citizens of their own country (McLauchlin 2010; Bellin 2012; Pion-Berlin et al. 2014; Barany 2016; Dragu and Lupu 2018). As a consequence, many military forces may not be dependable repressive agents when asked to shoot their fellow citizens in the event of mass anti-regime protests, and everyday authoritarian repression typically comes within the purview of domestic security agencies outside the military. Thus military spending figures may not include the funding that principally enhances domestic coercive capacity; and we lack systematic data on domestic security spending under these regimes. Remittances may not boost military spending, but they might still enhance repression by funding domestic security forces outside the military.

Second, the successful implementation of domestic repression may depend more on the loyalty of repressive security forces than on funding a mighty and capable coercive apparatus. One way to cement the loyalty of repressive security forces is to provide them with perks and privileges (Barany 2013). Military budgets contain several items that are in fact unrelated to coercive (or fighting) capacity, but rather constitute direct economic benefits to officers and soldiers. Indeed, Henk and Rupiya (2001) show that an overwhelming proportion of defense spending in sub-Saharan African countries actually goes on salaries and staff allowances. Still other expenditure on military equipment such as highly sophisticated weaponry that lacks immediate usefulness "due to a lack of adequate training or a lack of upkeep" (Powell 2014, 177), can be largely symbolic. If such benefits are unlikely to remain should the regime fall, they incentivize the security forces to pursue domestic repression to prop up the regime that provides them (Croissant et al. 2018). If remittances—via substitution—free up government resources to boost the perks and privileges of the security forces, and hence their incentives to side with and defend the incumbent regime, then remittances could indeed be said to increase repression.

Thus an implication of the substitution argument is that remittances may enhance authoritarian survival by increasing domestic state-led repression—either via additional (unobserved) direct spending on internal security forces that boosts their coercive capacity, or by augmenting government resources spent to ensure the loyalty of repressive agents. To test this proposition, we examine both high-intensity (violent) repression and low-intensity "preventive" repression. Repression takes multiple forms, that serve different purposes (Way and Levitsky 2006; Davenport 2007a; Escribà-Folch 2013). Violent or high-intensity forms involve violations of physical integrity rights, and include torture, forced disappearances, extrajudicial killings, imprisonment, and even targeted assassinations of rivals or opponents. Low-intensity, less violent, preventive repression, by contrast, consists in suppressing or restricting empowerment rights (or coordination goods), such as political and civil rights and press freedom (Bueno de Mesquita and Smith 2010). As Levitsky and Way (2010, 58) note, "whereas high-intensity coercion is often a response to an imminent—and highly threatening—opposition challenge, low-intensity coercion is often aimed at preventing such challenges from emerging in the first place."

### 3.4.1.  Do Remittances Enhance Violent Repression in Dictatorships?

We first examine data on high-intensity political repression, such as the torture and killing of political opponents, from the Varieties of Democracy project (Coppedge et al. 2011).[23] Our model attempts to take into account all differences between dictatorships, such as how they gained power and the strategies for survival—including repression—they are most likely to employ.[24] For example, some dictatorships are relatively "benign" and induce loyalty by providing avenues for expressing dissent and channeling societal input, while other regimes rely more on coercion or information-control to retain power (Davenport 2007b; Frantz and Kendall-Taylor 2014; Frantz et al. 2020). Our approach accounts for these and other differences between dictatorships.

Figure 3.4 shows the results.[25] First we test a specification that has no confounding variables. The estimate is small and not significant. A second adjusts

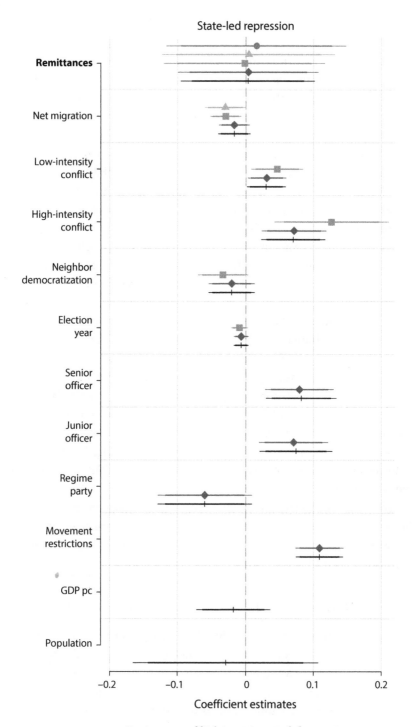

FIGURE 3.4. Remittances and high-intensity, state-led repression

for net migration (i.e., emigration) because repression may cause some of the population to exit, and this emigration could, in turn, account for remittances. Our focus is on financial remittances that stem from labor migration—not political migration—so we adjust for the potential exit of dissidents. Next we add standard measures of domestic conflict, both low- and high-intensity, as well as indicators for election years and democratization in a neighboring country. The conflict variables provide the model with stability, because they are excellent predictors of repression, as expected. Elections, meanwhile, may independently prompt state-led repression, especially if the regime is likely to lose, or the election is highly contested; and remittances increase during election periods (O'Mahony 2013). Democratization in neighboring countries may affect remittance flows from emigrants living in those countries; and regimes may respond to political change in neighboring countries by boosting repression.

Next we add potential confounders that autocratic governments may use to shape authoritarian control and repression. Having a military officer lead the regime may increase state-led repression while support parties, if they successfully co-opt potential dissenters and channel intra-elite disputes, may lower repression (Davenport 2007b; Frantz and Kendall-Taylor 2014; Escribà-Folch and Wright 2015). Movement restrictions are likely to influence remittances and may prompt violent repression, because enforcing these restriction requires state-led imprisonment and killing. Finally, we take into account structural features of countries—namely GDP per capita and population size.[26]

We find no relationship between remittances and repression.[27] The estimates for repression are small and not statistically significant, providing little support for the proposition that remittances increase violent, state-led repression against the political opposition in dictatorships.

### 3.4.2. Do Remittances Harm Civil Liberties and Political Rights?

Low-intensity repression, less visible than open violence, aims to prevent rivals and opponents from coordinating their behavior by mobilizing against the regime (Bueno de Mesquita and Smith 2010; Escribà-Folch 2013). In contrast to more visible coercion, low-level repression is thus mainly preventive (Dragu and Przeworski 2019). Yet, to be effective, such restrictions must be enforced, which requires a security apparatus with sufficient operational resources to collect intelligence about individuals' and clandestine groups' activities and act against them: surveilling rivals within the regime's support coalition; suppressing incipient organized dissent; censoring information; closing down critical media; and harassing, intimidating, or imprisoning activists.

If successful, "low-intensity coercion ... reduces the need for high-intensity coercion" (Levitsky and Way 2010, 58). Consequently, one view of hard repression—at least that which we can observe and record systematically—is that manifestations of this form of repression are reactive, and thus reflect the failure of the regime to deter opposition mobilization. If opponents know they will be defeated by mass repression or face a high cost for publicly challenging the regime in the streets, they may not mobilize in the first place; and as a result we would never observe overt state-led repression. Therefore the *absence* of observed high-intensity repression might reflect a loyal and high-capacity repressive force that effectively deters the opposition's capacity to organize and act collectively. If this were the case, then a null finding for a relationship between remittances and hard repression could still be consistent with the substitution argument—if substitution works by enhancing "soft," preventive repression that deters mobilization. For this reason, we also investigate low-intensity government repression, such as de facto restrictions on civil liberties and political rights, that may prevent anti-government mobilization from emerging. If remittances allow the regime to skim resources from public goods provision and divert the spending into repression that deters opposition mobilization, the implication in terms of the substitution argument is that soft repression can indeed be increased by remittances.

We examine whether remittances harm civil liberties and political rights using two measures of respect for civil liberties and political rights from the Varieties of Democracy project.[28] We employ these measures as proxies for civil liberties protections by the government. If substitution results in *more* preventive repression we would expect to observe *less* respect for these civil and political liberties.

The first two estimates in Figure 3.5 report results for remittances from tests of civil liberties and political rights. Both estimates are positive, but neither is statistically significant. Thus, similarly to other results reported in this chapter, we find evidence that is not just inconsistent with the substitution theory but rather points in the opposite direction.

Finally, if remittance income—via substitution—enhances authoritarian survival by boosting government resources to pay for softer forms of

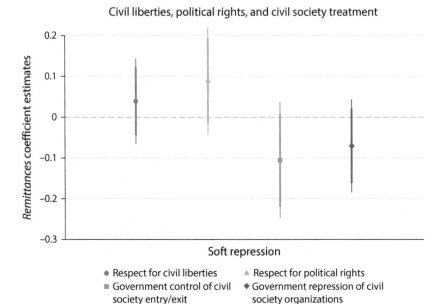

FIGURE 3.5. Remittances and "soft" repression

repression, such as infringements of civil liberties and political rights, then remittances may have a pernicious effect on democracy similar to that of oil wealth. And one manifestation of this pernicious consequence of oil wealth is what Ross (2001) and Friedman (2006) call "the group formation effect": "the government will use its largesse to prevent the formation of social groups that are independent from the state and hence that may be inclined to demand political rights" (Ross 2001, 334).[29] If this argument is adapted to remittances, the implication would be that remittance recipients with income from abroad are less invested in the domestic political economy than their fellow citizens who do not receive remittances. Further, the government may have more resources to repress and prevent independent groups from forming. Thus the effect of remittances could be to curtail the formation of civic and political groups, particularly those independent of the state. This version of the substitution mechanism suggests that remittances will lead to *more* government control over civil society, and more government repression of these groups.

We thus examine two additional outcomes: government control over entry to and exit from public life of civil society organizations, and government repression of such organizations.[30] Each concept taps into a slightly different aspect of the group-formation mechanism. Employing a test design similar to that utilized in prior tests for repression, we find negative estimates for the relationship between remittances and these two outcomes, as two right-hand vertical lines in Figure 3.5 show. Though neither estimate is statistically significant at conventional levels, together they nonetheless suggest that remittances are associated with, if anything, reduced government control over civil society and less repression.

Overall, we find no evidence that remittances adversely affect civil society groups. Together with the null findings for civil liberties and political rights, these tests provide little support for the proposition that remittance inflows in dictatorships increase softer forms of government repression.

## 3.5. Conclusion

This chapter has examined state-centered theories which argue that remittances extend the survival of dictatorships. To do so, we first investigated whether remittance flows increase the resources available to authoritarian governments, either directly via an increase in tax revenues or indirectly via a substitution effect. Such arguments build on the idea that, like other forms of foreign income such as oil revenues or foreign aid, remittances lead to a political "resource curse." However, remittance flows differ in important ways from these other sources of foreign income, because they are highly decentralized cross-country transfers between individuals, sent by migrants living abroad to relatives and friends at home. Remittance transfers therefore largely circumvent autocratic governments and channel funds directly to citizens.

Our findings cast doubt on the arguments connecting remittances to autocratic resilience. We find little evidence that monetary remittances increase tax revenue in dictatorships or alter government spending patterns. Indeed, we find that remittances have almost no effect on public health expenditure, and if anything decrease military spending. Further, remittances do not reduce one highly salient item of welfare expenditure: namely, subsidies to petrol consumption. We then explored the effect of remittances on various forms of state repression and, again, find no evidence to support the claim that remittances allow autocracies to bolster regimes' coercive apparatuses.

The chapter thus presents a series of mostly null findings. However, this set of empirical results is consistent with the proposition that remittances do not shape political outcomes by increasing autocratic regimes' resource advantage or changing government behavior. This should not be entirely surprising, because remittances do not flow to governments, but rather to citizens in countries ruled by autocratic governments. The next two chapters therefore examine the mechanisms through which remittances alter citizens' political behavior in ways that undermine autocratic power and promote democracy.

# 4

# Remittances Fund Opponents

The 1974 "Carnation Revolution" in Portugal that marked the start of a "Third Wave" of democratization followed by the revolutions of 1989 that ended Communist rule in Europe, democracy protest waves in Africa, the color revolutions in former Soviet states, the Arab Spring uprisings in 2011, and the 2019 and 2020 protests in cities as diverse as Algiers, Hong Kong, Khartoum, Caracas, and Minsk: all these suggest that mass anti-government protest campaigns are a pervasive and growing threat to authoritarian rule around the world (see, e.g., Zunes 1994; Schock 2005; Bunce and Wolchik 2011; Kendall-Taylor and Frantz 2014b; Chenoweth 2016). Indeed, headlines from across the world proclaim a burst of destabilizing protest activity, most often in countries ruled by autocratic governments: "Protests Rage around the World" (Safi 2019); "Global Wave of Protests Rattles Governments" (Lyons et al. 2019); "Do Today's Global Protests Have Anything in Common?" (BBC News 2019); "The Global Protest Wave" (Fisher and Taub 2019a); "Why Are There So Many Protests across the Globe Right Now?" (Zakaria 2019); and "Africa Uprising: The Rise of Popular Protest Continent-wide" (Davis 2015).

Despite these developments, research on the drivers of protest in autocracies remains relatively scarce—principally because of the low reliability of existing protest data or their limited geographical and temporal coverage. Moreover, existing research, mostly relying on country-level or event data, focuses on the domestic determinants of protest, pointing to causes such as economic crises, elections, technological advances, and other shocks to political opportunities for protest (Bratton and van de Walle 1997; Scarritt et al. 2001; Meyer 2004; Beaulieu 2014; Brancati 2014; Chenoweth and Ulfelder 2017; Ruijgrok 2017; Weidmann and Rød 2019). While some scholars point to international factors, such as economic globalization, the role of INGOs, and the diffusion of protest across borders, that might spur protest (e.g., Bunce and Wolchik 2006; Beissinger 2007; Bellinger and Arce 2011; Murdie and Bhasin 2011; Gleditsch and Rivera 2017), almost none of this research focuses on the potentially *destabilizing* role of migration; and to the extent that scholars look at migration, they focus on emigration policy, not financial flows (Barry et al. 2014).

The logic of "exit, voice, and loyalty" suggests, if anything, that emigration—in particular the exit of unemployed young men—should reduce the "pressure" of pent-up rage against incumbent governments, hurting the chances for protests to emerge. For example, emigration could result in a political "brain drain," undermining the capacity of local opposition groups to challenge the incumbent regime. According to this logic, emigration should *stabilize* dictatorships. This chapter argues and shows the opposite: out-migration boosts protest. Instead of serving as a "safety valve," emigration is a catalyst for mass-driven democratic revolution. The missing link between exit and protest in dictatorships, we argue, is the remittances migrants send home.

Consider the case of Zimbabwe. The United Kingdom hosts one of the largest Zimbabwean diaspora populations outside southern Africa; and that diaspora maintains strong transnational ties with its homeland. The number of Zimbabweans in the UK increased substantially in the late 1990s and early 2000s as a result of harsh government repression that followed the creation of a strong opposition party, the Movement for Democratic Change (MDC). The MDC had roots in the labor movement and a civic group, the National Constitutional Assembly—two organizations that leveraged discontent with government mismanagement, rampant corruption, and the initiation of controversial land reform to mobilize a competitive opposition party (Betts and Jones 2016).

Transnational ties between the diaspora and their families at home comprise a wide array of activities, including substantial economic support. Due to the mass exodus, remittances poured into Zimbabwe, with $1.2 billion flowing into the country in 2009 and another $2.1 billion in 2012, representing more than 10 percent of the country's GDP. A study of Zimbabweans living in the UK shows that nearly 80 percent of the diaspora remitted money back home, and that 10 percent made donations to community organizations (Bloch 2008). While the main motive for these remittances was undoubtedly to support family members in tough economic times, some respondents also stressed that they intended to support political activities with their remittance funds. Indeed, as Pasura (2010, 116) notes, "[d]iaspora politics in Britain is not divorced from homeland politics, but rather [is] about augmenting

REMITTANCES FUND OPPONENTS 99

political parties in the homeland, the more prominent grouping being appendages of opposition political parties or civic organizations in the country of origin."

A primary method of supporting political change back home, as several Zimbabwean migrants observed, was to channel funds to the MDC (Pasura 2009; 2010; Betts and Jones 2016). This organization—and later its splinter opposition groups—has numerous local branches in the UK that mobilize funds for the party back in Zimbabwe: "Membership fees, the selling of membership cards and party regalia as well as fundraising parties generate the financial resources to assist the opposition parties in Zimbabwe" (Kuhlmann 2010, 15). International support, financial and otherwise, was fundamental to the MDC's campaign activities as well as for other civil society organizations. In response to the growing international support and the increased mobilization capacity of the main opposition party, the ZANU-PF regime passed the Political Parties Finance Act in 2001, which prohibited parties from receiving foreign funding. Despite this, the MDC continued to gain in prominence, especially after the regime's defeat in the constitutional referendum of 2000. The last two decades have been marked by recurring mass protests—such as those in 2016–17—and the emergence of a sustained pro-democracy movement, despite major factional divisions and widespread violent repression (Taundi 2010).

Our claims draw on the resource model of political participation. As the example above illustrates, we posit that remittances increase the resources available to political opponents for mobilizing dissent against the government. First, they increase the private income of individuals and families back home, thereby lifting material constraints upon political action. Second, they directly fund opposition parties and civil society organizations. Our argument therefore contests not only the idea that emigration of unemployed young men reduces protest, but also claims that remittances reduce economic grievances, and therefore mobilization, against the government.

In this chapter we examine the evidence. At the micro-level, we show that remittance recipients are more likely to protest than citizens whose income is not supplemented by this external resource. Consistent with the theory positing that remittances fund political opponents of authoritarian regimes, we show that they mobilize resistance in opposition areas but not in regime-stronghold regions. Globally, meanwhile, we demonstrate that they boost anti-government protest mobilization in non-democracies. As popular mobilization against autocratic governments has become the most successful path to democracy in the past quarter-century, we document how global migration finances the political mobilization necessary for peaceful democratization.

## 4.1.  Remitted Income and the Global Rise in Protest

We first review competing explanations for how remittance inflows shape anti-government protest. One theory suggests that remittances should lead to less protest. The grievance model posits that social and political discontent breed protests. Because remittance recipients have more family income to purchase goods and services than those without remittances, the former should have fewer grievances against the government, which in turn should reduce the incentive to mobilize contentious political action.

Drawing on the resource model of political participation, a second argument claims the opposite: remittances boost the organizational resources and capacity of the opposition. Mobilizing and participating in protests is costly, and remittances provide individuals and groups with additional resources to overcome constraints to political activity. Remittances prompt participation in protests by increasing individual and household resources, and also by directly funding opposition groups, such as political parties and civil society organizations, in migrants' home countries.

A third argument posits that remittances fund a rising middle class that then demands democracy to protect its assets. Remittances, according to this logic, do not alter the capacity or resources required for protest mobilization, but simply provide an additional incentive for remittance recipients to demand political change.

### 4.1.1.  Anti-Government Protest

This section examines evidence linking remittances to anti-government protest, using a unique measure of global protest. Erica Chenoweth and her colleagues construct a latent protest variable from an item response theory (IRT) model that combines information from multiple existing data sets to estimate the value of yearly protest levels in each country in the world from 1960 to 2010 (Chenoweth et al. 2014).[1] This project thus produces anti-government protest data that are comparable across different periods of history as well as across the globe.

These data have several advantages over those generated by other approaches. First, the latent protest measure combines information from eight extant protest data sets—including the widely used Banks' Cross-National Times Series Data, as well as event data from the Social Conflict in Africa Data (SCAD) and the Armed Conflict Location and Event Data (ACLED) projects. Combining information from multiple extant sources mitigates the effect of estimates from any one data set possibly being biased. For example, the Bank's protest data, which have excellent historical coverage, are derived from just one source: articles on protest from *The New York Times*. It thus likely under-counts protests in small, poorer countries. Recent event data sets such as SCAD and ACLED, by contrast, exploit news reports from multiple sources but lack historical coverage. Further, the latent measure incorporates information from different types of sources, as some of the data sets used to construct the latent measure are sourced using computer-coded news reports while others are hard-coded by human researchers sifting through the historical record.

Second, the latent protest measure accounts for the fact that there are more news sources and likely more opportunity to observe protest in later periods—such as the 2000s—than during earlier periods. It is possible, for example, that a measure of protest primarily based on news sources might indicate a global rise in protests simply because we have more and better news information for more recent than for prior periods. Since remittances have been increasing during the most recent era of globalization, we might think erroneously that we observe a positive correlation between remittances and protest were we to use a measure of protest that mostly picks up the increase over time in the quantity of available information. The measure we actually employ, by contrast, takes into account changing standards in the observation of protest.

We utilize a measure of remittances per capita calculated from data from the World Bank with an inflation adjustment. To account for potential reverse causation—whereby protest in a particular year causes greater remittance inflows in that same year—we lag this variable by one year. Further, given the skewed distribution of remittances per capita, we use the logged value of the variable.[2] The sample period covers 130 autocratic regimes in eighty-four countries, from 1978 to 2010.

To model the relationship between worker remittances and protest, we account for potentially confounding factors that might explain both. In our preferred specification, we adjust for structural factors associated with protest capacity and the size of remittance flows: GDP per capita and population size, both logged and lagged by one year. Poor domestic economic growth may provoke grievances that fuel protest, while bad economic times may also cause citizens to elicit more remittances from abroad. We thus adjust for the lagged economic growth. Migrant flows—rather than remittances themselves—may explain protest levels, particularly if dissenting citizens exit rather than protest. Thus we adjust for for net migration (i.e., emigration) and regime control on foreign movement, again both lagged by one year.

Further, political protest in neighboring countries may spur protest via diffusion effects, as the Arab Spring and the color revolutions illustrate (Bunce and Wolchik 2006; Beissinger 2007; Gleditsch and Rivera 2017), while the economic factors in neighboring countries that produce such protests may, in turn, influence remittance flows. We therefore include neighbor protest and neighbor democratization measures.[3] Finally, we include an indicator of executive election years, because elections may spur anti-government protests (Hyde 2011; Daxecker 2012; Beaulieu 2014; Brancati 2014; Hafner-Burton et al. 2014), and there is evidence that they attract significant remittance inflows (O'Mahony 2013).[4]

Finally, different countries have different opportunities for labor migration and different protest opportunity structures. For example, North African countries are relatively close to Europe and so their citizens may migrate more and send more remittances than flow to countries in Central Africa. We therefore adjust for all differences between countries in the average levels of protest and remittances by modeling country effects.[5] Thus, the tests capture whether changes over time in remittance inflows within countries are associated with changes over time in their level of protest.

Figure 4.1 reports the results from three tests. The vertical axis lists the predictors and the horizontal axis measures the size of the coefficient estimates.[6] The first test only examines remittances, without adjusting for potential confounders. The second test adjusts for growth, and the third, our preferred specification, adjusts for an additional seven confounders. In all three tests, the estimate for remittances is positive and statistically significant, indicating that remittance inflows are associated with increased anti-government protest.[7]

We also find that economic growth—that is, good economic times—is associated with reduced protest. This is consistent with a common understanding of anti-incumbent protest as a reaction to bad economic times, such as periods of high unemployment or declining wages (see, e.g., Walton and Ragin 1990). While this finding corresponds to intuition, we use the estimate

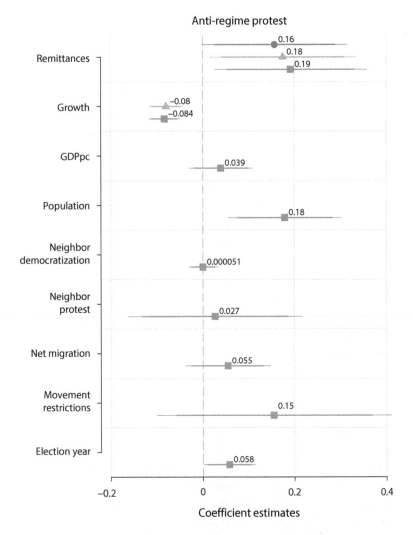

FIGURE 4.1. Remittances and anti-government protest

for the size of the growth effect to help understand the substantive effect of remittances, which is difficult to interpret because the protest variable is a latent measure. The estimates in Figure 4.1 suggest that a one-standard deviation increase in growth is associated with −0.08 units less protest, while a one-standard deviation increase in remittances is associated with an increase of 0.16 units of protest. Thus, at least according to these tests, the remittance effect is twice as large as the growth effect.

The online Technical Appendix discusses empirical tests that account for the possible endogeneity of remittances. Although the approach used thus far accounts for unobserved differences between countries that might jointly explain remittances and political protest, an association between remittances and protest may still reflect an endogenous relationship, either as the result of a mis-measured remittance variable or un-modeled strategic behavior that varies over time within countries. For example, if would-be protesters seek out external resources such as remittances to finance (or offset the costs of) protest behavior, an estimate of remittances is likely to be biased upwards. If, alternatively, regimes that are likely to face protests restrict the flow of private external resources in anticipation of anti-government activity, then an estimate of remittances would be biased towards zero.

We outline two strategies for addressing possible bias from endogeneity—one that models remittances from economic growth trends in OECD countries, and one that models remittances from world oil-price trends. Each of these strategies has strengths and drawbacks, which we discuss, but the upshot from both is that, if anything, the remittance estimates reported in Figure 4.1 are biased downwards, towards zero, meaning a true causal estimate is likely to be stronger than those reported here.

### 4.1.2. Pro-Government Mobilization

Not all protests are the same. Indeed, mass protest in dictatorships may in fact be a stabilizing social force if the regime mobilizes large groups of citizens to publicly demonstrate their support for it. The National Socialist Party in Germany, for example, convened annual mass rallies in Nuremburg in the 1930s; these pro-government rallies not only helped cement the participants' loyalty to the regime but also spread pro-regime propaganda via news coverage of the event and as participants relayed propaganda by word of mouth when they returned home (Sinclair 1938, 578, 582).

While pro-government rallies, in the form of collective displays of fealty to the leader, are often associated with Communist regimes—think the mass parades in Beijing in 1999 celebrating the fiftieth anniversary of the Communist Party's defeat of the Nationalists, or the adoring crowds lining the streets after Kim Jong Il's death in North Korea in 2011—many dictatorships hold mass pro-government protests, often in response to anti-government mobilization or around election time. After election-related anti-government protests in Iran in 2009, for instance, the government staged pro-government rallies in cities across the country, including Shiraz, Arak, Qom, and Tehran (Associated Press 2009). More recently, a pro-government union organized demonstrations supporting the military-led government in Algeria, ahead of the first post-Bouteflika elections (Ahmed 2019).

Informational models of protest emphasize that public demonstrations of either support for or antipathy against a government provide crucial signals about the level and intensity of sentiment of at least some citizens (Kuran 1989; Lohmann 1994). In turn, these signals—of either antipathy or support—influence the behavior of other individuals. For this reason, a pro-government rally may signal to would-be dissidents that organizing an anti-regime protest may be likely to fail, at a high personal cost to those contemplating mobilizing.

Even if participants in a pro-government rally do not, in private, support the government and only in fact show up to receive some compensation from it, or to avoid punishment, the public signal given out informs others—both co-participants in the pro-government demonstration and dissenters on the sidelines—that there possibly exist some citizens who truly support the government and might even fight to defend it. This public ambiguity as to the true, private preferences of participants in a pro-government rally may be sufficient to dissuade would-be anti-government protesters from mobilizing.

Just as informational theories of protest predict that small anti-government gatherings may quickly spiral into mass uprisings as more citizens' reveal their anti-government preferences by joining the dissenters in the street, they also predict that pro-government rallies will deter anti-government protest. Thus, pro-government rallies in dictatorships can potentially change the beliefs of non-participants (i.e., would-be dissenters) in ways that help sustain authoritarian rule.

Until recently, there have been no systematic data on pro-government mobilization in dictatorships, even though it has long been noted as a potentially decisive factor in sustaining autocratic rule (Friedrich and Brzezinski 1965). However, Weidmann and Rød (2019) collects event data for pro-government protests in all dictatorships throughout the world for the period from 2004 to 2015.[8] The Mass Mobilization in Autocracies Database (MMAD) contains data from a variety of news reports for mass mobilization events, defined as "public gathering[s] of at least 25 people with an expressed political motivation either opposing or supporting the government" (Hellmeier and Weidmann 2020), including counts, at the weekly level, of both pro- and anti-government rallies.

Given the prior analysis of the latent protest variable that is available covering a longer time series (1978–2010), we view analysis of the anti-government protest data from MMAD as a robustness test: we expect remittances to increase the likelihood of anti-government protests during the 2004–15 period. If the resource theory is correct—and citizens who receive additional private income from remittances support the government—we might, at first glance, expect remittances also to boost pro-government protest mobilization.

However, this logic assumes that the citizens who join pro-government rallies are genuine government supporters. If the government coerces or induces citizens into participating, however—through the threat of punishment or by paying them to show support—then additional private income from remittances may *reduce* participation in pro-government mobilization. This mechanism is similar to that envisaged by the argument that we investigate in the next chapter: remittances, we posit, decrease voters' dependency on government patronage and thus sever the clientelistic ties between regimes and the voters they mobilize. Indeed, autocratic governments often launch pro-government rallies during elections (Smyth et al. 2013; Hellmeier and Weidmann 2020); and we find that, according to the MMAD counts, pro-government demonstrations are twice as likely in election years as in other years. Thus, an alternative expectation, which is consistent with the broader proposition that remittances undermine authoritarian rule, is that remittances will be associated with fewer pro-government rallies.

Because we only have annual remittance data for a large group of autocracies, we aggregate the protest counts—for both pro- and anti-government rallies—from weekly events to yearly events. Even at this level of aggregation, there are still many observations with no protest, particularly for pro-government protest.[9] For these models, the outcome is the logged protest count, which addresses the skew in the count variables and makes a linear model more appropriate.[10] We adjust for GDP per capita, population size, neighbor democratization, net migration, movement restrictions, and elections.

Figure 4.2 reports the results for two predictors in the model: remittances and elections.[11] The vertical axis lists the two covariates; and the horizontal axis depicts the coefficient estimates. The first set of results, shown with circles and dark lines for confidence intervals, reports anti-government protest: both remittances and election years are associated with more anti-government protests.

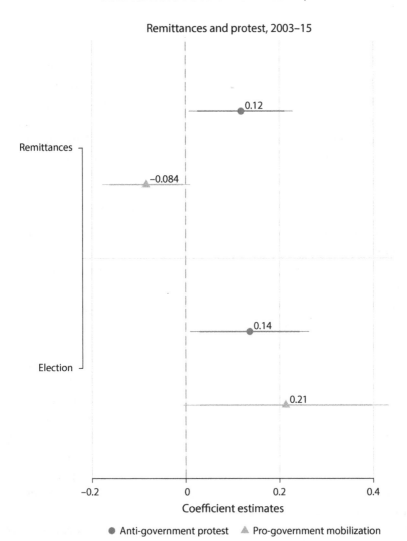

FIGURE 4.2. Remittances and pro-government mobilization

The second set of results, shown with triangles and lighter lines for confidence intervals, reports pro-government protest: while there are more pro-government rallies in election years, remittances are associated with *fewer* pro-government protests. This finding is consistent with the alternative expectation cited above, that remittances sever clientelistic ties between regimes and the citizens they mobilize to demonstrate support.

Together, the findings from the MMAD protest analysis suggest two pathways by which remittances shape protest behavior to undermine authoritarian rule: they both increase anti-government protest and decrease pro-government mobilization. This interpretation of the findings, of course, assumes that remittances mobilize some recipients—those who oppose the government—but de-mobilize others who might demonstrate support the regime absent the additional private income. These assumptions can only be examined, however, using individual-level data, to which we turn next.

## 4.2.  How Remittances Boost Protests

The previous section demonstrates that over the past four decades of globalization, remittances have increased protest in autocracies. However, research designs using macro-political data cannot adjudicate as to the mechanism linking the two. In particular, we want to know whether remittances increase protest in autocracies because they provide resources to regime opponents who previously could not afford to make investments in contentious activities (a resource mechanism); or alternatively, whether remittances increase protest because they enable individuals who were caught up in clientelistic exchanges to exit from those networks and reveal their political preferences (an extrication mechanism). In the first case, remittances should increase protest among citizens who live where clientelism is less pervasive: that is, in locations where individuals are less likely to support the regime. However, if remittances have a "liberating" effect, the increase in protest should be largest in pro-government areas where clientelistic networks are strongest.

While previous research shows that remittances induce electoral disengagement in dominant-party regimes (Pfutze 2014; Escribà-Folch et al. 2015), these findings are uninformative about costlier forms of dissent, such as protest. Regardless of whether remittances are conducive to a reduction in electoral engagement, if the severing of clientelistic ties—"extrication"—is the underlying mechanism linking remittances to protest, the effect should be evidenced in swing districts targeted by the regime with clientelism, or in traditional regime strongholds.

Further, if remittances enhance the capacity of rising middle-class citizens to protest against autocratic governments in an effort to protect their newly acquired economic gains (Ansell and Samuels 2010; 2014; Bastiaens and Tirone 2019; Bearce and Park 2019), we should find evidence that remittances indeed boost protest among such citizens. In the context of mostly low-income autocracies, this protection mechanism suggests that remittances should increase protest among citizens who can meet their basic material needs on a regular basis—that is, the *least* poor citizens. A resource mechanism, by contrast, posits that the marginal effect of remittances on protest should be highest among those with the fewest assets, namely the *poorest* citizens.

There are thus two dimensions along which we can test the mechanisms linking remittances and political protest: a "pro-government" dimension that distinguishes opposition areas from regime-stronghold areas; and a "poverty" dimension that distinguishes poor citizens from middle-class citizens. The resource mechanism suggests that remittances should increase protest the most in opposition areas and among those living in poverty. The extrication mechanism, alternatively, suggests that remittances should boost protest in regime-stronghold or swing-district areas where there is patronage-induced government support. The protection mechanism, finally, implies that while remittance receivers will be more likely to protest than their fellow citizens who do not receive income from abroad, this effect should be greatest for higher-income citizens who comprise the rising middle class.

To test for these micro-mechanisms linking remittances to protest, we focus on cases in Africa, because this region has a mix of democratic and autocratic governments, with many countries there having substantial political changes in the past two decades. Other regions, such as Latin America, contain mostly democracies, while still others, such as the the Middle East, have only autocracies.[12] We therefore turn to survey data from Africa: the Afrobarometer project fielded two waves of surveys that contain questions on remittances, in 2008 and 2016.

During this period, thirty of forty-seven African countries were ruled by autocratic governments, listed in Table 4.1 and shown in Figure 4.3.[13] The sample we use to test the remittances–protest connection covers over half (seventeen) of these thirty countries (in 2008, 2016, or both years). Some of these countries with autocratic governments in 2008, such as Burkina Faso, Gambia, and Tunisia, had democratized by 2016, in a process spurred by mass anti-government protest. Mass protests also toppled Hosni Mubarak's dictatorship in Egypt in 2011, but the new democracy was cut short in a 2013 coup, returning the country to the ranks of the autocracies by 2016. In other African countries with autocratic governments in 2008, mass protests toppled incumbent leaders, but this has led either to ongoing transition regimes (Algeria and Sudan) or a failed state (Libya). In still other countries in the region, such as

TABLE 4.1. African autocracies, 2008

| Country | Survey sample year(s) | Mass protest/ democratization |
|---|---|---|
| Algeria | 2016 | Protest |
| Angola | | No |
| Botswana | 2008, 2016 | No |
| Burkina Faso | 2008 | Protest |
| Burundi | 2016 | No |
| Cameroon | 2016 | No |
| Cen African Rep | | No |
| Chad | | No |
| Congo-Brz | | No |
| Congo/Zaire | | No |
| Egypt | 2016 | Protest |
| Eritrea | | No |
| Ethiopia | | No |
| Gabon | 2016 | No |
| The Gambia | | Protest |
| Guinea | | No |
| Ivory Coast | | No |
| Libya | | Protest |
| Morocco | 2016 | No |
| Mozambique | 2008, 2016 | No |
| Namibia | 2008, 2016 | No |
| Rwanda | | No |
| Sudan | 2016 | Protest |
| Swaziland | 2016 | No |
| Tanzania | 2008, 2016 | No |
| Togo | 2016 | No |
| Tunisia | | Protest |
| Uganda | 2008, 2016 | No |
| Zambia | 2008 | Election |
| Zimbabwe | 2008, 2016 | No |

Ethiopia, mass protest led to the resignation of a long-serving leader, though he was replaced by another member of the same ruling party. In Zimbabwe meanwhile, one of the longest-serving rulers on the continent was ousted in a coup in 2017: during the previous year, long-time opposition protesters had been joined by erstwhile allies of the regime, the war veterans, as well as large swathes of the diaspora, in calling for the president to go.[14] That leaves Zambia as the only country that democratized via an election without a mass protest campaign first toppling the incumbent ruler: the opposition won the 2011 election, ousting the incumbent leader and his party. Even here, however,

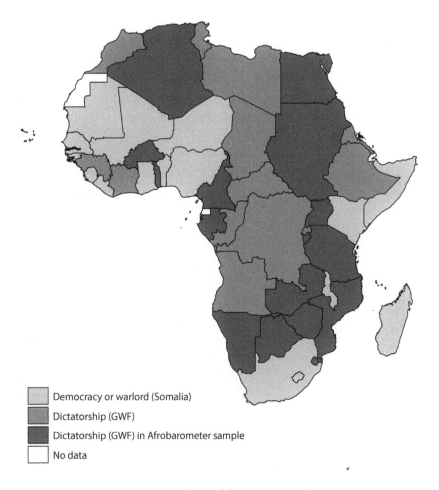

FIGURE 4.3. Dictatorships and democracies in Africa, 2008.

anti-regime sentiment in a neglected, high-poverty region fueled protest and demands for secession prior to the election.[15]

Thus political protest has been the primary driver of political change—and indeed democratic change—in Africa in the past two decades. This may be especially true in countries where ruling parties survived the third "wave of democracy" in the late 1980s and early 1990s, and where multiparty elections are unlikely to unseat incumbents. Further, some scholars have pointed out that a wave of large-scale protests in many parts of Africa preceded the 2011 Arab Spring uprisings by nearly a decade (Branch and Mampilly 2015, 54; Aidi 2018, 4). An important literature has now started to explain rising protest in Africa (Bratton et al. 2005; LeBas 2013; Branch and Mampilly 2015; Monyake 2016; Mueller 2018; Christensen 2019; Harris and Hern 2019); we add to this research by exploring how a growing source of private income— worker remittances—shapes protest in the region. Our approach therefore complements studies that explore how the growth of private businesses, as a result of neo-liberal reforms in the 1980s, contributed to a large pool of financial resources outside government control. This private income, albeit in the hands of a small group of wealthy business people, helped to fund multi-ethnic opposition coalitions that spurred electoral turnover in the 1990s (Arriola 2013a). Our argument focuses, by contrast, on the democratizing power of private income in the hands of mass citizens (not capital-owners) that transforms such newly resourced citizens into the agents of democratic political change.[16]

About two-thirds of sub-Saharan emigrants move to other African countries, while 90 percent of North African migrants move to Europe, the Middle East, or North America. Long-term migrant patterns reveal that intra-African migration has declined, while extra-continental migration has increased (Flahaux and de Haas 2016, 8). Migration in Africa is driven by the same motivating factors as in other world regions. Refugees and people in refugee-like situations account for 14 percent of international migrants in Africa, which means that the vast majority of emigrants move for family reasons or in search of job and educational opportunities (Flahaux and de Haas 2016, 2–3).

While protest has been driving democratic political change in Africa, remittances have become a large and increasing source of foreign revenue in the region: inward remittances in 2014 amounted to $34.5 billion, similar in size to FDI inflows ($36.5 billion) (World Bank 2016). These inflows grew by nearly 10 percent from 2017 to 2018, rising to $46 billion in 2018. Remittances are expected to continue to increase, albeit at a lower rate, in the coming decade (World Bank 2019a, 23). Many of the countries in our sample, such as The Gambia and Zimbabwe, are among the top ten emigrant-producing countries in the region; and our sample includes major migration corridors, such as Burkina Faso–Cote d'Ivoire, Zimbabwe–South Africa, and Mozambique–South Africa (World Bank 2016). Remittances have also seen a steady rise in North Africa. For example, those to Egypt increased by 17 percent in 2017 (World Bank 2019a, 20).

These remittance figures for Africa are likely underestimated, moreover, since most transactions are informal. For example, only 14 percent of remittances sent to Burkina Faso were sent through formal channels (Ratha et al. 2011, 5; Germano 2018, 80). And while most of the migration is intra-regional, with migrants settling in neighboring countries, remittances sent from outside sub-Saharan Africa far outweigh the remittances sent from within the region (Ratha et al. 2011, 74). These flows mostly finance current consumption, but also fund investments in health and education, housing, land, and farming equipment, and allow households to weather economic shocks by increasing savings. As in other regions, remittances reduce poverty (Ratha et al. 2011, 48).

Afrobarometer data show that on average, in African autocracies, recipients are less partisan, less supportive of incumbents, and vote less often. However, remittance recipients are also younger and more educated and have better access to mobile technologies—all factors that likely influence protest—than non-recipients. Mobile phones are not only becoming more frequently the instrument used to secure cross-border remittance transactions (Siegel and Fransen 2013), but also facilitate communication between regime opponents abroad and at home, making the organization of anti-government protest easier by scaling up activities and protests into pro-democracy campaigns on a global scale (Lyons 2012; Ruijgrok 2017; Christensen 2019). These demographic features are positively correlated with the likelihood of protesting, because they imply greater organizational skills and resources (Dalton et al. 2010; Campante and Chor 2014; Mueller 2018). There is, finally, no difference in the gender-balance as between remittance recipients and non-recipients, with females comprising about half of each group.

### 4.2.1. Capturing Political Preferences: Opposition and Regime Strongholds

To examine whether remittances augment resources for political opponents or "liberate" tacit supporters from clientelistic ties to the regime, we test whether the influence of remittances varies according to the *local political context* and, thus construct a measure of district-level support for the incumbent regime. We choose this geography-based strategy, rather than an individual-level measurement, for demarcating supporters from non-supporters for two related reasons.

First, clientelism in many sub-Saharan African countries entails the exchange of local-level electoral support for local public (i.e., locally non-excludable) goods (Ichino and Nathan 2013; Nathan 2016; Young 2009).[17] Indeed, studies of voting behavior and electoral dynamics in this region presume that the goods exchanged for votes take the form of local public goods, not private, excludable ones (see, e.g., Baldwin 2015; Carlson 2015;

Rozensweig 2015; Ejdemyr, Kramon, and Robinson 2016); and studies of ethnic favoritism suggest that this occurs via targeted spending on local public goods such as schools and boreholes (e.g. Baldwin 2015; Kramon and Posner 2016). This research indicates that clientelistic practices may require local elites (or brokers) to monitor local-level incumbent support and to supply local public goods (Koter 2013; Baldwin 2015). In short, a *local geographic* measure of incumbent support, we posit, captures a salient feature of clientelism in the seventeen countries concerned.

Second, using geographic location to capture the clientelistic operations that underpin incumbent support circumvents inference issues that arise when relying on individual-level survey data to distinguish between regime supporters and opponents in political contexts where opponents face the prospect of state-led violence. Indeed, scholars are well aware that asking politically sensitive questions, such as whether respondents support the government or will vote for the ruling party, may produce biased responses in autocratic contexts (Kuran 1997; Jiang and Yang 2016; Frye et al. 2017; Tannenberg 2017).

This sensitivity amounts to more than simply social-desirability bias, whereby respondents respond in a way they believe is the socially appropriate or expected norm for answering the question. (An example in the context of US politics would be that few respondents will admit, when asked directly, that they are racist.) While bias in response to sensitive questions in autocratic contexts is similar to this, it is likely to be stronger, because the consequences of providing an unfavorable response may be much more severe than the sort of social sanction the fear of which tends to account for a social-desirability bias: if respondents believe a repressive government is asking them about political affiliation or the identity of the party for which they vote, they may also believe that an unacceptable answer will result in punishments such as fines, losing a job, or even imprisonment. This fear is in our view likely to produce distortions stronger than the social-desirability bias in answers to politically sensitive questions. Indeed, Mares and Young (2016, 281) note that "[Afrobarometer survey] respondents who are exposed to violence are actually more likely to hide their political preferences for the opposition." We call this "fear bias", similar to the "preference falsification" identified by Kuran (1997).

Self-reported data on voting intentions or party affiliation, we posit, is likely to suffer from non-response and fear bias in non-democratic settings because there is a real threat of political violence against regime opponents.

Indeed, a non-trivial share of respondents refused to answer questions about which party they support. For example, in Zimbabwe, where the survey was implemented during an election period in which the regime targeted supporters of the political opposition, nearly a third of respondents refused to name the political party for which they vote. Clearly, therefore, questions that directly ask respondents to state which party they support or feel closest to are likely to produce biased responses.

We assess and address this issue in two ways. First, we show that non-response to sensitive questions is pervasive in our sample of countries with autocratic governments. This leads us to eschew variables that have high non-response rates when constructing a measure of political opposition and government support. Second, we utilize in the surveys a question that asks respondents—after they have finished the main questionnaire—to identify the group or organization they believe sponsored the survey. All respondents are told, at the start of the questionnaire, that the survey is conducted and paid for by an independent research organization that does not represent the government or any political party. However, a non-trivial share of respondents nonetheless indicate, at the end of the survey, that they believe the government sponsored the survey. We use this information to check whether the variables we test suffer from bias stemming from beliefs about the survey sponsor.

### 4.2.1.1. NON-RESPONSE RATES

First we examine non-response rates. The left plot in Figure 4.4 shows that the non-response rate for the question about the political party for which citizens vote (*Vote choice*) is considerably higher than for other questions in the survey. Over one-third of respondents did not answer this question by indicating a political party. While this high non-response rate may be due, in part, to lack of political knowledge, we find no evidence that respondent's level of education is correlated with non-response to this question.[18] In contrast to their reaction to the vote-choice question, nearly all respondents answered those on cell phone use and remittance receipt. Further, the political questions we test as outcome variables in this chapter (*Protest*) and the next (*Turnout*) have relatively low non-response rates. Finally, another potentially sensitive question, which asks whether respondents believe the president is corrupt, also has a relatively high non-response rate (17 percent). This suggests that there is a non-response bias in questions pertaining to vote choice and corruption

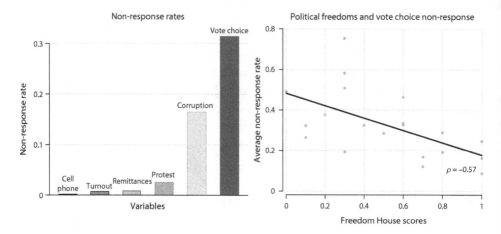

FIGURE 4.4. Non-response rates for Afrobarometer survey questions

perceptions, which are, plausibly, sensitive ones. Responses to questions regarding protest and turnout, however, are unlikely to suffer from the same kind of bias.

The right plot in Figure 4.4 shows how the average non-response rate in the sample countries varies with the level of political freedom, as measured by Freedom House scores. These scores measure political rights and civil liberties each year in each country.[19] The horizontal axis in the right plot identifies the Freedom House score; and the vertical axis is the average non-response rate for the vote-choice question in each country-year of the survey. Each point in the plot indicates one country-year in the sample; and the black line plots the linear fit. There is a strong negative correlation between non-response rate and political freedom, which is a rough proxy for expected punishment for answering the question "incorrectly" in an autocratic context. Thus not only does the vote-choice question have a high non-response rate relative to other, less sensitive questions in the survey, but this non-response rate is related to expected punishment, reinforcing the suggestion that the possibility that responses to this question are biased.

#### 4.2.1.2.  BELIEF THAT THE GOVERNMENT
#### SPONSORS THE SURVEY

Another way to account for bias in "sensitive" survey questions is to examine whether beliefs about *who sponsors* the survey are systematically related to responses (including non-response) to these questions. Tannenberg (2017), for example, shows that respondents who believe that the government administers the Afrobarometer survey systematically report higher levels of trust in the president and lower rates of presidential corruption—but only in more autocratic countries.

We adopt a similar approach by constructing a variable, *Government sponsor*, that indicates whether the respondent, when asked who s/he believes administered the survey, thinks the government is involved.[20] Respondents who report a government entity as the sponsor we code as 1, and others as 0.[21] In the 2008 and 2016 surveys combined, 40 percent of respondents in dictatorships believed the government sponsored the survey, while 42 percent of respondents in democracies thought so. Because these topline numbers are similar for autocracies and democracies, this indicator may not, in itself, be a good gauge of the "costliness of dissent" (Tannenberg 2017). However, Tannenberg shows that it may be a good proxy for the costliness of dissent in autocratic contexts specifically, where it correlates with increased expressed positive sentiments towards the government.

As a first test of whether this *Government sponsor* variable picks up potentially biased responses, we examine whether it predicts non-response on the vote-choice question as well as other political questions from the survey that we utilize, such as those concerning vote turnout and protest. We test a model of non-response on the vote-choice question using standard demographic variables (age, education, sex, employment, poverty, cell phone use, and ease of access to the border) as well as a variable that indicates whether the respondent "feels close to a political party." Crucially, this last question does not ask *which* party.

We find that belief that the government sponsored the survey is associated with *less* non-response on the vote choice question, in both democracies and dictatorships.[22] However, the effect is more than twice as large in dictatorships ($-4.5$ percent) as it is in democracies ($-2.1$ percent). This means that respondents who suspect that the government sponsored the survey are *more* likely to respond to the vote-choice question than those who do not believe this—and that this effect is stronger in dictatorships than in democracies. Thus it seems that belief in government sponsorship, corresponding to fear of repression for answering the vote-choice question in (from the government's perspective) an "undesirable" way, makes respondents more likely to report falsely—not simply refuse to respond—on sensitive questions. This suggests that not only may the vote-choice question result be biased by non-response, but that those who do respond may be engaging in preference falsification (Kuran 1997).

In a placebo test, we estimate the same model but change the outcome variable to non-response on questions of turnout, protest, and remittance receipt.[23] We find that believing the government to have sponsored the survey has no effect on non-response to any of these other questions, in either dictatorships or democracies. This suggests that results for these questions are unlikely to suffer from the same "fear-based" type of bias as those for more sensitive questions, such as vote choice.

### 4.2.1.3. MEASUREMENT

Because the response to the vote-choice question may be biased for autocratic contexts we do not use this information to construct a measure of pro-government sentiment in specific areas. Instead we turn to individual-level questions that tap into latent support for the incumbent regime or leader; and use this information to construct a continuous, district-level measure of local support for the government. The appendix to this chapter provides details on how we construct this measure, and examines the external validity of the data by comparing these with reported vote totals for the incumbent party in various elections. This validity check is *external* to our data, because it uses information on voting outcomes from outside the Afrobarometer survey; and we find that the measure we construct is highly correlated with vote totals in multiple countries and at different levels of aggregation.

In what follows, we use the district-level measure of government support, because it allows for wide application across very different contexts, including relatively fair elections (e.g., in Botswana) as well as elections that are rigged in favor of the incumbent (e.g., Algeria and Gabon). In principle, the measure we construct could also be useful for capturing relevant local variation in government support in autocratic contexts where elections are held infrequently or not at all.

At various points, we use the term "opposition" district, which we define as one with district-level government support of 50 percent or less. Similarly, we define a "swing" district as one in which government support is between 50 and 75 percent; and "stronghold" districts, then, are those with 75 percent of more government support. These cut-off points have intuitive appeal, insofar as they mirror normal usage of the term "opposition" to refer to a locality where incumbent support is not sufficient to win a majority, and "stronghold" to districts where incumbents hold at least a three-to-one advantage. Further, each of the three groups corresponds to roughly one-third of the sample: opposition districts are home to 32.4 percent, swing districts to 37.4 percent, and stronghold districts to 30.2 percent of our respondents.

## 4.2.2.  Testing the Micro-Logic Linking Remittances to Protest

Now that we have introduced the measure we use for pro-government districts, we explore the theoretical mechanisms linking remittances to political protest at the individual level. There are two dimensions along which we can test these mechanisms: a "pro-government" dimension that distinguishes opposition areas from regime-stronghold areas, and a "poverty" dimension that distinguishes poor citizens from middle-class citizens. The resource mechanism suggests that remittances should boost protest most in opposition areas and amongst the those living in poverty. The exit mechanism, alternatively, posits that remittances allow citizens caught up in clientelistic exchanges to escape those networks and reveal their political preferences; this suggests that remittances should increase protest in regime-stronghold areas, or possibly in swing districts where incumbents rely on a strategy of targeted clientelism. Finally, the asset-protection mechanism, which posits that middle-class citizens protest to demand protection of their economic gains, implies that the remittance effect should be strongest among the *least* poor citizens, who comprise the rising middle class.

### 4.2.2.1. DATA AND EMPIRICAL APPROACH

*4.2.2.1.1. Remittance and protest data*    To test whether there is an individual-level link between remittances and protest, we construct a binary indicator of political protest, derived from the following question: " [Have you attended] a demonstration or protest march?"[24] We group the three "Yes" outcomes ("Yes, once or twice," "Yes, several times," "Yes, often") together and group the two "No" responses together, while treating "Don't know" responses as missing. In 2008, just under 12 percent of respondents reported participating in a protest (in eight countries); this figure drops to 9 percent in 2016 (in fifteen countries). Thus roughly 10 percent of the sample reports protesting.

The main explanatory variable is an ordered measure of the frequency of remittance receipt from the following question: "How often did you receive remittances?"[25] Just over 14 percent of respondents reported receiving remittances in 2008, a figure that rises to over 20 percent in 2016, reflecting the global increase in remittances. In the sample including both rounds, roughly 14 percent of remittance receivers had protested, while 9 percent of non-receivers had done so. Thus the raw data indicate that remittance receivers are about 5 percent more likely to protest than non-recipients.

To offset potential confounders, we take into account cell phone usage, travel, age (log), education, poverty, gender, and employment status. In addition to standard demographic (gender, age, and education) and economic (poverty and employment) variables, the list includes cell phone usage because this technology facilitates protest by lowering coordination costs and is an essential tool for transferring remittances (Ebeke and Yogo 2013; Manacorda and Tesei 2016). Finally, respondents who travel more, either from individual preference or simply because they have greater economic resources, may view exit as a less costly form of dissent than voice. These individuals may also be more likely to have family abroad, enabling them both to travel more and to receive remittances.

We estimate a linear probability model with district-fixed effects. This approach departs from standard approaches when testing hypotheses using multi-country Afrobarometer data, which account for differences across countries with random effects (sometimes referred to as "multi-level models"). However, by our hypotheses there are strong reasons to believe that location conditions both protest opportunities and remittance receipt. For example, if protests are more likely to occur in opposition areas, there could be more opportunity for people to participate in them; and if citizens in opposition areas are more likely to emigrate and therefore have families back home who receive more remittances, a finding that remittances increase protest might be spurious if it simply indicates that grievances drive emigration (and hence remittances) from particular districts as well as protest opportunity in those same districts. This alternative argument focuses on differences in *location* that shape the opportunity structure for protest participation: *protest opportunity*, that is to say, may be an unobserved factor related to both protest and remittances.

Another variant of this location-based argument posits that emigration entails self-selection of more individualistic citizens for exit from the local political context (Knudsen 2019). This self-selection deriving from an individual personality trait leaves behind a higher proportion of citizens with "collectivist" attitudes in the areas most affected by emigration. This "relative push away from individualism, and towards collectivism, in migrant-sending locations" (Knudsen 2019, 1) could enhance anti-government collective action in some areas with high emigration, and hence remittance, rates because individuals with collectivist attitudes may be less likely to free-ride on the mobilization efforts of other citizens. This argument, though based on selection for emigration at individual level, implies an alternative logic according to which the inhabitants of locations with many emigrants (and hence more remittances) may better solve collective action problems, and thus protest more.

A third mechanism that might link emigration (and hence remittances) to protest is factor-price equalization: when low-skilled laborers emigrate from a location, fewer such workers remain there, which should, all else being equal, raise their incomes (Borjas 1989, 461–65). Hatton and Williamson (1998, ch. 9), for example, show that during the period of mass migration from Europe in the late nineteenth and early twentieth centuries, both farm and non-farm wages rose in emigrant-sending countries such as Ireland and Sweden; and it should be noted that they find this positive wage effect even after accounting for the possibility that capital can chase migrating labor.

Factor-price equalization is a direct income mechanism potentially linking emigration to protest that has nothing to do with remittances: as a consequence of emigration it is both chronologically and causally prior to remittance transfers. Thus, if we find an individual-level association between remittances and protest, this could simply be caused by a boost in private resources stemming from an increased wage for those left behind. However, a rise in local wages from factor-price equalization should affect *all* potential wage earners—both those who receive remittances and those who do not—within a local labor market that emigrants have left. To isolate the remittance channel as distinct from the factor-price-equalization mechanism, our identification strategy must therefore include comparison within any given location of respondents who receive remittances with those who do not.

Our empirical approach thus directly addresses alternative arguments that imply location-based differences in both migration and political protest behavior that could also explain an individual-level association between the two. We account for all unobserved location-based factors—including local protest opportunity structures, self-selection of "individualists" to leave local areas, and factor-price equalization that might increase local wages—by using a fixed-effects estimator.[26]

This approach addresses these alternative arguments inasmuch as the estimator compares individuals with remittances in a district $d$ to respondents without remittances *within the same district*, holding geographically specific conditions that influence protest and remittance receipt, including the composition and size of local emigration, constant. The estimator then calculates the (weighted) average of these individual-level comparisons within each district, for all districts.[27]

Finally, our empirical design addresses the additional concern that increased government support may, at the individual level, be be attributable to remittances themselves. For example, individuals who receive remittances may misattribute this income to government policy, resulting in a boost in support for incumbents. If the district-level measure is biased because remittance receivers are, on average, more pro-government (perhaps via such misattribution) than non-recipients, this could only bias our inference if this district-level bias shifts protest behavior differently as between recipients and non-recipients *in the same district*. If remittances increase (or decrease) government support amongst individuals in a systematic way, this would shift the district-level average up (or down), but would have no bearing on our inference, because any district-level bias is accounted for with the district-fixed effect.

#### 4.2.2.2. RESULTS

First, we test a specification without an interaction between remittances and government support to estimate the average marginal effect of remittances on protest across all districts—comprising opposition, swing, and stronghold districts. This estimate is positive (0.048) and statistically significant, indicating that remittance receipt is, on average, positively associated with protest behavior at an individual level. Substantively, a respondent with the maximum level of remittance receipt is 4.8 percent more likely to protest than a respondent who does not receive remittances. To put this estimate in context, the results indicate that cell phone use (1.3 percent), education (5.4 percent), poverty (3.0 percent), male (2.2 percent), and employment (1.4 percent) also increase protest participation; but age (1.5 percent) decreases it. Thus, on average, the boost to protest participation from remittances is substantively similar to demographic determinants of protest.

Next, we test a specification that allows for the marginal effect of remittances to vary across the district level of government support. The estimated

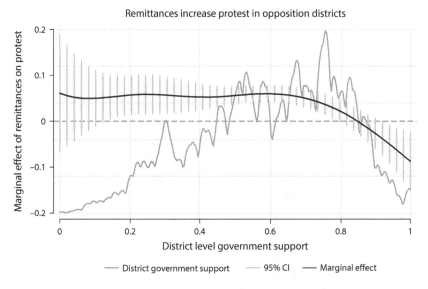

FIGURE 4.5. Remittances increase protest in opposition districts

interaction is negative and statistically significant, indicating that as district government support increases, the (generally) positive effect of remittances on protest diminishes. We plot this conditional relationship in Figure 4.5.[28] The horizontal axis displays the district level of government support, with districts with 50 percent or less of government support being "opposition" districts and those with 75 percent or more defined as "stronghold" districts. The vertical axis shows the marginal effects of remittances on protest. The black curved line is the estimated effect; and the vertical gray lines show the 90 (shorter) and 95 (longer) confidence intervals of the estimate. In the opposition districts, the marginal effect of remittances varies between 5 and 6 percent, which indicates that remittance recipients are roughly 5 to 6 percent more likely than non-recipients to protest. This positive effect of remittances then decreases as district government support increases. In a district with 75 percent government support, for example, the effect is 3.5 percent; and in stronghold districts with over 90 percent government support the effect turns negative. This finding remains robust through a battery of tests discussed in the online Technical Appendix.[29]

*4.2.2.2.1. Belief that the Government Sponsors the Survey*   As we discussed earlier, some respondents may fear that truthful answers to sensitive survey questions, particularly in an autocratic environment, may lead to government reprisals. They were therefore asked who they believed sponsored the survey, with about 40 percent indicating that they believe some government entity administered it. To ensure that the main results are not unduly influenced by this 40 percent of respondents, we conduct two additional tests.

First, we add the individual-level measure of belief in government sponsorship to the specification and include an interaction term between this variable and the country effect, thereby allowing any effect of this belief on reporting protest participation to vary by country. We do this because any potential bias in propensity to report protest participation is likely to vary by country, as citizens may have more fear of some governments, such as Zimbabwe's, and less fear of others, such as Botswana's. This test reveals findings nearly identical to those reported in the previous section.

Second, we test the main model, but this time drop respondents who state that they believe the government administered the survey. This leaves the sample 40 percent smaller, but excludes those who may be reporting false preferences in response to sensitive questions. We find that the interaction effect is slightly stronger than when using all respondents in the sample.

### 4.2.2.3. AN ALTERNATIVE MEASURE OF GOVERNMENT SUPPORT

Next, we test whether the positive effect of remittances is concentrated among opposition districts, using an alternative measure of the concept of *Opposition district*. Letsa (2019) matches district-level legislative election data in five countries—Cameroon, Tanzania, Togo, Uganda, and Zimbabwe—with the 2016 Afrobarometer survey. In doing so, she codes as opposition districts those in which an opposition legislature candidate had won the prior two elections. Swing districts, in her coding scheme, are those in which an opposition party and the ruling party have each won the legislative seat in prior elections; and, finally, a ruling-party district is one where the incumbent party has secured the legislative seat in past elections.[30]

This measure to identify an opposition district is more restrictive than the one we tested above, in which we categorized roughly 32 percent of respondents in nearly two thousand districts as living in opposition districts (i.e., those where less than half of the survey respondents were nominally pro-government). Letsa's measure, by contrast, only captures 11 percent of the 386 districts in her five-country sample. Thus, hers is a more restrictive measure of the concept "opposition district," potentially making for a stricter test

TABLE 4.2. Remittance estimates using an alternative measure of opposition district

| District type | All respondents | Respondents who do *not* believe government sponsored survey |
|---|---|---|
| Opposition | 3.6 (2.7) | 6.7* (3.3) |
| Swing | 3.3 (1.9) | 0.4 (2.6) |
| Ruling party | 5.4* (2.5) | 3.6 (3.2) |

Standard errors adjusted for district-level intra-cluster correlation reported in parentheses. * indicates that the estimate is statistically significant at the 0.05 level.

of the main proposition that the remittance effect is strongest in opposition districts.

We first test a specification without any interaction terms to estimate the average marginal effect across all districts in the five-country sample. The estimate for remittances is 3.7 percent, which is smaller than the estimate when using the full sample of twenty-three-country surveys (4.8 percent). Next we test a specification with an interaction between remittances and a binary indicator of opposition district as well as an interaction between remittances and an indicator of ruling-party district. This specification allows us to test whether the effect of remittances varies by different types of district (opposition, swing and ruling-party). A final test uses the same specification with the interaction terms, but restricts the analysis to those respondents who do not believe the government sponsored the survey, and who are thus less likely to report falsely.

Table 4.2 reports the estimated marginal effects of remittances from the latter two tests. The second column reports results from the sample of all respondents, including those who believe that the government sponsored the survey. While the estimate for remittances is positive in opposition districts (3.6 percent), it is also positive in swing districts (3.3 percent) and larger in ruling-party districts (5.4 percent). This is evidence *contrary* to our expectation that the marginal effect of remittances should be highest in opposition districts. The next column reports results from tests that exclude those who believe that the government sponsored the survey and are thus more likely to falsely report. Here, the estimate for remittances in opposition districts is large, positive, and statistically significant (6.7 percent). This estimate is nearly twice as large as the estimate in ruling-party districts (3.6 percent, but not statistically significant) and substantially larger than in swing districts (0.4 percent). Thus, once we restrict the analysis to respondents who are more likely to respond truthfully, the test reveals findings consistent with the expectation that remittances increase protest most in opposition districts.

### 4.2.3. Remittances, Poverty, and Protest

This section explores how poverty shapes the relationship between remittances and protest at the individual level. Prior sections have shown that remittances increase protest; and that the remittance effect is strongest in opposition districts. We argue that this set of findings is consistent with a resource theory of protest but inconsistent with either the substitution or grievance theories that suggest that remittances lead to political disengagement. However, if the resource theory is correct, we should also expect the marginal effect on protest of additional private income via remittances to be largest among citizens who have low initial levels of income from non-remittance sources: namely, those who are relatively poor.

This expectation is a standard theoretical implication of voting models, whereby the marginal effect of private income is largest for those with the lowest incomes (Dixit and Londegran 1996). This argument is also consistent with an entire class of economic development models which assume declining marginal returns, that underpins convergence theory; these theories posit that the marginal effect of investment (including foreign aid) should have the highest marginal return in the poorest countries, where the initial stock of investment is relatively low. Recently, Córdova and Hiskey (2019) showed that in Latin America, remittances shape recipients' political behavior at low levels of development. Thus, consistent with theoretical models that assume a diminishing marginal effect of additional income on political or economic outcomes, the resource theory of protest implies that the positive marginal effect of remittances on contentious behavior should be largest for the poorest citizens.

As we noted in chapter 2, there is an alternative argument linking remittances to political outcomes that has implications for how poverty might shape the remittance effect. Rising middle-class citizens who have newly acquired assets will seek protection—in the form of democracy—from autocratic governments likely to confiscate their economic assets (Ansell and Samuels 2014; Bastiaens and Tirone 2019; Bearce and Park 2019). An implication of this theory may be that, if remittances increase pro-democracy protest, the effect should be strongest among middle-class citizens. Applying this insight to our setting implies that remittances should have the strongest effect on protest for those at middle levels of poverty. Thus, while the resource theory suggest the remittance effect should grow stronger as poverty levels increase, the class-based theory suggests an inverted U-shaped relationship: remittances increase protest at middle levels of poverty but not at high or low levels.

That said, what we might consider a traditional "middle class" in Africa may not fall in the middle levels of the poverty index we construct. The term "middle class" might be more appropriately be applied to citizens with the lowest levels of poverty in these, mostly low-income, countries. Indeed, while the traditional middle class—made up of a rising middle-income group of citizens—may be increasing rapidly in Africa (Handley 2015; Ncube 2015), it is still relatively small compared with other regions of the world such as Latin America (Mueller 2018, 4), and probably not very similar to the classical conceptualization of the term (Handley 2015, 623).[31] As Handley (2015, 624) points out, what "principally defines" the middle class in Africa "and distinguishes it from the poor is its access to secure stable jobs," not membership of a rising entrepreneurial class or the proclivity of higher earners to save and invest. This conceptualization of the middle class echoes Mueller's (2018, 9), who defines it as those who meet their basic consumption needs with private income—that is, income not generated from the state. Thus, it could be that only the *least* poor citizens in our sample of mostly low-income countries might be categorized as "middle class," at least as Ansell and Samuels (2014) use the term; and even Mueller's definition of the African middle class departs from the "classical Marxist" version of a bourgeois class, insofar as the middle-class protesters in her theory are *not* the owners of the means of production who seek protection of their assets from the state (Mueller 2018, 10). Thus it could be that, if the class-based theory is correct, the marginal effect of remittances on protest will be greatest among the wealthiest respondents: those, that is, at the lowest poverty levels.

To test these competing expectations, we estimate a model using a specification that includes an interaction between remittances and poverty, which allows the marginal effect of remittances to vary across poverty levels. We measure poverty by a scaled index of individual responses to questions that ask about access to basic goods: food, water, cooking fuel, and medicine.[32] Because a large proportion of citizens in these countries participates in the informal labor market, and consumption of these basic goods is financed largely from private income, we view this index as a good proxy for individual poverty levels.[33]

Figure 4.6 shows the results from tests of three samples: all districts (top panel); opposition districts (middle panel); and regime-stronghold districts (bottom). The horizontal axes mark the individual-level poverty index, while the vertical axis shows the marginal effect of remittance receipt. The curved black line in each plot shoes the estimated effect of remittances, and the vertical gray lines the confidence intervals around the estimate. The top panel shows that the marginal effect of remittances increasing by poverty levels: for the lowest poverty level, the effect is less than 1 percent; at the middle level 5.8 percent; and at the highest level nearly 8 percent. This pattern is consistent with the resource theory of protest: as poverty increases the marginal effect of remittances increases. If we treat citizens in the middle levels of poverty as the middle class in these societies, we might interpret the positive effect of remittances as evidence consistent with the class-based theory of protest. However, in the context of such relatively low-income countries, it might be more accurate to describe only the *least* poor as a newly empowered middle class. In this view, the finding that the marginal effect of remittances is roughly zero for the wealthiest citizens in the sample is inconsistent with the class-based theory.

Next, we tested the model using only opposition districts, in which the government support measure is 50 percent or less. The middle panel of Figure 4.6 shows that the increasing marginal effect of remittances in poverty is even stronger in these districts. The estimated effects of remittances at the lowest, middle, and highest levels of poverty are, respectively, 1.2 percent, 6.5 percent, and 7.6 percent. By contrast, when we test the model on regime-stronghold districts, in which the government support is 75 percent or more, we find muted effects. Although the marginal effect of remittances increases with poverty, at no levels of poverty is the estimate statistically different from zero. The bottom two plots therefore show that findings for remittances, poverty, and protest are concentrated in opposition districts.

In sum, examining how individual-level poverty shapes the remittances–protest nexus yields findings consistent with the resource theory of protest.

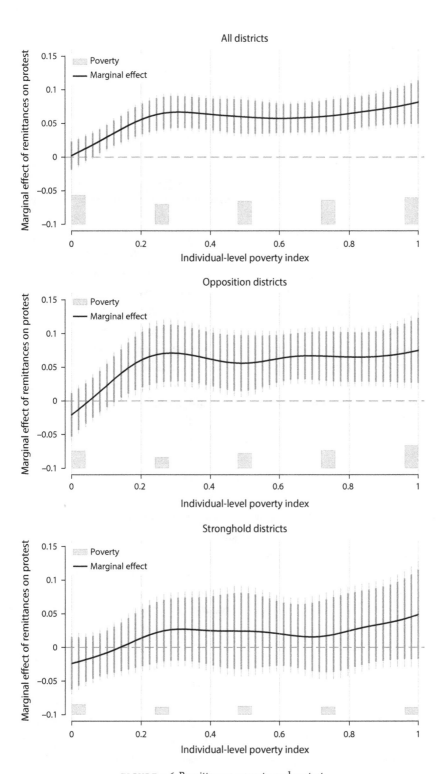

FIGURE 4.6. Remittances, poverty, and protest

As poverty increases, the effect of remittances gets stronger. Further, this relationship, as before, is strongest in opposition districts.

## 4.3.  Conclusion

Mass, anti-government protest is a growing threat to autocratic rule. While most dictatorships succumbed to the new norm of holding elections in the post–Cold War period, many have figured out how to sustain their rule despite elections, engineering a system of electoral autocracy that often better serves incumbent rulers than the citizens they rule. Dictatorships, however, must still face mass protest. Indeed, even though many dictators have learned to manipulate elections to yield favorable results, these events still pose a threat to autocratic governments because they provide a coordinating signal that helps mobilize anti-government protests and provide opportunities for legal opposition parties to form. In Algeria in 2019, for example, protests materialized when citizens demanded that their long-serving, senile president stand down as a presidential candidate. In The Gambia, elections led to incumbent defeat, but the leader refused to accept the results, and the resulting protests toppled his regime. In Burkina Faso, meanwhile, protesters mobilized—and ousted the regime—when the autocratic ruler attempted to change term limits that would allow him to rule for yet another decade. In all these cases, different parts of the election cycle served as a coordinating device for protesters who toppled dictatorships.

If aggrieved citizens can simply leave, why protest? The predominant view linking migration to protest—borne of the intuitive logic of the exit, voice, and loyalty framework—suggests that emigration sustains dictatorships by sapping the people and resources that would otherwise mobilize to demand political change. We argue and show the opposite: once one considers post-exit political dynamics, it appears that emigration enhances voice. The missing link in this process is, of course, remittances—a flow of income now reaching millions of individuals in the Global South.

When migrants send private income home to their friends and relatives, this boosts resources and the capacity to demand democracy in the streets. We have thus documented a strong empirical relationship, using both macro- and micro-data, linking remittances to protest. We then showed that this link is concentrated in opposition areas and among the poorest citizens—both factors that are consistent with a resource model of political protest. Emigration and the financial remittances migrant workers send home shift the balance of power in dictatorships towards citizens, fueling their capacity to demand democratic political change.

## 4.4. Appendix: Measuring Pro-Government Areas

This appendix discusses how we measure local political context to distinguish between pro-government and opposition areas. Recall that responses to the survey vote-choice question may be biased in autocratic contexts, due to fear of repression, by respondents either not answering a politically sensitive question or providing a false answer. We therefore do not use this information to construct a measure of pro-government sentiment in specific localities. Instead we turn to three individual-level questions that tap into latent support for the incumbent regime or leader, and use this information to construct a continuous, district-level measure of local government support. First, we combine responses from three Afrobarometer questions— Q49A: Trust the president, Q49E: Trust the ruling party, and Q70A: Presidential performance—to construct a scaled index at the individual level.[34]

Table 4.3 lists these three items. The second column shows the average non-response rate for each; these rates vary between 3 and 5 percent, substantially lower than the non-response rates for the *Vote choice* or *Corruption* variables in Figure 4.4. The third column shows the item–scale correlation, which is a measure of how well each item correlates with the constructed index or scale of government support. All three, as expected, correlate with the scaled index at high levels, indicating that they capture the same underlying concept. The final column shows the average level of support for each item: more respondents indicate positive trust and performance assessments of autocratic presidents (0.65 and 0.68 respectively) than trust in the ruling party (0.44).

TABLE 4.3. Items in the *Progovernment* measure

| Afrobarometer question | Non-response rate | Item–Scale correlation | Mean$^\alpha$ |
|---|---|---|---|
| Q49A: Trust president | 3.1 | 0.86 | 0.65 |
| Q49E: Trust the ruling party | 4.1 | 0.80 | 0.44 |
| Q70A: Performance: President | 5.2 | 0.76 | 0.68 |

$^\alpha$ treats non-response as non-affirmative; i.e., in the denominator.

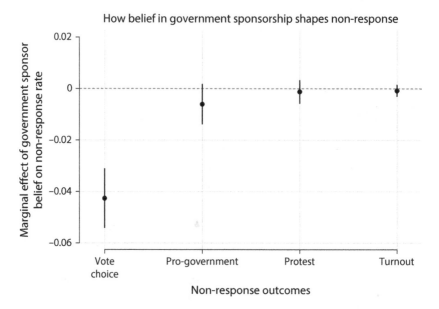

FIGURE 4.7. Predicting non-response rates for various outcomes

### 4.4.1. Vote Choice and Non-Response

While the non-response rates for these questions are relatively low when compared with the non-response for the vote-choice question, they are higher than for some of the demographic variables, including *Protest*. To further check for potential bias in these questions, we test whether the indicator of "government sponsorship," outlined in the previous section, predicts non-response. We compare the extent to which belief in government sponsorship predicts non-response on these questions to how well it predicts non-response in the vote-choice question, as well the non-response to the protest and vote-turnout questions. In these tests, the main explanatory variable is *Government sponsor*.[35]

Figure 4.7 shows the result for the *Government sponsor* explanatory variable. The vertical axis shows the estimated marginal effect of *Government sponsor* on the likelihood of non-response. The horizontal axis lists the four non-response outcome variables. The first test, shown on the left, uses non-response on the vote-choice question as the outcome variable. The negative and statistically significant marginal effect indicates that respondents who believe the government sponsored the survey are 4 percent *less* likely to

register a non-response than those who do not register this belief. Therefore, respondents who suspect the government sponsored the survey are *more*
likely to provide a response to this question, again suggesting potential bias
from falsifying responses to this question.

Second, we test whether *Government sponsor* predicts non-response for the
questions used to construct the individual-level "government support" scaled
index, where the outcome variable is non-response to any item. While the
estimate for *Government sponsor*, shown second from the left in Figure 4.7,
is negative, it is small and statistically insignificant. This suggests that belief
in government sponsorship does not affect non-response on these questions.
We conduct the same test for non-response in the protest and turnout questions, and find similar null results. In sum, the tests reported here suggest that
political fear—proxied by indicating a belief that the government sponsored
the survey—may influence non-response for the vote-choice question but not
for the items used to construct the government support measure or for the
outcome variables of interest, namely *Protest* and *Turnout*.

Even though the individual-level scaled index of government support is
less likely to be biased than the vote-choice information, there still may be
some bias if the small percentage who refused to respond to this question do
so because they are afraid of answering truthfully. Thus, as second step, we calculate the average level of individual-level support for the incumbent within
each district. If respondents refuse to respond to these questions because they
fear a reprisal for answering them, this non-response is registered by lowering the average level of incumbent support in the district. This provides a
continuous measure of local-level incumbent support (bounded at 0 and 1)
at the district level, which we call "Pro-government support." Thus, rather
than throwing out information from non-responses, which could systematically bias estimates, we use this information to measure district-level lack of
incumbent support.

The district-level measure varies across nearly five thousand local geographical units within the seventeen countries (over two years) in the autocracy sample. We also develop a similar geographical measure but instead
use (nearly seven hundred) regions (not districts) as the geographical unit
over which we calculate average government support. Although we focus
on the district-level measure in this and the next chapter, we report tests
using the region-level measure of government support in the online Technical
Appendix.

### 4.4.2. External Validity

Next, we assess *external validity*, for two reasons. First, despite our efforts to show that the individual-level information used to construct the district-level measure of government support is relatively unbiased, we can never prove this assumption without using techniques such as list experiments to ensure truthful survey responses.[36] Second, the survey data are not necessarily representative of the local area for which we aggregate them. The firms that conduct the survey are careful to implement a sampling design that captures national-level averages in individual-level political behavior and beliefs. Thus the sampling of individuals, neighborhoods, and towns within districts is not designed to produce representative district-level averages.

We use three types of voting results data: presidential election results at the provincial level in Gabon (2016); provincial National Assembly election results across two elections in Mozambique and Namibia (2009 and 2014); and district-level vote share data from five legislative elections in Cameroon, Tanzania, Togo, Uganda, and Zimbabwe (various years). We match election results data to the closest year of the Afrobarometer survey (either 2008 or 2016). For example, we match presidential election results from the 2016 election in Gabon to the Afrobarometer data from the same year. For Mozambique and Namibia, we match the 2009 legislative election data with the 2008 Afrobarometer data, and the 2014 legislative election data with the 2016 Afrobarometer data. The district-level vote share data from the other five countries comes from Letsa (2019), who carefully matches (thousands of) district names from multiple legislative elections in Cameroon, Tanzania, Togo, Uganda, and Zimbabwe across multiple elections in each country to the 2016 Afrobarometer survey.

Figure 4.8 shows the plots for four sets of correlations. The upper left plot shows the provincial-level presidential vote share data for Gabon along the horizontal axis and our measure of region-level government support constructed from the survey data on the vertical axis. The plot shows a strong positive correlation between the two measures of the same concept ($\rho = 0.74$). This presidential election was by no means fair, but it was highly contested, with the opposition candidate Jean Ping nearly defeating—at least in the officially announced results—the incumbent Ali Bongo.

The top right and bottom left panels show that our measure of region-level government support is also strongly correlated with legislative election data across regions in Mozambique and Namibia.[37] Finally, the district-level data

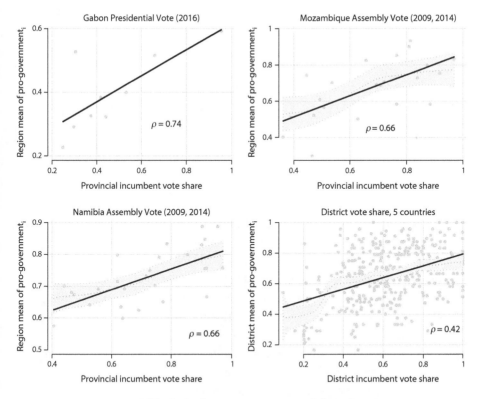

FIGURE 4.8. District-level government support and electoral support

on ruling-party vote share in five countries, shown in the bottom right plot, also correlates positively with our measure of government sentiment from the 2016 survey.[38] The correlations in Figure 4.8 indicate a strong positive association between our measure of local pro-government sentiment and reported election results. Neither measure is perfect given the difficulty of assessing private political preferences in autocratic contexts where respondents may fear to answer potentially politically sensitive questions. However, both indicators are highly correlated, suggesting that they are useful measures of the underlying concept.

# 5

# Remittances Demobilize Supporters

In the past three decades, autocratic governments have increasingly come to rely on mobilizing electoral support to survive in power (Gandhi and Lust-Okar 2009; Schedler 2013; Gandhi 2015). Indeed, by our count nearly 90 percent of autocratic regimes have held elections since 1980. Governments in China, Eritrea, Libya, North Korea, and Saudi Arabia are the only long-lasting regimes to eschew national elections in the past three decades.[1] Further, the electoral norm has become more pervasive over time: on average, dictatorships held an election once every five years in the 1980s; in the 1990s and 2000s this frequency jumped to once every four years. Over the 2010s, election frequency in autocracies ticked up even further.

Most non-democracies hold multiparty elections for strategic reasons, and they are most likely to emerge in places with stronger ties to democracies (Levitsky and Way 2010; Miller 2020). It is also true, however, that elections spread in those autocracies where it is easier for governments to control voters, in part because most voters are relatively poor. Thus while most dictatorships have adopted elections they have also developed strategies, such as clientelism targeted at poor voters, to minimize the risk of electoral loss.

Given the near ubiquity of elections in autocracies, this chapter examines how remittances shape electoral authoritarianism. We argue that remitted income from abroad erodes the electoral strength of the ruling parties by altering individuals' decisions about whether to show up at the polls. Many scholars have noted this link between electoral authoritarianism and patronage politics: what matters is "whether there is a large mass of poor voters that the regime can co-opt through clientelism and targeted public goods" (Miller 2020, 7). Similarly, Magaloni (2006, 16) stresses that "it is less expensive to buy off a large coalition of the very poor than a coalition of a wealthier middle class." Indeed, autocratic governments win elections—even relatively fraud-free multiparty contests—by distributing patronage to voters and, hence, by activating their constituencies through 'turnout buying' (Stokes et al. 2013; Gans-Morse et al. 2014). In countries as diverse as Cambodia, Malaysia, Mexico, Senegal, Tanzania, and Zimbabwe, autocratic governments' clientelistic networks mobilized voters to support the ruling party in elections. Parties in autocracies work not only as institutions that manage elite conflict but also, importantly, as mass mobilization machines (Magaloni and Kricheli 2010). Central to this latter function of building mass support is the control of state resources—along with an ample network of local party representatives—that are used to develop and sustain an extensive patronage system whereby citizens are enticed to support the ruling party via material inducements.

Extant theories of dominant-party erosion tend to concentrate on the supply side of clientelism and thus explain how this strategy for sustaining power remains viable in the long-term. Long-ruling autocratic parties only lose, according to these arguments, when the country experiences an external shock that erodes the government's resource advantage (Magaloni 2006; Greene 2007). Decreasing economic performance and recurrent crises, competition brought about by economic globalization, and pressure to liberalize from international financial institutions, according to these accounts, sap the resources that dominant parties deploy to sway voters.

This chapter articulates a theory to explain the demise of electoral authoritarian advantages that focuses rather on the demand side of the regime–citizen clientelistic relationship. Our key claim is that remittances decrease voters' dependence on government patronage and thus sever the clientelistic ties between electoral autocracies and the often low-income voters they mobilize (Pfutze 2012; 2014; Escribà-Folch et al. 2015). Money transfers from migrants abroad not only benefit recipient family and friends but also fund projects that benefit entire communities, including local services and public goods such as access to sewerage and clean water. Remittance income thus creates private substitutes for state-provided gifts, benefits, and services that ruling parties use to retain electoral support.

Further, as we have shown in chapter 3, remittances do not generate additional revenue for autocratic governments. This finding has important implications for the analyses which follow, because it means that while some voters receive additional external income—reducing the value of state-delivered goods—the state is unable to tap into remittances to boost transfer payments and thus keep those remittance recipients tied into the regime's clientelistic network (Pfutze 2014). As a result, in terms of Hirschman's EVL model, remittances weaken "loyalty" to the ruling party by undermining its ability to mobilize electoral support via clientelistic transfers.

We use these observations to explore how remittances influence individual-level voter turnout, demonstrating that remittances decrease turnout in swing districts where ruling parties are most likely to target (pro-government) voters in "turnout-buying" schemes. First though, we examine global patterns in remittance flows, to show that remittances not only decrease vote shares for autocratic governments but also reduce overall voter turnout—two related phenomena that erode ruling parties' electoral strength.

If remittances weaken loyalty to ruling regimes by lowering the vote turnout that underpins electoral authoritarianism, this suggests that remittances may demobilize some recipients and erode incumbent parties' dominance. This interpretation differs from that concerning the demobilizing effect of remittances suggested in prior research, such as, for example, Ebeke and Yogo (2013, 14), who conclude that rising remittances may be "bad news," because "[b]y reducing individuals' interest in elections, remittances [alter] the accountability [of] governments and strongly impede the benefits of having democratic systems in Sub-Saharan Africa." Similarly, in his work on the link between remittances and political engagement in Mexico, Bravo (2007, 23) argues that "by weakening the effects of political voice upon the disciplining of governments, [remittances] may perpetuate the political barriers to change that underpin the current low-quality equilibrium in which many Mexican localities are trapped." In authoritarian contexts, however, not only do migrant remittances boost the private income of democratic agents, thus undermining a key strategy that sustains many authoritarian governments throughout the world, but electoral demobilization can, in some circumstances, destabilize autocratic regimes and remittances, therefore, even if they demobilize, may offer "good news." Disengagement can work as a form of dissent, rather than of acquiescence (Croke et al. 2016). Moreover, as we show in chapter 6, electoral demobilization can co-exist with a remittance-driven increase in non-electoral forms of political activism, such as a greater propensity to join grassroots and civil organizations.

## 5.1. Remittances and the Electoral Fate of Ruling Parties

While ruling regimes increasingly hold elections, these contests nonetheless contain the potential to break ruling parties' hold on power.[2] Indeed, incumbents losing elections—and standing down afterwards—has been the primary *peaceful* path from dictatorship to democracy since 1990 (see Figure 2.1). Further, new democracies born from competitive elections tend to be the most peaceful and long-lasting (Wright 2008). In short, elections are important for understanding both how dictatorships endure and how they fall. Even if not totally defeated at the ballot box, significant loss of electoral support for incumbent parties signals growing regime weakness, providing additional incentives for regime insiders to defect and challenge the regime in future elections (Magaloni 2006). Importantly, weakening a dictator's ability to mobilize mass electoral support pushes elites to rely more on electoral fraud, which, in turn, can spark protests that ultimately topple the regime (Tucker 2007; Little et al. 2015).

Our task in this chapter is to understand how emigration—and the consequent private income provided by workers' remittances—reshapes the balance of power in autocracies that rely on elections to sustain their rule. We argue that worker remittances undermine autocratic ruling regimes by reducing citizens' dependence on government transfers and public goods. By giving individuals and households the option of exit from government patronage networks, remittances sever the clientelistic links between voters and incumbent dictators, causing defections from their support coalition. Further, by increasing the resources of opposition parties and civil society organizations, remittances may increase the capacity of these groups to challenge the regime in elections and, hence, narrow the resource gap between the incumbent and the opposition parties.

A party monopoly over state resources in most autocracies makes it possible for the regime to wield control over access to public housing, social services, property, fertilizers, subsidies, scholarships, jobs, and even food. And, most importantly, it allows the incumbent to make this access conditional on support for the regime. This ensures that important segments of society are economically dependent on that regime (Magaloni and Kricheli 2010).

Benefits to poor citizens typically take the form of private, tangible goods: in particular, gifts and handouts delivered during election campaigns. For example, the ruling Cambodian People's Party (CPP) relies on massive gift-giving programs to mobilize support in rural areas (Un 2005; Hughes 2006). Individual gifts normally include food, clothes, small money handouts, and utensils. The People's Action Party's (PAP) public housing programs in Singapore have long been a source of electoral support for the regime. During elections in Malaysia, workers from the ruling party, the United Malays National Organization (UMNO), visited rural households to dispense cash payments to supporters and deter opponent mobilization (Pepinsky 2007, 144). In Tanzania, after the transition to multiparty politics in 1992, the Chama Cha Mapinduzi (CCM) began relying on the widespread distribution of small gifts (*takrima*) such as food, drinks, money, and clothes, to cultivate support at campaign meetings and rallies; a practice that was even legalized prior to the 2000 election—but declared unconstitutional in 2006 (Croke 2017). Further, the benefits delivered from dominant parties can also take the form of targeted public goods and services. In Malaysia, federal politicians distributed grants for rural development to local clients to reward support for UMNO (Pepinsky 2007, 146). Blaydes (2010, 74) shows that during Mubarak's rule in Egypt, areas that voted for the opposition saw little improvement in sewerage and water coverage between the mid-1980s and 1990s. In Mexico, meanwhile, the PRI systematically directed PRONASOL funds, in the form of public works targeting municipalities, to ensure voters' loyalty in contested districts (Magaloni 2006, 68, 123).

Even military rulers get in on the act. The junta that ruled Brazil from 1964 to 1985 established a pro-military party in the mid-1970s to mobilize electoral support for the regime when it held multiparty elections. Far from ruling only by repressing the masses, the military engaged in the same electoral clientelism observed during periods of civilian rule (Desposato 2001, 305, 311). More recently, the ruling junta in Thailand formed a pro-regime party, Palang Pracharat, which did surprisingly well in rural constituencies in the deep south. The military-backed party won these constituencies by co-opting clan leaders, who in turn used well-established clientelistic networks to distribute payments that secured votes for the junta-led party (Utarasint 2019, 214).

In all these cases, voters received targeted benefits and public goods and services in exchange for supporting the regime. Transfers and investments are thus conditional. This support may entail tacit acquiescence or party membership, but most often involves endorsing the ruling party in elections. Ruling regimes use supporting parties and elections to deal with threats from both elites and the masses, and therefore intend to win them (Gandhi and Lust-Okar 2009). Consequently, among other strategies such as voter intimidation and restrictions on opposition parties, autocratic regimes exploit their resource advantage to fund clientelistic exchange of government goodies for electoral support (Greene 2007).

In this setting, financial remittances can weaken ruling regimes by reducing citizens' dependence on clientelistic transfers, and thus increase their economic autonomy (McMann 2006). By increasing private income, remittances reduce the marginal utility of state-provided targeted benefits as well as of local public goods and services. This "income effect" becomes manifest when the remittance boost to private income outweighs the benefits of siding with the ruling party in elections.

This argument builds on the stylized fact that remittances increase household capacity to acquire goods and thus represent a substitute for goods provided by the regime. As discussed in chapter 2, existing research shows that recipient households use remittance income to finance private consumption and access to welfare, and also to invest in housing, education, health, agriculture, and business. Additionally, remittances enable citizens to obtain local public goods that substitute for government welfare and infrastructure expenditure. As a result, with a new autonomous access to these goods, households can extricate themselves from the regime's clientelistic network (Díaz-Cayeros et al. 2003; Pfutze 2012; Escribà-Folch et al. 2015).

Two key assumptions underpin the logic of the income effect. First, remittance recipients have ideological preferences, and therefore care about which party they vote for. This condition is a standard assumption in models of clientelism. In these models, income increases voters' well-being and voting for the ruling party diminishes recipients' well-being when the voters' own ideological position is further from the ruling party's position. Hence, clientelistic transfers decrease (to zero at the limit) as a voter's support for the regime increases, or as s/he moves closer to the incumbent party's ideological position. Transfers, in these models, are the price the regime pays to alter individuals' political behavior. With increased economic autonomy thanks to alternative income sources, citizens might become more willing actually to challenge local authorities, instead of simply censoring their own preferences (McMann 2006; Magaloni and Kricheli 2010). Further, clientelistic networks easily trap poorer voters, as their lower incomes allow a reduction in the price the regime must pay in exchange for support. Substantial evidence suggests that remittances help reduce poverty. By increasing private income, and thus the monetary value of transfers needed to buy support, remittances weaken state clientelism, lowering the marginal utility of such transfers and increasing the importance of ideological preferences in voting.

The second assumption necessary for the income effect to hold is that the regime does not substantially augment its resources by capturing remittances, which it can then use to offset the increase in the price of continued support. Numerous studies—and our own analysis in chapter 3—suggest that remittances are largely non-taxable (Chaudhry 1989; Abdih et al. 2012; Pfutze 2012).

The World Bank, for example, notes (2006c, 93), that "[m]ost remittance-receiving countries today do not impose taxes on incoming remittances." In practice, governments rarely tax remittances, because they are highly sensitive to the tax rate, and those sending them can easily evade formal controls (Eckstein 2010). Thus, directly taxing remittances is likely simply to result in fewer of these being sent through formal channels (Freund and Spatafora 2008). For this reason, we follow the extant research and the findings reported in chapter 3 to suggest that remittances are generally not taxable and do not substantially increase government revenue in autocracies.

Empirical tests of electoral effect of remittances in Mexico show that they decrease votes cast for the incumbent and benefit the opposition by weakening the PRI's clientelistic networks (Pfutze 2012; 2014). In Senegal, migration and remittances helped transform an economy that had been dominated by the export of cash crops. These changes eroded the hegemony and control the ruling party had over the population (Dahou and Foucher 2009): the regime's distributional patronage networks connecting the state with the *marabouts* (local leaders of Muslim communities) in rural areas weakened (Fatton 1986), while, simultaneously, individuals and civil society—especially religious brotherhoods—gained autonomy and social power (Diedhiou 2015). By 2000, electoral support for the ruling Socialist Party in Senegal had dwindled so much that they lost the presidential election in the second round—the first time an incumbent had lost since independence.

In the next two subsections, we examine the evidence for a global sample of autocracies. First, we show that remittances are associated with lower vote shares for incumbent ruling parties in multiparty executive elections. We then look at turnout in autocratic elections and find that, consistent with the income effect, remittances also lower voter turnout. Together, these findings suggest that even when remittance flows are insufficient to boost opposition parties across the line to defeat ruling parties, these financial flows still decrease electoral support for autocratic governments.

### 5.1.1. Ruling Party Vote Share

Remittances, we argue, undermine dictatorships and promote democracy by reducing electoral support for ruling regimes and the parties that support them. While control of state resources allows the ruling party to reward loyalty through clientelism and targeted public goods, remittances have the opposite effect: these private financial flows weaken clientelistic ties by providing extra

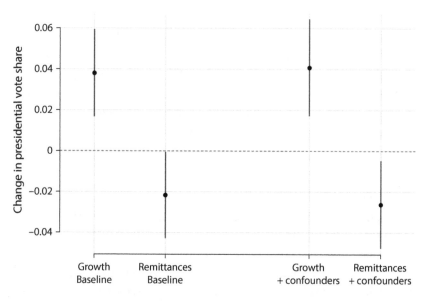

FIGURE 5.1. Remittances and presidential vote share

income to households. Because enjoying the spoils of clientelism depends on turning up to show electoral support for the incumbent, increasing remittances decrease electoral support for incumbent ruling parties. Citizens may vote for opposition parties or simply abstain from voting, both mechanisms reducing the vote share of the ruling party.

We examine remittances and changes in incumbent vote share in a global sample of autocracies from 1978 to 2017, with data on incumbent vote shares for each election and the prior election. The outcome variable is the change in vote share for the incumbent in a direct executive election; this means that we also pick up how well all opposition candidates fared in the election, because the opposition vote share is simply 100 percent minus the incumbent vote share. The measure of remittances is the lagged three-year moving average of remittances per capita. The base specification adjusts for lagged economic growth because remittances often increase growth, especially as remittance flows increase around election time; and domestic growth typically boosts incumbent vote share. The specification accounts for ceiling (and floor) effects by adjusting for the incumbent vote share in the prior election.[3]

Results from the baseline specification are shown in the first set of estimates in Figure 5.1. We report both the remittance estimate and the economic growth estimate for comparison. We find that a one-standard deviation increase in remittances is associated with a 2 percent decrease in the ruling party's vote share. By contrast, a one-standard deviation increase in economic growth is associated with a nearly four percent increase in incumbent vote share. A second specification adjusts for additional potential confounders: GDP per capita, population size, net migration, and movement restrictions. As shown in the second set of estimates in Figure 5.1, the results are almost identical to those reported in the baseline specification.

### 5.1.2.  The Turnout Contest

Authoritarian rulers who hold elections value not only margins of victory but also high turnout. Masses of citizens turning out to vote may not only signal the regime's strength, and therefore deter opposition mobilization, but may also enhance the authoritarian government's clientelistic strategies or contribute valuable information about local governance to the regime (Frantz 2018b). Jason Brownlee (2011, 818) nicely summarizes the benefits of turnout for dictatorships:

> If elections serve as a pressure valve for tempering elite or mass dissent, one would expect to find substantial turnout. Similarly, if elections distribute rents, the number of participants in a developing state will expectedly be substantial, for voting carries great incentives: from the single-day payoff of selling one's vote to the returns of serving the patron after Election Day. Finally, if elections generate an aura of invincibility around the ruler, voting would expectedly be widespread.

Thus high turnout in authoritarian elections can be interpreted as evidence of a release of pent-up anti-regime pressure, as an indication of effective rent distribution to secure mass loyalty, or even as a signal of regime strength. All these interpretations suggest that high turnout bolsters authoritarian power.

Even in contexts where there is no opposition party contesting the election, or when the opposition is weak, voting can still provide critical information for the regime that enhances its power. In Vietnam, for example, elections without an opposition do not necessarily yield "information on overall regime support and strength of opposition," but instead provide "information on the popularity of local notables and the compliance of local officials with central mandates" (Malesky and Schuler 2011, 491). If turnout is low, these one-party elections are less likely to yield this helpful information. Even in China, where the regime does not hold national-level elections, voting in local elections helps the ruling party keep tabs on local-level corruption. This is valuable information the regime can then use to improve local accountability (Martinez-Bravo et al. 2011) or bolster citizens' confidence in local leaders (Manion 2006)—two mechanisms likely to stem anti-regime mobilization. In short, even if everyone knows an authoritarian election is rigged and that the incumbent will win, high turnout in the election can still be very useful to the regime.

Many dictators rig elections, and many do so by fudging the numbers, including the tallies for turnout. Indeed, when everyone expects the ruling party to win, the election may be less of a vote-counting contest than one of turnout. This may be especially true for elections where turnout is the only meaningful metric: for example, when the opposition is not allowed to run. Indeed, if the regime does not allow opposition in an election, everyone knows the ruling party will win. However, if voters fail to show up, this sends a signal of regime weakness—either that the ruler is extremely unpopular, or that the government is unable to coerce citizens to the polls.

During the 2017 presidential election in Rwanda, for example, the regime reported over 98 percent turnout; and all ballots were cast for the ruling party, the Rwandan Patriotic Front. Technically, therefore, the regime could not "win" or "lose" the election. Rather, the ruling party wanted to demonstrate its strength. To this end, one voter recalls observing "voting officials sign[ing] ballots for at least 200 people who did not show up to vote" (Human Rights Watch 2017). And another voter reported that he "was forced to vote in the presence of a National Electoral Commission official" (Human Rights Watch 2017). Both strategies—outright ballot-stuffing and physical coercion—undoubtedly boost official turnout rates in many autocratic elections.

A more pernicious problem for our analysis of turnout data, however, is the possibility that incumbent rulers alter the turnout tally after the ballots are cast. For example, at the 2016 presidential election in Gabon, in which long-ruling president Ali Bongo faced a stiff challenge from a unified opposition, it appears the government rigged the election outcome by altering turnout tallies. The electoral contest was not just fought at the ballot box, with official results indicating that the incumbent had an edge over his opponent of 49.8 percent to 48.2 percent, but also on Wikipedia. On the night of the election, a Wikipedia page for Haut Ogooué, the Gabonese province from which President Bongo hails and where he presumably enjoyed substantial support, was altered more than a hundred times, with the reported population of the province fluctuating between 54,000 residents and 250,000 (Maclean 2016). When the Gabonese electoral commission released official results, it revealed that Bongo's home region was especially loyal, with 99.9 percent turnout and nearly 95 percent of voters plumping for the incumbent president. In contrast, average turnout in the other provinces, as reported by the election commission, was just 59 percent (Maclean 2016). To pull ahead in the vote count, it appears that the regime first tried to fudge population figures in a regime stronghold, and then, when thwarted in the Wikipedia battle, decided to boost the turnout tally in its stronghold province.

The fact that some rulers may rig election results and do so by fudging turnout tallies has implications for understanding what official turnout data can—and cannot—tell us. First, examining turnout is important for assessing authoritarian electoral strategies because so many elections in these regimes are not fair and free contests. Thus even tainted turnout data can help us evaluate the strength of the regime if incumbents value high official turnout—no matter how they construct the final count. While winning elections fairly sends an important signal of incumbent strength, rigging elections—by, for example, deterring opposition voter mobilization, ballot-stuffing in favor of the ruling party, and even altering turnout tallies—can also signal regime strength and thus deter investment in the opposition (Magaloni 2008; Gandhi and Lust-Okar 2009).

That said, if ruling parties manipulate the data, we might have less confidence in analysis that uses these official turnout tallies. However, we can think through how turnout-rigging is likely to effect this analysis. If the official turnout rates reflect a combination of both real turnout and incumbents changing turnout numbers to boost their vote shares, the way such fraud influences a test of remittances and turnout hinges on whether the incumbent alters turnout totals to boost support (at least on paper) in stronghold regions, or attempts to lower turnout in opposition areas, before and perhaps during the electoral contest. We posit that strategies to change vote tallies in opposition areas, such as decreasing the number of polling stations, purging opposition members from voter lists, jailing opposition politicians, and using targeted violent repression against opposition leaders and supporters, are more likely to occur either *before* election day or during the casting of ballots, but not afterwards when the government counts the ballots. In contrast, strategies to boost vote tallies in regime-stronghold areas are more likely to happen during the vote-counting stage *after* votes are cast and when the government constructs the final tallies to be reported publicly.

If, as we posit, remittances lower turnout in places that tend to support the regime, this might force the ruling party to fudge the official turnout results (as part of tinkering with official vote tallies) to ensure incumbent victory. This appears to be what occurred in Gabon in 2016. This scenario would boost official turnout figures and lead to an upwardly biased estimate of the effect of remittances on real turnout. That is to say, if we find that remittances increase official turnout, we should not have too much confidence in the estimate, because we would not be able to disentangle a null real effect resulting from the (false) positive effect resulting from the incumbent altering the tallies to boost turnout numbers in incumbent strongholds.

However, if we observe that remittances are associated with *lower* turnout, this is unlikely to result from the incumbent boosting the official turnout figures in regime-supporting districts after votes have been cast. Instead, tinkering with turnout tallies to boost vote totals for the incumbent would mean that a negative estimate of the remittance effect is too close to zero. Thus, if we find that remittances lower overall turnout, this is likely an *underestimate* of the true effect.

With these caveats in mind, we test how remittances shape vote turnout in autocratic elections, using turnout data from IDEA (2019). We examine turnout in 277 elections—both presidential and parliamentary contests—in 79 countries (105 distinct regimes) from 1978 to 2017.[4] Because, as noted above, turnout can be an important metric of regime strength even in uncontested elections, we include these events as well.

We know that electoral rules and country-specific factors, such as social cleavages, demographic factors, and conflict histories, shape turnout. Further, features of the electoral system and the configuration of cleavages may change, depending on which regime holds power in a particular country. For example, Mengistu's regime in Ethiopia effectively ruled as a one-party government, excluding sizable ethnic groups from power and employing mass repression to deter opposition mobilization. By contrast, the Ethiopian People's Revolutionary Democratic Front (EPRDF), although dominated by the Tigrayan ethnic group, played a game of legislative co-optation with opposition parties allied with larger ethnic groups. The EPRDF sometimes included these parties in the ruling legislative coalition, even allowing some of their representatives into the cabinet. These types of regime-specific factors not only shape election turnout but have implications for remittance flows. We therefore account for possible unobserved confounders by including the unit means of the key explanatory and outcome variables as proxies for unit effects.[5]

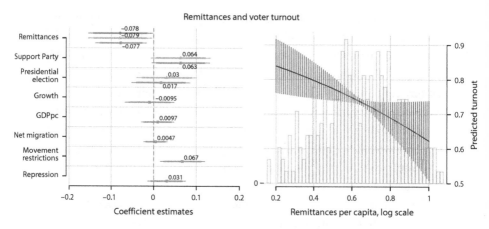

FIGURE 5.2. Remittances and turnout in executive elections

The baseline specification only accounts for time period effects and these unit means. The top estimate in the left panel of Figure 5.2 shows this result: the estimate for remittances is negative and statistically significant, indicating that remittances are associated with lower voter turnout in authoritarian executive elections.

Next we adjust for two possible confounding factors: an indicator of whether the election was a presidential one as opposed to a parliamentary election and an indicator for whether the regime has a supporting political party.[6] Next we add a standard set of potential confounders: economic growth, GDP per capita, Population, Net migration, Movement restrictions, and State-led repression.[7] The second and third set of estimates in the left panel of Figure 5.2 are the results from these specifications. Both yield estimates of remittances that are almost identical to the baseline estimate. Further, movement restrictions are associated with more turnout. This finding nicely illustrates how government manipulation of migration may boost turnout in executive elections in a way that strengthens the regime's grip on power. Remittances, in contrast, are associated with *less* turnout, suggesting an alternative pathway through which migration threatens authoritarian rule.

The plot in the right panel of Figure 5.2 shows large substantive effects on turnout across a range of observed values for remittances. However the estimated equation isolates changes over time in the level of remittances in each regime—not the effect of changes in the level of remittances across different dictatorships. Indeed, the average change in the level of remittances received within regimes is only 0.09 on the log scale, which, plotted around the median value of remittances, translates into a predicted decline in incumbent vote share from 74.4 percent to 71.8 percent—a roughly 2.5 percent decline. Even a 1–2 percent shift in turnout can matter, as the 2016 election in Gabon illustrates. Thus the remittance effect is not trivial.

The first part of this chapter (section 5.1) examines global patterns in remittance flows and autocratic elections. We find that, consistent with the contention that remittances undermine authoritarian rule, these flows are associated with lower vote totals for incumbent rulers and lower turnout in autocratic elections. These two mechanisms—vote share and turnout—are of course related, as lower turnout in areas supporting the regime should lower its share of the vote. However, the global patterns cannot reveal whether this is, in fact, the case: using data aggregated at the country level we cannot examine, for example, *where* turnout decreases.

The second half of this chapter (section 5.2) addresses this challenge by examining the micro-foundations of turnout in authoritarian elections. In doing so, we can look more closely at the places where voters live, to inform the question of whether remittances reduce turnout in areas where such turnout is most helpful to the regime.

While in an ideal world we would also examine the micro-foundations of voting for a particular party—the individual-level behavior that yields aggregate vote shares—doing so in an autocratic context is unlikely to yield reliable answers, because citizens are unlikely to respond truthfully to survey questions when they fear retribution for supporting the opposition. In contexts where rulers coerce voters to the polls, these same voters may not be willing to share their true voting preferences. The next section explores these issues among others, to pin down the micro-foundations linking remittances to electoral support for authoritarian regimes.

## 5.2. How Remittances Cut Clientelistic Ties to the Ruling Party

So far, we have shown that remittances reduce vote turnout and decrease incumbent vote share in electoral autocracies. This suggests that, at the macro-level, remittances undermine autocratic rule by threatening the electoral base of support for incumbent rulers and their dominant parties. This section explores how remitted money shapes the politics of election turnout at the individual level.

Recall from the last chapter that, in autocratic contexts, survey questions asking about vote choice contain substantial non-response, which is correlated, at the country level, with political repression. In addition, a relatively large share of respondents suspect the government sponsors the survey, despite being told otherwise. This belief, which we posit serves as a plausible proxy for fear of government reprisal, predicts non-response to the vote-choice question, as well as other politically sensitive questions. For these reasons, testing theories of remittances and vote choice at the individual level in repressive contexts is highly problematic. Therefore, we examine individual-level vote *turnout*. This survey question suffers much less from non-response than the vote-choice question; and fear of the government reprisal does not predict non-response on the turnout question.

In the prior section, we argued that remittances should sever clientelistic ties between ruling parties and the citizens who ostensibly support them at election time by turning out to vote for the incumbent. While the "extrication" mechanism implies that additional private income from remittances should "liberate" citizens from state-delivered goods, this may take the form either of disengagement from electoral politics, lowering turnout, or, alternatively, of a more active engagement, in the form of voting for the opposition. Ideally, we should test these competing expectations by exploring whether remittances are associated with lower turnout (disengagement) or with increased vote-switching from the incumbent to the opposition (engagement).

However, a direct test of the vote-switching expectation would require panel data on individuals that record remittance receipt and observed vote choice. Indeed, such a test would examine data on the same individuals' *unfalsified* vote choice at at least two points in time, since some individuals will move from the "no-remittance receipt" to "remittance receipt" category in the intervening period. Panel data for autocratic contexts that record plural responses from the same individuals about politically sensitive questions do not, to our knowledge, exist; and there remains the additional problem that some respondents will falsify their stated vote choice. If all respondents were equally likely to falsify, we might only have to adjust for this possibility when accounting for the average overall level of electoral support for ruling parties. However, falsification is likely to be more pernicious—from a research design standpoint—because those most likely to falsify their responses for fear of government reprisal may also be those most likely to switch their vote once "liberated" from the regime's clientelism. True vote-switchers, in other words, who presumably vote for the incumbent prior to receiving remittances but against the incumbent afterwards, are also those most likely to falsely report that they vote for the ruling party even after receiving remittances.

That said, we can use turnout data to test the contrasting implications of the disengagement and engagement arguments. If remittances reduce turnout by turning clients into non-voters (disengagement), then we should observe a decline in turnout. Alternatively, if remittances induce vote-switching, we will not necessarily see such a a change: rather, former regime clients newly liberated from the regime networks will still vote, but now *against* the ruling party now. The engagement expectation implies, then, that we should *not* observe lower turnout among citizens liberated by remittances.

These arguments thus yield straightforward, though contrasting, empirical expectations: lower turnout for disengagement and no change in turnout for engagement. These expectations, however, assume voters are targeted by the ruling party's clientelism; but we know that not all potential voters are equally likely to be targets, or at least not with the same intensity. The literature on clientelism, vote-buying, and turnout-buying suggests two dimensions in terms of which potential voters are most likely to be targeted by ruling parties for clientelistic exchange: individual income and political preference (for or against the incumbent regime) (Lindbeck and Weibull 1987; Dixit and Londegran 1996; Stokes 2005; Dunning and Stokes 2008; Stokes et al. 2013; Gans-Morse et al. 2014).

First, parties are most likely to target poor voters with clientelistic payments, since the marginal cost of doing so is lowest. Would-be voters who have the fewest resources apart from government payments—that is, low-income citizens—should be the most easily induced to turn out for the ruling party (Dixit and Londegran 1996; Diener and Biswas-Diener 2002; Magaloni 2006, 70; Stokes et al. 2013, 89, 161–63; Gans-Morse et al. 2014, 419; Kramon 2018, 62). This expectation assumes that the marginal benefit of income, from any source, is highest for those recipients of clientelist payments who have the lowest initial income; that is, there is a declining marginal utility of income. Further, from the ruling party's perspective, low-income citizens' votes are cheaper to buy than those of higher-income citizens, because the marginal benefit of additional income—from any source—is greatest for those with the least. Therefore, ruling parties will tend to target poor voters.

Second, parties engaging in clientelism are likely to target potential voters who are, ideologically speaking, the least costly to buy off (Dixit and Londegran 1996, 1,137, 1,143; Magaloni 2006, 69; Stokes et al. 2013, 66–67, 89–90). Voters with strong ideological convictions against the regime will require larger payments to persuade them to vote for it.[8] Would-be voters without strong ideological preferences, by contrast, should be more easily induced to vote for the ruling party. Vote-buying, whereby regimes attempt to persuade potential voters to switch their vote and cast a ballot in favor of the ruling party, should be aimed at those who weakly oppose the regime: namely, opposition voters who lack strong partisan attachments (Gans-Morse et al. 2014, 423–24). Combining this logic with the income argument suggests, then, that vote-switching schemes should focus on relatively poor opposition voters with weak ideological convictions.

On the other hand, turnout-buying, whereby parties attempt to mobilize non-voters who nonetheless might be induced to support the regime by turning out to vote, should target unmobilized, likely ruling-party supporters—or loyalists—who, again, are relatively poor.[9] However, if strength of ideological attachment and propensity to vote are correlated, then clientelistic parties should target *weak* supporters who need both a nudge both to to turn out in the first place and to vote for the ruling party when they do so. As Dunning and Stokes (2008, 5) state, if "voters with intense preferences for or against the machine (i.e., strong supporters and strong opponents) are more likely to turn out, whereas marginal voters or those with weaker preferences are more likely to abstain," then the ruling party should mobilize *weak*—not strong— supporters who find voting without inducement marginally too costly.[10] This logic is consistent with the more general theoretical expectation that ruling parties will target marginal districts, rather than core or loyalist constituents, with clientelism (Lindbeck and Weibull 1987).

In the context of voters interacting with ruling parties in sub-Saharan Africa, clientelistic exchange transpires at the local level, where local brokers mobilize electoral support in exchange for local public (i.e., locally non-excludable) goods (Young 2009; Ichino and Nathan 2013; Nathan 2016). Indeed, studies of voting behavior and electoral dynamics in this region demonstrate that the goods exchanged for votes take the form of local public, not private, individually-excludable ones (e.g., Baldwin 2015; Carlson 2015; Rozensweig 2015; Ejdemyr et al. 2016); and studies of ethnic favoritism suggest that this occurs via targeted spending on local public goods such as schools and boreholes (e.g., Baldwin 2015; Kramon and Posner 2016). This research indicates that clientelistic practices may require local elites (or "brokers") to monitor local-level incumbent support and to supply local public goods (Koter 2013; Baldwin 2015).

Stokes et al. (2013) explicitly incorporate the role of local vote-brokers into their theoretical model, in which they posit that local brokers act as agents of party elites: the local brokers know more about individual voters' preferences and behavior than do party elites; and thus brokers are better able to monitor voting. This principal–agent model yields the prediction that while local brokers have an incentive to mobilize non-voting loyalists—in part because brokers can better observe turnout than vote choice—party leaders, following standard swing-voter logic, will still have an incentive to target *marginal* districts. This yields the expectation that ruling party clientelism will "flow disproportionately to 'swing' (electorally competitive) districts," but target loyalists within those districts (Stokes et al. 2013, 92).

Because we focus on individual-level turnout rather than vote-choice, but use a local measure of the concept of "progovernment support," we posit that remittance receipt should decrease vote turnout in swing districts. If ruling parties target these districts, and if remittances undermine this electoral strategy that sustains authoritarian rule, then a finding that remittances decrease turnout in swing districts is consistent with the contention that remittances undermine electoral authoritarianism. Further, if, as most research suggests, clientelism targets relatively poor potential voters in swing districts, then we should observe any turnout effect in swing districts to be concentrated among relatively low-income respondents.

### 5.2.1. Testing the Micro-Logic of Remittances and Turnout

As in the last chapter, we use the Afrobarometer surveys from 2008 and 2016 to test the mechanisms linking remittance income to electoral politics. The outcome variable, *Turnout*, is a binary indicator of whether the respondent reports voting in the last election.[11] While only a minority of respondents report participating in a protest, over three-quarters claim to have voted in the last election.

We again test linear probability models with district-fixed effects, which allow us to account for all differences across districts that shape both voting propensity and remittance receipts. This approach thus directly models location-based differences that shape voting behavior, including geographical differences in access to public goods, maltreatment by the government, ethnicity, the local history of electoral participation, including past government sanctions for low local turnout, and the mobilization efforts of opposition groups. We chose this estimator over others precisely to address these and other location-based arguments that might explain patterns of both voting and remittance receipt.[12]

In addition to the standard demographic variables included as confounders in the models of protest, we add an indicator of partisanship, because politically motivated citizens who claim to feel "close to" a political party should garner intrinsic value from the experience of voting, fueling higher turnout. Partisans may also be more likely to seek out political remittances from abroad (Paarlberg 2017). It is important to note that this survey question on partisan attachment does *not* ask respondents to identify a particular party or politician to whom they "feel close," only whether they feel so. Responses to this question are therefore less likely to reflect preference falsification.

Our first test examines whether remittances increase voter turnout, on average. We find a small, negative and stastitically insignificant effect, suggesting that, across all districts, remittances have little influence on turnout.[13] Next, we test a specification that includes an interaction between remittances and the district level of government support, similar to the specification we tested in the previous chapter. This specification tests whether the marginal effect of remittances on turnout changes in a linear fashion as the level of government support changes. While the estimate for the interaction term is negative, implying that remittances have a larger negative effect when district government support is strong, this estimate is not statistically significant.

The linear interaction test cannot easily isolate the marginal effect of remittances in 'swing' districts, however. Therefore, we conduct a test that allows for the marginal effect of remittances to vary (potentially in a non-linear fashion) across levels of government support. This allows us to test whether the marginal effect of remittances is negative at middle levels of goverment support, but not at high or low levels; this approach is therefore a better test of whether remittances influence turnout in swing districts. Figure 5.3 shows the result when partitioning the district level of government support into five equally sized groups.[14] The horizontal axis depicts the district level of government support, with the density plot of this variable in the background. The vertical axis shows the estimated marginal effect of remittance receipt on vote turnout, for different levels of government support, which are shown as black points and vertical lines (indicating the 90 and 95 percent confidence intervals). The estimate at middle levels of government support, centered around 0.625 on the horizontal axis, is negative and statistically significant. It suggests that remittance receipt in these districts reduces voter turnout by roughly 5 percent.

The result reported in Figure 5.3 shows that the negative effect of remittances on turnout is concentrated in districts with middle levels of

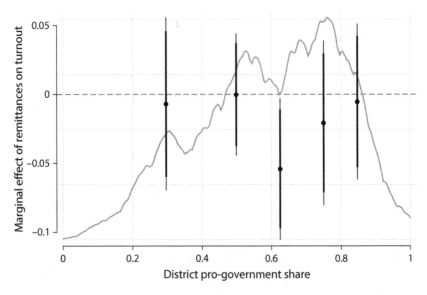

FIGURE 5.3. Remittances and vote turnout, by district-level government support

government support. This finding is consistent with our definition of swing districts as those that have between 50 and 75 percent government support, or roughly the middle third of the distribution. When we repeat this analysis but pre-determine three groups of districts as opposition (those with 50 percent or less government support), swing (those between 50 and 75 percent government support), and (regime-)stronghold (those with 75 percent or more government support), we find the same negative effect for remittances in swing districts, but not in opposition or stronghold districts. To simplify our analysis going forward, we use this three-category typology of districts. Next, we check whether the results for swing districts hold when we exclude respondents who believe that the government sponsored the survey. Recall that these respondents may be the most likely to falsely report positive responses on election turnout and negative responses on protest because they fear government reprisal for responding in a way that reflects poorly on the ruling party or president. Roughly 40 percent of respondents report believing the government sponsored the survey. Testing the model whilst excluding these respondents makes it more difficult to estimate effects precisely—because the sample size decreases substantially—but this test helps clarify whether the result holds among those respondents who are more likely to respond truthfully to questions about politically sensitive behavior. When we exclude these respondents who may fear government reprisal, however, we confirm that remittances are associated with lower turnout in swing districts: remittance receipt is associated with a 4 percent decline in turnout. And again, in non-swing districts there is no relationship between remittances and turnout.

### 5.2.2. Remittances, Poverty, and Turnout

This section explores how poverty shapes the relationship between remittances and turnout at the individual level. Prior sections show that remittances decrease turnout in swing districts. We argue that this finding is consistent with a disengagement theory of election turnout, whereby ruling parties aim turnout-buying schemes at would-be supporters in swing districts. When remittances reduce turnout in swing districts, this undermines the clientelistic stategy of ruling parties to mobilize support that is central to electoral authoritarianism. However, if this theory is correct, we should also expect the marginal effect of additional private income via remittances to be largest among citizens who have low initial income levels from non-remittance sources: those, that is, who are relatively poor. Thus, if remittances decrease turnout in swing districts, this effect should be stronger for high-poverty than for low-poverty respondents.

Recall from the last chapter that poverty is measured as an ordinal variable that captures access to basic goods, such as food, water, medical care, and housing. To examine whether the remittance effect in swing districts is concentrated among the poorest respondents, we test a model that allows for the marginal effect of remittances to vary across the five values of the individual-level poverty index. We then conduct this test for both  swing districts (i.e., those with between 50 and 75 percent government support) and non-swing districts (those outside this range). Figure 5.4 shows the results. The horizontal axis depicts five levels of individual poverty, from 0 to 1. For each level of poverty, the plot shows the marginal effect of remittance receipt on turnout—for both swing districts (in black) and non-swing districts (in gray). In swing districts, the estimates at the lower poverty levels (i.e., among higher-consumption respondents) are negative but relatively small (−2 to −3 percent) and not statistically significant. For the highest two levels of poverty in swing districts, however, the estimates are large, negative, and statistically significant—at around 6 percent. In non-swing districts, none of the estimates

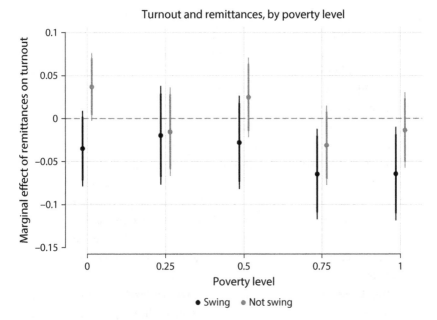

FIGURE 5.4. Remittances and vote turnout, by poverty level

is statistically different from zero, and they form no obvious pattern along the poverty index. This suggests that if remittance receipt lowers turnout in swing districts, this effect is strongest among higher-poverty respondents. This finding is consistent with a turnout-buying theory whereby ruling parties concentrate clientelism in swing districts and target lower income voters.

### 5.2.3. Remittances, Political Preferences, and Turnout in Swing Districts

Recall, from our discussion of why ruling parties are likely to invest in clientelism in swing districts, that parties have an incentive to target swing *districts* but local brokers have an incentive to target *loyalist voters* (Stokes et al. 2013, 92). One way for ruling parties to mitigate rent-seeking by local brokers is to concentrate investment in clientelism in locations where electoral contests are more competitive, on the assumption that brokers will apply more effort and resources to boosting turnout—as opposed to keeping this effort and these resources as rents—if they receive benefits from winning the district and when their efforts can be decisive in achieving this. Confirming these assumptions, Stokes et al. (2013) show that parties have an incentive to employ and provide resources to local brokers (intermediaries) in swing districts. Even when parties boost clientelism in swing districts, however, local brokers still have an incentive specifically to target loyalists within those districts, because monitoring individual-level turnout is easier than monitoring individual vote choices. This is the basis for our hypothesis presented in chapter 2: that remittances, by extricating individuals from clientelistic networks, result in a lower propensity to show up at the polls.

The main micro-finding in this chapter is that remittances decrease turnout in swing districts. Up to this point, however, we have not tested the additional implication of the theory—that brokers should target loyalists within swing districts—because, although we have an individual measure of government support, we suspect it may be upwardly biased, insofar as respondents who fear reprisal may falsely report support for the incumbent ruler and his/her party (Tannenberg 2017). Therefore, we encourage readers to evaluate the following result with appropriate caution.

Noting these caveats concerning the individual-level measure of government support, we proceed to test the following implication of the clientelism theory: that we should observe the negative effect of remittance receipt on turnout in swing districts to be concentrated among government supporters. The individual-level government support variable is a scaled index of three items that tap into trust and assessment of the ruler and his party (see Table 4.3). We then test whether an interaction between this variable and the remittance variable is negative, which would indicate that, in swing districts, an increase in remittances decreases turnout more among ruling party supporters than among opponents.

This test yields a result consistent with this additional implication of the theory: for opposition respondents (those with 0 on the individual pro-government index) remittances have no effect on turnout; but for regime supporters (those with 1 on the pro-government index) remittance receipt decreases turnout by between 4 and 6 percent, depending on the specification. Thus we find evidence that remittances decrease turnout in swing districts, and that this decrease is strongest for those who indicate they support the government. The evidence suggests, then, that if autocratic parties use clientelism to support their rule by targeting swing districts, and local brokers, who can more easily monitor turnout than vote choice, target loyalist voters, remittances undermine this strategy by reducing turnout among the regime supporters in swing districts.

### 5.2.4. An Alternative Measure of Government Support

As in the last chapter, we check our main findings using an alternative measure of district government support. Letsa (2019) codes as "stronghold", "opposition", and "swing" districts in five countries in the 2016 round of the Afrobarometer survey: Cameroon, Tanzania, Togo, Uganda, and Zimbabwe. Her operationalization of these concepts differs from ours insofar as she defines a swing district as one where both an opposition candidate and a ruling-party candidate have won a legislative seat in the recent past. Following this approach, opposition districts are those where opposition candidates won the legislative seats in prior elections; and stronghold districts are those where the ruling party won them. This measure of the concept of "swing district" thus uses information external to the survey, whereas our measure employs information from respondents about their support for the government to construct a district-level measure of that support. While Letsa's data have substantially less geographical and temporal coverage than our own, we nevertheless view their use as an important test of our own because it offers an external check on our measure for swing districts and the robustness of our findings.

With these data for five countries, we test whether the main findings of this chapter hold: do remittances indeed decrease turnout among the poor in swing districts? To this end, we conduct three sets of tests. First, we examine all districts and include an interaction term between remittances and poverty. This allows us to see if the effect of remittances varies by the level of poverty. The result of this test is reported in the two left-hand estimates in Figure 5.5. There appears to be little difference in the remittance effect between richest and poorest respondents: both estimates are negative, but small and insignificant. Next, we test the same specification, but look only at non-swing districts. These results are reported in the middle two estimates in Figure 5.5. Again, the estimated effect of remittances is roughly the same for both types of respondent, rich and poor. The last test restricts the analysis to swing districts, as identified by Letsa. The results, reported in the two left-hand estimates, indicate that remittances decrease turnout in these districts, but only among relatively poor respondents. In short, we find results similar to our own—remittances reduce turnout among the poor in swing districts—using this alternative measure of the concept of swing district.

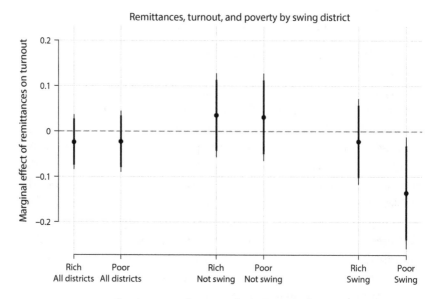

FIGURE 5.5. Remittances and turnout: alternative swing district measure

## 5.3.  Conclusion

The previous chapter showed that remittances increase anti-regime protests and that remittance recipients in areas with anti-regime preferences were more likely to join protests than non-recipients. This chapter has focused on another repertoire of contention, namely electoral behavior, and demonstrates that remittances reduce (some) recipients' propensity to participate in elections, which undermines authoritarian rule by sapping electoral support for ruling parties.

The key individual-level mechanism behind this outcome is the demobilization of poor supporters in swing districts, which, as our findings show, translates at the macro-level into reduced electoral support for incumbents. While prior research had already found that remittances reduce turnout in various contexts, none of these studies focused on autocratic regimes and specifically looked into the moderating effects of other variables. Our theoretical claims and analyses incorporate income and political preferences (along with local vote brokers), which allows for greater precision in explaining how and where remittances might influence individuals' electoral behavior. The results are consistent with our hypothesis that remittances erode clientelism, since the demobilization effect identified is concentrated among poor individuals in swing districts.

If electoral autocracy is increasingly common, and if dictators find ways to marshal their resource advantages to stack election results in their favor, then elections may be tools for autocracies to survive in power. Rather than undermining autocracies, multiparty elections may bolster autocratic governments. Remittances, however, undermine the strategies electoral autocracies employ to get voters to turn out at election time.

We find evidence in this chapter consistent with the proposition that remittances undermine dictatorship by causing recipients' loyalty to dwindle. Remittance-driven decline in support for incumbent parties opens the door to several pathways out of their dominance. First, it opens the possibility of an opposition victory at the polls that brings further and deeper political transformations. Second, even if the incumbent is not defeated, reduced support signals overall weakness, which may prompt defections by members of the elite, embolden opposition groups, lead to the use of electoral fraud, and spark protests in response to such irregular tactics. In sum, demobilization in these autocratic contexts does not necessarily favor the status quo and impede political change; instead, disengagement often works as a form of dissent and hence boosts democratization efforts.

# 6

# Remittances and Democratization

The myriad forces contained in the process of globalization are pulling the political dynamics in the Global South in different and even opposing directions. Some increasingly powerful global forces—such as trade with China or backlash against migration in Eastern Europe—may pull countries in the direction of authoritarianism and create new obstacles to democratization (Burnell and Youngs 2009). The end of the Cold War, with the resulting Western dominance and global economic integration, was supposed to entail the "end of history," that is, "the universalization of Western liberal democracy as the final form of human government" (Fukuyama 1989, 4). However, in the last couple of decades such optimism has faded because of what many consider the rise (or simply the return) of great non-democratic powers and the negative influence of these powerful countries on political liberalization throughout the world (Gat 2007). Some foreign policy pundits even warn of the beginning of a new Cold War (Kaplan 2019), which could alter geostrategic interests and undermine the spread of democracy. To make matters worse, Western democracies that face many internal challenges to democracy have been unwilling or unable to contain such efforts. President Trump's attempts to undermine democracy in the United States—not to mention his admiration, and even fondness, for several autocratic rulers—coupled with the EU's inability (or perhaps reluctance) to push back against anti-democratic politics in member countries has exacerbated the trend of global democratic decline.

Emerging global and regional powers such as China, Russia, and Saudi Arabia engage in foreign policy strategies that often work against Western efforts to promote democracy and subvert domestic liberalization, especially in target countries where they have strong strategic interests (Risse and Babayan 2015).[1] Although one might think in terms of military alliances or vetoes at the UN Security Council, the most pervasive form of authoritarian support to other governments is actually economic. For example, there is now ample evidence of Russian government interference in foreign elections to support non-democratic incumbents and far-right parties, not only in post-Soviet countries but also, since the mid-2010s, in established democracies in the West. The same is true of China's increasing involvement in Africa, where the Chinese government distributes billions in aid, loans, and investment programs, often without strings attached. Chinese economic adventurism abroad has now turned into a formal intergovernmental platform, the Forum on China–Africa Cooperation. The announcement in 2013 of the Belt and Road Initiative, a massive China-led investment plan to connect Asia, the Middle East, Africa, and Europe through a vast network of transportation and energy networks, poured fuel on the fire of Western concerns (Fontaine and Kliman 2018). The underlying fear is that growing Chinese involvement in countries ruled by autocratic governments may reduce the leverage that Western democracies have, in the past, used to entice these leaders to adopt multiparty elections.

Only a few global forces still pull developing countries in the direction of democratization and better governance. Crucially, while oil revenue, foreign aid, trade, and even investment flows so often reinforce the power of incumbent governments in recipient countries, global democratizing forces tend to shift power away from the government and towards citizens by empowering individuals, grassroots organizations, and social movements. Remittance flows to the Global South are one of these forces, a growing financial resource that, unlike the many other global monetary flows, accrues directly to agents of political change: citizens. This chapter examines how migration and the sizable remittances that flow from it shape democratization.

Our evidence so far demonstrated that remittances boost protest and undermine the electoral strategies that sustain authoritarian governments throughout the world. These two mechanisms suggest that remittances should also increase the chances of a democratic transition. This expectation is empirically grounded. As chapter 2 shows, protests and elections have become the main mechanisms of democratization. That is to say, citizen-led challenges to incumbent autocratic governments are now the most likely way for autocracies collapse, tending to result in democratic transitions. If this is correct, then democracy may be slipping into many developing countries through a back door that many dictatorships cannot keep fully closed, yet one that Western democracies may indirectly be helping to shut with their increasingly restrictive immigration policies.

Do remittances spur democratization, as our empirical findings so far suggest they do? This chapter answers this question by examining how remittances shape two types of political outcome. First, at the meso-level, we examine whether remittance flows increase the strength and mobilization capacity of opposition parties and civil society organizations. Second, at the highest level of analysis, we look at whether remittances boost the chances that a dictatorial regime may undergo a democratic transition. Before examining these global outcomes, we first discuss the implications of our results for resource-based theories of autocratic survival, and then illustrate how remittances shaped protest, voting, the development of opposition parties, and ultimately autocratic instability and democratization in two autocracies: the socialist regime that ruled Senegal until 2000, and the Cambodian regime under Hun Sen and the Cambodian People's Party (CPP).

## 6.1.  Closing the Resource Gap

What do our findings linking remittances to protest and voting behavior mean for autocratic survival and democratization? Central to our argument is the premise that remittance income from migration flows directly to citizens ruled by autocratic governments throughout much of the Global South. These remittances are thus an important financial resource for citizens to challenge their governments, which historically have retained power, in part, by monopolizing resources and using them to either buy political support or repress citizen challenges to their rule.

Many scholars and policy makers, as we document in chapter 3, assert that revenues from international oil sales and generous foreign aid receipts help entrench non-democratic regimes and impede democratic change. Central to these rentier theories is the vast volume of financial resources accruing to states, as well as the fact that these resources come from external, foreign sources—and not from taxing their own citizens. These external funds, the argument goes, allow governments to buy support from citizens via patronage networks and to fund more reliable and effective internal security forces that quell challenges to the government. The beneficiaries of government patronage, according to these theories, are members of dictators' inner circles, or perhaps middle-class groups, with the mass population forgoing democratic demands and government accountability when natural resource wealth or ample foreign aid reduce a government's need to tax its citizens. Some also suggest that resource rents enable autocracies to indulge in extensive welfare spending. Availability of, and control over, financial resources are thus an essential pillar of authoritarian survival.

Further, authoritarian governments often permit and strategically manipulate democratic-looking political institutions—such as elections, legislatures, and even opposition political parties—to sustain their rule. Predominant theories linking these institutions to authoritarian survival posit that political institutions sustain autocracies by reducing intra-elite conflicts and facilitating credible power-sharing between the ruler and crucial elite regime supporters. These political institutions, particularly political parties that support the regime, also help authoritarian governments to co-opt opposition organizations, by channeling their demands into regime-approved forms of dissent that do not ultimately challenge the regime itself.

Important among these democratic-looking political institutions are ruling parties, because they serve as centralized mechanisms to distribute patronage—that is, goods and services paid for by the regime, ultimately thanks to its substantial financial resource advantage. This patronage, in turn, generates mass-level political support for autocratic governments and expands social control over groups that might otherwise challenge the regime, in the process making citizens financially dependent on these governments (Slater and Fenner 2011).

In the context of most autocracies now holding regular multiparty elections, control and diversion of state resources results in "two types of dominant party advantages: the incumbent's resource advantages and its ability to raise the costs of participation in the opposition" (Greene 2007, 5). Such advantages allows governments to allocate state benefits and public goods strategically, privileging some regions or constituencies while systematically excluding others.[2] Dependence on state resources or jobs diminishes support for democracy, enticing citizens to instead vote for candidates from the ruling regime. Further, when autocratic governments exclude political opposition from state resources, this impedes investment in opposition activities. Díaz-Cayeros et al. (2003) describe this selective distribution of patronage and goods a "punishment regime," whereby autocratic governments use state resources "to reward the loyal and punish the disloyal" (Magaloni and Kricheli 2010, 128). Thus, the regime cultivates financial dependence as a mechanism to mobilize electoral support for the ruling party. Conversely, the regime deprives other groups of access to resources, limiting opposition parties' ability to campaign and organize, while, at the same time, deploying repression to raise the costs of participation in opposition groups. As Greene (2007, 5) explains,

> Dramatic resource advantages allow the incumbent to outspend on campaigns, deploy legions of canvassers, and, most importantly, to supplement policy appeals with patronage goods that bias voters in their favor. Dominant parties also impose two types of costs on candidates and activists who decide to affiliate with a challenger. One type of cost is the opportunity cost of foregoing the material advantages that they would have received by joining the dominant party, such as a stipend, kick-backs, or access to an old boys' network of business contacts and favors. The other cost is the cost associated with targeted physical intimidation, beatings, or even killings of opposition activists that occur episodically in some (but not all) dominant party systems.

Implicit in theories that pinpoint the ruling regime's resource advantage over its opponents as a crucial explanation for authoritarian durability is the understandable presumption that the cause of authoritarian collapse lies in the *loss* of these resources, perhaps brought about by local or global shocks such as economic crises, a decline in oil (or other commodity) prices, economic sanctions, or IFI-imposed structural adjustment plans that require the state to downsize. For resource theories of authoritarianism, external shocks that shrink the regime's resource advantage harm its capacity to strategically deploy patronage networks and repress challengers, paving the way for regime collapse and eventual democratization.

There are, however, other ways whereby the resource asymmetry might be reduced—even if state resources remain unaffected. The evidence reported in chapter 3 shows that remittances do *not* increase the government's budget or substantially alter the spending patterns of autocratic governments. Remittances thus do not amplify the regime's resource advantage by generating additional foreign rents that the government can capture. That said, the mechanisms underpinning resource theories of authoritarian durability may still explain authoritarian collapse when citizens increase their resources, even if regime resources do not decline.

Migrant remittances help to close the resource gap by increasing the resources available to citizens, the by-product of which is to undermine the regime's ability to employ state resources to mobilize support and prevent the emergence of organized dissent. Thus, remitted income weakens autocratic rule *from below*, by assisting popular mobilization. In fact, as our theory and empirical evidence indicate, remittances erode the "punishment regime" from both ends. Because they are a decentralized income flow accruing directly to individuals and groups within migrant-sending countries ruled by autocratic governments—and not to the governments themselves— remittances encourage the exercise of voice among those at the repression end of the punishment regime, as we show in chapter 4; whilst in addition, as our evidence in chapter 5 demonstrates, they reduce the effectiveness of the resources autocratic governments dole out to those at the reward, or material benefits, end. Remittances reduce the relative benefits of patronage distributed to maintain citizens' loyalty and to mobilize electoral support for the ruling party. Remittance inflows thus help to "level the playing-field," by both increasing citizens' financial autonomy and empowering dissenters and opposition organizations. In turn, these forces should increase the likelihood of democratic change.

## 6.2. Remittances, Voting, and Protests in Senegal and Cambodia

This section examines the key mechanisms in our argument linking remittances to autocratic instability and democracy in two particular cases: Senegal and Cambodia. These case studies are not meant to provide a test for our theory, but rather to illustrate how our argument works, by tracing the theorized causal mechanisms (Levy 2008). To do so, we consider one positive and one negative case of democratic change to illustrate how remittances were connected with increased levels of regime instability. In both cases, an increase in remittances coincided with important political transformations and increased likelihood of regime change, even though the regime collapsed and there was a transition to democracy in only one of the cases, Senegal.[3]

While the long-ruling Socialist Party of Senegal (Parti Socialiste du Sénégal, PS) lost its monopoly on power in a 2000 presidential election won by the candidate of the Senegalese Democratic Party, Abdoulaye Wade, its Cambodian counterpart, the Cambodian People's Party (CPP), has yet to lose, and its leader, Hun Sen, has consolidated the regime into a personal dictatorship (Morgenbesser 2018). However, the Cambodian opposition came very close to winning the 2013 election, with opposition groups uniting to mount a sustained campaign, complete with dozens of anti-government protests, both before and after the election. The Hun Sen regime only survived the 2013 contest by cheating; and in the election's aftermath the regime refused to investigate electoral fraud, eventually resorting to state-led violence to quell the protests and retain power.

### 6.2.1. Senegal

Migration has transformed Senegalese society in the past three decades and contributed to the demise of the Socialist Party's autocracy: in power for the first four decades after independence, the regime finally lost an election in 2000. Senegal is one of the top remittance recipients in Africa; and such inflows increased substantially during the 1990s and the years leading up to the crucial 2000 presidential election, as shown in Figure 6.1 (below).[4] The main destinations of Senegalese migrants include France, Spain, and the USA, but also neighboring countries such as Mauritania and Gabon.

The PS—previously known as Union Progressiste Sénégalaise—emerged as the hegemonic ruling party in post-independence Senegal, which "had as its base the support of the Muslim leaders and, in particular, the head of the powerful Mouride brotherhood" (Creevey et al. 2005, 479–480). Inherited from French colonial times, clientelism in Senegal was shaped by associations of Muslim brotherhoods, and their leaders, the marabouts, were instrumental in mobilizing electoral support for the PS and President Senghor in the decades after independence (Behrman 1970; Fatton 1986). In particular, the "powerful Muslim brotherhoods functioned as mechanisms for political integration in the countryside: in exchange for agricultural services and other resources channelled to client marabouts, the party-state could count on the votes of the disciples attached to these marabouts" (Dahou and Foucher 2009, 13). Marabouts would use the *ndigal*, a type of religious injunction or command, to instruct their followers to vote for the ruling party (Villalón 1995; Beck 2001; Galvan 2001).

Both migration and increasing opposition to the PS regime were a response to the economic crisis caused by the decline in the market for peanuts— the country's main cash crop—in the 1980s and 1990s. As in many developing countries, this crisis led international financial institutions to push for costly structural adjustment programs from the government. And these reforms—privatization of state-own businesses, liberalizing trade and foreign investment, and shrinking the size of the state—undermined the regime's traditional distributional networks, causing profound economic hardship that led many Senegalese to seek better opportunities abroad.

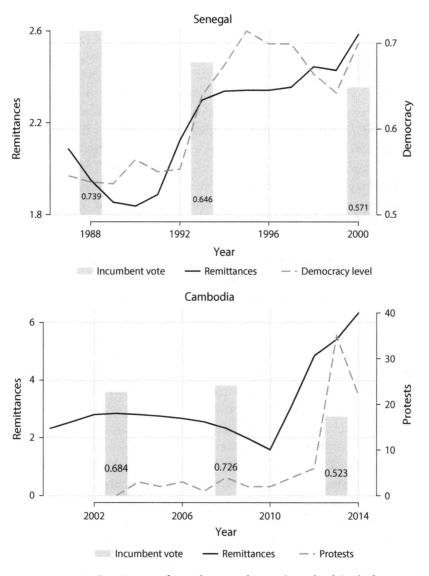

FIGURE 6.1. Remittances and incumbent vote shares in Senegal and Cambodia

Dahou and Foucher (2009, 17) emphasize that "[t]he shift of the Senegalese economy from groundnuts to migration and its increasing dependence on resources generated abroad could be seen as the final stage in the process of ending the hegemony once enjoyed by the state over Senegalese society."

Starting in the 1970s, the regime adopted several liberalizing reforms with the goal of preserving PS hegemony amidst economic problems and growing unrest (Vengroff and Magala 2001).[5] Under a system of managed pluralism, the Senegalese Democratic Party (Parti Démocratique Sénégalais, or PDS), headed by Abdoulaye Wade, was created in 1974 and allowed to officially register, assuming the role of a liberal, if loyal, opposition party (Creevey et al. 2005).[6] These incremental institutional reforms opened the door to the emergence of opposition parties under, initially, a competitive authoritarian system in which the ruling regime held regular multiparty elections.

Broader political space and growing international connections contributed to the emergence of a vibrant civil society, including new associations of young Murids (members of a Sufi brotherhood), called *dahiras*, with an urban base and strong desires for *sopi* (change), which became their political rallying cry. These social associations were initially created by young Murids from the same rural brotherhoods when they moved to urban areas (Beck 2001). The dahiras soon became providers of extensive safety nets for urban migrants, most often young men. As importantly, they transformed the traditional rural background of the brotherhoods into urban civil society groups comprised mostly of urban professionals (including university students), as well as transnational actors, especially as international migration increased (Diedhiou 2015). Many such organizations were created in cities outside Senegal such as New York, Paris, Rome, or Madrid; and today active dahiras can be found all over Europe and North America (Salzbrunn 2009).

These transformations eroded the ruling party's social control via the intermediary role of the marabouts. Even as early as the 1988 election, there is evidence that migration and the attendant changing social changes had weakened the power of marabouts to mobilize support for Abdou Diouf, the PS leader who replaced Senghor in 1981. And while the *ndigal* practice was still used "to reward Senghor's successor, Abdou Diouf, for the new roads and street lighting the state had installed" (Beck 2001, 612), it was waning. Villalón (1995, 197), for example, observes that "[m]any people, it seems, opted for abstention from voting rather than going against the *ndigal* or making the (to them) distasteful choice of casting a vote for the beleaguered president. Many others, however, simply disobeyed the marabout's command and voted as they saw fit." Moreover, allegations of irregularities and fraud during the 1988 election led to a wave of mass demonstrations against the government (Resnick and Casale 2011, 5).

These dynamics intensified in the following years and the vote share of the ruling PS gradually dwindled as a result, as illustrated in the top panel of Figure 6.1. Remittances increased the financial autonomy of the dahiras, the Murid brotherhoods in general, and their organizational capacity. The dahiras invested increased funds in providing basic services, building infrastructure, and even supplying consumption goods that had traditionally been delivered by the state (Diedhiou 2015). Simultaneously, the dahiras, located both in the cities and among the diaspora, were "becoming more concerned about the governance of their home country" (Diedhiou 2015, 175). The growing size of independently funded dahiras, combined with state shrinkage stemming from structural adjustment, weakened clientelism, especially for the state-sponsored marabout networks. In turn, this reduced citizens' loyalty to the ruling party.[7] Students and other youth in urban areas began mobilizing support for the opposition PDS among rural constituents—the opposite of the traditional marabout organizing that favored the ruling PS (Zeilig 2009). As Galvan (2001, 59) notes, "[i]n subsequent elections, the marabouts adopted a stance of political neutrality, neither supporting the ruling party nor mobilizing support for opposition candidates. By 2000, the PS, without the crucial backing of the *marabouts*, had become vulnerable, especially given the pent-up desire for *sopi*." In fact, he continues, "the 2000 elections sealed the collapse of the highways-for-ndigel patronage ties between the Socialists and the marabouts" (Galvan 2001, 60).

By the late 1990s, the number of migrants abroad and, as importantly, their financial and social influence had grown so important that the main opposition candidate, Abdoulaye Wade, launched his campaign for the 2000 presidential election among the diaspora. Indeed, obtaining the support of the diaspora was a top political priority (Salzbrunn 2009; Dedieu et al. 2013). In sum, migration and financial remittances not only undermined the traditional clientelistic ties between the PS and the marabouts, but also provided crucial resources to the opposition campaign. As Saine (2009, 53) observes,

[a]greement and support for the candidate by parties and leaders that constitute the coalition remain important but not a sufficient condition for victory. To win, it also means pooling limited resources, avoiding duplication of tasks to free-up finances and personnel to better position opposition candidates to win. With this come more financial and moral

support including monies from the Diaspora, who often are more willing to support a coalition rather than a single party candidate or several party coalitions . . . Wade's [victory in 2000] received strong financial support from . . . nationals abroad.

Wade and the main opposition party, the PDS, won with 58.7 percent of the vote in the second round of the presidential ballot. Turnout in this second round was 61 percent, slightly lower than in the first one, when it was 63 percent. The ruling PS was defeated and the incumbent president stepped down. All in all, as Mbow (2008, 162) summarizes it, "[t]he advent of political alternation was the achievement of citizens who, through a mobilization that brought together civil society groups, the media, and the Senegalese diaspora, became aware of their own strength."

### 6.2.2. Cambodia

At the time of writing, Cambodian prime minister Hun Sen, leader of the country since 1985, remains in power.[8] The 1993 elections, which were organized and supervised by the United Nations Transitional Authority in Cambodia, brought to its culmination the peace process ending the country's civil war, and put it on an apparent path to multiparty democracy. However, since the 1993 election, the CPP and its leader Hun Sen have steadily accumulated power, turning post-conflict Cambodia into an electoral authoritarian regime with Hun Sen firmly entrenched at its head (Morgenbesser 2017). The government now represses opposition leaders and voters and manufactures election results, all while employing an extensive clientelistic network to mobilize electoral support for the ruling party (Hughes 2003; Un 2005; Morgenbesser 2018).

Although the incumbent CPP lost the 1993 election, it was still part of the government coalition with the winner, the royalist FUNCINPEC, and Hun Sen was appointed "second prime minister." In 1997, tensions within the coalition mounted and a coup led by Hun Sen ousted the first prime minister, Norodom, Ranariddh, amid allegations that the latter had colluded with the Khmer Rouge to smuggle weapons. A new election was held in 1998, which the CPP won, but, without a strong majority, Hun Sen's party still had to form a coalition government with FUNCINPEC, this time, however, with Hun Sen as the sole prime minister. The same coalition was formed after the 2003 election; yet the results indicated increasing opposition strength, as the main opposition Sam Rainsy Party (SRP), founded in the mid-1990s, garnered

22 percent of the vote to become the second largest legislative party. Over the the next several years, the CPP excluded the opposition SRP from the government coalition; and by 2008, a highly irregular and heavily criticized national election resulted in a CPP majority with one-party government.

During the 2013 elections, however, the pro-democracy forces challenged the CPP's dominance for the first time, with the opposition experiencing a huge boost in electoral support. As the bottom panel of Figure 6.1 shows, the ruling CPP's share of the top two parties' votes dropped from roughly 70 percent in the 2000s to just 52 percent in 2013, meaning the ruling regime barely scraped a victory. Important socio-economic transformations during the 2000s favored the rise of a credible challenge to the CPP in the 2013 election. After the demise of the main opposition party from the 1990s, FUNC-INPEC, the opposition consolidated behind one candidate; and in 2012 the SRP joined forces with the smaller Human Rights Party (a former NGO) to create an electoral alliance, the Cambodia National Rescue Party (CNRP), in advance of the 2013 legislative elections. Forging a united opposition entailed communication and coordination as well as substantial resources, much of which came from abroad. Often opposition unification (or fragmentation) results from changes to the formal electoral rules, but in this case the leading opposition party led the process of opposition consolidation in the run-up to the 2013 election. After the CPP's victory in 2008 and its domination in local elections (Hughes 2015), the result of the 2013 election came as a surprise. The opposition campaigned using the simple slogan *Do!*, meaning "Change!" (McCargo 2014, 74), much as in Senegal. According to the official count, the CPP obtained about 49 percent of the vote (68 seats), and the CNRP 44.5 percent (55 seats). Importantly, the 2013 election was the record low point for turnout in national elections, at only 69.5 percent of the electorate (Schrey et al. 2013, 51).

The electoral dominance of the CPP is rooted in its deep patronage networks, which work in tandem with state-led violence and other political restrictions targeting opposition groups and leaders (Un 2005). Like many electoral regimes that rely on such strategies to mobilize support, the CPP's political base "is in the provinces, where the CPP uses its control of patronage and government resources (mainly derived from foreign aid) to keep power" (McCargo 2005, 100). Consistent with the key role of brokers in clientelism discussed in chapter 2, moreover, the mechanisms behind this electoral mobilization, as Hughes (2015, 10) describes it, "range from vote-buying, sponsoring of development initiatives and mass gift-giving programmes, to the formation of groups of households under a group leader who is responsible for finding out voting intentions of householders, and ensuring those that intend to vote CPP go and vote on the day." Relatively low-income, mostly rural voters are the primary targets of these strategies, with commune chiefs playing a crucial intermediary role. Around election time, the CPP uses ample state resources to invest in local infrastructure projects such as schools, roads, and irrigation schemes, and, crucially, to provide individual gifts, including food, small amounts of money, clothing, and utensils to potential voters. At the same time, to solidify the ruling party's advantage, opposition parties are not allowed to campaign or set up local offices in the rural provinces, or to interact with the media (Un 2005; Hughes 2006; Norén-Nilsson 2016). "All this is intended to create the sense amongst the public that there is no welfare state in Cambodia, only a philanthropic party—the CPP" (Hutt 2020).

Out-migration and remittances, however, along with demographic changes and growing conflict over land allocation, helped undermine these patronage networks in the years leading up to the 2013 election. Between 2000 and 2015, the number of Cambodian emigrants more than doubled, rising from around half a million to almost 1.2 million (OECD and CDRI 2017).[9] As McCargo (2014, 74) emphasizes, "[w]hile most Cambodians nominally live in rural areas, villagers of working age often spend much of the year selling their labor in and around Phnom Penh, in neighboring Thailand, or even further afield." Most migrants are young, low-skilled, and from rural areas (OECD and CDRI 2017). As a result, Cambodia is among the top four remittance-receiving countries in ASEAN.

This period of increasing migration was also one of rising anti-regime protests and decreasing electoral turnout. On the one hand, the change in demographics created an active support base for the opposition, which drew more support from urban than rural areas. As one pair of observers notes, "[t]he new generation of youth with different experiences and expectations has significantly loosened this personalized relationship of dependence. Young Cambodians benefit little from the CPP's gift-giving mechanism and are also much less likely to benefit from infrastructure development projects. They are also as a group less connected to these personalized networks, given their mobility and employment aspirations outside of their villages" (Eng and Hughes 2017, 405). Indeed, "[w]hile the CPP campaign was well-equipped and funded—most of those taking part were paid—CNRP activists were overwhelmingly volunteers" (McCargo 2014, 74). Furthermore, the CNRP's 2013 campaign stressed the need for change but also, importantly, attempted to alter public opinion by delegitimizing clientelistic exchange (Norén-Nilsson 2016).

As important as the demographic change was that the years preceding the 2013 election also saw a surge in remittances, which, as we argue, is likely to have undermined clientelism and reduced the resource advantage that the CPP traditionally wielded. The bottom panel in Figure 6.1 shows that remittances sent to Cambodia from migrants working abroad more than doubled in the three years from 2010 to 2013. Remitted income reduces households' poverty (Roth et al. 2015; Roth and Tiberti 2017), and in turn decreases voters' dependence on state-delivered basic goods, weakening clientelism (Hutt 2017).

In her study of voter perceptions in the 2013 Cambodian election, Norén-Nilsson (2016, 814) finds that "CPP gift giving is being undone from within," and that it was not very effective, as voters increasingly saw it as illegitimate and simply aimed at vote-buying. In fact, one of the key factors explaining the 2013 election results was not only the increase in support for the CNRP, but also the low turnout (69.5 percent), which indicates that CPP voters did not mobilize to the same extent as they did in previous electoral contests.[10]

Moreover, remittances constituted one the main external resources for opposition mobilization and campaigning (Un 2005). Having faced exile, several CNRP leaders and activists "carried out extensive outreach, established large networks and attracted financial support from overseas Cambodians, particularly from the Cambodian diaspora in the U.S., France, Canada and Australia" (Heng 2018). According to some estimates, about 60 percent of the party's funds for the 2013 election came from supporters living abroad (Sachsenröder 2018, 36). Thus, not only was the opposition more united for the 2013 election, but they were also better financed than earlier opposition campaigns, largely with funds from migrant remittances.

While Cambodian elections had often bred allegations of irregularities and prompted street protests prior to 2013, the electoral contest that year produced a much larger protest movement, that lasted for several months (Um 2014, 101). The protesters' main demand was for the creation of an independent committee to investigate the reports of widespread irregularities. The government responded with violent repression, as the state security forces cracked down on demonstrations. A few years later, in 2017, the CPP government arrested the opposition leader, Kem Sokha, and the Supreme Court dissolved the main opposition party amid accusations that they had conspired with the USA to topple the government.

### 6.2.3. Conclusion

While Hun Sen's regime ultimately survived the 2013 election, while the Senegalese Socialist Party stepped down after electoral defeat in 2000, we observe similar underlying mechanisms linking migration and democracy in both cases. Migration abroad helped shift the balance of power from governments to citizens, as remittances both helped to finance opposition mobilization and undermined the clientelism that underpinned the incumbents' respective electoral strategies. There is no doubt that other international factors also shaped the government response to electoral threats, which differed in each of these two cases: in Senegal, the government did not alter the election result and refrained from unleashing violence on the opposition, while the Cambodian People's Party opted for electoral manipulation and repression. Migration may not be able to explain this divergence in responses, but it does help us to understand why the incumbent autocrats in each case were faced with the choice between them in the first place: remittance-funded opposition mobilization and weakened clientelism led to close elections that threatened incumbent rule.

## 6.3. Meso-Level Analysis: Remittances, Civil Society, and Opposition Party Strength

In previous chapters, we documented macro-level and micro-level patterns for the key theoretical claims in this book: that financial remittances both weaken loyalty, which we observed as less voter turnout for incumbent ruling parties, and amplify voice, in the form of anti-government protest. The micro-analyses allowed us to scrutinize the pathways connecting remittances to different forms of political behavior at the individual level. They also help adjudicate between competing theoretical mechanisms, by examining how political preferences and socio-economic status shape the behavioral consequences of remittance receipt. We then documented, using global macro-analysis, that remittances are indeed related, at the country level, to increased protests and lower voter turnout in autocracies.

As the cases of Senegal and Cambodia suggest, however, not only do financial remittances influence individual behavior and possibly have macro-political consequences, but they also shape the autonomy and strength of opposition organizations such as parties and civil society groups. In fact, if our theory is correct, we should also observe a connection between remittances and the mobilization of political organizations in autocracies. The agents of political change are not simply individuals who engage in protest activities or who opt out of patronage networks during elections; they are also individuals collectively organized in opposition parties, grassroots associations, and civil society organizations that mobilize and demand democratic change. The rapid spread of multiparty politics in autocracies across the world has broadened the scope of political opportunities for regime opponents to organize. Remitted financial resources, we posit, contribute to this mobilization by boosting the organizational capacity of opposition forces in contexts where regimes typically enjoy a large resource advantage. In fact, a simple extension of the two micro-mechanisms—additional financial resources increasing protest participation (amplifying voice) and loosening clientelistic ties to the regime (weakening loyalty)—also informs our expectations as to how remittances shape political organizations.

The resource model suggests that financial remittances increase the resources flowing to home-country political organizations as a form of "political investment" (O'Mahony 2013). By providing recipient individuals with more resources and fiscal autonomy, remittances increase the pool of citizens who can contribute—with time, effort, and money—to political parties, NGOs, and other grassroots associations that mobilize politically and scrutinize government policies. Additionally, (pro-democratic) homeland organizations and politicians may receive direct economic support from migrants and diasporas, which channel funding from abroad. Political parties and civil society organizations often seek out this international financial support from diasporas, and many of them even have local branches in foreign countries to that end. It is also not uncommon for political candidates to campaign and raise funds in countries hosting large diasporas (Østergaard-Nielsen 2003b; Fitzgerald 2009; Delano 2011; Burgess 2014; Paarlberg 2017).

The clientelism model, which predicts that remittances will weaken loyalty by providing relatively poor voters with resources to extricate themselves from ruling parties' clientelistic networks, also suggests that private, decentralized remittance flows increase the autonomy of local political organizations. More resources and autonomy reduce the regime's ability to co-opt or repress these organizations and hence weaken the government's capacity to prevent the formation of social groups that are independent of the state.[11] We concur with Carothers (1999, 26), who notes that "[w]hen civil society groups wage a campaign for freedom in a dictatorship, a key element of their political bonafides is complete independence, financial and otherwise, from the government."

Additional financial resources and operational space help to emancipate a wide range of organizations from government control in autocracies because these groups often face substantial economic and legal constraints when pursuing their political and social activities, including election campaigns. Thus, similarly to other forms of investment, the marginal effect of remitted income should be higher in low-income, autocratic environments where these resources chip away at the often substantial incumbency advantage that autocratic parties and leaders enjoy (Escribà-Folch et al. 2018). By providing funding for training, campaigning, and coordinating activities, remittances should thus increase the strength, autonomy, and mobilizing capacity of opposition political parties and civil society organizations.

Do remittances strengthen domestic opposition groups? These potential meso-level consequences of remittance flows have not received scholarly attention thus far. Research so far has mostly explored either individual-level effects, such as political attitudes and behavior, or macro-outcomes, such as governance and corruption, but not political organizations themselves.

To test this meso-level mechanism, we examine the autonomy of opposition parties and the "vibrancy" of civil society organizations, using data from the Varieties of Democracy project (Coppedge et al. 2011).[12] The first variable measures the extent to which opposition parties are independent from and autonomous of the ruling regime.[13] The second measures the participatory environment of civil society organizations, their variety, the degree of autonomy from the regime, and the involvement of people in these organizations.[14]

In the following analyses, we examine a global sample of autocracies from 1976 to 2017.[15] We conduct three tests for each outcome. First, we estimate how remittances influence opposition party autonomy, and civil society strength during all periods. Then we restrict the sample to election periods, which we define as election years and the year prior to the election. This sample adjustment captures the idea that remittances may have a more substantial effect on these organizations around election time, including the run-up to elections when these groups may seek funds and other critical resources from abroad (O'Mahony 2013). Finally, we look at non-electoral periods, which are all years other than election years or the year prior to an election. The specification adjusts for the following potential confounders: economic growth, GDP per capita, population size, net migration, and foreign movement restrictions.

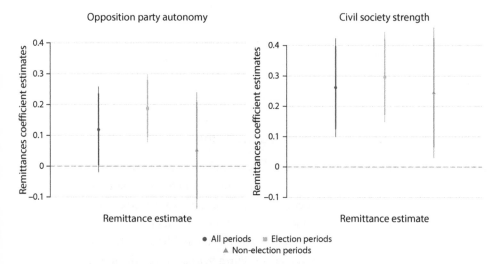

FIGURE 6.2. Remittances strengthen opposition parties and civil society organizations

Figure 6.2 reports the results. The left plot displays estimates for remittances for the three tests of opposition party autonomy. The full sample estimate, shown on the far left, is positive, but only statistically significant at the 0.10 level. In election periods, shown in the middle, the estimate is large and highly statistically significant. In non-election periods, however, the estimate is smaller and not significant. This suggests that there is a positive relationship between remittances and opposition party autonomy, but that it is concentrated in electoral periods. This should not be entirely surprising, because parties often mobilize most during these periods, making it easier to observe and record autonomy when it exists. Further, these organizations may seek such funds more actively during these periods, to increase resources that they can devote to organizing electoral campaigns.

The right plot shows results for civil society strength. In all three tests, the estimate for remittances is positive and significant. This suggests that not only do remittances bolster civil society organizations, but they do so even during non-election periods. This could be due to the fact that civil society organizations exist and operate to provide goods and services as well as to mobilize political pressure during periods between elections, and not just during election season.

Together these results point to a now familiar pattern: remittances boost the capacity and agency of non-state and opposition actors in altering the internal balance of power in autocracies. While the tests in this section cannot pinpoint whether the evidence reflects more a weakening of the loyalty of nominal regime supporters or amplification of dissenting voices, they nonetheless reveal meso-level global patterns consistent with our main theory that remittances undermine autocracy; in part, clearly, by bolstering opposition parties and civil society organizations.

## 6.4. Macro-Level Analysis: Remittances and Democratic Transitions

Our final empirical tests examine how remittances shape the prospects for democratic transition. Our theory and the evidence from analyses of electoral turnout, anti-government protest, and organizational strength all point to remittances as a *bottom-up cause of democratization*: remittances both lower vote turnout for incumbent ruling parties and boost anti-government mobilization in authoritarian regimes. Further, as chapter 2 documents, elections and protests (or a combination of the two) have been the primary paths to democracy during the era of mass migration over the past thirty years.

We examine the empirical link between inward remittance flows and democratic transitions using data on remittances per capita from the World Development Indicators (World Bank 2019b) and data on transitions to democracy from updates to Geddes et al. (2018). A "democratic transition" occurs in a given country-year when an autocratic regime collapses and the subsequent regime is "democratic." We distinguish democratic transitions from autocratic regime collapses where the new regime is not democratic but rather a new autocracy, governed by a different set of elite actors following different formal or informal (but non-democratic) rules of governance. It is important to note that the data-generating processes associated with democratic transitions and autocracy-to-autocracy transitions are fundamentally different: whereas mass anti-regime protest mobilization and election defeats are the primary ways in which democratic transitions occur, military defeat at the hands of armed insurgents and military coups d'état are the primary ways in which autocracies collapse into subsequent autocratic regimes.[16]

Dictatorships differ from each other, moreover, as much as they differ from democracies (Geddes 1999); and regimes arise from distinct historical political-cal economies and colonial histories (Slater 2010; Pepinsky 2014; Wantchekon and García-Ponce 2017). Some are preceded by democracy, or arise in countries with a long history of coups (Lehoucq and Pérez-Liñán 2014); others were constructed from the ruins of colonial empires (Owen 2004) or imposed by foreign military powers (Downes and Monten 2013). These differences both structure opportunities for protest (Wimmer 1997; Boudreau 2009) and shape the strategies—repression, co-optation, and elections—upon which regimes rely to survive in power (Gerschewski 2013). Further, different autocracies take distinct policy approaches towards emigration: some, such as Zimbabwe's government, attempt to curtail emigration, while others, such as those in Cambodia and Vietnam, encourage it (United Nations 2013, 68–70). We thus test an estimator that accounts for all differences between autocracies in the level of remittances, emigration policy, and in the baseline opportunity for democratic transition.[17] This approach means that we identify whether changes over time in the level of remittances in dictatorships are associated with the probability of democratic transition.

As regards accounting for confounders, first we test a specification that only includes a measure of remittance inflows. This ensures that our attempts to account for potential confounding factors are not in any way biasing results. A second specification adjusts for economic growth, because we know that remittances boost family incomes and may temporarily accelerate economic growth, which, in turn, may persuade citizens to forgo mobilizing protest and to vote for the incumbent. A third specification adjusts for additional potential confounders: neighbor democratization, GDP per capita, net migration, movement restrictions, and elections. Via diffusion effects, neighbor democratization both shapes regime survival and likely influences remittance receipt from neighboring countries; and level of development is one of the main structural features of polities shaping both democratization and the incentive for potential economic emigrants to leave in search of better opportunities. To ensure that financial remittances—and not migration itself or domestic migration policies—account for the result, we adjust for net migration and government restrictions on foreign movement. Finally, elections are an immediate occasion for democratic transitions, and we know that remittances increase around election time.

Figure 6.3 shows the results from these tests. All explanatory variables, save the *Election* variable, have been standardized so that estimates reflect the marginal effect of a one-standard deviation increase in the variable on the probability of democratic transition. In all three specifications, the estimate for remittances is positive and statistically significant; it varies between 1.6 percent and 2.1 percent, depending on the exact specification.[18]

To put this finding in context, we note that the baseline risk of democratic transition in the five-year period from 1982 to 1987 was 1.5 percent, but that during the wave of democratization at the close of the Cold War, during the

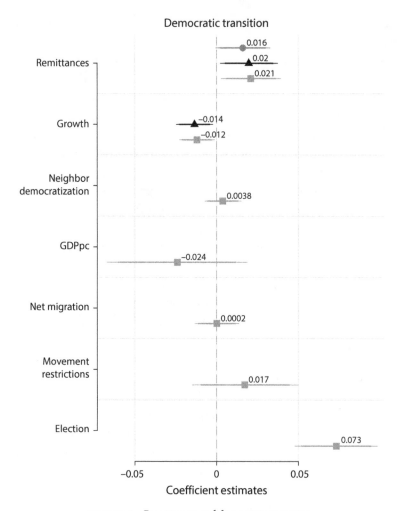

FIGURE 6.3. Remittances and democratic transitions

five-year period from 1987 to 1992, this risk increased to 5.2 percent. Thus from the mid-1980s to the collapse of the Cold War order, the rate of democratization increased by 3.7 percent. The remittance effect on democratization, as reported in Figure 6.3, is roughly half that size. So while we know that the collapse of the Cold War global order was a massive democratizing force, our findings indicate that the flow of remittances to dictatorships in the Global South could be as large as half that size.

Another way to interpret the remittance effect on democratization, is to compare the size of the remittance estimate to that for economic growth and elections. The growth effect varies between −1.2 to −1.4 percent; thus the remittance effect, according to these estimates, is larger than the growth effect. The estimate for elections, however, is much larger (7.3 percent). This suggests that the marginal effect of remittances on the prospect of democratic transition is larger than the growth effect, but considerably smaller than the direct effect of elections.

This empirical evidence linking remittances to democratization all points in the same direction: remittances increase the prospects of democratic transition in autocratic regimes. This macro-result is consistent with the micro-mechanisms—weakened loyalty and increased voice—that we have documented in prior chapters and that suggest that by receiving income from migrants, citizens become more likely to make use of bottom-up mechanisms of democratization: protests and elections. The results also conform with the meso-level patterns identified earlier in this chapter showing that remittances are associated with greater opposition party autonomy and stronger civil society organizations, which are essential collective actors in any bottom-up effort at political change.

## 6.5. Remittances and Democratic Transition in The Gambia

As a final illustration of the processes that we unpack in this chapter, consider the case of The Gambia. As in the cases of Cambodia and Senegal, we document how remittances shape the behavior of citizens and opposition groups, not the behavior of elite actors such as the state security forces, the incumbent president, or international agents.

The Gambia is one of the most remittance-dependent countries in sub-Saharan Africa and these monetary flows narrowed the resource gap between the regime and the opposition in the decade leading up to the 2016 election. The presidential election that year saw the opposition leader, Adama Barrow, and his 'Coalition 2016' grouping of opposition parties oust incumbent president Yahya Jammeh of the Alliance for Patriotic Reorientation and Construction (APRC), who had been in power for over twenty years. Although Jammeh initially accepted Barrow's victory, a week later he declared the election invalid due to irregularities. Barrow took refuge in the embassy of The Gambia in Senegal shortly afterwards, while Jammeh, following the threat of intervention by ECOWAS troops, negotiated his own exit to Equatorial Guinea (Hultin et al. 2017; Kora and Darboe 2017, 147–48). The defeat of Jammeh, which was largely unexpected, had multiple causes, but many scholars suggest that it resulted in part from deteriorating economic and political conditions and a subsequent increase in emigration, together with the mobilization of the diaspora during the election (Hultin et al. 2017; Kora and Darboe 2017).

The Gambia is one of the poorest countries in the world. During Jammeh's rule, the economy collapsed amid declining agricultural exports due to climate change, low tourism revenues, and high debt levels. Rising cost of living and massive youth unemployment translated into increasing poverty. Widespread illiteracy, especially in rural areas, led to persistent social and political exclusion (Kora and Darboe 2017, 150). As a consequence of economic mismanagement, the country saw persistent emigration from the 1990s, which intensified in the 2000s. By 2010, approximately 4 percent of the population had emigrated.[19] Gambians have a history of migrating to neighboring Senegal. Outside Africa, they have settled mostly in Spain, the USA, the UK, Germany, and Sweden (Hultin et al. 2017, 336). Much of this migration is irregular. For a large number of young Gambians, taking the "back way" (emigrating irregularly) expressed the frustration, anger, and despair they felt, as well as their desire for "change" (Hultin et al. 2017).

Jammeh's responses to increasing social unrest and demands for political change were erratic, often reacting to dissent with violent repression. As a result, besides the economic migration described above, Gambian asylum applications in Europe rose by 371 percent between 2012 and 2014 (Hultin et al. 2017, 338). This increase can be directly linked to Jammeh's heavy-handed response to opposition mobilization. Together with the large scale of irregular emigration, political emigration became a source of societal interest frequently discussed and diffused in social media, where it was directly linked to Jammeh's abuses. Gambians were literally "voting with their feet," and by so doing, were shaping "the electorate's composition and choice in December 2016" (Hultin et al. 2017, 340, 322).

In addition to criticizing and publicizing political repression and the regime's mismanagement of the economy, emigrants sent remittances. In The Gambia, remittances far surpass FDI inflows (Altrogge and Zanker 2019). In 2014, they amounted to 10 percent of the country's GDP, jumping to 14 percent in 2016 and reaching a peak in 2017.[20] This increase can be traced at least in part to the diaspora's strategy in support of a unified opposition in the 2016 election. Pressure from the diaspora and civil society groups pushed opposition groups to call a convention to hold a primary election that chose a single candidate from among seven opposition parties. Adama Barrow emerged as the winner of the convention, representing the "Coalition 2016."

Emigrants' remittances strengthened the opposition by financing parts of the election campaign, even paying the presidential candidate registration fee (Zanker and Altrogge 2019, 171), which Jammeh had increased tenfold in an attempt to raise the costs to the opposition of participation (Hultin et al. 2017; Kora and Darboe 2017). As Kora and Darboe (2017, 152) describe it, "in previous elections, the biggest opposition handicap had been lack of money and resources to match the APRC machine with its state assets. To close the gap, diaspora activists used crowd-funding apps and websites, raising enough to turn the wheels of a hard-driving opposition campaign. For the first time in Gambian history, opposition rallies eclipsed ruling-party gatherings all over the country."

Besides working with civil society to support a unified opposition with a chance of winning, the diaspora played a crucial role in helping to mobilize those left behind. A broad coalition of overseas Gambians comprising the highly skilled diaspora, irregular migrants, and political refugees used social media tools to inform their families and friends in their homeland about Jammeh's abuses, hoping "to influence them to vote against him" (Zanker and Altrogge 2019, 171). The extensive use of smartphones enabled diaspora political movements "to communicate freely with illiterate and previously disengaged Gambian voters in their own local languages" (Kora and Darboe 2017, 151). Thanks to migrant activism, the diaspora provided essential resources and opened spaces for debating and expressing dissent, shaping the political narrative. By working closely with Gambians back home, the diaspora provided crucial informational resources about the regime's abuses that "those on the ground were able to turn into action" against Jammeh (Altrogge and Zanker 2019, 36).

## 6.6. Conclusion

Remittances are the most tangible transnational flow that migrants generate, and one that, according to the evidence presented in this chapter, assists bottom-up efforts to democratize political rule in the Global South. Worried, if not indeed obsessed, by the socio-economic and political effects of migration in *migrant-host* countries, policy debates have largely overlooked the profound and positive transformations that migration, via remittances, contribute to democratization efforts in *migrant-sending* countries.

This chapter has provided evidence that the money migrants send back home contributes to democratization in the Global South—at both the meso- and the macro-levels. We first demonstrated that remittances boost the strength and autonomy of opposition political parties and civil society organizations, critical actors in the story of democratization who are largely overlooked by the literature on the political consequences of remittances. Second, we showed that financial remittances increase the chance of democratic transitions in a global sample of dictatorships, spanning four decades.

In previous chapters we argued that remittances increase protest and reduce electoral support for incumbents in autocracies. This chapter's evidence confirms that these dynamics do indeed undermine dictatorship, and have profound political consequences for democratization. In the next chapter, we test whether our findings hold once we take into account "social remittances." The final chapter then builds on these findings by discussing their implications for debates about the merits of globalization, and for understanding how migration policy can serve as a tool for the promotion of democracy.

# 7

# Social Remittances and Financial Remittances

While human migration has always been associated with increased communication and knowledge transfer, advances in information and communication technologies (ICT) have accelerated this trend during the most recent period of mass labor migration. New ICTs render the physical distance separating migrant families less relevant, as many digital alternatives to in-person meetings now exist. Indeed, many of the same technological advances that facilitate the rapid and decentralized transfer of monetary remittances also reduce the difficulty and cost of keeping in touch with relatives and friends in home countries. Globally, more than 4 billion people now use the internet; there are more than 5 billion unique mobile subscribers; and roughly 3.6 billion mobile internet users (GSMA 2012; International Telecommunication Union 2019). Almost the entire world population now lives within range of a mobile-cellular network signal, and broadband access continues to grow.

International calls are now routine for millions of families across the globe. According to some estimates, international over-the-top (OTT) voice traffic reached one trillion minutes in 2019; while international carrier traffic was estimated at 432 billion minutes (Telegeography 2020). Labor migration across borders accounts for a substantial portion of this global traffic (Perkins and Neumayer 2013). OTT communication services—such as WhatsApp, Facebook Messenger, WeChat, Skype, Viber, Line, and KakaoTalk—make cross-border communication cheaper and more accessible to migrants and their families. Social media and video chat are rapidly replacing international voice calls and roaming services.

Up to this point, we have argued that financial remittances, which for many countries ruled by autocratic governments is the largest source of foreign monetary flows, largely circumvent governments and instead flow to agents of democratic change, namely citizens. We then showed that remittance income in recipient autocracies increases political opposition resources and decreases government-dependence, two mechanisms that undermine dictatorships and foster democracy. In the previous chapter, we brought these arguments together to show that financial remittances do indeed boost opposition autonomy and increase the likelihood of democratic transition. Central to our argument and evidence are financial remittances.

However, most emigrants not only send their relatives back home financial resources, but also share their experiences and newly acquired beliefs about their societies of destination with them, including their political experiences. ICTs enable individuals to maintain personal and social relationships across countries and thus help redefine the identities, ideas, and values these individuals hold (Alonso and Oiarzabal 2010). The operation of these so-called "social remittances" presents a possible challenge to our main argument and evidence, which highlight the role of *financial* resources sent by migrants. The literature on social remittances contends that these informational exchanges might induce non-migrants to change their political behavior and/or preferences, potentially becoming and acting as "agents of social change."

These mechanisms bring forward not only the potential effect of nontangible cross-national flows, but also the importance of the regime type of migrants' destination countries, since pro-democratic values and practices need to be first acquired (or learned) by migrants in host societies before they can transmit these back home. Although, as we highlighted in chapter 1, most migrants go to high-income countries in the Global North, many seek new opportunities in countries governed by non-democratic regimes. In fact, according to recent data (International Organization for Migration 2020), of the top six international migrant destinations, three are democracies (the USA, Germany, and the UK) and three are dictatorships (Saudi Arabia, Russia, and the United Arab Emirates). Thus social remittances, especially those originating in democratic countries, rather than financial flows might explain why migration and the exchange between emigrant workers and their families back home facilitate the political behaviors—increasing protest and decreasing electoral support for incumbents—that we identify as the main micro-mechanisms linking out-migration from autocracies to democratization.

This chapter takes up this issue. We first articulate the predominant arguments linking social remittances to political behavior in migrant-sending countries. We then discuss how these theories may either challenge our findings—by suggesting that social remittances simply do the work that we attribute to financial remittances—or complement our argument—if they suggest that social remittances simply enhance the impact of financial remittances in boosting protest against autocratic governments and undermining electoral support for them. We then propose two empirical strategies, one suited for macro-analysis and the other for micro-level analysis, that help shed light on these issues. We find no significant differences between countries attributable to where remittances originate. We also find that the impact of remittances on political behavior is not explained by how remittances shape political discussion; however, political discussion magnifies the effect of remittances on the likelihood of protesting.

## 7.1. Social Remittances: Mechanisms and Evidence

Social remittances are "the ideas, behaviors, identities, and social capital that flow from receiving- to sending-country communities" (Levitt 1998, 927).[1] Based on Levitt's seminal work on social remittances, a more concrete strand of research focuses on political remittances, defined as "the act of transferring political principles, vocabulary and practices between two or more places, which migrants and their descendants share a connection with" (Krawatzek and Müller-Funk 2020, 1,004). The authors add that "political remittances are remoulded in a context of migration, and can, in turn, influence political behavior, mobilisation, organisation and narratives of belonging in places of destination and origin." In this chapter, we follow this slightly narrower definition of political remittances.

The types of norm that are communicated to those who remain in the home country depend on migrants' pre-departure characteristics and their integration in the country of destination, factors which in turn determine their exposure to domestic political life in the destination (Levitt and Lamba-Nieves 2011). Factors such as legal and employment status, length of stay, prospects of return, and connections with existing migrant networks all shape migrants' experience in destination countries and their propensity to remain engaged with their localities of origin (Waldinger 2008). The types of political institution and economic context migrants experience while abroad may also determine the kind of political socialization they undergo (Guarnizo et al. 2003; Itzigsohn and Villacres 2008; Escobar et al. 2015; Ahmadov and Sasse 2016). Simplifying somewhat, those emigrating to Gulf countries, where they may well experience severe restrictions upon their mobility and dire working conditions, are likely to transmit different experiences to relatives than emigrants based in advanced industrial countries where fundamental rights are by and large respected. However, even those emigrating to advanced countries often remain excluded from formal work and meaningful political participation, if not ostracized on account of the stigma of "crime" and illegality.

Political remittances might thus depend on whether emigration is politically motivated or whether it is mostly driven by economic necessity. While the distinction may be blurred in practice, it is important to consider it: an emigrant fleeing political repression in a dictatorship may be reluctant to choose another dictatorship as a destination country. Arguably, s/he may be more likely to transmit ideas and information about the existence of a "rights gap" between the home and the host countries. At the same time, however, s/he is also more likely to have developed or prioritized these ideas before leaving. Thus, in principle, an émigré to an advanced democracy is more likely to send resources to support democratization in the home country (Rother 2009; Pérez-Armendáriz 2014; Krawatzek and Müller-Funk 2020; Miller and Peters 2020; Fomina 2021).

Measuring "political" remittances in a convincing way remains an important challenge for this debate. In fact, empirical exploration of social and political remittances is in its infancy. Scholars have attempted to meet this challenge in various ways, such as by relying on survey data that explicitly ask about the frequency and content of communication between emigrants and their families and about remittance receipt. This research disentangles the effect of social remittances from economic remittances by exploring how they shape engagement in political persuasion, electoral turn out, and participation in civic associations back home see (see Goodman and Hiskey 2008; Pérez-Armendáriz and Crow 2010; Córdova and Hiskey 2015; Meseguer et al. 2016; Paarlberg 2017; Crow and Pérez-Armendáriz 2018). Others go by the totals of emigrants under different types of destination regime to make the implicit assumption that only those emigrants based in democratic countries are likely to send back "democratic remittances"—ideas, norms, and views that highlight the positives of democratic rule (see Mirilovic 2015; Barsbai et al. 2017; Maydom 2017; Miller and Peters 2020); whilst, by contrast, "undemocratic" political remittances may flow from those based in autocratic countries (Rother 2009; Barsbai et al. 2017). Finally, some rely on extensive historical evidence to show how democratizing ideas and resources flow from democracies to home countries, shaping institution-building in the latter. For instance, the emergence of labor movements in Germany (Schmidt 2020), the empowerment of workers in Norway (Moses 2011), and the weakening of Tsarist rule in Russia (Hartnett 2020) all have been traced back to active promotion from abroad by the respective diasporas.

We posit that remittances sent from democratic destinations may be sent with democratic intentions and thus support democratic causes: with the purpose, that is, of supporting anti-incumbent protests in dictatorships and facilitating the political autonomy of recipients from clientelistic regimes. Alternatively, remittances may simply be anti-incumbent, which suggests that those with emigrant experience, past or present, or with contact with emigrants, are more critical than non-migrants in judging the quality of politics in their home countries (Pérez-Armendáriz and Crow 2010; Crow and Pérez-Armendáriz 2018), independently of the origin of remittances (Rother 2009).[2]

In sum, while we know that remittances may be sent with political intentions, as suggested by their increase around election time (O'Mahony 2013; Nyblade and O'Mahony 2014; Paarlberg 2017), we unpack the social remittance debate from the perspective of the autocratic home countries where they are received. Thinking about financial remittances as in themselves carrying a democratic message helps to recast a debate that too often treats financial remittances as loose proxies substituting for social remittances to explain changes in political behavior. By contrast, we revisit the contention that social and financial remittances, or in other words, ideas and resources, may in fact reinforce each other (Levitt 1998; Lacroix et al. 2016). We explore whether their predominant origin in democratic host countries enhances the propensity to protest against and disengage electorally from autocracies. If financial remittances carry some democratizing message with them, this message should be transmitted through engagement in political discussions with relatives abroad and with others.[3] Finding that the impact of financial remittances on protest and voting is not magnified or entirely mediated by recipients' propensity to discuss politics will be evidence, even if indirect, that cash remittances impact behavior through the income effects spelled out in previous chapters.

## 7.2. Political Remittances and Destination Regime Type

Emigrants normally maintain close contact with their relatives. As Soehl and Waldinger (2010, 1,498) note, "the simple phone call . . . plays a central role for the majority of migrants." The internet and social media are increasingly important channels for migrants to keep connected with family and friends and for emigrants to become involved in home-country politics (Córdova and Hiskey 2015, 1,464). For instance, about 94 percent of Latin American households with a family member abroad communicate with that member at least occasionally, 65 percent do so at least once or twice a month, and 35 percent at least one or twice a week (Crow and Pérez-Armendáriz 2018, 251). Non-migrants with relatives abroad are more likely to follow national and international news (Pérez-Armendáriz 2014). These transborder conversations often concern political and social aspects of migrants' lives in their destination countries. Through circular travel, involvement in their communities, and distant communication, migrants discuss aspects of their daily life abroad and share them with their non-migrant co-nationals: topics such as their access to health and education, their experience in dealing with host bureaucracies, or their participation in their host communities are often the subject of transborder conversations. Citizens may talk with their emigrant relatives about alternative forms of participation beyond party politics, the value of tolerance, the perils of corruption, or equity in gender relations (Pérez-Armendáriz 2014). These exchanges shape the political behavior of recipients, altering their propensity to engage politically. Their influence may be most evident in shaping non-electoral political activities, such as attempting to persuade others to vote and participation in the political life of communities (Pérez-Armendáriz and Crow 2010; Careja and Emmenegger 2012; Córdova and Hiskey 2015; Paarlberg 2017).

An important corollary of these arguments is the suggestion that non-migrant co-nationals learn from migrants to depend less on the state for the undertaking of public works, searching instead for alternative, private ways of funding public goods (Pérez-Armendáriz 2014, 79). Because emigrants are important role models in their families and communities, and because of the asymmetric power relations that accompany the transmission of remittances, conversations and contact with migrants abroad shape the direction of relatives' vote at home (Kapur 2010; Vari-Lavoisier 2016). While the sending of remittances to the home country is unlikely to be conditional on voting, those who receive remittances appear more receptive to political influence from relatives abroad (Paarlberg 2017, 547). Transborder communication may thus reinforce the political consequences of monetary remittances, activating sympathizers and reinforcing partisan ties.

A crucial, yet still under-researched, extension of the social remittances debate concerns the political regime in the migrant-destination country.

International linkages and the nature of exchange networks influence domestic politics. It is important to take notice of evidence to suggests that while ties to democracies contribute positively to democratization, stronger ties to dictatorships may reinforce autocratic rule (see Levitsky and Way 2010; Tolstrup 2013; Goodliffe and Hawkins 2017; Tansey et al. 2017). Acknowledging that migrants live and work in both dictatorships and democracies begs the question of how the destination political regime shapes both socialization and integration, and subsequently the type of political remittances migrants send back home. First, emigrant self-selection may mean that those who value democracy more are the most likely to migrate to democratic destinations. This is most likely true of politically induced emigration, such as that of those who choose exile from autocracies amid armed conflict and political repression (Mirilovic 2015), but it is less clear whether it applies in the case of economic migration.[4] In the latter case, economic factors such as unemployment rates in the destination country, income expectations, physical distance, and existing migrant networks are the main factors shaping the decisions to leave (Hatton and Williamson 2008; Mayda 2010; Ferrie and Hatton 2013). For instance, in his study of overseas Filipino worker (OFW) returnees, Rother (2009, 272) asserts that "[i]t is unlikely that migrants consciously choose their destination country primarily according to democratic criteria, because their main motive is economic (and ... [in-depth interviews] confirm that migrants tend to take the first assignment abroad offered to them)." Second, while abroad, migrants experience different political contexts, which change their perception of the value of democracy in general, and of civil liberties in particular.

This extension to the debate tries to overcome the positive bias in the political-remittance literature, which too often portrays the transfer of ideas as necessarily favoring beliefs about the virtues of democracy and good governance. Rather, the types of regime prevailing in the destination country may have its effect: political remittances may sometimes be "undemocratic" (Rother 2009). For example, Moldovan emigrants either settle in Western destinations, mostly Italy, or head to Russia. High rates of emigration to Russia turn out to be a predictor of an increase in electoral support for the Moldovan Communist Party in migrants' municipalities of origin, while the opposite effect is produced by emigration to Western destinations (Barsbai et al. 2017). Eastern European natives with emigrant relatives based in Western destinations are more likely to participate in EU elections, an effect that is not evident in the case of the families of emigrants heading to non-Western destinations (Careja and Emmenegger 2012); Egyptian voters with emigrant relatives in the Gulf countries are more likely to vote for Islamist parties locally in what apparently reflects a transfer of religious norms (Karakoç et al. 2017); Malians who migrate to France have different attitudes toward Malian democracy than migrants based in undemocratic Côte d'Ivoire (Chauvet et al. 2016); and developing country elites based in Western democracies may transmit democratic values upon return (Spilimbergo 2009).[5]

Since sending funds is usually part and parcel of the political remittance bundle, political and financial remittances may reinforce one other. This logic suggests the benefit of exploring whether remittances sent by emigrants based in democratic countries have a particular effect on the political behaviors of stayers. Some recent research shows that emigration of political dissidents to Western democracies has often involved sending financial resources, along with ideas, to facilitate dissidents' activities and anti-incumbent social movements at home (Hartnett 2020; Fomina 2021).[6] For this chapter, the relevant question is whether the democratizing effect of remittances stems only from migrants settling in advanced democracies, or whether it occurs in relation to all sources of financial remittances. For example, it could be the case that financial remittances—at least as we have measured them in prior chapters—are simply a proxy for political remittances from democracies, and that these political remittances foster values that increase political participation, including anti-government protest. Further, perhaps only remittances sent from advanced democracies, and not those destination countries ruled by autocratic governments, reduce participation in autocratic elections at home, by liberating recipients from patronage networks. Or it could well be that extrication from clientelistic relationships happens independently of the autocratic or democratic character of the regime in the country from which remittances originate. In short, distinguishing between autocratic and democratic origins of remittances may serve as a proxy, if only approximate, to identify whether financial remittances come with some (presumably pro-democratic) political message attached to them.

Because political ideas are transmitted via transborder communication (Córdova and Hiskey 2015; 2019) or through a transnational relationship that alters beliefs that are then shared with others locally through political discussion (Crow and Pérez-Armendáriz 2018; Batista et al. 2019), we look at whether political discussion mediates or catalyzes the impact of financial remittances on political behavior. In so doing, we unpack the social remittance debate in regard to home-country dictatorships, a topic largely unexplored to date.

The next two sections examine two empirical implications of these arguments, one at the micro-level and one at the macro-level. The macro-tests employ global data on the migrant-destination country and bilateral remittance flows to distinguish between autocracies such as Mexico (coded as an autocracy in the 1990s) and Morocco, where remittance inflows largely come from family members residing in democracies (e.g., the USA and France, respectively), and autocracies such as Chad and Yemen, where most remittance inflows originate in Gulf countries ruled by autocratic governments. In these tests, we re-examine the macro-evidence from each of our main empirical chapters as to how or whether remittances boost anti-government protest, lower incumbent vote shares, and increase the chances of democratic transition. If the heart of evidence for these patterns stems from countries where most remittances originate in democracies, then we cannot be certain that our findings are *not* driven by social rather than financial remittances. However, if we find mixed evidence, or that the patterns largely derive from places where remittances tend to come from autocratic migrant-destination countries, it will be difficult to attribute our findings entirely to political remittances.

While it would be possible to pursue a similar strategy of dividing the sample for the micro-analysis, there are too few countries in the Afrobarometer sample that are both ruled by autocratic governments and also receive most of their remittances from autocracies to make reliable inferences.[7] Instead, we examine a micro-behavioral implication of the political remittances argument: that remittances either influence individual behavior through political discussion or that discussing politics amplifies a cash-remittance effect. These types of test allow for the possibility that financial and social remittances complement one another, rather than being alternative mechanisms, in the shaping of political behavior.

## 7.3. Remittances from Migrants Residing in Democratic and Autocratic Countries

In this section we re-examine macro-evidence presented in earlier chapters to see whether the main empirical result derives mostly from countries in the analysis that receive most of their remittances from democracies. To do this, we have to estimate the origins of remittances to autocracies. We calculate the relative share of remittances sent from democracies and from autocracies as a continuous variable, but conceptually, we can think of two groups of autocracies. The first comprises those where emigrants mostly reside in democracies, such that most of their inward flow of remittances is from democratic migrant-destination countries; we might call this group *democratic-remittance recipients*. The major emigrant-destination democracies include the USA and the EU countries, along with Nigeria (after 1999) and South Africa (after 1994). The second group comprises countries ruled by autocratic governments the majority of whose emigrants reside in countries also ruled by autocratic government, such that most of the inward flow of remittances comes from autocratic countries. Among the largest emigrant-destination autocracies are the Gulf monarchies and Russia; we might call this group *autocratic-remittance recipients*.[8]

The distinction between these groups of remittance recipient countries does not necessarily imply that all remittances from emigrants residing in democracies are, in fact, "political" remittances that come with a pro-democracy message. And similarly, all remittances sent from predominantly autocratic countries do not necessarily embody anti-democratic information that boosts support for autocratic government (or even any incumbent government) among recipients. Indeed, when we divide the sample of countries with autocratic governments into democratic-remittance recipients and autocratic-remittance recipients, this distinction parallels other differences as regards migration regimes and remittances in addition to any relating to possible "democratic" norms transfers.

For example, democratic countries hosting migrants from developing countries tend to have more restrictive migration policies, limiting the number and type of migrants legally permitted to enter the country and work there (Ruhs 2013); however, such destination democracies also tend to provide more legal rights to the migrants who do live and work within their borders. By contrast, countries with autocratic governments that host many migrants tend to have more permissive migration policies, that permit entry to more low-skilled migrant labor (Shin 2017); but these same destination countries also tend to severely restrict the social and economic rights of these migrant workers. Ruhs (2013, ch. 4) provides substantial cross-country evidence that Gulf countries (ruled by autocratic governments) have more permissive low-skilled labor immigration policies than the largest democratic migrant destinations such as the USA and the EU. Paralleling this finding, he also shows that democratic migrant destinations tend to provide more legal economic and social rights for immigrants than do migrant destinations ruled by autocratic governments, such as the Gulf monarchies and Russia.

Thus Ruhs's (2015) analysis suggests that there is a trade-off, at least empirically, between migrant rights in destination countries and the "openness" of these countries' migration policies. For our purposes, these two dimensions, migrant rights in the destination country and migration policy openness, map onto our empirical distinction between democratic-remittance and autocratic-remittance recipient countries. That is, migration to and remittances from more democratic destinations may not only transmit democratic norms and practices via "social remittances" but may also transmit beliefs about social and economic rights, as well as beliefs about the value of "openness" and globalization. In short, when we divide destination countries into categories based on whether they are ruled by democratic or autocratic governments, this variation also corresponds to variation in migrants' experiences of rights protection in their destination countries, and perhaps even their notions of liberalization and globalization.

These other dimensions of migrant experience—rights protection in destination countries and openness—may confound any interpretation of empirical results that implies that democratic norms account for differences that we might observe between the political consequences of remittances in democratic-remittance and in autocratic-remittance recipients respectively. That said, we can still use this exercise to search for some evidence that remittances we know mostly to come from autocratic destinations nevertheless boost protest, lower electoral turnout, and increase the chances of democratization. If we can find such evidence, we can rule out the possibility that our main findings derive solely from "political" rather than financial remittances. However, given the various caveats noted above, we cannot necessarily take evidence that remittances from mostly democratic countries shape politics in autocracies as confirmation of the political remittances argument as other norms too may flow in along with cash from these destinations.

### 7.3.1. Remittances Flows from Democratic and Autocratic Origins

The appendix to this chapter discusses how we measure remittance inflow from different migrant-destination countries. We calculate remittances from democracies and autocracies by reorganizing bilateral remittance matrices using weights constructed by Azizi (2018, 385). We then classify migrant-destination countries by whether they are democratic or autocratic; and

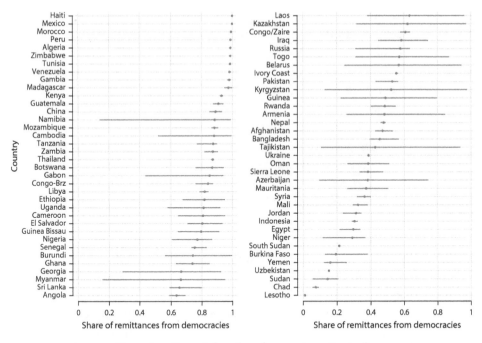

FIGURE 7.1. Share of remittance inflows from democracies: estimates for 1990–2015

finally calculate remittances from democracies as a share of all remittances as a country-level average from 1990 to 2015.

Figure 7.1 shows this average *Democratic share of remittances* for all autocracies in the sample, as a gray dot. Horizontal black lines represent the minimum and maximum values of the *yearly* shares for each country. The country names are ordered from those with the highest *Democratic share of remittances* in the left plot to those with the lowest in right plot.

Three important points emerge that help explain these patterns. First, countries that are geographically close to the USA and EU and also relatively distant from Gulf monarchies receive most of their remittances from democracies, as expected; this applies to countries such as Algeria, Haiti, Mexico, and Morocco that received nearly all their remittances from democracies. Conversely, countries such as Chad, Sudan, and Yemen, located nearer to the Persian Gulf, receive most remittances from autocracies. Second, some countries, such as Cambodia, Namibia, and Tajikistan, appear to have substantial yearly variation in their share of remittances from democracies. This is less likely to stem from shifting migration patterns as from changes in the type of regime in the migrant-destination country, as in South Africa in 1994 and Thailand in 1991–92 and 2006–7. Other countries show less variation over time. Lesotho, for example, which was ruled by an autocratic government until 1993, receives nearly all of its remittances from South Africa, which was ruled by a dictatorship until 1994. Thus for Lesotho's years as an autocracy during the sample period (1990–93), all remittances come from an autocracy (South Africa), and this share of remittances from autocracy does not shift during these years.

Finally, this measure, of *Democratic share of remittances*, shows that the majority of the autocracies listed received most of their remittances during the 1990s and 2000s from democracies: almost two-thirds of these countries (46 of 71) received half or more of their remittances from democracies, while nearly half (33 of 71) received more than two-thirds from democracies. Only 18 percent (13 of 71) of these countries received more than two-thirds of their remittances from autocracies rather than democracies.

While yearly data on remittances from different destinations have some advantages, because annual data capture possible changes in migration destination patterns as well as changes in political regime type in destination countries, we view the averaging approach as superior for our purposes. The case of Haiti illustrates this point: the yearly data are missing for the 1990s, but not the 2000s. By using the country-average, we recover observations for Haiti during the 1990s and we do not think that the migrant destination preference changed much between the two decades: in both periods the vast majority of Haitian emigrants left for the USA and most remittances flowing into Haiti thus came from a democracy in both periods. We lose more information and introduce more possible bias, we posit, when we exclude Haiti in the 1990s than when we include it but attribute the estimated share remittances from democracies in the 2000s also to the 1990s. For migrant-destination countries that change political regime type during the sample period, moreover, thus altering whether remittances sent from these countries come from a democracy or an autocracy, averaging destination regime type over two or more decades captures the fact that these destination countries are not, in fact, long-standing durable democracies (or autocracies) with well-entrenched democratic (or autocratic) political practices, norms, and values. By averaging over decades, our approach places these countries somewhere in the middle of the distribution of *Democratic share of remittances*.

### 7.3.2.   Revisiting the Macro-Evidence

So what does the evidence suggest? To examine whether the main macro-results are concentrated among countries with a relatively high *Democratic share of remittances*, we re-estimate the empirical models for three outcomes introduced in previous chapters: anti-government protest, incumbent vote share, and democratic transition. Instead of dividing the sample into countries with low and high *Democratic share of remittances*, which would rely on an arbitrary delineation of what constitutes "low" and "high" in this context, we utilize an approach that estimates—and allows us to visualize—the marginal effect of remittances for each data point in the respective samples.[9] For anti-government protest, we examine a sample from 1990 to 2010, and for the other two outcomes the sample extends from 1990 to 2017.

Figure 7.2 reports the results. Each plot shows the marginal effect of remittances for each level of *Democratic share of remittances*. The shaded histogram along the horizontal axis displays the in-sample distribution of *Democratic share of remittances*, and the lines and confidence intervals display the marginal effects of remittances. Each plot also reports the average marginal effect of remittances—across all levels of *Democratic share of remittances*—as a coefficient estimate $(\beta)$. In a standard regression, this average marginal effect is typically what we interpret. In these plots, we visualize how the marginal effect of remittances varies as the *Democratic share of remittances* changes.

Recall that if the main macro-results are concentrated among countries with higher *Democratic share of remittances*, then we should observe stronger marginal effects along the right-hand side of each plot (higher values along the horizontal axis); and we could interpret this as possibly showing that political remittances, which presumably only transmit pro-democracy information and norms when originating in democracies, account for the main findings. However, if we find that the marginal effect of remittances is relatively stable across all values of *Democratic share of remittances*, or if the effects are strongest for countries with low values of *Democratic share of remittances*, then we can rule out the possibility that the main macro-findings result solely from political remittances.

The top plot shows the result for anti-government protest. The average marginal effect of remittances is 0.144, indicating that, from 1990 to 2010, remittances increase protest, similar to the result we found in chapter 4 for a sample period that extends back to the late 1970s. Across a range of values for *Democratic share of remittances*, this estimate remains relatively stable. The confidence interval, for example, never falls below 0.10 or increases to more than 0.17. This indicates that, since 1990, remittances are associated with more anti-government protest for countries that receive most remittances from democracy, but also for countries that receive most remittances from

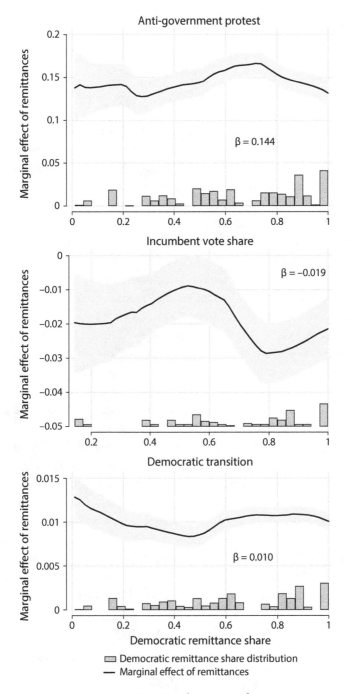

FIGURE 7.2. Revisiting the macro-evidence

autocracies and those that receive a mix of remittances, from both democratic and autocratic countries. In short, there is little evidence that the remittance effect is concentrated among countries with high *Democratic share of remittances*.

The middle plot in Figure 7.2 shows results for incumbent vote share; the average marginal effect of remittances is −0.019. At the lowest levels of *Democratic share of remittances*, the remittance effect is roughly the same as the average (about −0.02); and at the highest levels it is slightly stronger than average (between −0.03 and −0.02). Finally, the remittance effect is weakest at middle levels of *Democratic share of remittances*. However, even here the marginal effect is still negative and significant. Again, there is little evidence here that the main remittance effect on incumbent vote share is concentrated among countries that receive most of their remittances from democracies.

The bottom plot shows the results for democratic transition. Recall that democratic transitions are low-likelihood events to begin with, occurring at about 3.8 percent a year in autocracies from 1990 to 2017. Given this, the average marginal effect during the period is estimated at 1 percent. This marginal effect appears to be strongest for countries at the lowest levels of *Democratic share of remittances*, weakest in the middle, and about average for the highest levels. Nevertheless, the estimated effect never strays too far from the average effect of 1 percent. As with the other two outcomes, these tests for democratic transition provide little evidence that the remittance effect is isolated among countries with high *Democratic shares of remittances*.

In sum, in view of this evidence, there are few grounds to assert that only countries with high levels of *Democratic share of remittances* are more likely to experience the processes described so far. Moreover, since our indicator of *Democratic share of remittances* is correlated with social and economic rights and with immigration policy regime in destination countries, "political remittances" may be a concept too narrow to describe the range of experiences that emigrants transmit. Having said that, the tests above should be taken as a "first cut" in exploring political remittances, since our measure *Democratic share of remittances* is necessarily crude due to missing bilateral remittance data.

## 7.4. Does Political Discussion Mediate or Moderate How Remittances Shape Behavior?

The section examines the possibility that remittance receipt, which in addition to being a transfer of resources may also imply a transfer of norms, shapes individual political behavior—protest and vote turnout—by working through interpersonal discussions of politics. If sending financial remittances carries a message along with the funds, social and financial remittances would not be two alternative mechanisms, but rather two factors that reinforce one other (Levitt 1998; Kapur 2010; Carling 2014; Lacroix et al. 2016). Because the impact of changed beliefs may be shared via political discussions, we want to know whether, net of the ideational transfer that may accompany financial remittances, the resource aspect of remittances continues to play a role.

Empirical research in this area overwhelmingly focuses on Mexico and Latin America, because superior survey instruments are available for these regions. This means that most of what we know about social remittances concerns democratic home countries.[10] Typically, social remittances are measured using questions that ask respondents whether they have any relatives abroad and how often they communicate with them. Cash remittances, by contrast, are addressed by questions about whether the recipient or household receive money from migrant relatives (Pérez-Armendáriz and Crow 2010; Córdova and Hiskey 2015; Paarlberg 2017; Crow and Pérez-Armendáriz 2018; Córdova and Hiskey 2019). However, this approach masks the fact that resources and ideas are closely intertwined, and often reinforce one other. The knot that ties resources and ideas together is that of political discussion, with or without a transborder component. While a transborder component is important to understanding attitudinal and behavioral change in remittance recipients, political discussion between transnational household members and non-migrants may produce spillover effects and magnify attitudinal and behavioral changes (Crow and Pérez-Armendáriz 2018). As Pérez-Armendáriz and Crow (2010, 125) state, "[t]he information transmitted through the social networks produces an aggregate effect on attitudes and behaviors in entire communities, which transcends those personally tied to migration."

Research categorizes political discussion as either a mediating (Córdova and Hiskey 2019) or an intervening variable (Crow and Pérez-Armendáriz 2018; Batista et al. 2019) in shaping attitudes and behaviors. Regardless of the approach adopted and despite discussion often being framed as an alternative mechanism to that of financial remittances, these studies show that political discussion and financial remittances tend to reinforce and amplify each other. For instance, remittances may have stronger political effects in less developed countries, because households' high remittance dependence makes contact with relatives abroad more intense, favoring the transfer of political norms (Córdova and Hiskey 2019). Similarly, emigrants' power to shape stayers' political views is connected with remittance dependence. The transborder transfer of ideas via political discussion may thus gain more relevance the more a recipient depends on remittances. This influence is not coercive, but rather derives from power asymmetries that make emigrants worth listening to in the eyes of stayers (Pérez-Armendáriz 2014; Vari-Lavoisier 2016; Paarlberg 2017).

The mere fact of engaging in transnational relationships *and* discussing politics with others may be enough to trigger changes in political behavior. Belonging to a "transnational household" reorients non-migrant family members towards a transnational sphere in which family members learn about the lives and sacrifices their relatives experience abroad. Knowledge of their difficulties as well as dependence on the resources they provide makes those who stay behind more critical of the workings of their political systems. This effect is magnified by discussing politics with others (Crow and Pérez-Armendáriz 2018). For instance, in their study of the 2009 Mozambican election (2019), Batista et al. report that merely chatting with transnational households members, even if they are not family, increased electoral engagement and demands for more political accountability. Note then that *transborder* conversations have the capacity to mold the behaviors of those engaged in those conversations, while *domestic* political discussion may magnify that effect at the meso-level. Unlike accounts that frame ideational and monetary transfers as two opposing mechanisms, ours posits that they are likely to operate in tandem.

To test these propositions, we would ideally have individual-level survey data that provided two crucial pieces of information. First, a survey would have questions about whether a respondent is a "transnational household member" (Crow and Pérez-Armendáriz 2018; Batista et al. 2019); that is, whether s/he has a migrant relative. This information would help us distinguish informal social mechanisms from cash remittances. Similarly, the survey would ideally have questions asking whether respondents engage in transborder conversations with those relatives (Córdova and Hiskey 2015; Paarlberg 2017; Córdova and Hiskey 2019) and even better, about the content of those transborder conversations. Unfortunately, the Afrobarometer does not include these types of question. Second, an ideal test would compare cash transfers from democracies with cash transfers from autocracies to examine how they (separately) influence individual behavior. This information would further isolate the concept of "democratic" social remittances from other types of norm transfer that originate from emigrants residing in autocratic countries. However, as noted earlier, an overwhelming number of the African autocracies we study receive most of their remittances from democracies, making it challenging to reach solid conclusions about remittances flowing from autocratic regimes.

Instead, we opt for a second-best strategy, given the survey data we have: we examine the role of political discussion. A first test posits that individual political discussion mediates the relationship between financial remittance receipt and political behaviors such as protest and voting. A second asks whether political discussion amplifies the resource effects of financial remittances such that informal communication and financial resources reinforce each other to shape protest and turnout.

### 7.4.1. Political Discussion as a Mediator

If cash remittances increase political discussion and this political discussion, in turn, shapes citizens' behavior, then political discussion could mediate the relationship between financial remittances and political outcomes. Given this scenario, we might not be confident that our main findings result from the fact that remittances provide additional financial resources. Instead, remittances might only be a proxy for transnational engagement that shapes norms and ideas and, in turn, political behavior, irrespective of the financial resources remittances provide. Note too that while in previous research being part of a transnational network was shown to shape activities such as political discussion and persuasion (Córdova and Hiskey 2015), the possibility of engaging in political discussion may be compromised in autocratic settings.

Alternatively, if we find that remittance receipt, even after accounting for the mediating role of political discussion, predicts more protest and less turnout, then we could interpret this as evidence consistent with the premise that financial—and not social—remittances shape behavior. That is, if there remains a direct relationship between remittances and behavior even after adjusting for the fact that the social component of remittance receipt boosts political discussion and that this remittance-induced discussion may drive behavior, then we can plausibly ascribe this direct effect as the causal effect of financial remittances, net of any indirect social remittance effect.[11]

As in chapters 4 and 5, we used the Afrobarometer survey data for countries ruled by autocratic governments during the survey periods (2008 and 2016), and test the same specification with the same estimator.[12] The two outcomes we model are participation in protest and vote turnout.

TABLE 7.1. Remittances, political discussion, and behavior

| Outcome | Protest | | | Vote turnout | | |
|---|---|---|---|---|---|---|
| Sample | All districts | Stronghold | Opposition | All districts | Swing | Non-swing |
| Mediated effect | 0.2 | 0.2 | 0.2 | 0.2 | 0.2 | 0.2 |
| Direct effect | 4.5 | 0.0 | 4.8 | −1.1 | −3.8 | 0.5 |
| Total effect | 4.7 | 0.2 | 5.0 | −0.9 | −3.6 | 0.7 |

Table 7.1 shows the results of this analysis. The left-hand columns report the causal mediation results for *Protest* for all local districts in the seventeen sample countries. The direct effect of remittances increases protest by 4.5 percent, while the total effect is a 4.7 percent increase. This means that the indirect effect of remittances—mediated through political discussion—is only 0.2 percent, suggesting that most of the work of remittances shown in the model comes directly from cash remittances and is not mediated through political communication. The second and third columns report the results for (regime-)stronghold and opposition districts respectively. As we found in chapter 4, the remittance effect on protest is largely confined to opposition districts; and the causal mediation analysis for these areas again suggests that the direct effect of remittances is much larger than the effect mediated through political discussion.

The right-hand columns of Table 7.1 show the results for *Turnout*. Analysis that looks at all districts shows a small negative effect of remittances on turnout, with the direct effect (−1.1) and the indirect effect (even smaller at 0.2) working in opposite directions. The fifth column reports results for swing districts only, which are the places where we most expect remittances to harm turnout if incumbents direct clientelism to these districts. The direct negative effect of remittances is larger, reducing turnout by −3.8 percent; and, again, the indirect effect is small and works in the opposite direction. For non-swing districts, the remittance effect is negligible.

Similar to the micro-results reported in chapters 4 and 5, the mediation analysis shows that remittances are associated with more protest in opposition districts and less turnout in swing districts. For the purposes of this chapter, though, these results largely indicate that the direct remittance effect is much larger than the indirect effect mediated through political discussion. This suggests that remittance receipt does not necessarily work through political discussion to explain the main micro-findings in this book. Instead, we interpret these results as evidence to suggest that financial remittances have important consequences for political behavior that cannot be explained simply in terms of the remittance of norms that diffuse through political discussion. However, this evidence does not necessarily mean that social remittances understood as norms transmitted via transborder political discussion play no role, since unfortunately we do not have information on transborder communication. Further, political discussion may be a factor that can help us to understand the connection between remittances and political behavior, if it amplifies the remittance resource effect.

## 7.4.2. *Political Discussion as an Amplifier*

While the mediation analysis shows that political discussion does not mediate the observed relationship between remittance receipt and protest or vote turnout, it is still possible that remittance receipt works in concert with political discussion. If cash remittances carry a political message, political discussion with others could *magnify* the resource effect of remittances on protest and turnout, creating spillover effects. To examine this possibility, we test a specification with an interaction between political discussion and remittance receipt. This allows us to see whether the resource effect of remittance receipt is heterogeneous. If the marginal effect of remittances is higher for respondents who also discuss politics than for those who do not, this would suggest that these two phenomena work in concert: the social component of remittances, captured by political discussion, amplifies the financial remittance component and generates spillover effects beyond the recipient. Alternatively, if the remittance effect is the same irrespective of whether respondents engage in political discussion, this would cast doubt on the possibility that social remittances work in concert with financial remittances to shape behavior.

We again use the Afrobarometer survey data to test whether remittances influence protest and vote turnout. To examine possible heterogeneous remittance effects, we divide the sample into respondents who report participating in political discussion (roughly two-thirds of them) and those who do not (roughly one-third). We then re-estimate the main protest and turnout models.[13]

Table 7.2 shows the results of this analysis. The first three columns report results for protest. In all districts, the remittance effect is much higher for those who discuss politics (4.4 percent) than for those who do not (1.2). This

TABLE 7.2. Remittances and behavior: Heterogeneous effects

| Outcome | Protest | | | Vote turnout | | |
|---|---|---|---|---|---|---|
| Sample | All districts | Stronghold | Opposition | All districts | Swing | Non-swing |
| *with* political discussion | 4.4 | 4.5 | 1.5 | −1.5 | −4.1 | −0.1 |
| *without* political discussion | 1.2 | 0.7 | 0.2 | −3.1 | −4.8 | −1.9 |

indicates that political discussion indeed has an amplifying effect on remittance receipt, suggesting that the two phenomena work in concert to facilitate anti-incumbent protests. The next two columns examine the evidence from (regime-)stronghold and opposition districts, separately. Again, remittances boost protest in stronghold districts but not in opposition ones, and this boost is much larger among respondents who report discussing politics than among those who do not.

The final three columns of Table 7.2 report results for vote turnout. As before, remittance receipt is associated with lower turnout, and this effect is concentrated in swing districts and nearly absent in non-swing districts. However, in contrast to the protest findings, the negative effect of remittance receipt is roughly the same among respondents who do *not* report discussing politics as among those who do. This indicates that the remittance effect on turnout is not different for those who discuss politics and those who do not, and thus suggests there is no amplifying effect of political discussion. The results make sense given the different nature of these activities. While the decision to vote is taken in the private sphere, protesting is a collective activity that requires not only resources but also coordination. Remittance recipients create spillover effects by discussing politics with others, with implications for protest, but not necessarily for vote turnout.

If political discussion is an individual-level proxy for a more socially engaged respondent, then it may not be surprising that this individual-level trait facilitates protest and amplifies a cash remittance resource effect. More socially engaged respondents may by contrast be *less* likely to turn out to vote; and in unreported tests we find this to be the case. For this reason, social engagement may not alter how financial remittances enable citizens to extricate themselves from incumbent clientelistic networks. In fact, when we re-run this analysis with an ordered measure of remittances, we find that the remittance effect is strongest among respondents in swing districts who do *not* report discussing politics. Again, this makes sense if social engagement more closely entwines voters with clientelistic networks in local communities.

Overall, we find evidence consistent with an amplification effect of political discussion for protest, but not for turnout. It is important, moreover, to emphsasize that remittances do not impact political behavior only through political discussion. To reiterate, tests ideally should ask questions about relatives abroad and transborder conversations; lacking these survey items, our tests still suggest, however, that remittances have a direct impact on political behavior that, in the case of protest, is amplified by discussing politics with non-migrants.

## 7.5.  Conclusion

This chapter has tested an important alternative explanation that might account for our main findings. The changes in political behavior we have documented could result, rather than from cash remittances, from another type of transfer: that of norms and ideas that migrants develop or acquire in host countries. Exposure to democratic institutions in developed countries could result in remittances being sent with the intent to foster political changes in home countries. Communication between emigrants and those who stay at home could alter remittance recipients' views about home-country politics and thereby boost protest and induce electoral apathy, as we have documented throughout the book.

While we do not have the ideal data for making solid inferences, we offer a battery of tests that provide little support to this alternative explanation. First, our macro-results are stable regardless of the share of remittances that originate in democracies. Second, the individual-level effect of remittances on protest and turnout is not explained by the impact that remittances have on political discussion. However, political discussion appears to magnify the effect of monetary remittances on protest in autocracies. While none of these findings is necessarily conclusive, we hope they provide a first step towards the study of political remittances in autocratic sending countries.

## 7.6.  Appendix: Measuring Remittances by Origin

Remittances from democracies and autocracies were obtained by reorganizing bilateral remittances matrices for the period 1990 through 2015. Azizi (2018, 385) constructed weights by calculating the share that remittances from destination country $j$ represent over the total of remittances received by a particular home country $i$ in year $t$.[14]

$$W_{ijt} = \frac{\text{Remittances from country } j \text{ to country } i \text{ in year } t}{\text{Total remittances received by country } i \text{ in year } t} \qquad (7.3)$$

We multiplied the weights, $W_{ijt}$, by the total remittances received by country $i$ to obtain the amount of remittances flowing from country $j$ to country $i$. Once we got those figures, we classified the destination country—or in other words, the country of origin of remittances—as either an autocracy or a democracy according to the Polity Score (Polity IV).[15] We then added up all the remittances arriving in a given origin country $i$ from different destinations, according to regime type. This in turn allowed to obtain the share of remittances arriving in each country from democracies and from autocracies.[16]

$$RemittancesShare_{i,t}^{D} = \frac{Remit_{i,t}^{D}}{Remit_{i,t}^{D} + Remit_{i,t}^{A}} \qquad (7.4)$$

where $Remit_{i,t}^{D}$ is the constant dollar amount of estimated annual remittances from democracies $(D)$ while $Remit_{i,t}^{A}$ is the same total from autocracies $(A)$.

This process provides us with a measure of the share of remittances from democracies for each remittance recipient country-year observation, with a range between 0 and 1: $Remittances\ Share_{i,t}^{D}$. A benefit of using this yearly measure is that it captures (possible) changing migration patterns over time. Some countries with autocratic governments may send more migrants to autocracies, for example, if nativist attitudes in democratic migrant-destination countries shift to such an extent that these democracies begin to restrict labor migration. This could lead to a decrease in remittances from democratic destination countries and a relative increase in remittances from destination autocracies. More likely, though, is for some autocracies to send many migrants to countries that shift from autocracy to democracy (e.g., South Africa) or from democracy to autocracy (e.g., Thailand, multiple times) during the sample period. This means, for example, that remittances sent from South Africa to Namibia will be classified as autocratic until 1994, when South Africa transitioned to democracy, and then these same remittance flows to Namibia will be classified as democratic afterwards. The yearly measure therefore picks up both shifts in migration patterns between countries and, more importantly, shifts in the political regime type of the migrant-destination country.

The drawback of this approach is that data are substantially missing for some periods for some countries. For example, for a fairly large number of countries there are data for the 2000s, but not the 1990s (e.g., Algeria, Angola, Burkina Faso, The Gambia, Haiti, Ivory Coast, Kazakhstan, Laos, Libya, Mozambique, Syria, Russia, Tanzania, Uganda, and Yemen); for others, there are data for the 1990s, but not the 2000s (Mauritania); or for the 2000s, but not the 2010s (Rwanda, Togo, Venezuela, and Zimbabwe). Indeed, just over a quarter of the possible sample (1990 to 2015) is missing data on this yearly share of remittances from democracies. More worryingly, this lack is negatively correlated with anti-government protest and democratic transition, potentially biasing results.

As a last step, we therefore average the yearly share of remittances from democracies over twenty years (1990–2010) or twenty-five years (1990–2015), depending on the macro-sample we use:[17]

$$DemocraticShareRemittances_i = \sum_{t=1}^{T} RemittancesShare_{i,t}^{D} \qquad (7.5)$$

where $RemittancesShare_{i,t}^{D}$ is the annual share of all remittances that come from democracies and $T$ is the number of years over which we average. We call this average measure, which varies by country, the *democratic share of remittances*.

# 8

# Conclusion

Scholars and policy makers have long noted the negative consequences of the "brain drain" that may result when high-skilled workers leave their home country to seek better opportunities abroad. The home country loses not only its most skilled workers, who would otherwise increase productivity and pay substantial taxes, but also the return on the human capital invested in those workers. In Guyana, for example, it is estimated by some scholars that nearly half of all native-born Guyanese live and work abroad, the majority of these being high-skilled. If these skilled workers are also those who are most likely to value, foster, and sustain the democratic rule and open access societies that underpin sustained economic growth, then the consequences of the brain drain become political as well as economic, and all the more pernicious in the long run.

The counter-argument would be that labor mobility—especially for high-skilled workers—increases the incentive to invest in human capital in home countries, because the return on this investment should increase when such workers leave, for two related reasons. First, high-skilled workers who migrate presumably earn even higher wages abroad than at home, which raises the return on their skills; and second, the scarcity of the high-skilled workers left at home should raise their wages, in turn raising the return on skills development. Thus free labor movement for high-skilled workers in low-income countries should, in theory, increase investment in human capital in these countries. The only downside to the migration of high-skilled labor from poor to rich countries, according to this logic, is a lowering of wages for high-skilled workers in rich countries, who would face more competition from an increased supply of high-skilled (likely service) workers. In the United States, one could imagine, professional associations of doctors, which already restrict domestic labor supply in their field to prop up wages, would fight fiercely to block mass immigration of, for example, high-skilled Indian or Jamaican healthcare workers (Malhotra et al. 2013; Peterson et al. 2014).

Is there a political counterpart to the economic brain drain? The logic of the exit, voice, and loyalty framework would suggest that the answer is "yes": those most likely to demand political change, particularly if mass political protest and opposition voter mobilization are the most effective methods to advance democracy, may in fact exit rather than express the voice necessary to see through democratic political change. This book shows the opposite, however: that exit funds voice and weakens loyalty, and thus undermines dictatorship by boosting protests, weakening electoral authoritarianism, and strengthening opposition parties as well as civil society organizations. The key to this argument, of course, is the financial remittances migrants send home. This private income from abroad flows to citizens and not to governments, and therefore shifts the balance of power in autocracies away from governments and towards citizens.

Globalization is changing the political dynamics of societies throughout the world, but especially in the Global South. Domestic actors—both elites and citizens—are influenced by international factors, including, as this book shows, migrants and the remittances they send back home. Before moving to discussion of the implications, let us briefly summarize the main findings presented in the book.

Remittances are the largest source of foreign income in most autocratic countries. Our main argument is that this substantial flow of private income alters the internal balance of power in dictatorships, making it possible for recipients to become the protagonists of democratic change. Mass mobilization has played an increasingly important role in democratic transitions in recent decades. Remittance flows, we argue, are a fundamental force behind this increase in bottom-up political change, both boosting voice, manifested as more protest, and weakening loyalty, manifested as lower electoral turnout.

Our empirical analyses first tackle the state-centric claims that remittances empower autocracies by increasing (either directly or indirectly) their resources, which can in turn be used to increase patronage or repression. After revisiting the various mechanisms that supposedly link foreign income to a political resource curse, we find no evidence consistent with these arguments. Remittances, we show, do not substantially boost government revenue, alter public spending patterns, or correlate with state-led repression, and do not prevent the formation of social groups independent from the state. In contrast to revenue from natural resource exports, foreign aid, and even international investment, remittances flow directly to citizens and bypass the government, so they do little to directly alter the behavior of those who rule.

A central contribution of this book is that it tests the micro-mechanisms through which remittances shape individual political behaviors (protest and voting) using micro-data and then explores their aggregate macro-level consequences. Consistent with our theory that remittances boost the resources and capacity to mobilize for democracy, we find substantial evidence, using both macro- and micro-data, linking remittances to protest in dictatorships. This link is concentrated in opposition areas and among the poorest citizens. Further, our findings show that remittances erode electoral support for ruling parties in autocracies. At the micro-level, we demonstrate that this outcome results from weakening of clientelistic ties between citizens and the government, and, hence, the demobilization of poor supporters in swing districts.

These two sets of findings suggest that remittances undermine dictatorships, which we demonstrate in chapter 6 by showing a global link between remittance inflows and democratization. At the meso-level, we document how remittances boost the strength and autonomy of opposition political parties and civil society organizations. Crucially moreover, at the macro-level, we find that migrant remittances increased the chance of democratic transitions in a global sample of dictatorships spanning four decades. A series of tests in chapter 7 provide little evidence consistent with an alternative explanation, that social—not monetary—remittances explain our findings.

In what follows we examine the implications of our argument and findings for debates in four related research areas. First, in section 8.1, we discuss how our main conclusion—that citizens exiting dictatorship improve the prospects for democracy—has implications for important debates about the ethics of migration policies, both in relatively wealthy destination countries and for the developing countries from which most international migrants hail. Second, in section 8.2, we propose how our theory might inform immigration policy in democratic migrant-destination countries, by reframing immigration as an important tool for the promotion of democracy.

Our theory pertains to migration *from dictatorships*, and the evidence we marshal to test it comes exclusively from countries ruled by autocratic governments. However, the mechanisms we propose as linking financial remittances to democracy, namely protest and voting, are central to the practice of democratic politics as well. We therefore ask, in section 8.3, whether our theory is really about a more general phenomenon whereby financial remittances fuel *anti-incumbent* political behavior, with implications for whether our theory applies to democracies as well as dictatorships.

Finally, in section 8.4, we explore how our theory of democratic migration might inform debates about globalization. We demonstrate how our evidence helps reframe migration as an element of globalization categorically different from other international factors, such as trade and investment, insofar as migration and the consequent financial remittances constitute a *decentralized* flow of income across borders, in contrast to the much more centralized movement of money that transpires when firms trade with or invest in other countries. We close by discussing the implications of our argument for understanding the next wave of globalization.

## 8.1. Remittances and the Ethics of Migration Policy

Ethical debates about emigration and, perhaps more pointedly, immigration policy have for the most part ignored how remittances shape *political* outcomes in migrant origin countries (see, e.g., Pogge 1997; Carens 2013; Collier 2013; Ruhs 2013; Brock and Blake 2015; Oberman 2015; Miller 2016; Song 2018). Our theory and findings have implications for these normative theories, particularly insofar as they address, either directly or indirectly as background assumptions, the empirical question of whether migration influences socio-economic development in the Global South. Further, understanding whether migration boosts long-term development in origin countries has implications for how scholars think about migration in debating ethical demands in relation to global poverty, equality, and redistribution (see, e.g., Unger 1996; Sen 1999; Pogge 2005; Singer 2010; Oberman 2015).

To highlight how the evidence in this book speaks to these debates, we revisit a point that Collier (2013, 187) articulates: "[a]lthough migrants themselves do well from migration, it can only be truly significant in addressing hardcore global poverty if it accelerates transformation in countries of origin. In turn, that transformation is at base a political and social, rather than economic, process. So the potential for migration to affect the political process for those left behind really matters."

This book makes a clear statement about how migrants shape political outcomes in their countries of origin: via financial remittances, migration boosts democracy in origin countries ruled by autocratic governments. This point bears emphasis, because it forces those involved in normative debates to think critically about how migration—and hence migration policy in rich democracies—shapes broad-based development outcomes, including with regard to global poverty and inequality. If, as our evidence suggests, migration from dictatorships fosters democracy, and if democracy yields sustained economic development and domestic security for its citizens, then migration must be considered alongside other policy tools, such as foreign aid or boosting trade, that may also shape democracy and development, with implications for global justice. We touch on the relative effectiveness of migration and policies in these other areas later in this chapter; first we discuss how our theory and evidence have implications for normative debates about migration policy.

We revisit two debates pertaining to migration. The first concerns *emigration* and addresses long-held suspicions that emigration may hurt migrant origin countries via "brain drain." The second, much larger, debate concerns the ethics of *immigration* policy in rich, developed democracies in the Global North.

### 8.1.1. *Emigration*

As noted at the outset of this chapter, we offer evidence that remittances help to counter a potentially pernicious "political brain drain." One argument suggesting ethical limits on emigration, as articulated by Brock and Blake (2015, 17), points out that highly skilled emigrants "are important sources of demand and supply for better [political and economic] institutions" in migrant-sending countries.[1] Building on this point, Brock and Blake offer an ethical rationale for asking those who leave to compensate those left behind for the developmental and institutional damage caused, in part, by the exit of citizens with productive skills—indeed, skills that may reflect human capital investments made by origin-country governments. Such compensation could be a period of compulsory service in the sending country, or taxes levied on emigrants or the migrant-receiving countries. More pointedly, Miller (2016, 108) argues, without reference to any empirical findings, that even if remittances compensate families of migrants, "these are unlikely to fill the gaps in health provision [in migrant origin countries] that the brain-drain creates."

However, this view overlooks the fact that emigrants often contribute to the economic well-being of those left behind by, precisely, sending remittances to them, enabling investment in community development, and, as we show in this book, providing resources that those left behind use to demand democratic political change. Sending remittances is central to the implicit and symbolic contract that emigrants "sign" with their relatives: sending house-holds support—both materially and emotionally—the emigration of some family members in the expectation that their emigration will bring a steady flow of remittances in return (Lucas and Stark 1985; Carling 2008; 2014). Emi-grants are aware of their obligations to those left behind and they meet those obligations precisely by sending remittances.[2]

These decentralized and private contracts involving the moral obligation to remit do not necessarily need to be supplemented by compulsory taxes, in part because such taxation is likely to be implemented by corrupt and ille-gitimate governments.[3] Moreover, research on transnational political engage-ment shows that more educated migrants are often the ones most likely to engage in the kinds of activity that contribute to the autonomy and mobiliza-tion of the political opposition in autocracies (Guarnizo et al. 2003; Smith and Bakker 2005; Burgess 2014). With their greater financial and intellectual resources, highly-skilled migrants are uniquely positioned to engage with the "meso-level" activities we described in previous chapters, helping to counter any negative effects of political brain drain entailed by their exit.

### 8.1.2. *Immigration policy*

Those involved in debates about ethical limits on immigration—and hence the moral dimensions of immigration policy in rich and mostly democratic destination countries—often overlook the role of remittances in develop-ment writ large, and remain largely unaware of the possible political conse-quences of migration *in origin countries*. We discuss the implications of our theory and evidence for two points made in this literature.

First, some scholars argue that remittances may harm development in migrant origin countries, either by exacerbating inequality or by aiding recip-ient governments. For example, Song (2018), in presenting an ethical argu-ment in support of "closed borders but open doors" to particular groups, emphasizes that inward remittance flows may increase inequalities in migrant origin countries. Inequality, according to this logic, results when either wealthy or middle-income citizens emigrate and send remittances back home, leaving the very poorest, who do not receive remittances, worse off relative to remittance-receiving families (Kapur and McHale 2012). Miller (2005, 198) similarly argues that migration "will do little to help the very poor, who are unlikely to have the resources to move to a richer country." In the scenario whereby remittances increase inequality in migrant origin countries, they may even contribute to communal and political divisions between remittance recipients and non-recipients.

Further, in critiquing labor migration programs, Miller (2016, 98) notes that the governments of migrant-sending countries lack a political incentive to advocate for migrant workers' rights in destination countries "because [these governments] benefited indirectly from remittances and were anxious that their own people might be substituted by [migrant] workers from elsewhere." This critique both reflects the assumption that sending-country governments benefit from remittances and, building on this assumption, argues that host countries leverage competition between migrant sending-countries that enables host countries to treat migrant labor poorly.[4]

Second, some argue that we cannot justify open migration—or the remittances that flow from it—as a valid way to meet the ethical demand to address global inequality when there are other, it is presumed better, methods for wealthy democracies to combat poverty in the Global South. Song (2018, 91), for example, argues that "it is both more desirable and feasible to turn to development assistance aimed at addressing global poverty rather than opening borders to everyone." While the relative benefits from migration and foreign aid for reducing poverty is ultimately an empirical question, as Oberman (2015, 247) points out, Pogge (1997, 13) and Song (2018, 90) also argue that mass migration of all low-income citizens from poor to rich countries is unfeasible: there are simply too many living in poverty throughout the world for all these human beings to migrate to wealthy democracies.

These theories largely ignore the role of migrant remittances in contributing to global justice. We show in this book how migration can foster democratic political change, which, many argue, is the institutional foundation for long-term economic development, and will thus help reduce global inequality. For one thing, arguments that focus on inequality in migrant origin countries overlook the overwhelming empirical evidence that remittances are effective in lifting recipients out of poverty (Adams and Page 2005; World Bank 2006d; Fajnzylber and López 2007; Acosta et al. 2008; Chami et al. 2008).[5] There is also substantial evidence of spillover economic effects of remittances in high-emigration communities, thanks both to collective involvement of emigrants in co-production projects and to the multiplier effect generated by remittance recipients' activities at the local level (Adida and Girod 2011; Aparicio and Meseguer 2012; Meseguer and Aparicio 2012; Duquette-Rury 2014). Moreover, remittance recipients exhibit more prosocial behavior, such as volunteer work, than non-recipients. These flows strengthen norms of reciprocity and trust, transcending the recipient house-hold and generating organizational spillover effects at the community level (Pérez-Armendáriz and Crow 2010; Fransen 2015; Mendola 2017).

Our theory builds on this latter point, but goes further. If remittances foster democratic development in migrant origin countries, the majority of which are ruled by authoritarian governments, and if democracy does in fact reduce domestic inequality in migrant origin countries,[6] then the ethical argument might turn inequality-based critiques on their head. If remittances reduce inequality or produce more public trust within local communities in migrant origin countries, one could indeed argue in favor of *more* migration.

Second, proposals that prioritize development assistance over migration to address global inequality overlook the fact that, unlike remittances, development aid too often falls into the hands of corrupt dictators, who then use it to distribute patronage, as we illustrated in the case of Cambodia.[7] Further, as we discuss in the next section, democracy assistance suffers from flaws as regards the building of better democratic institutions. Because remittances are a decentralized income flow, they are more likely to reach the hands of those that need them. Remittances have consequences in terms not only of poverty alleviation, but also, as we demonstrate, of increasing political autonomy and voice.

Finally, if democracy—that is, government that is both accountable and responsive to citizens and that preserves open economic and politi-cal access—is the key to sustained development (North et al. 2009; Ace-moglu and Robinson 2012), then employing migration as a tool to alleviate global poverty need not entail all the poor citizens of the world migrating to rich countries, as Song implies it does. Instead, some migration—assuming resulting remittances flow to agents of democratic change in migrant origin countries—may be enough to undermine the autocratic governments that hinder development and breed insecurity in many parts of the world.

Our argument and evidence rely on the assumption that migrants can access foreign labor markets and have de facto rights to earn wages and make financial transfers to their home countries safely and cheaply. Some scholars argue that by increasing legal admissions and granting the right to work, afflu-ent countries would meet their responsibilities towards global justice, at least in part (Cheneval and Rochel 2012; Ruhs 2013; Brock and Blake 2015). The expansion of Temporary Migrant Programs (TMPs), as advocated by Martin Ruhs, to mobilize the emigration of low-skilled workers could be viewed as a compromise along the lines of "opening more doors to labor migration while still controlling borders," in Song's (2018) phrase.[8] However, these programs may imply temporarily sacrificing migrant labor protections in exchange for the right to work legally for a period of time. Even so, Ruhs (2013, 169–70) views these programs as a realistic and better alternative to closing doors to all economic migrants. In defending TMPs, Ruhs highlights the ethical imperative of granting emigrants "moral standing" by considering their economic interests and those of non-emigrants in origin countries. While exploitation of workers in these temporary programs raises ethical issues (Carens 2013) and all governments must work to prevent and punish such abuse, TMPs offer an opportunity for low-skilled migrants to raise their own incomes and those of their families left behind.

Of course, allowing migrants to work and send remittances home in an effort to address global injustices is not the sole purpose of immigration policy. Such policies must balance migrant rights and opportunities with the impact of immigration on inequality, the wages of low-income workers, and public trust in destination countries. In light of this, some scholars argue that, after we consider the positive aspects of remittance flows, temporary migration offers advantages over more permanent immigration, as temporary migrants often remit more (Collier 2013, 212–13). For those concerned about destination societies' self-determination, TMPs may represent a pragmatic tool with which to calibrate the number of migrants and the rights of labor migrants according to the receiving society's needs and preferences.

This book is not concerned to argue one way or another on the ethical merits of migration policies, or to advocate for any particular emigration or immigration policy. Rather, we present a theory and empirical evidence that, we hope, informs this debate by examining some of the assumptions about the costs and benefits of migration and remittances for politics in migrant origin countries. We show that by sending remittances and thus making recipients politically autonomous, emigrants contribute to institution-building and political change from afar. By funding protests, strengthening civil society, reducing support for dominant parties, and ultimately facilitating democratization, migrants' remittances contribute to political transformations that set migrant origin countries on the path to democracy and sustained economic development. Tackling global inequality will, of course, require the orchestration of multiple strategies, including improving the way development aid, democracy assistance, and migration policies are designed and deployed.

The evidence we present in this book suggests that the political consequences of remittances should be factored into debates about immigration policy in wealthy democracies. In short, we agree with Cheneval and Rochel's (2012, 16) view, that normative approaches to migration should integrate remittances—and, as we highlight, the political consequences of remittances—into ethical frameworks.

## 8.2. Immigration as Democracy Promotion

Our argument and findings have implications for understanding how domestic immigration policies in destination countries—which are often rich, democratic polities—can be reframed as a tool for democracy promotion abroad. Western democracies and international organizations have historically used a broad range of policy instruments aimed at spreading democracy abroad: from coercive policies, such as economic sanctions and military intervention, to a variety of less violent tools of statecraft, including financial assistance, diplomacy, and soft-power persuasion. The existing evidence indicates that in this regard, coercive politics are, on balance, more likely to fail than not; and that the success they do achieve is highly dependent on local conditions and the interests of the countries adopting them. Moreover, even when some coercive international policy tools such as sanctions and military interventions contribute to the collapse of autocratic regimes, democracy rarely follows in its wake; instead, new dictatorships typically replace the old, or, worse yet, state failure ensues (Escribà-Folch and Wright 2015); and although making traditional development aid conditional on political change has helped to buy democratic reforms—mostly the introduction of multiparty elections—in many countries, many of these electoral regimes have fallen short of becoming full-fledged democracies.

The late 1980s and especially the 1990s saw the rise of a new aid modality: democracy assistance. To this, official and private donors have devoted billions of dollars to date. Nevertheless, guided by some initial cases during the third wave of democratization, donors have embraced a limited and even misleading transition model or paradigm that focused on toppling long-standing leaders and holding multiparty elections (Carothers 2002, 6). Transitions to democracy, many thought, stemmed from splits within ruling groups of autocratic elites, followed by an election, and then a consolidation period when liberal democracy would become entrenched. Viewing any liberalizing reform as the beginning of a transition, and equating elections with the emergence of democracy, donors concentrated their efforts on the latter—via election monitoring and administration support. Then, after elections, they turned their efforts to fostering more robust state institutions, principally the judiciary and parliaments. Supporting elections and funding state institutional reform proved insufficient, however. Autocratic incumbents largely resisted reforms that could jeopardize their grip on power, and soon found ways of retaining political office despite facing electoral competition. Further, the bulk of foreign-funded investments in governance and state capacity targeted governments and, in turn, ended up bolstering incumbent regimes (Dietrich and Wright 2015).

Donors then began to realize that assisting civil society groups could help overcome these limitations, by focusing on a non-state actor with an interest in democratic political reform. Consequently, since the late 1990s, aid programs have often focused on groups that stand outside the state; but even so, the share of funds targeting civil society groups remains small compared to the share aimed at institution-building. Although it initially looked like a powerful tool to promote democracy, civil society aid has numerous limitations in relation to both donors and recipients (Ottaway and Carothers 2000a). On the donor side, this aid mostly supports advocacy or service-delivery NGOs—especially highly professionalized ones that can fulfill reporting requirements—not political parties and other grassroots political associations. Focusing funding on advocacy and service limits its power to reshape the internal balance of power. The ambition of aid programs weakens further, moreover, whenever the goal of promoting democracy clashes with other foreign policy objectives deemed more important (Risse and Babayan 2015; Peterson and Scott 2018).

In relation to recipients, democracy aid to civil society organizations faces a growing and more insurmountable obstacle. Not only do democracy promoters have to face countervailing policies of non-democratic regional powers; but since the early 2000s, numerous governments have started to put in place legal prohibitions or restrictions on foreign funding for NGOs (Christensen and Weinstein 2013; Buyse 2018). Since democracy aid can harm incumbents if it strengthens civil society organizations and opposition groups, most dictatorial governments do not allow aid to flow to such groups, especially those with strong links to opposition parties or with a clear pro-democracy agenda (Dietrich and Wright 2015). As a result, not only has assistance to countries with such prohibitions decreased, but, as Bush (2015) notes, democracy assistance programs have been purposely "tamed" to be more pleasing and less threatening to recipient governments. That is to say, over time democracy assistance has become less politically confrontational towards host governments and, as a consequence, less likely to support dissidents or foster regime change. This development, Bush observes, is rooted in the survival instincts of the NGOs carrying out the assistance programs.

While several studies find that democracy aid increases democracy levels,[9] these may not in fact provide much ground for optimism.[10] The evidence from these studies does not necessarily indicate that democracy aid increases the chances of autocratic governments being voted out of power in a democratic transition.[11] Rather, they may simply identify partial liberalizing reforms that please donors but nevertheless do not threaten incumbent governments, and thus do little to boost the prospects of a democratic transition. Indeed, case study research in numerous regions has concluded that democracy aid has had at best very limited effects (Ottaway and Carothers 2000b; De Zeeuw and Kumar 2006).

This book has shown that, in contrast to one of the most widely used tools of Western democracy promotion, namely foreign aid, *remittances* empower citizens and promote democratic regime change, by undermining the regime's resource advantage. Not only do financial remittances boost resources for millions of citizens, but these flows erode the mobilizing capacity of ruling parties and strengthen opposition parties and civil society organizations. They have several advantages over democracy aid. Most importantly, remitted income flows are a *decentralized* and flexible source of foreign funding for individuals, households, and organizations in autocratic recipient states. The source of this funding is millions of individuals living outside their countries, not a handful of Western donors. Moreover, while Westerns donors have responded to government-imposed restrictions by reducing democracy aid or taming it, remittances have been growing consistently for years (until the 2020 global pandemic). As importantly, money sent by nationals living abroad raises fewer suspicions among incumbent autocratic governments in recipient states. By contrast, dictators now routinely label any association with Western democracy aid programs as colllusion in foreign-funded schemes to topple popular leaders. Similarly, funding via remittances is less likely to undermine the perceived legitimacy of NGOs and political groups among local populations, who might view official funding from Western countries as foreign interference or antithetical to local values.

Second, because democracy aid typically flows through centralized, official channels it is easier for autocratic governments to track and block. Remittances, conversely, because they are highly decentralized and their senders use a wide variety of channels to transfer the money are much more difficult for incumbent governments to control. Furthermore, in contrast to democracy aid, which mostly targets specific professionalized advocacy NGOs, remittances flow to a diverse group of citizens, including *both* regime opponents who use the funds to mobilize protest *and* nominal regime supporters who disengage from regime-supporting clientelistic networks. While some remittances may be sent directly to NGOs, parties, and voluntary associations from abroad, much of the remitted income in the hands of opposition groups first flows to individuals who receive it from overseas. Remittance resources can be transferred to these actors formally, but also informally, which makes it nearly impossible to trace and control them. As our findings demonstrate, the anti-incumbent effects of remittances can be observed at the micro-level, among individual citizens, but also the meso-level: we have shown that they boost civil society groups. While there is little systematic evidence demonstrating that civil society aid increases the strength and autonomy of such organizations, we provide evidence that remittances do so—amongst other things, by boosting the electoral strength of opposition parties.

Overall, the evidence in this book suggests that remittances can be a powerful instrument for the promotion of democracy. Policymakers routinely examine foreign aid, trade, and investment policies (including economic sanctions) through the lens of democracy promotion; we propose that they should think equally carefully about immigration policy as a method to promote democracy and further the development of open access societies throughout the world (North et al. 2009).

## 8.3.  Do Remittances Fund Anti-Incumbent Politics?

Our theory and empirical findings focus on *autocratic regimes*; incumbent rulers and parties in these contexts are autocratic inasmuch as they do not allow fair and free elections in a contest for executive power. We argue that remittances empower citizens to protest against autocratic governments and to disengage from clientelistic networks that underpin dictatorships' electoral strength.

Protests and voting, however, are central to democracy as well. This raises the question of whether our theory has implications for understanding how emigration shapes politics *in democracies*. If we conclude that emigration—because remittances boost voice and undermine loyalty mechanisms—harms incumbent rule and boosts democracy in autocratic contexts, then perhaps the more general phenomenon we uncover is simply that emigration undermines incumbent rule, irrespective of whether those incumbent rulers are autocratic or democratic. If this is correct, then emigration from countries ruled by democratic (or even semi-democratic) governments may have consequences for democratic consolidation and survival.

For example, if emigration from migrant-sending countries and the resulting remittances increase the chances of incumbents losing elections in a democracy, this could pave a path for new, potentially autocratic, rulers to win elections, consolidate their party's power, and ultimately undermine democracy. We discuss this possibility in two contexts: firstly, intra-European migration and the rise of populist parties in Europe, focusing on the case of Fidez in Hungary; and secondly, a long-standing democracy—India—where a nationalist party, the Bharatiya Janata Party (Indian People's Party, or BJP), won power and has subsequently begun to dismantle liberal, democratic rule.

### 8.3.1. Intra-European Migration and the Rise of Populist Parties

Until the migration crisis of 2015 and the global pandemic of 2020, intra-European borders were left largely "open" under the Schengen Agreement, permitting labor migration throughout the political bloc. This led to substantial migration from Central and Eastern European (CEEU) countries to their western and northern counterparts. By 2015, nearly 20 million EU residents, representing roughly 4 percent of the EU birth population, lived in another EU country (Pew Research Center 2017). While there has been much debate over how *immigration* may undermine democracy in migrant-*host* countries, particularly in the EU, scholars and policymakers have only recently begun to address the consequences of this migration for EU *sending* countries, many of which are relatively young democracies.

Two theories linking emigration and democracy in CEEU countries suggest that migration has hurt democracy in the region. One argument posits that emigration from CCEU to richer European countries signals a malaise back home, which, in turn, breeds disillusion with the liberal democratic model created after the collapse of Communist states (Krastev and Holmes 2018; 2019).[12] This lowers citizens' support for liberal democracy. Further, if remittances that flow back to CEEU countries also weaken recipients' support for the redistributive social states in new democracies established in the 1990s, these financial flows could undermine democracy by lowering electoral support for traditional, centrist parties and boost support for new parties led by populist leaders such as Viktor Orbán in Hungary and Jarosław Kaczyński in Poland.[13] If this argument is correct, then emigration may harm democracy.

This scenario points to the central role of political context: where incumbents are liberal centrists and the opposition are populist authoritarians, then perhaps private financial flows from remittances could contribute to higher anti-incumbent, anti-establishment sentiment, paving the way for the electoral success of populist candidates. In other contexts, where long-ruling autocratic parties are incumbent, anti-incumbent funding via remittances should further democracy, consistently with our theory.

The second argument (Keleman 2020, 486–87) draws on the standard exit, voice, and loyalty framework to posit that labor migration from, for example, Hungary serves as a safety valve for discontent against Orbán's increasingly authoritarian rule. Dissenters exit, according to this logic, leaving only those more inclined to support the incumbent behind. Further, Keleman claims that remittances decrease grievance among recipients back home, who misidentify the source of the benefit they provide, giving some political credit to the incumbent, which again, in the Hungarian case, is the increasingly autocratic Orbán government.

Emigration of dissenters, or the "safety valve" argument, is consistent with Krastev and Holmes's stagnation argument, insofar as both invoke increased levels of grievance; but Keleman's argument points to emigration aiding incumbent populists, while stagnation, in Krastev and Holmes's account, undermines liberal, centrist incumbents. Thus, these theories suggest that emigration both helps incumbents and undermines them, depending on whether the incumbent is a populist authoritarian or a centrist party. While both arguments suggest emigration hurt democracy in CEEU countries, the mechanisms underpinning each argument are in fact the opposite: one anti-incumbent and the other pro-incumbent. Our theory is closer to the stagnation argument offered by Krastev and Holmes, because we too posit that emigration is an anti-incumbent force. Neither the safety-valve theory nor the stagnation idea necessarily work through remittances, however.

In short, while it is possible that in a democratic or semi-democratic context emigration and the consequent remittances either sap support for liberal, centrist governments or finance political mobilization against such governments, there is, as yet, no comparative empirical analysis that sorts out the relative weight of these competing (indeed sometimes contradictory) mechanisms that link emigration to democratic demise.

### 8.3.2. Remittances and Democracy in India

In a manner similar to one of the mechanisms that may link emigration to democratic decline in CEEU countries, emigration and attendant remittances may undermine secular incumbent parties in democracies and pave an electoral path for nationalist or religious parties that subsequently undermine democratic rule. In India, a secular incumbent party, Congress, had ruled from a position of strength for decades, and the diaspora that helped fund the main religious opposition party was well educated and relatively wealthy.

In 2014, the Bharatiya Janata Party (BJP: Indian People's Party) won parliamentary elections, making Narenda Modi prime minister. The 2014 election marked only the second time since independence in 1947 that the long-ruling, secularist Congress party had lost.

The BJP was originally formed in 1980 by merging several Hindu-nationalist organizations, including the political wing of the Rashtriya Swayamsevak Sangh (RSS). Growing from a small electoral base in the early 1980s, a BJP-led coalition won control of parliament in 1998 and BJP leader Atal Bihari Vajpayee became prime minister, leading the country until an electoral defeat in 2004. In the intervening decade, between 2004 and 2014, the BJP expanded its electoral base to include many lower-caste voters and much of the ideological right, culminating in a large victory over the Congress party in 2014. During this time, Modi, who was chief minister of Gujarat province, built his political base on Hindu nationalism, with a history of condoning anti-Muslim violence. Since coming to power, the BJP has eroded basic democratic rights (Varshney 2019, 70; Maerz et al. 2020, 917). The BJP-led government initially targeted protesters who promoted liberal democratic values (e.g., anti-death penalty organizers, and students rallying for academic freedom), but has since extended political repression to include mass censorship in Muslim-majority areas, jailing journalists, attacking judicial independence, and, perhaps most perniciously, strategically promoting and exonerating anti-Muslim violence (Ganguly 2019; McDonnell and Cabrera 2019; Varshney 2019; Ayyub 2020; Chacko and Talukdar 2020).

The BJP has received substantial monetary and organizational support from the Indian diaspora, particularly from high-skilled, relatively wealthy emigrants. As one observer writes, "[t]he wealthy segments of the overseas Indian and the People of Indian Origin (PIOs)—many of whom identify with BJP's Hindutva ideology—are sources of large remittances into

India" (Palit 2019, 3). Similarly to politicians in other countries with large overseas populations BJP politicians travel abroad to solicit financial contributions to the party and to organize electoral support. For example, the BJP has held campaign events in Australia, the UK, and the USA (Schrank 2019; Shankar 2019; Smyth and Findlay 2019). The BJP's affiliate political organization, the RSS, has deep roots in the diaspora, stemming from earlier periods when some Hindu nationalists were forced into exile during Indira Gandhi's (Congress party) "emergency" in the mid-1970s, when she shut down parliament and arrested political opponents (Shankar 2019).

Much of the diaspora support for the BJP is from emigrants from Gujarat, an Indian state where the BJP had its strongest showing in the 2014 election and one of its traditional electoral strongholds. Over the prior decade, the BJP government in Gujarat had established political and financial ties to the diaspora and then created the Non-Resident Gujarati Foundation (NRG) to channel money towards their objectives, which included establishing a database of overseas Gujaratis and facilitating technical and professional skills transfer between the diaspora and their counterparts at home (Singh and Rajan 2015, 138–39). This suggests that relatively wealthy emigrants, particularly from Gujarat, may have helped fund BJP party organization with remittances and other resources.

Further, the BJP won the 2014 election in part by broadening its electoral support to include many new voters in scheduled tribes and castes: the first time the BJP had bested the Congress party among these groups of voters (Chhibber and Verma 2014, 50). In the run-up to the election, the Indian diaspora in the USA funded anti-poverty and development efforts in India by contributing to the India Development Relief Fund (IDRF), a tax-exempt relief effort. However, as Bose (2015, 36) notes, "the bulk of funds raised [by the IDRF] have gone to RSS-affiliated organizations and have been directed at promulgating *Hindutva* beliefs under the guise of relief and development activities, especially in tribal or marginalized areas." This suggests that diaspora funding funneled through BJP-linked organizations to relatively low-income voters may have boosted their electoral support for the BJP in 2014.

For the past decade, India has been the top recipient of remittances globally.[14] However, diaspora funding of the BJP, primarily from relatively wealthy emigrants, does not reflect the entire remittance story in India. Many Indian emigrants live and work in wealthy Gulf states: by one estimate, nearly one-third of immigrants in Gulf countries hail from India; and 70 percent of these migrants work in either construction or household service (Singh and Arimbra 2019). Thus while some of the remittances sent from the Gulf may come from relatively wealthy ex-pat supporters of the BJP, most are likely sent back to India by low-skilled migrants.

Indian remittance inflows from the Gulf suggest another pathway through which these resources may have shaped electoral politics. If Gulf remittances to low-income voters back home made them less dependent on state benefits from Congress-led governments, this may have decreased electoral support for the Congress party by 2014—a mechanism that resonates with our main argument. If emigration and remittances lower electoral support for long-established democratic parties by helping low-income voters to extricate themselves from incumbent-party dependency networks, we might conclude that in this case remittances aided the rise of an authoritarian (Hindu-nationalist) party.

If we interpret this narrative as demonstrating that remittances, by aiding the rise of the BJP, harm democracy in India, the two mechanisms we offer in our theory—the undermining of electoral support for incumbent parties and the increasing of resources for political opposition—work via two very different groups there. Remittances from relatively wealthy emigrants helped fund an opposition party (the BJP prior to 2014), and remittances from relatively low-skill emigrants in the Gulf may have reduced the economic rationale for some low-income Congress supporters to turn out at the polls. Our micro-evidence in chapters 4 and 5 also points to two different groups of remittance recipients: those who reside in opposition districts (more protest) and those who reside in swing districts (lower vote turnout).

This account, suggesting that remittance inflows to India both helped fund BJP electoral campaigns and reduced turnout for the incumbent Congress party, validates the mechanisms linking remittances to political change that we propose, and illustrates how our larger argument—that remittances foster democracy by undermining autocratic rule—may be context-dependent. That is to say, the Indian case points to the anti-incumbent nature of the causal mechanisms we propose, irrespective of whether the incumbent is a long-ruling democratic party or an authoritarian one.

Finally, the Indian case also illustrates the potential for opposition parties, once in power, to channel diaspora resources into development schemes (such as the India Development Relief Fund) to bolster the party's electoral campaigns. When political parties win power and control remittance inflows, they may use them to undermine democracy and entrench their own power. This part of the Indian narrative, however, points to one of our central themes: it is unlikely that remittances will further democracy if incumbent governments control this resource.

The Hungarian and Indian cases point to areas for future research. First, if emigration signals a malaise in the status quo, as Krastev and Holmes argue, and remittances empower citizens to mobilize against incumbent governments in democracies—two theories that yield similar macro-predictions— then we might test these competing mechanisms with micro-data on political behavior. Second, the Indian case suggests the possibility that different types of emigrant may influence politics back home in distinct ways, a possibility we have not explored. Finally, as these two cases highlight, our theory largely ignores what comes next, after democratic transitions occur, affording ample opportunity to explore how emigration and remittances shape democratic consolidation and survival.

## 8.4. What Does This Mean for Globalization?

Migration is perhaps the oldest form of globalization. Ancient humans moved across continents, and in doing so they settled and later colonized different regions, shaping the civilizational landscape of the world. Furthermore, prior to settled agriculture and the economic surplus it generated, trade across long distances could only occur when humans themselves migrated. In the contemporary era, non-remittance monetary flows between countries, particularly between the Global North and Global South, largely follow the path first trodden by migrants. For example, OECD countries provide more foreign aid to developing countries that send many migrants to the donor countries (Bermeo and Leblang 2015); and migration often paves the way for international investment flows (Leblang 2010). Thus migration is a central component of other aspects of economic globalization, including trade, investment, and foreign aid. However, policy and even much academic discussion about the liberalizing potential of globalization assumes that trade and investment are the only factors that transform politics in autocratic political regimes.

### 8.4.1. How Migration Differs from Trade and Investment Liberalization

The main argument of this book speaks to the debate about globalization and its impacts on democracy: the remittances that flow from migration, unlike capital flows or international trade, move across borders in ways that shift the balance of power towards citizens and away from governments in migrant-sending countries. This, according to the evidence presented in this book, opens opportunities for bottom-up democratization. A brief look at the possible political consequences of globalization in a few cases points to ways in which financial flows from remittances differ from trade and investment flows.

At the start of the post–Cold War era, many policy-makers and pundits thought globalization would enhance democracy. This became clear, for example, during discussion prior to China's accession to the World Trade Organization (WTO) in 2001. The bet at the time was that economic openness would bring political change to China, undermining Communist Party (CCP) rule by reducing the party's economic control over society and building a strong middle class that would demand democracy. In a speech in March 2000 at the Paul H. Nitze School of Advanced International Studies of the Johns Hopkins University, President Bill Clinton affirmed, "By joining the WTO, China is not simply agreeing to import more of our products; it is agreeing to import one of democracy's most cherished values: economic freedom. The more China liberalizes its economy, the more fully it will liberate the potential of its people—their initiative, their imagination, their remarkable spirit of enterprise. And when individuals have the power, not just to dream but to realize their dreams, they will demand a greater say." Interestingly, he also emphasized that "[w]e know how much the Internet has changed America, and we are already an open society. Imagine how much it could change China." These remarks highlight the hope placed on the power of modernization to bring political change. Increased economic integration would lead to growth and this, in turn, would bring democracy. International trade, investment, and the internet would, according to this account, transform China politically.

So far this has not turned out to be the case, despite the fact that China is now the world's second largest economy and second largest FDI recipient (UNCTAD 2019).[15] Instead, rapid economic growth and technological change in China have led to a rising middle class but also to authoritarian retrenchment, the emergence of a mass surveillance and digital repression system, and, under the presidency of Xi Jinping, increasingly personalistic rule.[16] While the explanations for the failure of economic globalization to lead to democracy in China are undoubtedly complex (and outside the scope of our project), we note that throughout the period of rising globalization in the past three decades, the CCP maintained control over domestic capital flows, retained a large state-owned banking sector, adjusted its party institutions to co-opt many new economic elites, and never allowed multiparty, national electoral contests.

China is not the only country where the economically liberalizing aspects of globalization have had political consequences. According to some scholars, economic liberalization in sub-Saharan Africa moved substantial financial resources away from states—and the long-standing ruling autocratic parties that controlled them—and to private business people. These newly private economic resources, according to this argument, helped finance opposition parties central to the story of democratization in the post-1990 decades (Arriola 2013b).[17]

This economic liberalization, while perhaps breaking party monopolies on power in many countries, has limits, however, because newly empowered actors are not necessarily pro-democratic. Take the example of Benin, a democratic "success story" in post–Cold War Africa. Patrice Talon, a businessman who grew wealthy in the wake of privatization (he consolidated Beninois cotton distribution), helped finance the political campaigns of a two-time president, former banker and bureaucrat Thomas Boni Yayi. Yayi stepped down after winning two terms in office, respecting term limit rules put in place during democratization in the 1990s, but not before opening a corruption investigation into Talon. Talon then turned against Yayi, bankrolled his own presidential campaign, and, since his election in 2016, has "stuffed the courts with cronies, excluded opposition parties from elections, shut down the internet, and arrested journalists" (*The Economist* 2020b).[18] If economic liberalization yielded substantial non-state financial capital that funded opposition parties and broke the power of long-ruling autocratic parties, this financial capital was often controlled by only a handful of wealthy business people, leaving a legacy of centralized financial power.

Remittances, as private income that flows to millions of citizens, offer a type of non-state financial resource very different from gains from privatization or trade and investment liberalization, because it is (nearly) effortlessly decentralized. While some remittance income may flow directly to political parties, the vast majority accrues to individual citizens who may fund parties or otherwise devote time and resources to political organization. But even by this account it is citizens, not party elites who ultimately control the resources—a picture far different from that of financial liberalization breeding a handful of super-wealthy individuals who use this new wealth to fund opposition parties, or the autocratic party co-opting newly wealthy elite "red capitalists," as in China. In short, remittances are a diffuse flow of international financial resources, and thus differ from concentrated financial resources. The winners from trade and investment liberalization are much more concentrated, and thus easier for autocratic governments to co-opt or control.

### 8.4.2. Political Implications for the Next Wave of Globalization

The decades of increasing globalization—from roughly the 1980s to the 2010s—may be coming to a close, at least in the short term. Even before the global pandemic largely halted international migration, backlash against globalization had produced political and policy changes, with support for populist parties rising and global powers clashing over trade and investment openness (Broz et al. 2021).

However, a leading thinker on globalization, Richard Baldwin, recently conjectured that globalization in the long twenty-first century is likely to take the form of mass movement of low-cost labor across international borders, but without humans actually *migrating* across those borders (Baldwin 2016).[19] He posits that advances in communications technology—particularly virtual presence and telerobotics—will substantially reduce the costs of face-to-face interaction, allowing low-skilled labor residing in the Global South to provide services directly to consumers in rich-world countries. While today many low-wage services are still conceived of as "in-person" (i.e., non-tradable), requiring a human being in close physical proximity to the consumer, and hence resident in the consumer's country, future globalization may decouple the service provision from the human being providing it. As the 2020 global pandemic unfolds and government orders to "shelter in place" proliferate, these trends may accelerate. Baldwin writes (2006, 283) that

> salaries and wages are much higher in rich countries and there are billions of people who would like to earn those wages. They are, today, unable to do so, since they find it hard to get into rich nations. If technology opens a sluice-gate that allows these people to offer their labor services in advanced economies without actually being there, the impact on jobs could be shocking. And the necessary technology is . . . not too far away.

Telerobotics, by this account, "would allow workers based in developing nations to provide labor services inside developed nations without actually being there" (297). This will lead, Baldwin argues, to the "virtual offshoring" of many jobs in what are now considered non-tradable sectors: labor services will be "physically unbundled from laborers" (298).

The global pandemic of 2020 is likely to accelerate technological change, as more of the economy moves to digital products and workers move online. Despite stagnating trade between the 2008 global financial crisis and the onset of the pandemic in 2020, the World Bank still believes that global value chains will continue to boost growth and reduce poverty in developing countries, because technological advancements will move further down global supply chains, boosting the productivity of low-wage workers (World Bank 2020, 4). Artuc et al. (2018), for example, find that roboticization of production in the Global North is likely to boost incomes in the Global South by increasing imports to rich countries sourced from developing countries. As importantly, as Baldwin and Forslid (2020) argue that if globalization and robotics boost incomes in the Global South, this will most likely stem from rising employment and wages in service—not manufacturing—sectors. Indeed, a "global digital labour market, spurred by firms' investments in technology, might unleash a new wave of innovation," with cross-border provision of digital education and health care at the forefront (Curr 2020, 14).

If this new twist to globalization—"virtual" labor in rich countries in exchange for real remittance earnings in developing countries—becomes a reality, it has profound implications for the sources of income for citizens in countries ruled by authoritarian governments. Indeed, if Baldwin is correct, the findings in this book suggest an overlooked implication of the next wave of globalization: when citizens of dictatorships earn wages in foreign economies even without physical migration, this may provide a large infusion of private income that shifts the balance of power away from authoritarian governments enabling those citizens to mobilize against repressive regimes. Globalization, in this scenario, would spur a wave of opposition mobilization undermining electoral autocracies throughout the world. This implication, of course, assumes that citizens retain control over these income flows and that authoritarian governments do not develop the technologies to capture and control them.

There may be a parallel with global information flows. The Chinese government, for example, places real limits on the cross-border flow of information on the internet and on social media in an effort to censor information that could lead citizens to mobilize against the regime (King et al. 2013). While the censorship is not foolproof, Chinese government efforts to control information flows have raised the costs of accessing some forms of international information sufficiently to deter most citizens from consuming it (Roberts 2018). By allowing and encouraging the types of cross-border information flow that facilitate global manufacturing supply chains, the Chinese government has helped to boost the incomes of hundreds of millions of its citizens; but while the government enabled these information flows, it also raised the costs of accessing information flows harmful to "social stability." Thus the Chinese government benefited enormously from the ICT revolution, while minimizing the risks to itself.

If autocratic governments can similarly block or shift to their balance sheet the bulk of worker remittances from a global digital labor market, this new form of globalization may not threaten their grip on power, but might instead bolster it. Indeed, one could imagine authoritarian governments implementing a technology to control "virtual" labor migration by restricting access to these markets or taxing the flow of this income. By excluding citizens deemed least loyal while permitting regime supporters to supply labor in a virtual international labor market—thus boosting their incomes but not those of political opponents—autocratic governments could transform such virtual labor migration into yet another international financial flow that sustains their rule.

Again, returning to the Chinese example, in 2019 the government implemented a new payments regulation requiring mobile deposits to be cleared through the People's Bank of China, thus allowing the government access to user data from the mobile payments platforms on Alibab (Alipay) and Ten-Cent's Wechat. By one estimate, over 40 trillion dollars flowed through these apps in 2018.[20] The government is also working to integrate WeChat into the Chinese government's electronic ID system, which will permit real-time government surveillance of users' personal financial data, including payment deposits. Further, Ant Financial, the parent company for Alibab, exploits enormous amounts of information on consumers' financial transactions and income flows to strengthen its consumer lending and insurance arms.[21] It would be possible for such information to be connected to other forms of digital and personal surveillance so that the government could directly monitor the sources of income for those it deems loyal, as well as those it does not.

Our theory argues that international financial remittances undermine autocratic rule; but this story presumes these remittances remain firmly in the hands of citizens, not the government. If either access to virtual international labor markets or information about remittance income come to be within the purview of autocratic governments, this key assumption fails; and remittances become much more like oil export revenue: an external source of income that flows directly to autocrats. Our theory thus parallels debates about how technology influences the relative power of citizens and governments, particularly in autocratic contexts. Broadly speaking, when technological change favors better information for the mass of citizens—for example in mobilizing anti-regime protest—this informational advantage undermines autocratic rule. However, as autocratic governments use technological advances to gain (or regain) informational advantages over citizens—for example, through government surveillance and social media disinformation campaigns—then technology is likely to stabilize and even strengthen autocratic rule.[22]

Thus, when policymakers grapple with technological change, globalization, and new forms of labor migration, they should bear in mind who controls not only access to these labor markets, but also the flow of income from them: that is, whether it is citizens, or governments. In the past two decades, the United Nations, the World Bank and other international organizations have set a policy goal of reducing the transaction costs of remittance transfers across borders (World Bank 2017, 4; Method and Owuor 2018). By lowering these costs, new transfer mechanisms ensure workers receive more of this income, reduce the share of these flows accruing to the "middleman", and may even increase overall remittance flows (Ahmed et al. 2020). If international development organizations continue to invest in remittance transfer mechanisms, they should think carefully about the extent to which governments in recipient countries control access to these transfer technologies, especially if money transfer platforms transform into "virtual labor markets" which are the site of both virtual service provision and real foreign remittance payments. For remittances to remain a liberalizing financial flow, virtual labor markets and remittance transfer technologies must remain outside the control of autocratic governments.

We close, then, by emphasizing that migrants' financial remittances, should they fall under the sway of authoritarian governments, would be unlikely to threaten dictators' grip on power and foster democracy. As long as remittances flow to citizens and help finance opposition political activity, however, tipping the resource imbalance in their favor, migration may yet undermine dictatorship and pave the way for democracy.

## Chapter 1: Introduction

1. Further tens of millions of people migrated from various parts of Asia to other territories within that continent.

2. See Davis et al. (2018).

3. Note, moreover, that official figures for remittances underestimate the true amount of such flows, due to the extensive use of informal channels for sending them.

4. For a relatively recent analysis of the effect of immigration on democratization, see Bearce and Hutnick (2011). They argue that immigration facilitates redistributive concessions that reduce social unrest, thus fostering political stability, not change.

5. Urdal (2006), for example, finds that "youth bulges" (in population) increase the risk of political violence. Youth bulges, he explains, "provide greater opportunities for violence through the abundant supply of youths with low opportunity costs, and with an expectation that stronger motives for violence may arise as youth bulges are more likely to experience institutional crowding, in particular unemployment" (Urdal 2006, 607).

6. Barry et al. (2014) find that more freedom of foreign movement is associated with less anti-government protest activity in authoritarian states when there are attractive opportunities abroad.

7. See also Moses (2012). Karadja and Prawitz (2019) find empirical evidence for this mechanism in nineteenth-century Sweden.

8. Some note, however, that the transmission of ideas might be detrimental to democracy if migrants transmit anti-democratic social remittances when they settle in countries ruled by non-democratic governments (Rother 2009; Barsbai et al. 2017).

9. The shutdown of many economies during the global pandemic of 2020, however, has not only closed many borders but has also caused cross-border remittance flows to plummet. Migrant workers are much more likely to work outside the home than native workers but also much less likely than native residents to receive economic support from host governments, making the economic impact of the global pandemic much worse, on average, for migrant workers than for native ones.

10. Developing countries only received about one-third of total global investment flows.

11. On the link between oil and autocratic rule see, among many others, Ross (2001); Smith (2004); Ulfelder (2007); Morrison (2009); Omgba (2009); Tsui (2011); Ross (2012); Andersen and Ross (2014); and Wright et al. (2015). On the stabilizing effect of aid see, for example,

Djankov et al. (2008); Smith (2008); Kono and Montinola (2009); and Bueno de Mesquita and Smith (2010).

12. While foreign aid may have helped prop up autocratic governments during the Cold War period, when donors prioritized stability in allied autocratic regimes and former colonies over the official goal of promoting development and reducing poverty, most of the evidence from the post-1990 period shows that foreign aid may in fact promote democracy (or at least multiparty politics) in recipient countries (Dunning 2004; Wright 2009; Bermeo 2011; Escribà-Folch and Wright 2015; Carnegie and Marinov 2017).

13. Even if governments do not directly control the firms involved in the export of natural resources and cash crops, these products are more easily taxed by governments than income or other goods and services, because they tend to flow through only a few export locations. This makes it much easier for governments to observe, measure, and ultimately tax these goods as they leave the country.

14. In several cases, these incentives have even led MNCs to cooperate with non-democratic host regimes to reduce union activity, control internal opposition groups, and suppress workers' protests.

15. "A diaspora can be defined as a social collectivity that exists across state borders and that has succeeded over time to (1) sustain a collective national, cultural or religious identity through a sense of internal cohesion and sustained ties with a real or imagined homeland and (2) display an ability to address the collective interests of members of the social collectivity through a developed internal organizational framework and transnational links" (Adamson and Demetriou 2007, 497). While there are data on collective remittances for individual cases, we are not aware of cross-national data on collective remittances or data on remittances that distinguish individual from collective remittances; collective remittances are "virtually impossible to systematically track" (Duquette-Rury 2019, 20).

16. See Hirschman (1993) for a reformulation of his framework suggesting that exit and voice can reinforce each other.

## Chapter 2: Migration and Repertoires of Contention: How Remittances Undermine Dictatorship

1. See Nordlinger (1977); Geddes (1999); Geddes et al. (2014b), and Singh (2014) on the military's advantage in solving collective action problems.

2. We use 'dictatorship', 'autocracy', and 'autocratic regime' interchangeably. Throughout the book we use data on dictatorships from Geddes et al. (2014a); they define an autocratic regime as "a set of formal and/or informal rules for choosing leaders and policies." Dictatorships thus include both regimes that regularly hold multiparty elections (e.g., Belarus, Malaysia prior to 2018, and Uganda during President Museveni's rule), regimes that only have one-party elections (e.g., Vietnam), and regimes that do not hold elections for national office (e.g., China and Saudi Arabia). According to this definition of autocracies, dictatorships can, but do not necessarily, fall into a "grey area" between democracy and autocracy. "Grey-area" regimes, typically referred to as "competitive authoritarian regimes," are coded as non-democratic if the criteria for identifying democracies are not met. Regimes coded as "autocratic" thus include electoral—or competitive—autocracies but are not limited to these. Further, there can be

multiple specific regimes within spell of autocracy, where this is constituted by the consecutive calendar years during which an autocracy in any form rules the country. Once an observation-year is coded as authoritarian, successive years in the same country are regarded as coming under the same regime until a regime-transition (i.e., regime-collapse) event occurs.

3. A regime collapse occurs when the group currently in power is ousted. Regime collapse may lead to a transition to democracy, such as the electoral defeat for the ruling PRI in Mexico in 2000; or the regime may collapse and be replaced by a subsequent dictatorship: for example, Mobutut Sese Seko ruled the former Zaire as a dictatorship from the 1960s to 1997, when a rebel group chased his government from power and established a new autocratic regime. The total number of autocratic collapse events in each of the three periods shown in Figure 2.1 is 158, 65, and 25, respectively.

4. There is, however, debate about the political consequences of coups: some suggest that coups can promote democratization (Thyne and Powell 2016) and lead to multiparty elections (Marinov and Goemans 2014); while others question the evidence for the "democratic coup" claim (Miller 2011; Derpanopoulos et al. 2016; Tansey 2016b).

5. Some evidence suggests that not only is there a strong association between nonviolent protest campaigns and democratic transitions, but also that democracies emerging from such campaigns are more stable and less prone to breakdown (Bayer et al. 2016).

6. Weidmann and Rød (2019) show that internet penetration increases protests in the short term but diminishes them in the long term. Similarly, Kendall-Taylor et al. (2020) argue that dictatorships increasingly deploy digital repression to quash protests, perhaps, as the Chinese case suggests, by providing regimes with better information about political opponents (Xu 2021).

7. Not all international factors, of course, advance democracy. An emerging research agenda examines how authoritarian governments devise strategies to support other autocratic governments and promote their model of government abroad. See, for example, Tolstrup (2013); Vanderhill (2013); Bader (2015); von Soest (2015), and Tansey (2016a). Ample research shows, moreover, that international trade in natural resources helps to prop up resource-rich dictatorships.

8. For a review, see Krasner and Weinstein (2014).

9. For example, the Trump administration shifted US immigration policy in attempts to block migration to the States. However, this is not the first time the US government has gone down this path. The wave of migration at the end of the nineteenth and early twentieth centuries also provoked an anti-immigrant policy backlash, including the institution of literacy tests, exclusion of Chinese, enforcement of strict quotas, and immigrant taxes (Williamson 1998); not to speak of the terrorist campaigns targeting immigrants in the USA during this period (see, e.g., Jew 2002; Pfaelzer 2007).

10. This is not to say, of course, that foreign actors never play a role in state-led violence, military coups, or elections (Huggins 1987; Thyne 2010; Bubeck and Marinov 2019).

11. Between 1946 and 2010, not even 5 percent of all autocratic regime collapse events resulted from direct foreign military invasion, according to Geddes et al.'s (2014) data. See Figure 2.1.

12. Likewise, revolutions as drivers of democratic change only featured prominently in game-theoretic accounts aimed at understanding how structural factors such as economic

development and inequality shape democratization (Boix 2003; Acemoglu and Robinson 2006; Ansell and Samuels 2014). Again in these models however, political change was assumed to be elite-driven, and revolutions—as well as other crises—were seen only as shaping elite behavior once they arise as credible threats that give elites little choice but to open the regime so as to prevent revolts from toppling it.

13. Some argue that elections constitute a top-down pathway of autocratic breakdown because they require insider agreement to be held (Kendall-Taylor et al. 2019, 144). However, for elections to destabilize autocracies, the behavior of the public is central, since a defeat at the polls is only possible when voters withdraw their support for incumbent parties or decide to protest electoral manipulation.

14. In some cases this support may even include military assistance for armed rebel groups.

15. See Brancati and Lucardi (2019) for an opposing view.

16. As Farrell (1983, 598) notes, "loyalist behavior may constitute an independent course of action between exit and voice or it may be a transitory form giving way to other behaviors as the situation continues."

17. A recent empirical evaluation of these claims finds that autocracies adopt more open emigration policies when economic migration is high, but restrict emigration if citizens leave for democracies (Miller and Peters 2020).

18. For example, contrary to popular understanding, over 60 percent of migrants in Germany's guest-worker program are, in fact, temporary and often circular migrants, meaning they return home (Constant and Zimmermann 2011).

19. Political-economic models of democratization have long emphasized the role of redistributive pressures in explaining democratization. Inequality increases the threat of social unrest, by these accounts, forcing elites to respond by committing to credible future income redistribution and, hence, democracy (Acemoglu and Robinson 2006).

20. See Wright and Bak (2016) for a discussion.

21. Geddes et al. (2018, 142) note that "[i]n most dictatorships, low turnout means either that local officials and activists have not done their job of making sure that people go to the polls or that people are hostile enough to risk penalties for failing to vote."

22. Repression-induced fear may indeed discourage the public expression of dissent (Young 2019). At the same time, disproportionately harsh repression may strengthen group cohesion and solidarity, deepen existing grievances, and act as a catalyzing event that sparks further mobilization (Lichbach 1987; Francisco 1995; 2006; Blaydes 2018). Dictators may be quite aware of the mobilizing backlash from pursuing repression against prominent opponents. Esberg (2021) finds, for example, that in Chile the Pinochet regime exiled prominent opposition politicians rather than torturing and imprisoning them because the latter strategies might prompt widespread anti-regime mobilization. For less well-known opponents, however, the regime did not refrain from torture or imprisonment.

23. Some protests, however, may even be strategically tolerated by the regime, in order to gather relevant information on existing grievances and discontented groups—all in an effort to prevent more widespread challenges from emerging (Lorentzen 2013).

24. Similarly, in so-called "violent democracies," which are also highly risky environments for protesting, migrant resources help recipients to organize against crime. For example, during the drug war in Mexico, some recipients opted to keep a low profile to avoid attracting

attention from criminals; yet, others relied on household and collective remittances to organize protests against criminal organizations. Both monetary resources and migrant-induced
social learning facilitated a collective response against crime and often against the Mexican
state, which was unable (or unwilling) to fight violence (Ley et al. 2021; Pérez-Armendáriz 2021;
Pérez-Armendáriz and Duquette-Rury 2021).

25. This need not be the case for remittances to boost *individual* capacity, however without
intending to influence home country politics, senders can nonetheless increase their family
members' capacity for contentious political engagement when they remit income.

26. Others find that remittances increase the risk of civil war and terrorist attacks, by boosting resources available to armed groups (Collier and Hoeffler 2004; Mascarenhas and Sandler
2014; Miller and Ritter 2014; Van Hear and Cohen 2017). As an external "political investment" that funds opposition political activity and mobilizes citizens, remittances are a form of
transnational political engagement (O'Mahony 2013). Conflict-generated diasporas often fund
anti-government mobilization and protection of relatives left behind, sometimes contributing
to conflict perpetuation but also to regime collapse and post-conflict reconstruction processes
(Koinova 2009; Lindley 2009; Brinkerhoff 2011; Carling et al. 2012; Lyons 2012; Moss 2016;
Van Hear and Cohen 2017; Carment and Calleja 2018; Koinova 2018).

27. The literature on diaspora engagement with homelands is vast and by no means suggests a simplistic, positive relationship between diasporas and democratization. Diasporas are
not only "actors" but also "objects" of homeland politics, whereby groups at home, including
autocratic governments, craft, court, or repress diaspora communities to pursue their own
advantage. Further, diasporas are not necessarily unambiguously supportive of democracy.
Instead, their involvement in homeland politics depends on the often complex political and historical processes through which they originated, as well as on windows of opportunity offered
by host countries (Shain 1999; Gamlen 2014; Glasius 2018; Koinova 2018; Adamson 2019a,b).
While all these are necessary caveats, diasporas do often nevertheless support pro-democracy
leaders and social movements financially.

28. This argument resonates with research showing that remittance recipients, at least in
Latin America, tend to align on the ideological right, opposing redistribution, than on the left
(Doyle 2015).

29. Scholars debate how best to define clientelism and patronage (Hicken 2011), especially
when applied to democratic politics. Some treat the concepts as synonymous, using them
interchangeably. Others consider patronage to be a sub-class of clientelism, while still others
consider patronage to be a broader condition that enables clientelism. Alternative distinctions
between the two concepts focus on whether the recipient is a party member or simply a voter;
whether the political actor delivering benefits holds office or is a private actor; and whether
the benefit is a public job or some consumable state resource. To avoid confusion, we use
Stokes's (2007, 605) definition of clientelism: "proffering of material goods in return for electoral support, where the criterion of distribution that the patron uses is simply: did you (will
you) support me?" Meanwhile patronage is: "proffering of public resources (most typically,
public employment) by office holders in return for electoral support" (Stokes 2007, 606). In
the case of autocratic contexts, where incumbent ruling parties monopolize control over state
resources and use them to mobilize electoral support with little constraint, the two concepts
largely overlap and we use them interchangeably.

30. Chapter 4 explains in detail why we use a geographical approach to measuring pro- and anti-regime preferences.

31. Brady et al. (1995) also stress the role of recruitment and mobilization, to which resources accruing to opposition parties, civil society organizations, and other voluntary associations can also contribute.

32. Others posit that risk-aversion explains why clientelism targets low-income citizens: poorer voters, more than wealthy ones, discount the future more strongly and prioritize receiving immediate benefits over possibly uncertain, future redistribution and other programmatic promises (Kitschelt 2000; Stokes 2007).

33. A recent literature addresses how political parties react to voters who receive remittances. These studies suggest that party machines are aware of the risk of electoral demobilization among remittance recipients, which increases the likelihood that parties will target them more than those who do not receive remittances. However, this implies that governments, and in particular brokers, know who remittance recipients are. As Germano (2018, 134) explains, once in the field, there are evident signs, such as owning a better home or luxury goods as well as driving cars with foreign plates, that a household receives remittances. Further, emigrants often visit family back home and participate in community projects with their relatives and local authorities (Aparicio and Meseguer 2012; Meseguer and Aparicio 2012; Duquette-Rury 2016; 2019; Danielson 2018). Compared to other information that models of clientelism often attribute to brokers, knowing who receives remittances is relatively easy for local brokers who are "well embedded" in their communities. See González-Ocantos et al. (2018, 692–93) for a discussion, and Álvarez Mingote (2019).

34. A ruling party may, however, attempt to buy abstention in opposition areas even though what we observe more often is intimidation to prevent individuals in such areas from voting (Mares and Young 2016, 269). Theoretically, remittances might erode abstention-buying, resulting in increased levels of electoral participation in opposition districts.

35. Indeed, this is exactly what Kramon (2009) finds in Kenya: targets tend to be poor "individuals in more electorally competitive areas."

36. Again, see chapter 4 for discussion of how we operationalize government support in the micro-level analyses.

37. The figure omits the unclear predictions of the grievance model concerning voting. It also excludes the potential positive effect of remittances on protest predicted by the weakened-clientelism model. This expectation would appear in the lower-left cell (pro-government and low-income), but we expect this potential impact to be rather weak.

38. Escribà-Folch et al. match individuals based on four possible sources of individual-level grievance: *anti-government sentiment*; material *deprivation*; *fear* of the regime; and paying *bribes*. The first source of grievance captures individual-level sentiment towards the incumbent national government and thus accounts for the possibility that the regime targets particular individuals according to their personal sentiment vis-á-vis the government. Anti-government individuals, for example, may be more likely targets of government efforts to stymie remittance flows to political opponents. The second source of grievance, relative material deprivation, accounts for the possibility that individuals who have fewer material goods than others in their country are more likely to emigrate and to protest. The third source of grievance, fear of the regime, accounts for the possibility that individuals already targeted by the government

as known opponents are more likely to come from families that have emigrants and that are more likely to protest. These individuals may also be targets of government efforts to obstruct remittance receipt. Finally, corruption—one manifest indicator of which is paying bribes—is a potential source of individual grievance (Hiskey et al. 2014). If individuals who experience more corruption are more likely to seek out remittances and to protest, this could confound the micro-analysis.

39. Some scholars use an instrumental variable—a factor such as exposure to disaster or civil war that is empirically correlated with the decision to migrate but that purportedly does not influence political behavior—to address individual selection effects (e.g., Batista et al. 2019).

## Chapter 3: Remittances, Revenue, and Government Spending in Dictatorships

1. Autocratic governments often control cash-crop revenue from, for example, cocoa, cotton, and coffee production by relying on government-owned marketing boards to capture exports (Bates 1984).

2. Final-point-of-purchase taxes and VAT, if enforced, generate government revenue irrespective of whether the private income used in these transactions is from foreign or domestic sources.

3. Abdih et al. (2008, 6) write that "[t]he assumption that remittances are non-taxed accords with the general practice of avoiding taxing these flows by governments in the recipient countries."

4. Ahmed (2012) re-specifies the game-theoretic model in Abdih et al. (2008) but argues that a substitution-driven increase in patronage goods increases autocratic stability.

5. Remittances could decrease government's need to collect tax revenue if remitted income served as a substitute for labor income and, hence, reduced labor supply, which in turn would reduce observed income tax receipts.

6. See Asatryan et al. (2017) for a study that also uses ICTD tax-revenue data. In reproduction files, we attempt to replicate this study using a similar exogenous instrument: oil price × distance from oil producers. Our sample has sixty-two countries with autocratic governments, from 1980 to 2017. Using the same specification, the instrument strength is generally stronger than that reported in Asatryan et al. (2017). We find that remittances are negatively associated with sales tax revenue (goods and services tax), though the estimate is not statistically significant. Bastiaens and Rudra (2018) also use ICTD tax revenue data, but their research does not focus on remittances.

7. We still find non-random missingness in the ICTD data. Roughly 20 percent of the data with no missingness in remittances lacks information on total tax revenue. Missingness occurs more often for resource-rich countries with *less* emigration and *fewer* remittances.

8. We estimate and report the long-run multiplier, which is the overall change in the equilibrium level of tax revenue, and captures remittance effect over multiple time periods. We report estimates from sixty-eight country-panels that are at least five years in length (5–37 years), though this choice does not materially effect the results. The number of country-year observations is 1,143. By excluding short-panels, for which dynamic estimates will be more imprecise, we increase the chances of finding a statistically significant estimate for remittances.

The dependent variables are logged to reduce the skew and provide a more normal distribution for the least-squares estimator. Finally, we report panel-corrected standard errors that account for panel heteroskedasticity and AR(1) error processes.

9. Extant literature on remittances, taxation, and spending also use two-way fixed effects estimators (Singer 2012; Ebeke 2014; Easton and Montinola 2017).

10. Specifications that drop additional covariates or use the exact specification in Singer (2012) yield similar, null results. We also note that this specification does not adjust for economic growth, because one mechanism through which remittances might augment government tax revenue is by boosting economic growth. Including growth could therefore lead to post-treatment bias. However, in our reproduction files we report estimates from specifications that adjust for growth and also yield null results.

11. One version of the political resource curse argument claims that resource rents lower domestic tax-revenue collection from the non-resource sector, dampening citizens' demand for representation and accountability.

12. The sample includes sixty-four country panels (1,001 observations) with panel sizes ranging from five to thirty-seven years.

13. In this sample period (1990–2009), Mexico (1990–2000), Peru (1992–2000), and Venezuela (2006–2009) are the only autocracies among the eighteen countries. All three regimes had relatively fraud-free and competitive executive and legislative elections during these periods.

14. We report estimates for the square root of this measure to ensure a more normal distribution of the dependent variable. Using the untransformed series and excluding an extreme outlier produce the same results. The sample covers seventy-six unbalanced panels from 1978 to 2017 for a total of 1,501 observations. Again, this sample excludes panels with less than five years of data. Only 7 percent of the data with non-missing remittance values lacks data on government spending.

15. Singer (2012) and Doyle (2015) both employ ECMs to examine remittances and government spending.

16. When we use an untransformed outcome measure, the finding is negative; when omitting country-fixed effects, the finding is positive. Together with the null finding with fixed effects, these diverging results suggest inconsistency.

17. Again we restrict analysis of health and military spending to panels of five years or more, but this choice does not alter the results. The health-spending sample contains data on fifty-five unbalanced (five to twenty-one years) country panels (802 observations) with autocratic governments. Our sample thus has nearly three times as many observations as the sample (275 observations) analyzed in Ahmed (2013), which includes both autocracies and democracies. The military-spending sample contains data for seventy-three unbalanced panels (1,338 observations). For both outcomes we again estimate an ECM with two-way fixed effects and panel-corrected errors that allow for panel heteroskedasticity and AR(1) errors.

18. The estimate is statistically significant at the 0.075 level.

19. In reproduction files, we examine the ratio of health to military spending and find null results for remittances.

20. The point of congestion, and thus that at which the subsidy becomes rivalrous, occurs when the government can no longer afford the subsidy and must make fiscal decisions that may hurt some consumers.

21. The data cover autocracies in fifty-four countries. However, after restricting analysis to panels with five or more years of data, there are forty-two panels. Including short panels does not alter the results. As with the analysis of other types of spending, we estimate an ECM with two-way fixed effects, and panel-corrected errors that allow for panel heteroskedasticity and AR(1) errors.

22. If petrol subsidies forestall social unrest but remittances increase protest, as in the next chapter we show they do, then the evidence that remittances are associated with larger government subsidies is consistent with our theory, because autocratic governments, in the face of rising protest, may opt to boost subsidies.

23. The variable is $v2x\_clphy$, which measures the extent to which individual physical integrity—freedom from political killings and torture by the government—is protected. The measure reflects state repression not directly referring to elections. We flip the scale so that larger values can be interpreted as *more* repression.

24. We propose a two-way fixed-effects OLS model whereby we treat the autocratic regime—which is nested with the country unit—as the cross-section unit. We also include time-period effects and report cluster-robust error estimates. The sample comprises 101 regimes from 1978 to 2017, with panel sizes varying from five to forty years.

25. In these tests we measure remittances in the prior year, to mitigate concerns about reverse causation. Additional confounders are lagged by one year, with the exception of the conflict and election indicators.

26. Because these features of countries do not vary much over time, they are unlikely significantly to affect changes in repression in a fixed-effects model.

27. These reported tests estimate the long-term effect of remittances, which we believe is consistent with the substitution theory; we also test dynamic models that estimate a short-term relationship between remittances and repression, using first-difference models, again with null results.

28. These variables are $v2x\_civlib$ and $v2x\_clpol$. The civil liberties measure is a composite of the absence of physical violence committed by government agents and the absence of constraints upon private liberties and political liberties by the government. It therefore contains some conceptual overlap with the measure for hard repression, $v2x\_clphy$. Political liberties are conceptualized representatively as freedom of association and freedom of expression. For both measures, higher values mean *more* government respect for civil and political liberties—that is, the opposite of 'soft' repression. We propose the same model and specification as the test for hard repression.

29. This mechanism linking remittances to a dearth of political opposition—via substitution—is also consistent with an expectation taken directly from the study of the direct political consequences of increased remitted income, namely that remittances reduce electoral turnout (Goodman and Hiskey 2008; Bravo 2009; Ebeke and Yogo 2013; Germano 2018).

30. Both variables are from the Varieties of Democracy project. The first, $v2cseeorgs$, measures the extent to which the government achieves control over civil society organizations' entry into and exit from public life. The second, $v2csreprss$—government repression of civil society organizations—measures the extent to which the government violently and actively pursues members of (independent) civil society organizations, in an effort not just to curb the activity of such groups, but to eliminate them entirely. We flip the scales of these variables such that larger values correspond to *more* government control and repression.

## Chapter 4: Remittances Fund Opponents

1. The latent estimates are derived from an IRT model that is dynamic in the treatment of the item-difficulty cut-points of the latent variable (Fariss 2014). The model employs a Poisson distribution to model count data. The online Technical Appendix provides more information on the construction of this variable; the Appendix is accessible via https://press.princeton .edu/books/paperback/9780691199375/migration-and-democracy.

2. This reduces the potential that outliers drive estimates, and helps ensure that the data are more appropriate for a linear estimator.

3. Neighboring countries are regarded as being those with capital cities within 4,000 km of the target country's capital.

4. Election years are those with parliamentary or presidential elections; data from Coppedge et al. (2019).

5. We estimate a linear model; random and fixed-effects models yield similar estimates for remittances. The specification also includes time period effects:

$$Protest_{i,t} = \alpha_0 + \beta_1 Remit_{i,t-1} + \beta_3 X_{i,t-1} + \eta_t + \zeta_i + \varepsilon_{i,t} \tag{4.1}$$

where $Protest_{i,t}$ is the latent mean of the protest variable, $Remit_{i,t-1}$ is the lagged measure of remittances (logged constant dollars), $X_{i,t-1}$ is a set of covariates, $\eta_t$ are period-fixed effects, $\zeta_i$ country-fixed effects, and $\varepsilon_{i,t}$ is the error term that allows for clustering on leaders.

6. We standardize all explanatory variables so that the estimates reflect the marginal effect of a one-standard deviation increase in the variable.

7. See reproduction files and Escribà-Folch et al. (2018) for results from: altering the specification; adding additional confounders, including other global flows in the specification (e.g., aid, FDI, trade, refugees); different ways of modeling the calendar time trend; and in an error-correction model that accounts for short- and long-term effects. Further, we find that the remittance effect is strongest in later decades (2000s) than in earlier ones (pre-1990).

8. By design, the sample matches the updated data on autocratic regimes from Geddes et al. (2014a).

9. While 34 percent of the time there is no recorded anti-government protest, MMAD records pro-government rallies for less than 10 percent of the observations. In reproduction files, we test random-effects negative binomial estimators for both raw protest counts, which yield similar results to those reported here.

10. Tests for normality in the distribution of the logged counts indicate a much closer-to-normal distribution than the raw counts. We take the quadratic root of the logged pro-government count.

11. As before, "elections" includes years in which either a presidential or parliamentary election was held. Other confounders in these specifications (GDP per capita, population size, neighbor democratization, net migration, and movement restrictions) are not reported. We report results from a random-effects linear estimator rather than a fixed-effects one because the panel is relatively short (thirteen years), implying less within-unit variation. Results from a "within" kernel regression estimator are consistent with those reported here.

12. Cuba and Venezuela were the only two countries in Latin America classified as autocracies in 2008, while by 2016 Nicaragua had become a third. Further, migration from Cuba,

historically at least, and Venezuela more recently, has been political: those most likely to migrate are dissidents. Thus relatively few migrants from Cuba and Venezuela would be classified as economic migrants or climate refugees.

13. Autocracy–democracy coding uses an updated version of Geddes et al. (2014a).

14. Leaders in Algeria, Burkina Faso, Egypt, Sudan, and Tunisia were also ousted by military officers; these coups occurred during mass protest campaigns, as a direct response to protesters filling the streets of the capital cities for days, if not weeks.

15. See, for example, Economist Intelligence Unit (2011).

16. Some scholars argue that families that receive remittances are more likely to be targets of government officials' (including police) corruption, particularly bribery (Konte and Ndubuisi 2019); and this experience of corruption could, in turn, cause protest. However, Lewis (2020) shows that protest is more likely to be driven by elite corruption rather than everyday experience of corrupt police.

17. Clientelistic exchange based on local public goods provision is prevalent in many parts of the world (Stokes et al. 2013).

18. See the online Technical Appendix.

19. We combine the scores from the two indices into one fourteen-point scale, flip the scale, and then re-scale it on (0,1) so that higher scores correspond to *more* political freedom.

20. At the start of the survey, interviewers state that the survey is administered by an independent research organization. The last question they ask is: "Just one more question: Who do you think sent us to do this interview?" (Carter 2010, 56; Isbell 2017, 66).

21. We count the following responses (see Afrobarometer 2008, "Merged Round 4 Codebook (20 countries)," 56) as indicating of belief that the government administered the survey: "Government (general)"; "National/federal gov"; Provincial/regional; "Local government"; "President/PM's office"; "Parliament/National"; "Government census/st"; "National Intelligence"; and "Political party/poli."

22. See the online Technical Appendix for details of this test and reported results. We test a linear probability model with country and survey-year fixed effects.

23. See the online Technical Appendix for detail and reported results.

24. This question is Q23C in the 2008 survey and Q27E in the 2016 survey.

25. This question is Q87 in the 2008 survey and Q9 in the 2016 survey. In robustness tests, we employ a binary indicator of remittance receipt that groups the positive responses ('Less than once a year', 'At least once a year', 'At least every 6 months', 'At least every 3 months', and 'At least once a month') together and groups negative responses together, while treating 'Don't know' as missing.

26. Other location-based differences include: ease of migration; geographical variation in access to public goods, maltreatment by the government, and ethnicity; the local history of protest mobilization; local labor-market conditions; local cultural attributes; and the local mobilization efforts of opposition groups.

27. For ease of interpretation, we report tests of linear probability models with fixed effects, even though we confirm results with non-linear estimators, reported in the online Technical Appendix. The specification is the following, where $i$ indexes individual respondents within district $d$; $Remit_{i,d}$ is an ordinal variable measuring the frequency of remittance receipt; $Progovernment_d$ is the district-level measure of government support; $X_{i,d}$ are individual-level

confounders; $\delta_d$ are the district-fixed effects; and $\epsilon_{i,d}$ is a noise parameter:

$$Protest_{i,d} = \beta_1 Remit_{i,d} + \beta_2(Remit_{i,d} \times Progovernment_d) + \beta_3 \chi_{i,d} + \delta_d + \epsilon_{i,d} \qquad (4.2)$$

We omit the district level measure of $Progovernment_d$ from the specification because this variation is subsumed in the district effects, $\delta_d$.

28. The reported marginal effects estimates are from a kernel regression estimator to ensure common support across all parameter values; the bandwidth was selected via cross-validation.

29. Robustness tests include: using region-level government support in lieu of the district-level measure; using a binary, rather than an ordinal, measure of remittance receipt; using an ordinal, rather than a binary, measure of protest; estimating a conditional logit model; using a non-linear estimator with district means to proxy for fixed effects; and excluding a potential outlier country survey in Zimbabwe 2008, when a campaign of state-led violence was conducted during the period the survey was in the field.

30. Letsa (2019) also matches data—on the individual level—for each respondent to the party to which they feel close; she then codes a partisanship type variable to record: (1) non-partisan; (2) pro-government partisan; and (3) opposition partisan. While we might suspect these data to be biased at the individual level, tests using this variable indicate that remittances increase protest among non-partisan and opposition partisans but not among pro-government partisans. This result is consistent with the theory that remittances increase protest among opposition but not among regime supporters. We encourage readers to interpret this finding with appropriate caution, given the caveats with regard to using an individual-level measure of government support that may be upwardly biased (Tannenberg 2017).

31. Of the twenty-three country-years in the sample, only four were classified as middle-income by the World Bank in 2016: Algeria, Botswana, Morocco, and Gabon.

32. See, for example, Harding (2010, 12) and Mattes et al. (2016, 2–3). The latter compiles a "lived index of poverty" using multiple rounds of the Afrobarometer survey. Their index includes the same four items as we do, plus access to "cash income." We exclude this item from the index to avoid conflating it with remittance receipt, which may correspond directly to access to "cash income."

33. The poverty index has five ordinal values, re-scaled on (0,1). Each of the five categories contains between 16 and 23 percent of the sample. Other consumption items, particularly services such as education and agricultural inputs such as seeds or fertilizer, are often heavily subsidized by national governments. The basket of basic consumption goods in our index, by contrast, includes items that all citizens, irrespective of income levels, are likely to consume.

34. We create a binary indicator of incumbent support from the responses for each question such that "somewhat"/"approve" and "a lot"/"strongly approve" indicate support. The three items have an alpha score of 0.73.

35. We test a linear probability estimator with district-level fixed effects and adjust for individual-level demographic covariates.

36. See, for example, Corstange (2009) and Frye et al. (2017).

37. There are nine regions in Mozambique, and fifteen in Namibia. Data assembled from http://www.electionpassport.com.

38. There are 386 districts, in five countries.

## Chapter 5: Remittances Demobilize Supporters

1. If war-torn countries are included, to this list can be added Taliban rule in Afghanistan, Buyoya's seven years of rule in Burundi after the 1996 coup, Liberia during the civil war, and South Sudan.

2. See Gandhi and Lust-Okar (2009) for an excellent review of the methods by which elections enhance authoritarian power, and Knutsen et al. (2017) for a detailed analysis of the short-term costs and long-term benefits of elections for autocracies.

3. The specification thus has a lagged dependent variable, which (via differencing) isolates over-time variation. The specifications also include a linear time trend to account for temporal trends in migration (and thus remittances) as well as the global increase in authoritarian elections over time. Standard errors are clustered by regime-case. Because of the bounded nature of the outcome variable, we use Beta regression, which allows the variance of the mean response function to be large. Thus, this estimator is better for dealing with over-dispersion in the distribution of presidential vote share than a GLM with a logit link function. Using Bayesian information criteria, we select the cloglog link function. GLM with a logit link function yields similar results, as does a kernel regression estimator.

4. Election data are from Coppedge et al. (2019), `v2xel_elecpres` and `v2xel_elecparl`. Again we use a beta regression estimator to model bounded data with dispersion in the distribution of turnout tallies. BIC tests indicate a loglog function is the best link. GLM estimators with logit link functions yield similar results. All models employ cluster-robust standard errors.

5. We show in the reproduction files that results hold in specifications without unit effects.

6. Some autocracies, such as those in Botswana, Ethiopia, and Malaysia, have parliamentary elections for (indirectly) selecting the executive. Most executive elections (74 percent) in the sample are presidential, however. Some autocracies do not have supporting political parties, as is the case for many military juntas and monarchies.

7. Reproduction files show the result remains when adjusting for additional possible confounders: regime duration, civil war, aid, oil rents, FDI, trade openness, capital account openness, age dependency ratio, urban population, urbanization rate, government spending, opposition autonomy, party institutionalization, political rights and civil liberties protections, an index of participatory democracy, and state protections for free expression and freedom of association. Some of these factors may be post-treatment.

8. Theoretically, the basis of ideological conviction can take the form of positive or negative partisanship. See Levitsky and Way (2012) on non-patronage, often ideological, sources of attachment to autocratic ruling parties, particularly revolutionary or independence parties.

9. Stokes et al. (2013) use the terms "persuasion" and "loyalists."

10. See too Stokes et al. (2013, 66–67).

11. The survey question asks, "Understanding that some people were unable to vote in the most recent national election in [year], which of the following statements is true for you?" We treat "Don't know" responses as missing as well as responses that indicate the voter was too young to vote in the last election. The variable is Q23D in the 2008 round, and Q21 in the 2016 round.

12. The specification is the following, where $i$ indexes individual respondents within district $d$; $Remit_{i,d}$ is an ordinal variable measuring the frequency of remittance receipt;

*Progovernment$_d$* is the district-level measure of government support; $\chi_{i,d}$ are individual-level confounders; $\delta_d$ are the district-fixed effects; and $\epsilon_{i,d}$ is a noise parameter:

$$Turnout_{i,d} = \beta_1 Remit_{i,d} + \beta_2 (Remit_{i,d} \times Progovernment_d) + \beta_3 \chi_{i,d} + \delta_d + \epsilon_{i,d} \qquad (8.6)$$

We omit the district-level measure of *Progovernment$_d$* from the specification because this variation is subsumed in the district effects, $\delta_d$.

13. In the online Technical Appendix we report estimates from a hierarchical estimator (i.e., district-random effects): remittances decrease turnout by 2.5–2.8 percent on average; this result is statistically significant at conventional levels.

14. We find the same result when we use three equal bins.

## Chapter 6: Remittances and Democratization

1. See Yakouchyk (2019) for a review of the literature on autocracy promotion.

2. For studies demonstrating how autocracies distribute state resources and patronage to deter protests, mobilize electoral support, and reduce pro-democratic demands, see Magaloni (2006); Greene (2007); Chen (2013); Frye et al. (2014); Pan (2020); Rosenfeld (2020).

3. All major comparative data sets identifying political regimes and regime failure code the events in Senegal in 2000 as a democratic transition. These include, for example, Cheibub et al. (2010); Boix et al. (2013), and Geddes et al. (2014a).

4. Note that the bar corresponding to the year 2000 reports the vote share obtained in the first round of the presidential election. In the second round, Diouf, the PS candidate, obtained only the 41.3 percent of the vote.

5. Further electoral reforms were introduced in the 1980s, undermining electoral support for the main opposition party, the PDS.

6. The role of a Marxist-Leninist party was assumed by the Parti Africain d'Indépendence (PAI).

7. Even merchants in Touba, a marabout stronghold, revolted against new taxes adopted by the local council (Beck 2001). Merchants had strong links with the diaspora and many of them were return migrants (Diedhiou 2015).

8. Hun Sen was second prime minister and therefore not the de iure leader of the country for a roughly four-year period from 1993 to 1997.

9. Thailand is the main destination country, followed by Malaysia and South Korea.

10. Turnout in previous national elections had been 93.7 percent (1998), 83.2 percent (2003), and 75.2 percent (2008), illustrating a gradual decrease in mobilization.

11. Recall that, in chapter 3, we did not find evidence that remittances prevent civil society groups from forming, contrary to what the "group formation effect," often associated the resource curse, would predict.

12. While civil society organizations need not always be normatively "pro-democratic" (see, for example, Jamal 2009), in autocratic contexts civil society groups are predominantly anti-incumbent and thus more likely to demand more political competition and accountability rather than less. In mobilizing for political change, they tend to weaken the regime's hold on power (Bernhard 1993; Gyimah-Boadi 1996; Oxhorn 2010).

13. The values of the variable, v2psoppaut, are: "0: Opposition parties are not allowed"; "1: There are no autonomous, independent opposition parties. Opposition parties are either selected or co-opted by the ruling regime"; "2: At least some opposition parties are autonomous and independent of the ruling regime"; "3: Most significant opposition parties are autonomous and independent of the ruling regime"; and "4: All opposition parties are autonomous and independent of the ruling regime". The variable we test is a continuous, standardized transformation of this index.

14. The values of this variable, v2csprtcpt, are: "0: Most associations are state-sponsored, and although a large number of people may be active in them, their participation is not purely voluntary"; "1: Voluntary CSOs exist but few people are active in them"; "2: There are many diverse CSOs, but popular involvement is minimal"; and "3: There are many diverse CSOs and it is considered normal for people to be at least occasionally active in at least one of them". Again we test a continuous, standardized transformation of this index.

15. As in prior empirical analyses, we test a linear model with regime-case fixed effects, time period effects, and robust clustered standard errors. Random-effects models produce similar results.

16. While migration and remittance inflows likely influence rebel insurgency, this process is not the focus of this book, because the individual-level causal mechanisms we propose—weakening loyalty and resourcing the political opposition—mainly shape mass-level electoral participation and protest mobilization that underpin democratic transitions. Further, regime collapses due to successful insurgency are relatively rare events, accounting for less than 8 percent of autocratic regime collapses, and typically result in autocratic transitions or state failure (in 82 percent of cases). The online Technical Appendix lists, in Table (A-1), the autocratic regime cases in the analysis. The estimating sample spans 127 autocracies in ninety countries from 1976 to 2017, covering 1,803 country-year observations, and identifies fifty-one democratic transitions. To ensure that these findings point to *democratic transitions* rather than all forms of autocratic regime collapse (i.e., democratic autocracy-to-autocracy transitions combined), we test the same set of models reported as in Figure 6.3, but change the outcome to autocracy-to-autocracy transitions. We report these results in the Technical Appendix, but note here that the estimates for remittances are very close to zero and not statistically significant, which indicates no relationship between remittances and the likelihood of autocracy-to-autocracy transitions in the global analysis. This makes sense, because autocracy-to-autocracy transitions typically do not result from bottom-up mobilization in the form of mass protest or election defeats of the incumbent.

17. We estimate linear probability models with regime-case fixed effects and five-year time-period effects to account for common temporal shocks. To account for duration dependence, all specifications adjust for regime duration with third-order polynomials. All estimated errors are clustered by regime-case.

18. The online Technical Appendix reports results from two sets of tests that address the potential endogeneity of remittances, either due to mismeasurement of remittance flows or unmodeled strategic behavior on the part of the regime or citizen agents of democratic change. As described in the online Technical Appendix for chapter 4, we adopt two instrumental-variables approaches. One uses the intra-OECD trend in remittances to model the flow of remittances to non-OECD autocracies, weighting this time trend by distance to the coast in

the migrant-sending country with an autocratic government. The second approach uses the time trend in world oil prices and weights this trend by distance to major oil producers.

19. This figure is likely an underestimate, with at least one suggestion that it could be as high as 7 percent of the population (Altrogge and Zanker 2019, 13).

20. https://data.worldbank.org/indicator/BX.TRF.PWKR.DT.GD.ZS?locations=GM, accessed 10 November 2020.

## Chapter 7: Social Remittances and Financial Remittances

1. See also Levitt and Lamba-Nieves (2011).

2. Moreover, migrants may discriminate between various aspects of destination countries that affect their daily lives, regardless of regime type. For instance, they may strongly dislike restrictions on their mobility in the most draconian autocracies such as Saudi Arabia, yet approve of the regime's approach to guaranteeing security, and prefer a dictatorial regime that provides jobs to a flawed democracy that does not (Rother 2009).

3. See Goodman and Hiskey (2008); Córdova and Hiskey (2015); Paarlberg (2017); Crow and Pérez-Armendáriz (2018); Batista et al. (2019); Córdova and Hiskey (2019).

4. That said, political emigration from military dictatorships in South America during the Cold War period often took an ideological form, with many self-exiles migrating to countries with sympathetic governments, such as Cuba and Mexico, even though these governments were autocratic as well. Further, we acknowledge that migration policies shape the migration decision. For instance, Fitzgerald et al. (2014) found that aspects of migrant policy such as residence requirements and an anti-immigrant political climate are as relevant as economic factors in the choice of destination. See also Mayda (2010).

5. Many autocratic governments appear to be aware of the perils of mobilized diasporas; and autocratic governments may be particularly sensitive to the destabilizing potential of émigrés' transnational involvement (Glasius 2018). Autocracies thus deploy a repertoire of actions, from outright repression to co-optation strategies, in an effort to both legitimize their non-democratic rule and to sustain emigrants' loyalty (Kovács 2020). Alternatively, these governments may cultivate diaspora relations to use them as carriers of autocrats' soft power (Tsourapas 2015; Bruce 2020). For example, because migrants heading towards democratic destinations may send "democratic remittances," these migrants are more likely to face tighter emigration restrictions (Miller and Peters 2020); and autocratic countries are less likely to grant dual citizenship to highly educated emigrants living in democracies—an effort to limit potential "voice after exit" (Mirilovic 2015). Morocco planted state agents among their exiled university students and migrant associations abroad in an attempt to control the opposition's activities; and Moroccan governments have deployed several more subtle strategies, too, facilitating the diaspora's participation in domestic matters through state-controlled institutions (Brand 2006; Dalmasso 2018). Finally, autocracies export professionals abroad, generating their own diasporas with the purpose of legitimizing themselves (Del Sordi 2018) or spreading some creed, be it pan-Arabism or socialist revolution (Adamson and Tsourapas 2019). The wide range of autocratic government policies towards their emigrants demonstrates that dictators are aware of the potentially destabilizing influence of diasporas abroad.

6. Except for Maydom (2017), we are not aware of any research exploring whether the origin of remittances as between democratic and autocratic countries has a differential impact on the type of political behaviors that may undermine autocracies.

7. Emigrants from only three of seventeen countries in the Afrobarometer sample of autocracies reside predominantly in countries ruled by autocratic governments: Burkina Faso (survey year 2008), Egypt (2016), and Sudan (2016).

8. The majority of migrants from Burkina Faso (and to a lesser extent Mauritania and Mali) work in Côte d'Ivoire, which was ruled by an autocratic government until 2011; and most emigrants from Lesotho, an autocracy until 1993, reside in South Africa, which was ruled by dictatorship until 1994. Thus Lesotho's inward remittances would be categorized as coming from an autocracy up to 1994.

9. We test a kernel regression least squares (KRLS) estimator, which minimizes over-fitting and reduces the variance and fragility of estimates, while estimating point-wise marginal effects for covariates (Hainmueller and Hazlett 2013). In tests of protest and democratic transition, we incorporate country-fixed effects in the estimator by adjusting for the unit means of all explanatory variables. The incumbent vote share model includes a lagged outcome variable. All specifications adjust for time trends and potential confounders.

10. But see Karakoç et al. (2017) on Egypt, and Batista et al. (2019) on Mozambique.

11. The design assumptions for this inference, conditional on adjustment for potential observed confounders, are: (1) Treatment assignment (whether a respondent receives remittances) is statistically independent of both the outcome behavior (protest or turnout) and the mediating phenomenon (discussing politics); and (2) given treatment assignment (conditional on remittance receipt) the mediating phenomenon (discussing politics) is independent of the outcome behavior (protest or turnout). These are potentially strong assumptions that cannot be completely verified empirically.

12. Specifications adjust for the following: age, education, travel, cellphone use, poverty, and sex. In lieu of district fixed effects we adjust for the unit mean values of remittances and protest, which isolates the "within"-district variation, similar to a fixed effects estimator.

13. Again we estimate linear probability models with district-fixed effects to account for all country, region, and district-level confounders. We test a binary remittance indicator.

14. Azizi uses the method proposed by Ratha and Shaw (2007, Appendix B), using UN data on bilateral migration and remittance inflows. As Ratha and Shaw (2007) explain, these are proxies based on assumptions about migrants' remitting behavior. Migrants living in host country $j$ send remittances to their home country, denoted by subscript $i$. The average remittance sent by any given migrant is designated as $r_{ij}$ and directly depends on the income per capita in both nations. Specifically:

$$r_{ij} = f(\bar{Y}_i, Y_j) = \begin{cases} \bar{Y}_i & \text{if } Y_j < \bar{Y}_i \\ \bar{Y}_i + (Y_j - \bar{Y}_i)^\beta & \text{otherwise} \end{cases} \tag{7.1}$$

where $Y_j$ refers to the GNI per capita in host country $j$, $\bar{Y}_i$ to the GNI per capita in home country $i$, and $\beta$ is a parameter between 0 and 1. Ratha and Shaw's (2007) research on the twenty largest remittance-receiving nations set the value of $\beta$ at 0.75. In other words, this assumes that if the average migrant moves to a poorer country than the home country, the remittance sent home will equal the GNI per capita of the home country. If instead the migrant moves to a richer country, the remittances sent home will be higher and depend on the adjusted difference in average income between home and host countries. The formula therefore takes into account the fact that most people migrate with the expectation that they will earn more in their chosen destination than they would at home. The total amount of remittances received by any given country $(R_i)$ will then equal:

$$R_i = \sum_j r_{ij} M_{ij} \qquad (7.2)$$

where $M_{ij}$ is the number of migrants from home country $i$ living in host country $j$. Data on the weights is from https://www.researchgate.net/publication/341204891_Weight_of _remittance_sending_countriesxlsx.

15. Following polity definitions in Marshall & Gurr (2018), we classified autocracies as the regimes with polity values between −10 and −6; anocracy as the regimes with polity values between −5 and +5 as well as −66 (interruption), −77 (interregnum), and −88 (transition); and democracies as regimes with polity values between +6 and +10. Our category "dictatorships" adds together autocracies and anocracies.

16. These figures are rough estimates of bilateral remittance data because, as the prior footnote details, they are based on assumptions about migrants' behavior, with weights calculated from estimates of migrants' income made in the destination country and sent back home and equally noisy data on migrant stocks in destination countries.

17. For this average, we weight each year equally, even if remittances received in a country rise or falls over time. This allows us to preserve the full temporal variation in the remittances series for each country, without mixing in information on primary origin of these remittances.

## Chapter 8: Conclusion

1. Song (2018, 90) also raises this issue when she expresses concern about the departure of those "who possess the skills necessary to demand and build better institutions in their home country."

2. For a discussion of the ethical questions raised by the moral obligation to remit, see Simoni and Voirol (2021).

3. In chapter 3 above we provide evidence that remittances do *not* contribute to revenue and spending for autocratic governments.

4. This argument parallels "race-to-the-bottom" theories that suggest trade and international capital flows harm human rights and labor protections; see, for example, Rudra (2008); also Davies and Vadlamannati (2013) and Olney (2013).

5. Oberman (2015) makes a similar point to ours.

6. There is a voluminous empirical literature on this question. See Acemoglu et al. (2015) for a review and recent evidence.

7. Oberman (2015, 248) argues that if development assistance and reforming global financial institutions fail to alleviate global poverty, then rich democracies should simply make cash transfers to poor, foreign citizens, to fulfill the moral duty to address global injustice.

8. Collier (2013, 220) describes such policy as "not a door that is open or closed, but one that is ajar."

9. See Finkel et al. (2007); Kalyvitis and Vlachaki (2010); Scott and Steele (2011); Cornell (2013).

10. On the multiple challenges of assessing the impact of democracy aid, see Green and Kohl (2007).

11. The outcomes in these studies measure aggregate democracy levels without distinguishing democratic transitions from liberalizing reforms by incumbent autocrats. These studies also focus on democracy aid from different donors—such as USAID, the NED, and the OECD—seperately, making it difficult to understand the aggregate effect of aid.

12. To explain the illiberal turn in CEEU countries, Krastev and Holmes (2018, 125) argue that "[t]he combination of an ageing population, low birth rates, and an unending flow of out-migration is the ultimate source of demographic panic in Central and Eastern Europe." The Great Recession of 2008 accelerated this process: they note that the number of CEEU citizens who migrated to Western Europe after the recession exceeds the number of non-European refugees who fled to Europe (126).

13. Doyle (2015) argues that remittances reduce demand for social welfare spending in Latin America; and lower support for redistribution could undermine electoral support for centrist parties that advocate for redistributive policies.

14. India is the largest remittance recipient country only in *absolute* terms (*Economic Times* 2019). As a share GDP, however, official remittances have fluctuated between 2 and 4 percent for the past decade.

15. China is largest FDI recipient if Hong Kong is included as part of China.

16. For example, see Dickson (2003) for an examination of how the Communist Party of China co-opted ascendant economic elites, Chen (2013) for an explanation of why a growing class does not demand democracy, Shirk (2018) for discussion of increasingly personalist rule under President Xi, Xu (2021) on surveillance, and Kendall-Taylor et al. (2020) on digital repression.

17. Others note that economic liberalization, particularly privatization, led to social protest, that in turn, helped unseat ruling autocratic governments and pave the way for democracy (Walton and Ragin 1990; Bratton and Van de Walle 1992).

18. See also *Africa Confidential* (2019a,b).

19. Baldwin postulates that early periods of globalization in the nineteenth century separated production and consumption, by facilitating rapid transportation of consumer goods from the places where they were most efficiently produced to the consumers that bought them. Falling transportation costs for traded goods "unbundled" production and consumption. The more recent wave of globalization, starting in the late twentieth century, took off when the cost of moving ideas fell rapidly. The ICT revolution, by facilitating massive and rapid information flows, allowed producers to unbundle fabrication of goods and from the design, management, and marketing of those goods, as firms built global supply chains. This process of unbundling the stages of manufacturing production—what Baldwin calls the "global value chain revolution"—meant that some countries in the Global South (or really regions within some countries) specialized in the fabrication of goods designed and managed by high-skilled labor in the Global North. Parts sourced from myriad suppliers in different countries could be assembled in other countries, with the design and management of the process residing in still other countries. This second wave of globalization, in Baldwin's account, married high-skill

knowledge in rich countries to low-wage labor in some parts of the Global South. While this process may have lowered wages for low-skilled labor in the Global North, it also boosted incomes for a large swathe of humanity in the Global South, leading to the "Great Convergence" of the income gap between newly globalized economies (e.g., China, Indonesia, and Mexico) and advanced industrial nations (Milanovic 2016). This second phase of globalization, in which low-wage labor in the Global South was matched with high-skill know-how in the same global supply chain but not in the same country, has boosted income, for example, for hundreds of millions of internal migrant laborers in China. In turn, this rising income reduces the incentive of these workers to migrate physically across international borders in search of higher wages.

20. See Baiyu (2019); according to CGAP (2019), Alipay and WeChat Pay account for more than 90 percent of all mobile payments in China.

21. As *The Economist* (2020a) notes, Ant "identifies and assesses borrowers, but passes them on to banks which extend loans." Many of these banks are either state-owned or beholden to state financial backing.

22. See, for example, Roberts (2018), Guriev and Treisman (2019), Xu (2021), Chang and Lin (2020), Kendall-Taylor et al. (2020), and Dragu and Lupu (2021).

# REFERENCES

Abdih, Yasser, Ralph Chami, Jihad Dagher, and Peter Montiel. 2008. "Remittances and Institutions." IMF Working Paper WP 08/29.

Abdih, Yasser, Ralph Chami, Jihad Dagher, and Peter Montiel. 2012. "Remittances and Institutions: Are Remittances a Curse?" *World Development* 40(4), 657–66.

Acemoglu, Daron and James A. Robinson. 2006. *Economic Origins of Dictatorship and Democracy*. New York: Cambridge University Press.

Acemoglu, Daron and James A. Robinson. 2012. *Why Nations Fail: The Origins of Power, Prosperity, and Poverty*. New York: Crown Publishers.

Acemoglu, Daron, Suresh Naidu, Pascual Restrepo, and James A. Robinson. 2015. "Democracy, Redistribution, and Inequality." In *Handbook of Income Distribution*, vol. 2. Amsterdam: Elsevier, 1,885–996.

Acemoglu, Daron, Suresh Naidu, Pascual Restrepo, and James A. Robinson. 2019. "Democracy Does Cause Growth." *Journal of Political Economy* 127(1), 47–100.

Acosta, Pablo, Cesar Calderón, Pablo Fajnzylber, and Humberto López. 2008. "What Is the Impact of International Remittances on Poverty and Inequality in Latin America?" *World Development* 36(1), 89–114.

Adams, Richard H. 2007. *International Remittances and the Household : Analysis and Review of Global Evidence*. World Bank Policy Research no. 4,116.

Adams, Richard H. and John Page. 2005. "Do International Migration and Remittances Reduce Poverty in Developing Countries?" *World Development* 33(10), 1,645–669.

Adamson, Fiona B. 2019a. "Non-State Authoritarianism and Diaspora Politics." *Global Networks* 20(1), 150–69.

Adamson, Fiona B. 2019b. "Sending States and the Making of Intra-Diasporic Politics: Turkey and Its Diaspora(s)." *International Migration Review* 53(1), 210–36.

Adamson, Fiona B. and Madeleine Demetriou. 2007. "Remapping the Boundaries of 'State' and 'National Identity': Incorporating Diasporas into International Relations Theorizing." *European Journal of International Relations* 12(4), 489–526.

Adamson, Fiona B. and Gerasimos Tsourapas. 2019. "Migration Diplomacy in World Politics." *International Studies Perspectives* 20(2), 113–28.

Adida, Claire L. and Desha M. Girod. 2011. "Do Migrants Improve Their Hometowns? Remittances and Access to Public Services in Mexico, 1995–2000." *Comparative Political Studies* 44(1), 3–27.

*Africa Confidential*. 2019a. "A Talon for Authoritarianism." *Africa Confidential* 60(10). Available at: https://tinyurl.com/ydx6pnxt [accessed 1 January 2020].

*Africa Confidential.* 2019b. "Talon Turns Back the Clock." *Africa Confidential* 60(9). Available at: https://tinyurl.com/y8bqqlnd [accessed 1 January 2020].

Agarwal, Reena and Andrew W. Horowitz. 2002. "Are International Remittances Altruism or Insurance? Evidence from Guyana Using Multiple-Migrant Households." *World Development* 30(11), 2,033–44.

Ahmadov, Anar K. and Gwendolyn Sasse. 2016. A Voice Despite Exit: The Role of Assimilation, Emigrant Networks, and Destination in Emigrants' Transnational Political Engagement. *Comparative Political Studies* 49(1), 78–114.

Ahmed, Faisal Z. 2012. "The Perils of Unearned Foreign Income: Aid, Remittances and Government Survival." *American Political Science Review* 106(1), 146–65.

Ahmed, Faisal Z. 2013. "Remittances Deteriorate Governance." *The Review of Economics and Statistics* 94(4), 1,166–82.

Ahmed, Faisal Z. 2017. "Remittances and Incumbency: Theory and Evidence." *Economics and Politics* 29(1), 22–47.

Ahmed, Hamid Ould. 2019. "Pro-Government Supporters Rally in Algeria to Back Planned Elections." *Reuters* 30 November. Available at https://tinyurl.com/sbnku6w [accessed 12 December 2019].

Ahmed, Junaid, Mazhar Mughal, and Inmaculada Martínez-Zarzoso. 2020. "Sending Money Home: Transaction Cost and Remittances to Developing Countries." University of Goettingen, Department of Economics, Center for European, Governance and Economic Development Research Discussion Papers, no. 387. Available at: https://ideas.repec.org/s/zbw/cegedp.html [accessed 14 June 2021].

Aidi, Hisham. 2018. "Africa's New Social Movements: A Continental Approach." Available at: https://www.africaportal.org/publications/africas-new-social-movements-continental-approach/ [accessed 14 June 2021].

Albertus, Michael and Victor Menaldo. 2012. "Coercive Capacity and the Prospects for Democratization." *Comparative Politics* 44(2), 151–69.

Albertus, Michael and Victor Menaldo (eds). 2018. *Authoritarianism and the Elite Origins of Democracy.* New York: Cambridge University Press.

Alemán, José and Dwayne Woods. 2014. "No Way Out: Travel Restrictions and Authoritarian Regimes." *Migration and Development* 3(2), 285–305.

Allen, Susan H. 2008. "The Domestic Political Costs of Economic Sanctions." *Journal of Conflict Resolution* 52(6), 916–44.

Almeida, Paul D. 2003. "Opportunity Organizations and Threat-Induced Contention: Protest Waves in Authoritarian Settings." *American Journal of Sociology* 109(2), 345–400.

Alonso, Andoni and Pedro J. Oiarzabal (eds). 2010. *Diasporas in the New Media Age: Identity, Politics, and Community.* Reno: University of Nevada Press.

Altrogge, Judith and Franzisca Zanker. 2019. *The Political Economy of Migration Governance in the Gambia.* Arnold Bergstraesser Institute, Freiburg: Mercato Dialoque in Asylum and Migration.

Álvarez Mingote, Cristina. 2019. "How Do Remittances Shape Electoral Strategies Back Home? Evidence from Mexico's 2006 Presidential Election." *Latin American Politics and Society* 61(3), 55–79.

Ambrosius, Christian. 2019. "Government Reactions to Private Substitutes for Public Goods: Remittances and the Crowding-out of Public Finance." *Journal of Comparative Economics* 47(2), 396–415.

Amburn, Brad. 2009. "The Remittance Curse." *Foreign Policy* 7 October. Available at: https://foreignpolicy.com/2009/10/07/the-remittance-curse/ [accessed 14 June 2021].

Andersen, Jørgen J. and Michael L. Ross. 2014. "The Big Oil Change: A Closer Look at the Haber–Menaldo Analysis." *Comparative Political Studies* 47(7), 993–1,021.

Ansell, Ben W. and David J. Samuels. 2010. "Inequality and Democratization: A Contractarian Approach." *Comparative Political Studies* 43(12), 1,543–74.

Ansell, Ben W. and David J. Samuels, 2014. *Inequality and Democratization: An Elite-Competition Approach.* Cambridge: Cambridge University Press.

Aparicio, Javier and Covadonga Meseguer. 2012. "Remittances and the State: The 3 × 1 Program in Mexican Municipalities." *World Development* 40(1), 206–22.

Arriola, Leonardo R. 2013a. "Capital and Opposition in Africa: Coalition Building in Multiethnic Societies." *World Politics* 65(2), 233–72.

Arriola, Leonardo R. 2013b. *Multi-Ethnic Coalitions in Africa: Business Financing of Opposition Election Campaigns.* New York: Cambridge University Press.

Artuc, Erhan, Paulo Bastos, and Bob Rijkers. 2018. "Robots, Tasks and Trade." World Bank Policy Research Working Paper no. 8674.

Asatryan, Zareh, Benjamin Bittschi, and Philipp Doerrenberg. 2017. "Remittances and Public Finances: Evidence from Oil-Price Shocks." *Journal of Public Economics* 155, 122–37.

Associated Press. 2009. "Pro-Government Rallies Call for Death of Iran's Opposition Leaders." *The Guardian*, 30 December. Available at: https://tinyurl.com/uuhwxbu [accessed 12 December 2019].

Ayyub, Rana. 2020. "Narendra Modi Looks the Other Way as New Delhi Burns." *Time Magazine* 28 February. Available at: https://time.com/5791759/narendra-modi -india-delhi-riots-violence-muslim/ [accessed 8 June 2020].

Azizi, Seyedsoroosh. 2017. "Altruism: Primary Motivation of Remittances." *Applied Economics Letters* 24(17), 1,218–21.

Azizi, Seyedsoroosh. 2018. "The Impacts of Workers' Remittances on Human Capital and Labor Supply in Developing Countries." *Economic Modelling* 75, 377–96.

Bader, Julia. 2015. *China's Foreign Relations and the Survival of Autocracies.* London: Routledge.

Baiyu, Gao. 2019. "China's Mobile Payment Transaction Volume Hits $41.51 Trillion in 2018." *Caixin*, 22 March. Available at: https://tinyurl.com/yyk9e76w [accessed 10 June 2020].

Bak, Daehee, and Chungshik Moon. 2016. "Foreign Direct Investment and Authoritarian Stability." *Comparative Political Studies* 49(14), 1,998–2,037.

Baker, Peter. 2019. "Trump Declares a National Emergency, and Provokes a Constitutional Clash." *The New York Times* 15, February. Available at: https://tinyurl.com/y4ngfkyz [accessed 12 April 2020].

Baldwin, Kate. 2015. *The Paradox of Traditional Chiefs in Democratic Africa.* Cambridge: Cambridge University Press.

Baldwin, Richard. 2016. *The Great Convergence.* Cambridge, MA: Harvard University Press.

Baldwin, Richard, and Rikard Forslid. 2020. *Globotics and Development: When Manufacturing is Jobless and Services are Tradable.* National Bureau of Economic Research

Working Paper no. w26731. Available at: https://papers.ssrn.com/sol3/papers.cfm?abstract_id=3535321 [accessed 14 June 2021].

Bank, World. 2019. *World Development Indicators*. Washington, D.C.: World Bank.

Barajas, Adolfo, Ralph Chami, Connel Fullenkam, Michae Gapen, and Peter Montiel. 2009. "Do Workers' Remittances Promote Economic Growth?" IMF Working Paper WP 09/153.

Barany, Zoltan. 2013. "Armies and Revolutions." *Journal of Democracy* 24(2), 62–76.

Barany, Zoltan. 2016. *How Armies Respond to Revolutions and Why*. Princeton: Princeton University Press.

Barry, Colin M. K. Chad Clay, Michael E. Flynn, and Gregory Robinson. 2014. "Freedom of Foreign Movement, Economic Opportunities Abroad and Protest in Non-Democratic Regimes." *Journal of Peace Research* 51(5), 574–88.

Barsbai, Toman, Hillel Rapoport, Andreas Steinmayr, and Christoph Trebesch. 2017. "The Effect of Labor Migration on the Diffusion of Democracy: Evidence from a Former Soviet Republic." *American Economic Journal: Applied Economics* 9(3), 36–69.

Bastiaens, Ida and Nita Rudra. 2018. *Democracies in Peril*. New York: Cambridge University Press.

Bastiaens, Ida and Daniel C. Tirone. 2019. "Remittances and Varieties of Democratization in Developing Countries." *Democratization* 26(7), 1,132–53.

Bates, Robert H. 1984. *Markets and States in Tropical Africa: The Political Basis of Agricultural Policies*. Berkeley: University of California Press.

Bates, Robert H. and Da-Hsiang Donald Lien. 1985. "A Note on Taxation, Development, and Representative Government." *Politics and Society* 14(1), 53–70.

Batista, Catia, Julia Seither, and Pedro C. Vicente. 2019. "Do Migrant Social Networks Shape Political Attitudes and Behavior at Home?" *World Development* 117, 328–43.

Bayer, Markus, Felix S. Bethke, and Daniel Lambach. 2016. "The Democratic Dividend of Nonviolent Resistance." *Journal of Peace Research* 53(6), 758–71.

BBC News. 2017. "Cambodia Top Court Dissolves Main Opposition CNRP Party." BBC, 16 November. Available at: https://www.bbc.com/news/world-asia-42006828 [accessed 13 April 2020].

BBC News. 2019. "Do Today's Global Protests Have Anything in Common?" BBC, 11 November. Available at: https://www.bbc.com/news/world-50123743 [accessed 12 December 2019].

Bearce, David H. and Jennifer A. Laks Hutnick. 2011. "Toward an Alternative Explanation for the Resource Curse: Natural Resources, Immigration and Democratization." *Comparative Political Studies* 44(6), 689–718.

Bearce, David H. and Seungbin Park. 2019. "Why Remittances Are a Political Blessing and Not a Curse." *Studies in Comparative International Development* 54(1), 164–84.

Beaulieu, Emily. 2014. *Electoral Protest and Democracy in the Developing World*. New York: Cambridge University Press.

Beck, Linda J. 2001. "Reining in the Marabouts? Democratization and Local Governance in Senegal." *African Affairs* 100(401), 601–21.

Behrman, Lucy. 1970. *Muslim Brotherhoods and Politics in Senegal*. Cambridge, MA: Harvard University Press.

Beissinger, Mark R. 2007. "Structure and Example in Modular Political Phenomena: The Diffusion of Bulldozer/Rose/Orange/Tulip Revolutions." *Perspectives on Politics* 5(2), 259–76.

Bellin, Eva. 2000. "Contingent Democrats: Industrialists, Labor, and Democratization in Late-Developing Countries." *World Politics* 52(2), 175–205.

Bellin, Eva. 2012. "Reconsidering the Robustness of Authoritarianism in the Middle East: Lessons from the Arab Spring." *Comparative Politics* 44(2), 127–49.

Bellinger, Paul T. and Moisés Arce. 2011. "Protest and Democracy in Latin America's Market Era." *Political Research Quarterly* 64(3), 688–704.

Berkowitz, Leonard. 1972. "Frustrations, Comparisons, and Other Sources of Emotion Arousal as Contributors to Social Unrest." *Journal of Social Issues* 28(1), 77–91.

Bermeo, Sarah B. 2011. "Foreign Aid and Regime Change: A Role for Donor Intent." *World Development* 39(11), 2,021–31.

Bermeo, Sarah Blodgett and David Leblang. 2015. "Migration and Foreign Aid." *International Organization* 69(3), 627–57.

Bernhard, Michael. 1993. "Civil Society and Democratic Transition in East Central Europe." *Political Science Quarterly* 108(2), 307–26.

Betts, Alexander and Will Jones. 2016. *Mobilising the Diaspora: How Refugees Challenge Authoritarianism*. Cambridge: Cambridge University Press.

Blaydes, Lisa. 2006. "Who Votes in Authoritarian Elections and Why? Determinants of Voter Turnout in Contemporary Egypt." Paper presented at the Annual Meeting of the American Political Science Association, Philadelphia, August 31–September 3.

Blaydes, Lisa. 2010. *Elections and Distributive Politics in Mubarak's Egypt*. New York: Cambridge University Press.

Blaydes, Lisa. 2018. *State of Repression: Iraq under Saddam Hussein*. Princeton: Princeton University Press.

Bloch, Alice. 2008. "Zimbabweans in Britain: Transnational Activities and Capabilities." *Journal of Ethnic and Migration Studies* 34(2), 287–305.

Boix, Carles. 2003. *Democracy and Redistribution*. New York: Cambridge University Press.

Boix, Carles. 2011. "Democracy, Development, and the International System." *American Political Science Review* 105(4), 809–28.

Boix, Carles, Michael Miller, and Sebastian Rosato. 2013. "A Complete Data Set of Political Regimes, 1800–2007." *Comparative Political Studies* 46(12), 1,523–54.

Borjas, George J. 1989. "Economic Theory and International Migration." *International Migration Review* 23(3), 457–85.

Bose, Pablo Shiladitya. 2015. *Urban Development in India: Global Indians in the Remaking of Kolkata*. London: Routledge.

Boudreau, Vincent. 2009. *Resisting Dictatorship: Repression and Protest in Southeast Asia*. Cambridge: Cambridge University Press.

Brady, Henry E. Sidney Verba, and Kay Lehman Scholzman. 1995. "Beyond SES: A Resource Model of Political Participation." *American Political Science Review* 89(2), 271–94.

Brancati, Dawn. 2014. "Pocketbook Protests: Explaining the Emergence of Pro-Democracy Protests Worldwide." *Comparative Political Studies* 47(11), 1,503–30.

Brancati, Dawn and Adrián Lucardi. 2019. "Why Democracy Protests Do Not Diffuse." *Journal of Conflict Resolution* 63(10), 2,354–89.

Branch, Adam and Zachariah Mampilly. 2015. *Africa Uprising: Popular Protest and Political Change*. London: Zed Books Ltd.

Brand, Laurie A. 2006. *Citizens Abroad: Emigration and the State in the Middle East and North Africa*. Cambridge: Cambridge University Press.

Bratton, Michael. 2008. "Zimbabwe's Long Agony." *Journal of Democracy* 19(4), 41–55.

Bratton, Michael and Nicolas Van de Walle. 1992. "Popular Protest and Political Reform in Africa." *Comparative Politics* 24(4), 419–42.

Bratton, Michael and Nicolas van de Walle. 1997. *Democratic Experiments in Africa: Regime Transitions in Comparative Perspective*. New York: Cambridge University Press.

Bratton, Michael, Robert Mattes, and E. Gyimah-Boadi. 2005. *Public Opinion, Democracy, and Market Reform in Africa*. New York: Cambridge University Press.

Bravo, Jorge. 2007. "Emigration and Political Engagement in Mexico." Unpublished Ms, Nuffield College, University of Oxford.

Bravo, Jorge. 2009. "Emigración y Compromiso Político en México." *Política y Gobierno* vol. temático no. 1, 273–310.

Brinkerhoff, Jennifer M. 2011. "Diasporas and Conflict Societies: Conflict Entrepreneurs, Competing Interests or Contributors to Stability and Development?" *Conflict, Security and Development* 11(2), 115–43.

Brinks, Daniel and Michael Coppedge. 2006. "Diffusion Is No Illusion: Neighbor Emulation in the Third Wave of Democracy." *Comparative Political Studies* 39(4), 463–89.

Brock, Gillian and Michael Blake. 2015. *Debating Brain Drain: May Governments Restrict Emigration?* New York: Oxford University Press.

Broz, J. Lawrence, Jeffry Frieden, and Stephen Weymouth. 2021. "Populism in Place: The Economic Geography of the Globalization Backlash." *International Organization* 75(2), 464–94.

Bruce, Benjamin. 2020. "Imams for the Diaspora: The Turkish State's International Theology Programme." *Journal of Ethnic and Migration Studies* 46(6), 1,166–83

Bubeck, Johannes and Nikolay Marinov. 2019. *Rules and Allies: Foreign Election Interventions*. New York: Cambridge University Press.

Bueno de Mesquita, Bruce and Alastair Smith. 2010. "Leader Survival, Revolutions and the Nature of Government Finance." *American Journal of Political Science* 54(4), 936–50.

Bunce, Valerie and Sharon Wolchik. 2006. "International Diffusion and Postcommunist Electoral Revolutions." *Communist and Postcommunist Studies* 39(3), 283–304.

Bunce, Valerie J. and Sharon L. Wolchik. 2010. "Defeating Dictators: Electoral Change and Stability in Competitive Authoritarian Regimes." *World Politics* 62(1), 43–86.

Bunce, Valerie J. and Sharon L. Wolchik. 2011. *Defeating Authoritarian Leaders in Postcommunist Countries*. New York: Cambridge University Press.

Burgess, Katrina. 2012. "Migrants, Remittances, and Politics: Loyalty and Voice after Exit." *The Fletcher Forum of World Affairs* 36(1), 43–55.

Burgess, Katrina. 2014. "Unpacking the Diaspora Channel in New Democracies: When Do Migrants Act Politically Back Home?" *Studies in Comparative International Development* 49(1), 13–43.

Burnell, Peter and Richard Youngs (eds). 2009. *New Challenges to Democratization*. London: Routledge.

Bush, Sarah S. 2015. *The Taming of Democracy Assistance: Why Democracy Promotion Does Not Confront Dictators.* Cambridge: Cambridge University Press.

Buyse, Antoine. 2018. "Squeezing Civic Space: Restrictions on Civil Society Organizations and the Linkages with Human Rights." *The International Journal of Human Rights* 22(8), 966–88.

Calero, Carla, Arjun S. Bedi, and Robert Sparrow. 2009. "Remittances, Liquidity Constraints and Human Capital Investments in Ecuador." *World Development* 37(6), 1,143–54.

Calvo, Ernesto and Maria Victoria Murillo. 2004. "Who Delivers? Partisan Clients in the Argentine Electoral Market." *American Journal of Political Science* 48(4), 742–57.

Campante, Filipe R. and Davin Chor. 2014. " 'The People Want the Fall of the Regime': Schooling, Political Protest, and the Economy." *Journal of Comparative Economics* 42(3), 495–517.

Careja, Romana and Patrick Emmenegger. 2012. "Making Democratic Citizens: The Effects of Migration Experience on Political Attitudes in Central and Eastern Europe." *Comparative Political Studies* 45(7), 875–902.

Carens, Joseph H. (ed.) 2013. *The Ethics of Immigration.* New York: Oxford University Press.

Carling, Jørgen. 2008. "The Determinants of Migrant Remittances." *Oxford Review of Economic Policy* 24(3), 581–98.

Carling, Jørgen. 2014. "Scripting Remittances: Making Sense of Money Transfers in Transnational Relationships." *International Migration Review* 48(s1), 218–62.

Carling, Jørgen, Marta Bivand Erdal, and Cindy Horst. 2012. "How does Conflict in Migrants' Country of Origin Affect Remittance-Sending? Financial Priorities and Transnational Obligations Among Somalis and Pakistanis in Norway." *International Migration Review* 46(2), 283–309.

Carlson, Elizabeth. 2015. "Ethnic Voting and Accountability in Africa: A Choice Experiment in Uganda." *World Politics* 67(2), 353–85.

Carment, David and Rachael Calleja. 2018. "Diasporas and Fragile States—Beyond Remittances: Assessing the Theoretical and Political Linkages." *Journal of Ethnic and Migration Studies* 44(8), 1,270–88.

Carnegie, Allison and Nikolay Marinov. 2017. "Foreign Aid, Human Rights, and Democracy Promotion: Evidence from a Natural Experiment." *American Journal of Political Science* 61(3), 671–83.

Carothers, Thomas. 1999. "Civil Society." *Foreign Policy* 117, 18–24 + 26–29.

Carothers, Thomas. 2002. "The End of the Transition Paradigm." *Journal of Democracy* 13(1), 5–21.

Carter, Danielle. 2010. "Afrobarometer Data Codebook for Round 4 Afrobarometer Surveys." *Afrobarometer* Round 4, 1–83.

Catrinescu, Natalia, Miguel Leon Ledesma, Matloob Piracha, and Bryce Quillin. 2009. "Remittances, Institutions, and Economic Growth." *World Development* 37(1), 81–92.

CGAP. 2019. "China: A Digital Payments Revolution." *CGAP* September. Available at: https://tinyurl.com/yb4nlwdo [accessed 10 June 2020].

Chacko, Priya and Ruchira Talukdar. 2020. "Why Modi's India has Become a Dangerous Place for Muslims." *The Conversation* 2 March. Available at: https://tinyurl.com/y9v2lwej [accessed 8 June 2020].

Chami, Ralph, Adolfo Barajas, Thomas Cosimano, Connel Fullenkamp, Michael Gapen, and Peter Montiel. 2008. *The Macroeconomic Consequences of Remittances.* Washington: International Monetary Fund Occasional Paper 259.

Chang, Chun-Chih and Thung-Hong Lin. 2020. "Autocracy Login: Internet Censorship and Civil Society in the Digital Age." *Democratization* 27(5), 874–95.

Chaudhry, Kiren A. 1989. "The Price of Wealth: Business and State in Labor Remittance and Oil Economies." *International Organization* 43(1), 101–45.

Chauvet, Lisa, Flore Gubert, and Sandrine Mesplé-Somps. 2016. "Do Migrants Adopt New Political Attitudes from Abroad? Evidence Using a Multi-Sited Exit-Poll Survey during the 2013 Malian Elections." *Comparative Migration Studies* 4, 19.

Cheibub, José Antonio, Jennifer Gandhi, and James Raymond Vreeland. 2010. "Democracy and Dictatorship Revisited." *Public Choice* 143(1–2), 67–101.

Chen, Jie. 2013. *A Middle Class Without Democracy: Economic Growth and the Prospects for Democratization in China.* New York: Oxford University Press.

Cheneval, Francis and Johan Rochel. 2012. "An Ethical View on Remittances and Labor Migration." *Global Justice: Theory, Practice, Rhetoric* 5, 16–30.

Chenoweth, Erica. 2016. "The Rise of Nonviolent Resistance." *PRIO Policy Brief* 19, 1–4.

Chenoweth, Erica and Maria J. Stephan. 2011. *Why Civil Resistance Works: The Strategic Logic of Nonviolent Conflict.* New York: Columbia University Press.

Chenoweth, Erica and Jay Ulfelder. 2017. "Can Structural Conditions Explain the Onset of Nonviolent Uprisings?" *Journal of Conflict Resolution* 61(2), 298–324.

Chenoweth, Erica, Vito D'Orazio and Joseph Wright. 2014. "A Latent Measure of Political Protest." Paper presented at the International Studies Association's 55th Annual Convention, Toronto, March 26–9.

Chhibber, Pradeep and Rahul Verma. 2014. "The BJP's 2014 'Modi Wave': An Ideological Consolidation of the Right." *Economic and Political Weekly* 49(39), 50–6.

Chinn, Menzie D. and Hiro Ito. 2008. "A New Measure of Financial Openness." *Journal of Comparative Policy Analysis* 10(3), 309–22.

Christensen, Darin. 2019. "Concession Stands: How Mining Investments Incite Protest in Africa." *International Organization* 73(1), 65–101.

Christensen, Darin and Francisco Garfias. 2018. "Can You Hear Me Now? How Communication Technology Affects Protest and Repression." *Quarterly Journal of Political Science* 13(1), 89–117.

Christensen, Darin and Jeremy M. Weinstein. 2013. "Defunding Dissent: Restrictions on Aid to NGOs." *Journal of Democracy* 24(2), 77–91.

Chubb, Judith. 1983. *Patronage, Power, and Poverty in Southern Italy: A Tale of Two Cities.* New York: Cambridge University Press.

Clemens, Michael A. and David McKenzie. 2018. "Why Don't Remittances Appear to Affect Growth?" *The Economic Journal* 128(612), F179–F209.

Cocco, Federica, Jonathan Wheatley, Jane Pong, David Blood, and Andrew Rininsland. 2019. "Remittances: The Hidden Engine of Globalisation." *Financial Times* 28 August. Available at: https://tinyurl.com/y3kddq9h [accessed 16 December 2019].

Collier, Paul. 2013. *Exodus: How Migration is Changing Our World.* Oxford: Oxford University Press.

Collier, Paul and Anke Hoeffler. 2004. "Greed and Grievance in Civil War." *Oxford Economic Papers* 56(4), 563–95.

Collier, Paul and Anke Hoeffler. 2007. "Unintended Consequences: Does Aid Promote Arms Races?" *Oxford Bulletin of Economics and Statistics* 69(1), 1–27.

Combes, Jean-Louis and Christian Ebeke. 2011. "Remittances and Household Consumption Instability in Developing Countries." *World Development* 39(7), 1,076–89.

Conrad, Courtenay R. 2011. "Constrained Concessions: Beneficent Dictatorial Responses to the Domestic Political Opposition." *International Studies Quarterly* 55(4), 1,167–87.

Constant, Amelie F. and Klaus F. Zimmermann. 2011. "Circular and Repeat Migration: Counts of Exits and Years away from the Host Country." *Population Research and Policy Review* 30(4), 495–515.

Coppedge, Michael, John Gerring, David Altman, Michael Bernhard, Steven Fish, Allen Hicken, Matthew Kroenig et al. 2011. "Conceptualizing and Measuring Democracy: A New Approach." *Perspectives on Politics* 9(2), 247–67.

Coppedge, Michael, John Gerring, Carl Henrik Knutsen, Staffan I. Lindberg, Jan Teorell, David Altman, Michael Bernhard et al. 2019. "V-Dem [Country-Year/Country-Date] Dataset V.9." *Varieties of Democracy (V-Dem) Project* 9.

Córdova, Abby and Jonathan Hiskey. 2015. "Shaping Politics at Home: Migrant Networks and Political Engagement." *Comparative Political Studies* 48(11), 1,454–87.

Córdova, Abby and Jonathan Hiskey. 2019. "Development Context and the Political Behavior of Remittance Recipients in Latin America and the Caribbean." *Political Behavior*. Online first: DOI: 10.1007/s11109-019-09574-5.

Cornell, Agnes. 2013. "Does Regime Type Matter for the Impact of Democracy aid on Democracy?" *Democratization* 20(4), 642–67.

Corstange, Daniel. 2009. "Sensitive Questions, Truthful Answers? Modeling the List Experiment with LISTIT." *Political Analysis* 17(1), 45–63.

Creevey, Lucy, Paul Ngomo, and Richard Vengroff. 2005. "Party Politics and Different Paths to Democratic Transitions: A Comparison of Benin and Senegal." *Party Politics* 11(4), 471–93.

Croissant, Aurel, David Kuehn, and Tanja Eschenauer. 2018. "The 'Dictator's Endgame': Explaining Military Behavior in Nonviolent Anti-Incumbent Mass Protests." *Democracy and Security* 14(2), 174–99.

Croke, Kevin. 2017. "Tools of Single Party Hegemony in Tanzania: Evidence from Surveys and Survey Experiments." *Democratization* 24(2), 189–208.

Croke, Kevin, Guy Grossman, Horacio A. Larreguy, and John Marshall. 2016. "Deliberate Disengagement: How Education Can Decrease Political Participation in Electoral Authoritarian Regimes." *American Political Science Review* 110(3), 579–600.

Crow, David and Clarisa Pérez-Armendáriz. 2018. "Talk Without Borders: Why Political Discussion Makes Latin Americans with Relatives Abroad More Critical of Their Democracies." *Comparative Political Studies* 51(2), 238–76.

Curr, Henry. 2020. "Special Report on The World Economy: The Role of Government." *The Economist* 10 October, 5–14.

Czaika, Mathias and Hein. de Haas 2014. "The Globalization of Migration: Has the World Become More Migratory?" *International Migration Review* 48(2), 283–323.

Dahou, Tarik and Vincent Foucher. 2009. "Senegal since 2000: Rebuilding Hegemony in a Global Age." In Abdul Raufu Mustapha, and Lindsay Whitfield (eds), *Turning Points in African Democracy*. Cambridge: Boydell & Brewer, 13–30.

Dalmasso, Emanuela. 2018. "Participation Without Representation: Moroccans Abroad at a Time of Unstable Authoritarian Rule." *Globalizations* 15(2), 198–214.

Dalton, Russell, Alix Van Sickle, and Steven Weldon. 2010. "The Individual–Institutional Nexus of Protest Behaviour." *British Journal of Political Science* 40(1), 51–73.

Dalton, Russell J. 2017. *The Participation Gap: Social Status and Political Inequality*. New York: Oxford University Press.

Dancygier, Rafaela M. 2010. *Immigration and Conflict in Europe*. New York: Cambridge University Press.

Danielson, Michael S. 2018. *Emigrants Get Political: Mexican Migrants Engage Their Home Towns*. New York: Oxford University Press.

Davenport, Christian. 2007a. "State Repression and Political Order." *Annual Review of Political Science* 10, 1–23.

Davenport, Christian. 2007b. "State Repression and the Tyrannical Peace." *Journal of Peace Research* 44(4), 485–504.

Davies, Ronald B. and Krishna Chaitanya Vadlamannati. 2013. "A Race to the Bottom in Labor Standards? An Empirical Investigation." *Journal of Development Economics* 103, 1–14.

Davis, Julie Hirschfeld, Sheryl Gay Stolberg, and Thomas Kaplan. 2018. "Trump Alarms Lawmakers with Disparaging Words for Haiti and Africa." *The New York Times*, 11 January. Available at: https://tinyurl.com/vwaa9xub [accessed 18 June 2021]

Davis, Rebecca. 2015. "Africa Uprising: The Rise of Popular Protest Continent-Wide." *Daily Maverick*: 4 November. Available at: https://tinyurl.com/tok577q [accessed 12 December 2019].

Dawsey, Josh. 2018. "Trump Derides Protections for Immigrants from 'Shithole' Countries." *The Washington Post* 12 January. Available at: https://tinyurl.com/ybspu5qa [accessed 12 April 2020].

Daxecker, Ursula E. 2012. "The Cost of Exposing Cheating: International Election Monitoring, Fraud and Post-Election Violence in Africa." *Journal of Peace Research* 49(4), 503–16.

De Zeeuw, Jeroen and Krishna Kumar. 2006. *Promoting Democracy in Postconflict Societies*. Boulder: Lynne Rienner.

Dedieu, Jean-Philippe, Lisa Chauvet, Flore Gubert, Sandrine Mesplé-Somps, and Étienne Smith. 2013. "Les 'Batailles' de Paris et de New York: Une analyse du comportement électoral transnational des migrants sénégalais en France et aux États-Unis." *Revue Française de Science Politique* 63(5), 865–92.

Del Sordi, Adele. 2018. "Sponsoring Student Mobility for Development *and* Authoritarian Stability: Kazakhstan's Bolashak Programme." *Globalizations* 15(2), 215–31.

Delano, Alexandra. 2011. *Mexico and Its Diaspora in the United States Policies of Emigration since 1848*. Cambridge: Cambridge University Press.

Della Porta, Donatella. 2014. *Mobilizing for Democracy: Comparing 1989 and 2011*. Oxford: Oxford University Press.

Derpanopoulos, George, Erica Frantz, Barbara Geddes, and Joseph Wright. 2016. "Are Coups Good for Democracy?" *Research and Politics* 3(1), 1–7.

Desai, Raj M. Anders Olofsgard, and Tarik M. Yousef. 2009. "The Logic of Authoritarian Bargains." *Economics and Politics* 21(1), 93–125.

Desierto, Desiree A. 2018. "What Resource Curse? The Null Effect of Remittances on Public Good Provision." *Journal of Theoretical Politics* 30(4), 431–50.

Desposato, Scott W. 2001. "Legislative Politics in Authoritarian Brazil." *Legislative Studies Quarterly* 26(2), 287–318.

Díaz-Cayeros, Alberto, Beatriz Magaloni, and Barry R. Weingast. 2003. "Tragic Brilliance: Equilibrium Hegemony and Democratization in Mexico." Working paper, Stanford University.

Díaz-Cayeros, Alberto, Federico Estévez, and Beatriz Magaloni. 2016. *The Political Logic of Poverty Relief: Electoral Strategies and Social Policy in Mexico*. Cambridge: Cambridge University Press.

Dickson, Bruce J. 2003. *Red Capitalists in China: The Party, Private Entrepreneurs, and Prospects for Political Change*. Cambridge: Cambridge University Press.

Diedhiou, Alpha. 2015. "Remittances, Transnational Dahiras and Governance in Senegal." *International Migration* 53(1), 171–86.

Diener, Ed and Robert Biswas-Diener. 2002. "Will Money Increase Subjective Well-Being?" *Social Indicators Research* 57(2), 119–69.

Dietrich, Simone. 2014. "Bypass or Engage? Explaining Donor Delivery Tactics in Foreign Aid Allocation." *International Studies Quarterly* 57(4), 698–712.

Dietrich, Simone and Joseph Wright. 2015. "Foreign Aid Allocation Tactics and Democratic Change in Africa." *Journal of Politics* 77(1), 216–34.

DiGiuseppe, Matthew and Patrick E. Shea. 2016. "Borrowed Time: Sovereign Finance, Regime Type, and Leader Survival." *Economics and Politics* 28(3), 342–67.

Dillman, Bradford. 2002. "International Markets and Partial Economic Reforms in North Africa: What Impact on Democratization?" *Democratization* 9(1), 63–86.

Dixit, Avinash and John B. Londregan. 1996. "The Determinants of Success of Special Interests in Redistributive Politics." *Journal of Politics* 58(4), 1,132–55.

Djankov, Simeon, Jose G. Montalvo, and Marta Reynal-Querol. 2008. "The Curse of Aid." *Journal of Economic Growth* 13(3), 169–94.

Docquier, Frédéric, Elisabetta Lodigiani, Hillel Rapoport, and Maurice Schiff. 2016. "Emigration and Democracy." *Journal of Development Economics* 120, 209–23.

Downes, Alexander B. and Jonathan Monten. 2013. "Forced to be Free?: Why Foreign-Imposed Regime Change Rarely Leads to Democratization." *International Security* 37(4), 90–131.

Doyle, David. 2015. "Remittances and Social Spending." *American Political Science Review* 109(4), 785–802.

Dragu, Tiberiu and Yonatan Lupu. 2018. "Collective Action and Constraints on Repression at the Endgame." *Comparative Political Studies* 51(8), 1,042–73.

Dragu, Tiberiu and Yonatan Lupu. 2021. "Digital Authoritarianism and the Future of Human Rights." *International Organization*. Online first: DOI: 10.1017/S0020818320000624.

Dragu, Tiberiu and Adam Przeworski. 2019. "Preventive Repression: Two Types of Moral Hazard." *American Political Science Review* 113(1), 77–87.

Dunning, Thad. 2004. "Conditioning the Effects of Aid: Cold War Politics, Donor Credibility and Democracy in Africa." *International Organization* 58(2), 409–23.

Dunning, Thad and Susan Stokes. 2008. "Clientelism as Persuasion and as Mobilization." In *Annual Meeting of the American Political Science Association*, 1–31.

Duquette-Rury, Lauren. 2014. "Collective Remittances and Transnational Co-Production: The 3 × 1 Program for Migrants and Household Access to Public Goods in Mexico." *Studies in Comparative International Development* 49(1), 112–39.

Duquette-Rury, Lauren. 2016. "Migrant Transnational Participation: How Citizen Inclusion and Government Engagement Matter for Local Democratic Development in Mexico." *American Sociological Review* 81(4), 771–99.

Duquette-Rury, Lauren. 2019. *Exit and Voice: The Paradox of Cross-Border Politics in Mexico.* Oakland: University of California Press.

Earl, Jennifer. 2006. "Introduction: Repression and the Social Control of Protest." *Mobilization: An International Quarterly* 11(2), 129–43.

Easton, Malcolm R. and Gabriella R. Montinola. 2017. "Remittances, Regime Type and Government Spending Priorities." *Studies in Comparative International Development* 52(3), 349–71.

Ebeke, Christian. 2012. "Do Remittances Lead to a Public Moral Hazard in Developing Countries? An Empirical Investigation." *Journal of Development Studies* 48(8), 1,009–25.

Ebeke, Christian and Thierry Yogo. 2013. "Remittances and the Voter Turnout in Sub-Saharan Africa: Evidence from Macro and Micro Level Data." African Development Bank Group Working Paper no. 185.

Ebeke, Christian Hubert. 2014. "Do International Remittances Affect the Level and the Volatility of Government Tax Revenues?" *Journal of International Development* 26(7), 1,039–53.

Eckstein, Susan. 2010. "Remittances and Their Unintended Consequences in Cuba." *World Development* 38(7), 1,047–55.

Eckstein, Susan Eva and Adil Najam (eds). 2010. *How Immigrants Impact their Homelands.* Durham: Duke University Press.

*Economic Times.* 2019. "India Highest Recipient of Remittances at $79 bn in 2018." *Economic Times*, May. Available at: https://tinyurl.com/ycufyn96 [accessed 5 June 2020].

Economist Intelligence Unit. 2011. "Violent Protests in Western Province." *Economist Intelligence Unit* 3 February. Available at: https://bit.ly/2nxx9c1 [accessed 26 September 2019].

Edelbloude, Johanna, Farid Makhlouf, and Charlotte Fontan Sers. 2016. *L'impact du Printemps arabe sur les transferts de fonds des migrants tunisiens.* HAL Available at: https://hal-univ-pau.archives-ouvertes.fr/hal-01885143 [accessed 14 June 2021].

Eichengreen, Barry and David Leblang. 2008. "Democracy and Globalization." *Economics and Politics* 38(7), 1,047–55.

EJF. 2005. *White Gold: The True Cost of Cotton.* London: Environmental Justice Foundation.

Elkink, Johan A. 2011. "The International Diffusion of Democracy." *Comparative Political Studies* 44(12), 1,651–74.

Eng, Netra and Caroline Hughes. 2017. "Coming of Age in Peace, Prosperity, and Connectivity: Cambodia's Young Electorate and Its Impact on the Ruling Party's Political Strategies." *Critical Asian Studies* 49(3), 396–410.

Esberg, Jane. 2021. "Anticipating Dissent: The Repression of Politicians in Pinochet's Chile." *Journal of Politics* 83(2), 689–705

Escobar, Cristina, Renelinda Arana, and James A. McCann. 2015. "Expatriate Voting and Migrants' Place of Residence: Explaining Transnational Participation in Colombian Elections." *Migration Studies* 3(1), 1–31.

Escribà-Folch, Abel. 2013. "Repression, Political Threats, and Survival under Autocracy." *International Political Science Review* 34(5), 543–60.

Escribà-Folch, Abel. 2017. "Foreign Direct Investment and the Risk of Regime Transition in Autocracies." *Democratization* 24(1), 61–80.

Escribà-Folch, Abel and Joseph Wright. 2015. *Foreign Pressure and the Politics of Autocratic Survival.* Oxford: Oxford University Press.

Escribà-Folch, Abel, Covadonga Meseguer, and Joseph Wright. 2015. "Remittances and Democratization." *International Studies Quarterly* 59(3), 571–86.

Escribà-Folch, Abel, Covadonga Meseguer, and Joseph Wright. 2018. "Remittances and Protest in Dictatorships." *American Journal of Political Science* 62(4), 889–904.

Fajnzylber, Pablo and J. Humberto López. 2007. *Close to Home: The Development Impact of Remittances in Latin America.* Washington, DC: The International Bank for Reconstruction and Development, World Bank.

Fariss, Christopher J. 2014. "Respect for Human Rights Has Improved over Time: Modeling the Changing Standard of Accountability." *American Political Science Review* 108(2), 297–318.

Farrell, Dan. 1983. "Exit, Voice, Loyalty, and Neglect as Responses to Job Dissatisfaction: A Multidimensional Scaling Study." *The Academy of Management Journal* 26(4), 596–607.

Fassihi, Farnaz and Rick Gladstone. 2019. "With Brutal Crackdown, Iran Is Convulsed by Worst Unrest in 40 Years." *The New York Times* 1 December. Available at: https://tinyurl.com/u8nxbom [accessed 12 March 2020].

Fatton, Robert. 1986. "Clientelism and Patronage in Senegal." *African Studies Review* 29(4), 61–78.

Ferrie, Joseph P. and Timothy J. Hatton. 2013. *Two Centuries of International Migration.* IZA Discussion Paper no. 7,866.

Feyzioglu, Tarhan, Vinaya Swaroop, and Min Zhu. 1998. "A Panel Data Analysis of the Fungibility of Foreign Aid." *The World Bank Economic Review* 12(1), 29–58.

Finkel, Steven E., Aníbal Pérez-Liñán, and Mitchell A. Seligson. 2007. "The Effects of US Foreign Assistance on Democracy Building, 1990–2003." *World Politics* 59(3), 404–39.

Fisher, Max and Amanda Taub. 2019a. "The Global Protest Wave, Explained." *The New York Times,* 10 December. Available at: https://tinyurl.com/tkfcnpq [accessed 12 December 2019].

Fisher, Max and Amanda Taub. 2019b. "Trump's Immigration Approach Isn't New: Europe and Australia Went First." *The New York Times* 18 July. Available at: https://tinyurl.com/spx45xw [accessed 16 December 2019].

Fitzgerald, David. 2009. *A Nation of Emigrants: How Mexico Manages Its Migration.* Berkeley: University of California Press.

Fitzgerald, Jennifer, David Leblang, and Jessica Teets. 2014. "Defying the Law of Gravity: The Political Economy of International Migration." *World Politics* 66(3), 406–45.

Flahaux, Marie-Laurence and Hein de Haas. 2016. "African Migration: Trends, Patterns, Drivers." *Comparative Migration Studies* 4(1), 1–25.

Fomina, Joanna. 2021. "Voice, Exit and Voice Again: Democratic Remittances by Recent Russian Emigrants to the EU." *Journal of Ethnic and Migration Studies* 47(11), 2,439–58

Fontaine, Richard and Daniel Kliman. 2018. "On China's New Silk Road, Democracy Pays A Toll." *Foreign Policy* 16 May. Available at: https://foreignpolicy.com/2018/05/16/on-chinas-new-silk-road-democracy-pays-a-toll/ [accessed 23 February 2020].

Fox, Jonathan A. 2007. *Accountability Politics: Power and Voice in Rural Mexico*. Oxford: Oxford University Press.

Francisco, Ronald A. 1995. "The Relationship between Coercion and Protest: An Empirical Evaluation in Three Coercive States." *Journal of Conflict Resolution* 39(2), 263–82.

Francisco, Ronald A. 2006. "After the Massacre: Mobilization in the Wake of Harsh Repression." *Mobilization: An International Quarterly* 9(2), 107–26.

Frankel, Jeffrey. 2011. "Are Bilateral Remittances Countercyclical?" *Open Economies Review* 22(1), 1–16.

Fransen, Sonja. 2015. "Remittances, Bonds and Bridges: Remittances and Social Capital in Burundi." *Journal of Development Studies* 51(10), 1,294–308.

Frantz, Erica. 2018a. *Authoritarianism: What Everyone Needs to Know*. New York: Oxford University Press.

Frantz, Erica. 2018b. "Voter Turnout and Opposition Performance in Competitive Authoritarian Elections." *Electoral Studies* 54, 218–25.

Frantz, Erica and Andrea Kendall-Taylor. 2014. "A Dictator's Toolkit: Understanding how Co-optation Affects Repression in Autocracies." *Journal of Peace Research* 51(3), 332–46.

Frantz, Erica, Andrea Kendall-Taylor, Joseph Wright, and Xu Xu. 2020. "Personalization of Power and Repression in Dictatorships." *Journal of Politics* 82(1), 372–77.

Freeman, Richard B. 2006. "People Flows in Globalization." *Journal of Economic Perspectives* 20(2), 145–70.

Freund, Caroline and Nikola Spatafora. 2008. "Remittances, Transaction Costs and Informality." *Journal of Development Economics* 86(2), 356–66.

Friedman, L. Thomas. 2006. "The First Law of Petropolitics." *Foreign Policy* 154, 28–36.

Friedrich, Carl J. and Zbigniew K. Brzezinski. 1965. *Totalitarian Dictatorship*. New York: Praeger Publishers.

Frye, Timothy, Ora John Reuter, and David Szakonyi. 2014. "Political Machines at Work: Voter Mobilization and Electoral Subversion in the Workplace." *World Politics* 66(2), 195–228.

Frye, Timothy, Scott Gehlbach, Kyle L. Marquardt, and Ora John Reuter. 2017. "Is Putin's Popularity Real?" *Post-Soviet Affairs* 33(1), 1–15.

Fukuyama, Francis. 1989. "The End of History?" *The National Interest*, 3–18.

Galvan, Dennis. 2001. "Political Turnover and Social Change in Senegal." *Journal of Democracy* 12(3), 51–62.

Gamlen, Alan. 2014. "Diaspora Institutions and Diaspora Governance." *International Migration Review* 48(Fall), S180–S217.

Gandhi, Jennifer. 2015. "Elections and Political Regimes." *Government and Opposition* 50(3), 446–68.

Gandhi, Jennifer and Ellen Lust-Okar. 2009. "Elections under Authoritarianism." *Annual Review of Political Science* 12, 403–22.

Ganguly, Sumit. 2019. "India Under Modi: Threats to Pluralism." *Journal of Democracy* 30(1), 83–90.

Gans-Morse, Jordan, Sebastián Mazzuca, and Simeon Nichter. 2014. "Varieties of Clientelism: Machine Politics during Elections." *American Journal of Political Science* 58(2), 415–32.

Gat, Azar. 2007. "The Return of Authoritarian Great Powers." *Foreign Affairs* 86(4), 59–69.

Geddes, Barbara. 1999. "What Do We Know about Democratization after Twenty Years?" *Annual Review of Political Science* 2, 115–44.

Geddes, Barbara, Joseph Wright, and Erica Frantz. 2014a. "Autocratic Breakdown and Regime Transitions: A New Data Set." *Perspectives on Politics* 12(2), 313–31.

Geddes, Barbara, Erica Frantz, and Joseph Wright. 2014b. "Military Rule." *Annual Review of Political Science* 17, 147–62.

Geddes, Barbara, Joseph Wright, and Erica Frantz. 2018. *How Dictatorships Work*. New York: Cambridge University Press.

Germano, Roy. 2013. "Migrants' Remittances and Economic Voting in the Mexican Countryside." *Electoral Studies* 32(4), 875–85.

Germano, Roy. 2018. *Outsourcing Welfare: How the Money Immigrants Send Home Contributes to Stability in Developing Countries*. New York: Oxford University Press.

Gerschewski, Johannes. 2013. "The Three Pillars of Stability: Legitimation, Repression, and Co-optation in Autocratic Regimes." *Democratization* 20(1), 13–38.

Gingerich, Daniel W. 2013. "Can Institutions Cure Clientelism? Assessing the Impact of the Australian Ballot in Brazil." Inter-American Development Bank Working Paper no. IDB-WP-428.

Glasius, Marlies. 2018. "Extraterritorial Authoritarian Practices: A Framework." *Globalizations* 15(2), 179–97.

Gleditsch, Kristian S. and Mauricio Rivera. 2017. "The Diffusion of Nonviolent Campaigns." *Journal of Conflict Resolution* 61(5), 1,120–45.

Gleditsch, Kristian S. and Michael D. Ward. 2006. "Diffusion and the International Context of Democratization." *International Organization* 60(4), 911–33.

Gleditsch, Nils Petter, Peter Wallensteen, Mikael Eriksson, Margareta Sollenberg, and Havard Strand. 2002. "Armed Conflict 1946–2001: A New Dataset." *Journal of Peace Research* 39(5), 615–37.

Global Burden of Disease Health Financing Collaborator Network. 2019. Past, Present, and Future of Global Health Financing: A Review of Development Assistance, Government, Out-of-Pocket, and Other Private Spending on Health for 195 Countries, 1995–2050. *The Lancet* 393(10,187), 2,233–60.

Goldring, Luin. 2002. "The Mexican State and Transmigrant Organizations: Negotiating the Boundaries of Membership and Participation." *Latin American Research Review* 37(3), 55–99.

González-Ocantos, Ezequiel, Chad Kiewiet de Jonge, and Covadonga Meseguer. 2018. "Remittances and Vote Buying." *Latin American Research Review* 53(4), 689–707.

Goodliffe, Jay and Darren Hawkins. 2017. "Dependence Networks and the Diffusion of Domestic Political Institutions." *Journal of Conflict Resolution* 61(4), 903–29.

Goodman, Gary L. and Jonathan Hiskey. 2008. "Exit without Leaving: Political Disengagement in High Migration Municipalities in Mexico." *Comparative Politics* 40(2), 169–88.

Green, Andrew T. and Richard D. Kohl. 2007. "Challenges of Evaluating Democracy Assistance: Perspectives from the Donor Side." *Democratization* 14(1), 151–65.

Greene, Kenneth F. 2007. *Why Dominant Parties Lose: Mexico's Democratization in Comparative Perspective*. New York: Cambridge University Press.

Greitens, Sheena Chestnut. 2017. "Rethinking China's Coercive Capacity: An Examination of PRC Domestic Security Spending, 1992–2012." *The China Quarterly* 232, 1,002–25.

GSMA. 2012. *The Mobile Economy 2019*. Tecnical report, GSMA Mobile Economy Series. London: GSM Association.

Guarnizo, Luis Eduardo, Alejandro Portes, and William Haller. 2003. "Assimilation and Transnationalism: Determinants of Transnational Political Action among Contemporary Migrants." *American Journal of Sociology* 108(6), 1,211–48.

Gunitsky, Seva. 2017. *Aftershocks: Great Powers and Domestic Reforms in the Twentieth Century*. Princeton: Princeton University Press.

Guo, Xuezhi. 2012. *China's Security State: Philosophy, Evolution, and Politics*. Cambridge: Cambridge University Press.

Guriev, Sergei and Daniel Treisman. 2019. "Informational Autocrats." *Journal of Economic Perspectives* 33(4), 100–27.

Gurr, Ted R. 1970. *Why Men Rebel*. Princeton: Princeton University Press.

Gyimah-Boadi, Emmanuel. 1996. "Civil Society in Africa." *Journal of Democracy* 7(2), 118–32.

Hadenius, Axel and Jan Teorell. 2007. "Pathways from Authoritarianism." *Journal of Democracy* 18(1), 143–57.

Hafner-Burton, Emily M. Susan D. Hyde, and Ryan S. Jablonski. 2014. "When Do Governments Resort to Election Violence?" *British Journal of Political Science* 44(1), 149–79.

Haggard, Stephan and Robert R. Kaufman. 2016. *Dictators and Democrats: Masses, Elites, and Regime Change*. Princeton: Princeton University Press.

Hainmueller, Jens and Chad Hazlett. 2013. "Kernel Regularized Least Squares: Reducing Misspecification Bias with a Flexible and Interpretable Machine Learning Approach." *Political Analysis* 22(2), 143–68.

Hale, Henry E. 2013. "Regime Change Cascades: What We Have Learned from the 1848 Revolutions to the 2011 Arab Uprisings." *Annual Review of Political Science* 16(1), 331–53.

Handley, Antoinette. 2015. "Varieties of Capitalists? The Middle-Class, Private Sector and Economic Outcomes in Africa." *Journal of International Development* 27(5), 609–27.

Harding, Robin. 2010. "Urban-Rural Differences in Support for Incumbents across Africa." Afrobarometer Working Paper no. 120.

Harris, Adam S. and Erin Hern. 2019. "Taking to the Streets: Protest as an Expression of Political Preference in Africa." *Comparative Political Studies* 52(8), 1,169–99.

Hartnett, Lynne Ann. 2020. "Relief and Revolution: Russian Émigrés' Political Remittances and the Building of Political Transnationalism." *Journal of Ethnic and Migration Studies* 46(6), 1,040–56

Hatton, Timothy J. and Jeffrey G. Williamson. 1998. *The Age of Mass Migration: Causes and Economic Impact*. New York: Oxford University Press.

Hatton, Timothy J. and Jeffrey G. Williamson. 2008. *Global Migration and the World Economy: Two Centuries of Policy and Performance*. Cambridge, MA: MIT Press.

Hellmeier, Sebastian and Nils B. Weidmann. 2020. "Pulling the Strings? The Strategic Use of Pro-Government Mobilization in Authoritarian Regimes." *Comparative Political Studies* 53(1), 71–108.

Heng, Sreang. 2018. "Elections Under Oppression in Cambodia: A Predictable Outcome?" *Yale McMillan Center* 4 September. Available at: https://tinyurl.com/rjcd6mr [accessed 13 April 2019].

Henk, Daniel W. and Martin R. Rupiya. 2001. *Funding Defense: Challenges of Buying Military Capability in Sub-Saharan Africa*. Carlisle: Strategic Studies Institute, US Army War College.

Hicken, Allen. 2011. "Clientelism." *Annual Review of Political Science* 14(1), 289–310.

Hirschman, Albert O. 1970. *Exit, Voice, and Loyalty: Responses to Decline in Firms, Organizations, and States*. Cambridge: Harvard University Press.

Hirschman, Albert O. 1978. "Exit, Voice and the State." *World Politics* 31(1), 90–107.

Hirschman, Albert O. 1993. "Exit, Voice, and the Fate of the German Democratic Republic: An Essay in Conceptual History." *World Politics* 45(2), 173–202.

Hiskey, Jonathan, Jorge D. Montalvo, and Diana Orcés. 2014. "Democracy, Governance and Emigration Intentions in Latin America and the Caribbean." *Studies in Comparative International Development* 49(1), 89–111.

Hoffmann, Bert. 2010. "Bringing Hirschman Back In: 'Exit,' 'Voice,' and 'Loyalty' in the Politics of Transnational Migration." *The Latin Americanist* 54(2), 57–73.

Horz, Carlo M. and Moritz Marbach. 2020. "Economic Opportunities, Emigration and Exit Prisoners." *British Journal of Political Science*. Online first: DOI: 10.1017/S0007123420000216

Houle, Christian, Mark A. Kayser and Jun Xiang. 2016. "Diffusion or Confusion? Clustered Shocks and the Conditional Diffusion of Democracy." *International Organization* 70(4), 687–726.

Howard, Marc M. and Philip G. Roessler. 2006. "Liberalizing Electoral Outcomes in Competitive Authoritarian Regimes." *American Journal of Political Science* 50(2), 365–81.

Huggins, Martha K. 1987. "US-Supported State Terror: A History of Police Training in Latin America." *Crime and Social Justice* 27/28, 149–71.

Hughes, Caroline. 2003. *The Political Economy of Cambodia's Transition 1991–2001*. London: Routledge.

Hughes, Caroline. 2006. "The Politics of Gifts: Tradition and Regimentation in Contemporary Cambodia." *Journal of Southeast Asian Studies* 37(3), 469–89.

Hughes, Caroline. 2015. "Understanding the Elections in Cambodia 2013." *AGLOS: Journal of Area-Based Global Studies. Special Issues: Workshop and Symposium 2013–2014*, 1–20.

Hultin, Niklas, Baba Jallow, Benjamin N. Lawrance, and Assan Sarr. 2017. "The Gambia's 'Unpredecedented' 2016 election." *African Affairs* 116, 149–71.

Human Rights Watch. 2017. "Rwanda: Politically Closed Elections." *Human Rights Watch* 18 August. Available at: https://tinyurl.com/rtjww47 [accessed 12 December 2019].

Huntington, Samuel P. 1991. *The Third Wave: Democratization in the Late Twentieth Century*. Norman: University of Oklahoma Press.

Hutt, David. 2017. "The Fall of Cambodia's Patron-Client Politics?" *The Diplomat* 19 May. Available at: https://tinyurl.com/vpubs7q [accessed 16 April 2020].

Hutt, David. 2020. "Hun Sen's Art of Giving." *Southeast Asia Globe* 4 February. Available at: https://tinyurl.com/vpubs7q [accessed 16 April 2020].

Hyde, Susan D. 2011. *The Pseudo-Democrat's Dilemma: Why Election Observation Became an International Norm*. Ithaca: Cornell University Press.

Hyde, Susan D. and Nikolay Marinov. 2012. "Which Elections Can Be Lost?" *Political Analysis* 20(2), 191–210.

Ichino, Nahomi and Noah L. Nathan. 2013. "Crossing the Line: Local Ethnic Geography and Voting in Ghana." *American Political Science Review* 107(2), 344–61.

IDEA. 2017. *The Global State of Democracy 2017: Exploring Democracy's Resilience*. Stockholm: International Institute for Democracy and Electoral Assistance.

IDEA. 2019. *Voter Turnout Database*. Stockholm: International Institute for Democracy and Electoral Assistance.

IMF. 2005. *World Economic Outlook: Globalization and External Imbalances*. Washington, DC: International Monetary Fund.

Inglehart, Ronald and Pippa Norris. 2017. "Trump and the Populist Authoritarian Parties: The Silent Revolution in Reverse." *Perspectives on Politics* 15(2), 443–54.

International Crisis Group. 2007. "Uzbekistan: Stagnation and Uncertainty." *Asia Briefing* 67(1), 1–19.

International Organization for Migration. 2020. *World Migration Report 2020*. New York: United Nations.

International Telecommunication Union. 2019. *Measuring Digital Development: Facts and Figures 2019*. Geneva: ITU Publications.

Isbell, Thomas A. 2017. "Afrobarometer Survey Data Codebook for Round 6." *Afrobarometer* Round 6, 1–110.

Iskander, Natasha. 2010. *Creative State: Forty Years of Migration and Development Policy in Morocco and Mexico*. Ithaca: Cornell University Press.

Itzigsohn, José and Diana Villacres. 2008. "Migrant Political Transnationalism and the Practice of Democracy: Dominican External Voting Rights and Salvadoran Home Town Associations." *Ethnic and Racial Studies* 31(4), 664–86.

Jablonski, Ryan S. 2014. "How Aid Targets Votes: The Impact of Electoral Incentives on Foreign Aid Distribution." *World Politics* 66(2), 293–330.

Jamal, Amaney A. 2009. *Barriers to Democracy: The Other Side of Social Capital in Palestine and the Arab world*. Princeton: Princeton University Press.

Jew, Victor. 2002. "Exploring New Frontiers in Chinese American History: The Anti-Chinese Riot in Milwaukee, 1889." Susie Lan Cassel (ed.), *The Chinese in America: A History from Gold Mountain to the New Millennium*. Rowman & Littlefield Publishers.

Jiang, Junyan and Dali L. Yang. 2016. "Lying or Believing? Measuring Preference Falsification from a Political Purge in China." *Comparative Political Studies* 49(5), 600–34.

Judis, John. 2018. *The Nationalist Revival: Trade, Immigration, and the Revolt Against Globalization*. New York: Columbia Global Reports.

Kalyvitis, Sarantis and Irene Vlachaki. 2010. "Democratic Aid and the Democratization of Recipients." *Contemporary Economic Policy* 28(2), 188–218.

Kaplan, Robert D. 2019. "A New Cold War Has Begun." *Foreign Policy*, 7 January. Available at: https://foreignpolicy.com/2019/01/07/a-new-cold-war-has-begun/ [accessed 23 February 2020].

Kapur, Devesh. 2010. *Diaspora, Development and Democracy: The Domestic Impact of International Migration from India*. Princeton: Princeton University Press.

Kapur, Devesh. 2014. "Political Effects of International Migration." *Annual Review of Political Science* 17, 479–502.

Kapur, Devesh and John McHale. 2012. "Economic Effects of Emigration on Sending Countries." In Marc R. Rosenblum and Daniel J. Tichenor (eds), *The Oxford Handbook of the Politics of International Migration*. Oxford: Oxford University Press, 131–52.

Karadja, Mounir and Erik Prawitz. 2019. "Exit, Voice, and Political Change: Evidence from Swedish Mass Migration to the United States." *Journal of Political Economy* 127(4), 1,864–925.

Karakoç, Ekrem, Talha Köse, and Mesut Özcan. 2017. "Emigration and the Diffusion of Political Salafism: Religious Remittances and Support for Salafi Parties in Egypt during the Arab Spring." *Party Politics* 23(6), 731–45.

Katz, Eliakim and Oded Stark. 1986. "Labor Migration and Risk Aversion in Less Developed Countries." *Journal of Labor Economics* 4(1), 134–49.

Kelemen, R. Daniel. 2020. "The European Union's Authoritarian Equilibrium." *Journal of European Public Policy* 27(3), 481–99.

Kendall-Taylor, Andrea and Erica Frantz. 2014a. "Autocrats Now More Vulnerable to Being Ousted by Revolt." *The Washington Post*, 9 April. Available at: https://tinyurl.com/qwvn3gb [accessed 20 September 2019].

Kendall-Taylor, Andrea and Erica Frantz. 2014b. "How Autocracies Fall." *The Washington Quarterly* 37(1), 35–47.

Kendall-Taylor, Andrea, Natasha Lindstaedt, and Erica Frantz. 2019. *Democracies and Authoritarian Regimes*. Oxford: Oxford University Press.

Kendall-Taylor, Andrea, Erica Frantz, and Joseph Wright. 2020. "The Digital Dictators: How Technology Strengthens Autocracy." *Foreign Affairs* 99(2), 103–15.

Kim, Nam Kyu and Alex M. Kroeger. 2019. "Conquering and Coercing: Nonviolent Anti-Regime Protests and the Pathways to Democracy." *Journal of Peace Research* 56(5), 650–66.

King, Gary, Jennifer Pan, and Margaret E. Roberts. 2013. "How Censorship in China Allows Government Criticism but Silences Collective Expression." *American Political Science Review* 107(2), 326–43.

Kitschelt, Herbert P. 1986. "Political Opportunity Structures and Political Protest: Anti-Nuclear Movements in Four Democracies." *British Journal of Political Science* 16(1), 57–85.

Kitschelt, Herbert P. 2000. "Linkages between Citizens and Politicians in Democratic Polities." *Comparative Political Studies* 33(6/7), 845–79.

Kitschelt, Herbert and Steven I. Wilkinson. 2007. "Citizen–Politician Linkages: An Introduction." In Herbert Kitschelt and Steven I. Wilkinson (eds), *Patrons, Clients and Policies: Patterns of Democratic Accountability and Political Competition*. Cambridge: Cambridge University Press, 1–49.

Klotz, Audie. 1995. "Norms Reconstituting Interests: Global Racial Equality and US Sanctions against South Africa." *International Organization* 49(3), 451–78.

Knudsen, Anne Sofie Beck. 2019. "Those Who Stayed: Selection and Cultural Change during the Age of Mass Migration." *Stanford University*. Available at: https://economics.stanford.edu/sites/g/files/sbiybj9386/f/thosewhostayed.pdf [accessed 11 December 2019].

Knutsen, Carl Henrik, Håvard Nygård, and Tore Wig. 2017. "Autocratic Elections: Stabilizing Tool or Force for Change?" *World Politics* 69(1), 98–143.

Kobrin, Stephen J. 1985. "Diffusion as an Explanation of Oil Nationalization: Or the Domino Effect Rides Again." *Journal of Conflict Resolution* 29(1), 3–32.

Koinova, Maria. 2009. "Diasporas and Democratization in the Post-Communist Word." *Communist and Post-Communist Studies* 42(1), 41–64.

Koinova, Maria. 2018. "Diaspora Mobilisation for Conflict and Post-Conflict Reconstruction: Contextual and Comparative Dimensions." *Journal of Ethnic and Migration Studies* 44(8), 1,251–69.

Kono, Daniel Yuichi and Gabriella R. Montinola. 2009. "Does Foreign Aid Support Autocrats, Democrats, or Both?" *Journal of Politics* 71(2), 704–18.

Kono, Daniel Yuichi and Gabriella R. Montinola. 2013. "The Uses and Abuses of Foreign Aid: Development Aid and Military Spending." *Political Research Quarterly* 66(3), 615–29.

Konte, Maty and Gideon Ndubuisi. 2019. "Remittances and Bribery in Africa." United Nations University—Maastricht Economic and Social Research Institute on Innovation and Technology, MERIT Working Paper 2019-043.

Kora, Sheriff and Momodou N. Darboe. 2017. "The Gambia's Electoral Earthquake." *Journal of Democracy* 28(2), 147–56.

Koter, Dominika. 2013. "King Makers. Local Leaders and Ethnic Politics in Africa." *World Politics* 65(2), 187–232.

Kovács, Eszter. 2020. "Direct and Indirect Political Remittances of the Transnational Engagement of Hungarian Kin-Minorities and Diaspora Communities." *Journal of Ethnic and Migration Studies* 46(6), 1,146–65.

Kramon, Eric. 2009. *"Vote Buying and Turnout in Kenya's 2002 Elections."* PhD dissertation, University of California, Los Angeles.

Kramon, Eric. 2018. *Money for Votes: The Causes and Consequences of Electoral Clientelism in Africa*. New York: Cambridge University Press.

Kramon, Eric and Daniel N. Posner. 2016. "Ethnic Favoritism in Education in Kenya." *Quarterly Journal of Political Science* 11(1), 1–58.

Krasner, Stephen D. and Jeremy M. Weinstein. 2014. "Improving Governance from the Outside In." *Annual Review of Political Science* 17(1), 123–45.

Krastev, Ivan and Stephen Holmes. 2018. "Explaining Eastern Europe: Imitation and its Discontents." *Journal of Democracy* 29(3), 117–28.

Krastev, Ivan and Stephen Holmes. 2019. *The Light that Failed: A Reckoning*. London: Penguin Books.

Krawatzek, Félix and Lea Müller-Funk. 2020. "Two Centuries of Flows between 'Here' and 'There': Political Remittances and their Transformative Potential." *Journal of Ethnic and Migration Studies* 46(6), 1,003–24.

Kuhlmann, Jenny. 2010. "Political Activism of the Zimbabwean Diaspora: Opportunities for, and Challenges to, Transnational Mobilisation." Working Paper Series of the Graduate Centre Humanities and Social Sciences of the Research Academy Leipzig no. 5.

Kuran, Timur. 1989. "Sparks and Prairie Fires: A Theory of Unanticipated Political Revolution." *Public Choice* 61(1), 41–74.

Kuran, Timur. 1997. *Private Truths, Public Lies: The Social Consequences of Preference Falsification*. Cambridge: Harvard University Press.

Kwok, Chuck and Soloman Tadesse. 2006. "The MNC as an Agent of Change for Host-Country Institutions: FDI and Corruption." *Journal of International Business Studies* 37(6), 767–85.

Lacroix, Thomas, Peggy Levitt, and Ilka Vari-Lavoisier. 2016. "Social Remittances and the Changing Transnational Political Landscape." *Comparative Migration Studies* 4, article 16. Available online: DOI: 10.1186/s40878-016-0032-0.

LeBas, Adrienne. 2013. *From Protest to Parties: Party-Building and Democratization in Africa*. Oxford: Oxford University Press.

Leblang, David. 2010. "Familiarity Breeds Investment: Diaspora Networks and International Investment." *American Journal of Political Science* 104(2), 584–600.

Lehoucq, Fabrice and Aníbal Pérez-Liñán. 2014. "Breaking Out of the Coup Trap: Political Competition and Military Coups in Latin America." *Comparative Political Studies* 47(8), 1,105–29.

Letsa, Natalie W. 2019. "The Political Geography of Electoral Autocracies: The Influence of Party Strongholds on Political Beliefs in Africa." *Electoral Studies* 60, 1–12.

Levitsky, Steven and Lucan A. Way. 2006. "Linkage versus Leverage. Rethinking the International Dimension of Regime Change." *Comparative Politics* 38(4), 379–400.

Levitsky, Steven and Lucan A. Way. 2010. *Competitive Authoritarianism: Hybrid Regimes after the Cold War*. Cambridge: Cambridge University Press.

Levitsky, Steven R. and Lucan A. Way. 2012. "Beyond Patronage: Violent Struggle, Ruling Party Cohesion, and Authoritarian Durability." *Perspectives on Politics* 10(4), 869–89.

Levitt, Peggy. 1998. "Social Remittances: Migration Driven Local-Level Forms of Cultural Diffusion." *International Migration Review* 32(4), 926–48.

Levitt, Peggy. 2001. *The Transnational Villagers*. Berkeley: University of California Press.

Levitt, Peggy and B. Nadya Jaworsky. 2007. "Transnational Migration Studies: Past Developments and Future Trends." *Annual Review of Sociology* 33(1), 129–56.

Levitt, Peggy and Deepak Lamba-Nieves. 2011. "Social Remittances Revisited." *Journal of Ethnic and Migration Studies* 37(1), 1–22.

Levy, Jack S. 2008. "Case Studies: Types, Designs, and Logics of Inference." *Conflict Management and Peace Science* 25(1), 1–18.

Lewis, Jacob S. 2020. "Corruption Perceptions and Contentious Politics in Africa: How Different Types of Corruption Have Shaped Africa's Third Wave of Protest." *Political Studies Review*. Online first: DOI:10.1177/1478929920903657.

Lewis-Beck, Michael S. and Mary Stegmaier. 2007. "Economic Models of Voting." In Russell Dalton and Hans-Dieter Klingemann (eds), *The Oxford Handbook of Political Behavior*. Oxford: Oxford University Press, 518–37.

Ley, Sandra, J. Eduardo Ibarra-Olivo, and Covadonga Meseguer. 2021. "Family Remittances and Vigilantism in Mexico." *Journal of Ethnic and Migration Studies* 47(6), 1,375–94.

Li, Quan and Rafael Reuveny. 2009. *Democracy and Economic Openness in an Interconnected System: Complex Transformations*. New York: Cambridge University Press.

Lichbach, Mark I. 1987. "Deterrence or Escalation?: The Puzzle of Aggregate Studies of Repression and Dissent." *Journal of Conflict Resolution* 31(2), 266–97.

Lim, Sokchea and A.K.M. Mahbub Morshed. 2017. "Fiscal Policy in a Small Open Economy with Cross-Border Labour Mobility." *Journal of Macroeconomics* 52, 147–74.

Lindbeck, Assar and Jörgen W. Weibull. 1987. "Balanced-Budget Redistribution as the Outcome of Political Competition." *Public Choice* 52(3), 273–97.

Lindley. 2009. "The Early-Morning Phonecall: Remittances from Refugee Diaspora Perspective." *Journal of Ethnic and Migration Studies* 35(8), 1,315–34.

Little, Andrew T. 2016. "Communication Technology and Protest." *Journal of Politics* 78(1), 152–66.

Little, Andrew T., Joshua A. Tucker and Tom LaGatta. 2015. "Elections, Protest and Alternation of Power." *Journal of Politics* 77(4), 1,142–56.

Lohmann, Susanne. 1994. "The Dynamics of Informational Cascades: The Monday Demonstrations in Leipzig, East Germany, 1989–91." *World Politics* 47(1), 42–101.

Lorentzen, Peter L. 2013. "Regularizing Rioting: Permitting Public Protest in an Authoritarian Regime." *Quarterly Journal of Political Science* 8(2), 127–58.

Lucas, Robert E. B. and Oded Stark. 1985. "Motivations to Remit: Evidence from Botswana." *Journal of Political Economy* 93(5), 901–18.

Lust-Okar, Ellen. 2006. "Elections under Authoritarianism: Preliminary Lessons from Jordan." *Democratization* 13(3), 456–71.

Lyons, John, Nazih Osseiran, and Margherita Stancati. 2019. "Global Wave of Protests Rattles Governments." *Wall Street Journal*, November 22. Available at: https://tinyurl .com/waf7xnv [accessed 12 December 2019].

Lyons, Terrence. 2006. "Transnational Politics in Ethiopia: Diasporas and the 2005 Elections." *Diaspora: A Journal of Transnational Studies* 15(2/3), 265–84.

Lyons, Terrence. 2007. "Conflict-Generated Diasporas and Transnational Politics in Ethiopia." *Conflict, Security and Development* 7(4), 529–49.

Lyons, Terrence. 2012. "Transnational Politics in Ethiopia. Diaspora Mobilization and Contentious Politics." In Terrence Lyons and Peter Mandaville (eds), *Politics from Afar: Transnational Diasporas and Networks*. London: Hurst & Company, 141–56.

Machado, Fabiana, Carlos Scartascini, and Mariano Tommasi. 2011. "Political Institutions and Street Protests in Latin America." *Journal of Conflict Resolution* 55(3), 340–65.

Maclean, Ruth. 2016. "Violence Erupts after Gabon Election as Incumbent Ali Bongo Named Victor." *The Guardian*, August 31. Available at: https://tinyurl.com/hmbhh6h [accessed 12 December 2019].

Maerz, Seraphine F., Anna Lührmann, Sebastian Hellmeier, Sandra Grahn, and Staffan I. Lindberg. 2020. "State of the World 2019: Autocratization Surges—Resistance Grows." *Democratization* 27(6), 909–27.

Magaloni, Beatriz. 2006. *Voting for Autocracy: Hegemonic Party Survival and its Demise in Mexico*. Cambridge: Cambridge University Press.

Magaloni, Beatriz. 2008. "Credible Power-Sharing and the Longevity of Authoritarian Rule." *Comparative Political Studies* 41(4/5), 715–41.

Magaloni, Beatriz and Ruth Kricheli. 2010. "Political Order and One-Party Rule." *Annual Review of Political Science* 13, 123–43.

Magee, Gary B. and Andrew S. Thompson. 2006. " 'Lines of Credit, Debts of Obligation': Migrant Remittances to Britain, c. 1875–1913." *The Economic History Review* 59(3), 539–77.

Malesky, Edmund. 2009. "Foreign Direct Investors as Agents of Economic Transition: An Instrumental Variables Analysis." *Quarterly Journal of Political Science* 4(1), 59–85.

Malesky, Edmund and Paul Schuler. 2011. "The Single-Party Dictator's Dilemma: Information in Elections without Opposition." *Legislative Studies Quarterly* 36(4), 491–530.

Malhotra, Neil, Yotam Margalit, and Cecilia Hyunjung Mo. 2013. "Economic Explanations for Opposition to Immigration: Distinguishing between Prevalence and Conditional Impact." *American Journal of Political Science* 57(2), 391–410.

Manacorda, Marco and Andrea Tesei. 2016. "Liberation Technology: Mobile Phones and Political Mobilization in Africa." Working paper, Queen Mary University of London.

Manion, Melanie. 2006. "Democracy, Community, Trust: The Impact of Elections in Rural China." *Comparative Political Studies* 39(3), 301–24.

Mares, Isabela and Lauren Young. 2016. "Buying, Expropriating, and Stealing Votes." *Annual Review of Political Science* 19, 267–88.

Marinov, Nikolay and Hein Goemans. 2014. "Coups and Democracy." *British Journal of Political Science* 44(4), 799–825.

Martinez-Bravo, Monica, Gerard Padró i Miquel, Nancy Qian, and Yang Yao. 2011. "Do Local Elections in Non-Democracies Increase Accountability? Evidence from Rural China." National Bureau of Economic Research, Working Paper no. 16948.

Mascarenhas, Raechelle and Todd Sandler. 2014. "Remittances and Terrorism: A Global Analysis." *Defence and Peace Economics* 25(4), 331–47.

Mattes, Robert, Boniface Dulani, and E. Gyimah-Boadi. 2016. "Africa's Growth Dividend? Lived Poverty Drops Across Much of the Continent." Afrobarometer Policy Paper no. 29.

Maxfield, Sylvia. 1998. "Understanding the Political Implications of Financial Internationalization in Emerging Market Countries." *World Development* 26(7), 1,201–19.

Mayda, Anna M. 2010. "International Migration: A Panel Data Analysis of the Determinants of Bilateral Flows." *Journal of Population Economics* 23(4), 1,249–74.

Maydom, Barry. 2017. "Migrant Remittances and Democracy." PhD thesis, University of Oxford.

Mbow, Penda. 2008. "Senegal: The Return of Personalism." *Journal of Democracy* 19(1), 156–69.

McCargo, Duncan. 2005. "Cambodia: Getting Away with Authoritarianism?" *Journal of Democracy* 16(4), 98–112.

McCargo, Duncan. 2014. "Cambodia in 2013: (No) Country for Old Men?" *Asian Survey* 54(1), 71–77.

McCarthy, John D. and Mayer N. Zald. 1977. "Resource Mobilization and Social Movements: A Partial Theory." *American Journal of Sociology* 82(6), 1,212–41.

McDonnell, Duncan and Luis Cabrera. 2019. "The Right-Wing Populism of India's Bharatiya Janata Party (and Why Comparativists Should Care)." *Democratization* 26(3), 484–501.

McFaul, Michael. 2002. "The Fourth Wave of Democracy and Dictatorship: Noncooperative Transitions in the Postcommunist World." *World Politics* 54(2), 212–44.

McKeown, Adam. 2004. "Global Migration 1846–1940." *Journal of World History* 15(2), 155–89.

McLauchlin, Theodore. 2010. "Loyalty Strategies and Military Defection in Rebellion." *Comparative Politics* 42(3), 333–50.

McMann, Kelly M. 2006. *Economic Autonomy and Democracy: Hybrid Regimes in Russia and Kyrgyzstan*. Cambridge: Cambridge University Press.

Mendola, Mariapia. 2017. "International Migration and Informal Social Protection in Rural Mozambique." *Research in Economics* 71(2), 282–90.

Meseguer, Covadonga and Francisco Javier Aparicio. 2012. "Supply or Demand? Migration and Political Manipulation in Mexico." *Studies in Comparative International Development* 47(4), 411–40.

Meseguer, Covadonga, Sebastián Lavezzolo, and Francisco Javier Aparicio. 2016. "Financial Remittances, Trans-Border Conversations, and the State." *Comparative Migration Studies* 4(1), 1–30.

Method, Sierra and Victor Odundo Owuor. 2018. "Understanding SDG 10.C. Global Market on Remittances." *One Earth Future Research*. Available at: https://tinyurl.com/yaf8mp4c [accessed 11 June 2020].

Meyer, David S. 2004. "Protest and Political Opportunities." *Annual Review of Sociology* 30, 125–45.

Milanovic, Branko. 2016. *Global Inequality: A New Approach for the Age of Globalization*. Cambridge: Harvard University Press.

Miller, Andrew C. 2011. "Debunking the Myth of the 'Good' Coup d'Etat in Africa." *African Studies Quarterly* 12(2), 45–70.

Miller, David. 2005. "Immigration: The Case for Limits." In Andrew I. Cohen and Christopher Heath Wellman (eds), *Contemporary Debates in Applied Ethics*. Malden, MA: Blackwell, 193–206.

Miller, David. 2016. *Strangers in Our Midst: The Political Philosophy of Immigration*. Cambridge, MA: Harvard University Press.

Miller, Gina Lei and Emily Hencken Ritter. 2014. "Emigrants and the Onset of Civil War." *Journal of Peace Research* 51(1), 51–64.

Miller, Michael K. 2020. "The Strategic Origins of Electoral Authoritarianism." *British Journal of Political Science* 50(1), 17–44.

Miller, Michael K. and Margaret E. Peters. 2020. "Restraining the Huddled Masses: Migration Policy and Autocratic Survival." *British Journal of Political Science* 50(2), 403–33.

Mina, Wasseem. 2019. "Diaspora and Government Welfare Spending: Do Migrant Remittances Increase Public Social Protection?" *Economic Notes* 48(3), 1–18.

Mirilovic, Nikola. 2015. "Regime Type, International Migration, and the Politics of Dual Citizenship Toleration." *International Political Science Review* 36(5), 510–25.

Mohapatra, Sanket. 2010 (December). "Taxing Remittances Is Not a Good Idea." World Bank Blogs, 18 December. Available at: https://blogs.worldbank.org/peoplemove/taxing -remittances-is-not-a-good-idea [accessed 14 June 2021].

Mohapatra, Sanket, Blanca Moreno-Dodson, and Dilip Ratha. 2012. "Migration, Taxation, and Inequality." Economic Premise no. 80. Washington, DC: World Bank.

Monyake, Moletsane. 2016. "Does Personal Experience of Bribery Explain Protest Participation in Africa?" Afrobarometer Working Paper no. 167.

Moore, Barrington. 1966. *Social Orgins of Dictatorship and Democracy*. Boston: Beacon Press.

Morgenbesser, Lee. 2017. "The Failure of Democratisation by Elections in Cambodia." *Contemporary Politics* 23(2), 135–55.

Morgenbesser, Lee. 2018. "Misclassification on the Mekong: The Origins of Hun Sen's Personalist Dictatorship." *Democratization* 25(2), 191–208.

Morrison, Kevin. 2009. "Oil, Non-Tax Revenue, and the Redistributional Foundations of Regime Stability." *International Organization* 63(1), 107–38.

Morrison, Kevin M. 2014. *Nontaxation and Representation: The Fiscal Foundations of Political Stability.* New York: Cambridge University Press.

Morse, Yonatan L. 2018. *How Autocrats Compete: Parties, Patrons, and Unfair Elections in Africa.* Cambridge: Cambridge University Press.

Moses, Jonathon W. 2011. *Emigration and Political Development.* New York: Cambridge University Press.

Moses, Jonathon W. 2012. "Emigration and Political Development: Exploring the National and International Nexus." *Migration and Development* 1(1), 123–37.

Mosley, Layna and David A. Singer. 2015. "Migration, Labor, and the International Political Economy." *Annual Review of Political Science* 18, 283–301.

Moss, Dana M. 2016. "Transnational Repression, Diaspora Mobilization, and The Case of the Arab Spring." *Social Problems* 63(4), 480–98.

Mueller, Lisa. 2018. *Political Protest in Contemporary Africa.* Cambridge: Cambridge University Press.

Munshi, Kaivan and Mark Rosenzweig. 2015. *Insiders and Outsiders: Local Ethnic Politics and Public Goods Provision.* Tech. rept. National Bureau of Economic Research.

Muradov, Bakhodyr and Alisher Ilkhamov. 2014. "Uzbekistan's Cotton Sector: Financial Flows and Distribution of Resources." Open Society Foundations Working Paper. Available at: https://www.opensocietyfoundations.org/publications/ [accessed 14 June 2021].

Murdie, Amanda and Tavishi Bhasin. 2011. "Aiding and Abetting: Human Rights INGOs and Domestic Protest." *Journal of Conflict Resolution* 55(2), 163–91.

Nathan, Noah L. 2016. "Local Ethnic Geography, Expectations of Favoritism and Voting in Urban Ghana." *Comparative Political Studies* 49(14), 1,896–929.

Ncube, Mthuli. 2015. "Introduction." In Mthuli Ncube and Charles Leyeka Lufumpa (eds), *The Emerging Middle Class in Africa.* London: Routledge, 1–9.

Nichter, Simeon. 2008. "Vote Buying or Turnout Buying? Machine Politics and the Secret Ballot." *American Political Science Review* 102(1), 19–31.

Nordlinger, Eric A. 1977. *Soldiers in Politics: Military Coups and Governments.* Englewood Cliffs: Prentice Hall.

Norén-Nilsson, Astrid. 2016. "Good Gifts, Bad Gifts, and Rights: Cambodian Popular Perceptions and the 2013 Elections." *Pacific Affairs* 89(4), 795–815.

North, Douglass C., John Joseph Wallis, Barry R. Weingast et al. 2009. *Violence and Social Orders: A Conceptual Framework for Interpreting Recorded Human History.* Cambridge: Cambridge University Press.

Nyblade, Benjamin and Angela O'Mahony. 2014. "Migrants' Remittances and Home Country Elections: Cross-National and Subnational Evidence." *Studies in Comparative International Development* 49(1), 44–66.

Oberman, Kieran. 2015. "Poverty and Immigration Policy." *American Political Science Review* 109(2), 239–51.

O'Donnell, Guillermo and Philippe Schmitter. 1986. *Transitions from Authoritarian Rule: Tentative Conclusions about Uncertain Democracies.* Baltimore: Johns Hopkins University Press.

OECD, and CDRI. 2017. *Interrelations between Public Policies, Migration and Development in Cambodia*. Paris: OECD.

Oette, Lutz and Mohamed Abdelsalam Babiker. 2017. "Migration Control à la Khartoum: EU External Engagement and Human Rights Protection in the Horn of Africa." *Refugee Survey Quarterly* 36(4), 64–89.

Olney, William W. 2013. "A Race to the Bottom? Employment Protection and Foreign Direct Investment." *Journal of International Economics* 91(2), 191–203.

O'Mahony, Angela. 2013. "Political Investment: Remittances and Elections." *British Journal of Political Science* 43(4), 799–820.

Omgba, Luc D. 2009. "On the Duration of Political Power in Africa: The Role of Oil Rents." *Comparative Political Studies* 42(3), 416–36.

Ong, Lynette H. and Donglin Han. 2019. "What Drives People to Protest in an Authoritarian Country? Resources and Rewards vs Risks of Protests in Urban and Rural China." *Political Studies* 67(1), 224–48.

Open Source. 2015. "Rustam Inoyatov: The Most Feared Man in Uzbekistan." Open Source Investigations. Available at: https://www.opensourceinvestigations.com/uzbekistan/ [accessed 14 June 2021].

Orozco, Manuel and Michelle Lapointe. 2004. "Mexican Hometown Associations and Development Opportunities." *Journal of International Affairs* 57(2), 31–51.

Østergaard-Nielsen, Eva (ed.). 2003a. *International Migration and Sending Countries: Perceptions, Policies and Transnational Relations*. London: Palgrave Macmillan.

Østergaard-Nielsen, Eva. 2003b. "The Politics of Migrants' Transnational Political Practices." *International Migration Review* 37(3), 760–86.

Ottaway, Marina and Thomas Carothers. 2000a. "The Burgeoning World of Civil Society Aid." In Ottaway and Carothers (eds) 2000b, 3–17.

Ottaway, Marina and Thomas Carothers. (eds). 2000b. *Funding Virtue: Civil Society Aid and Democracy Promotion*. Washington: Carnegie Endowment for International Peace.

Owen, Roger. 2004. *State, Power and Politics in the Making of the Modern Middle East* (3rd edn). London: Routledge.

Oxhorn, Philip D. 2010. *Organizing Civil Society: The Popular Sectors and the Struggle for Democracy in Chile*. University Park: Penn State University Press.

Paarlberg, Michael A. 2017. "Transnational Militancy. Diaspora Influence over Electoral Activity in Latin America." *Comparative Politics* (49)4, 541–59.

Palit, Parama Sinha. 2019. "Modi and the Indian Diaspora." RSIS Publications, Nanyang Technical University, Singapore. Available at: https://www.rsis.edu.sg/rsis-publication/rsis/modi-and-the-indian-diaspora/ [accessed 14 June2021].

Pan, Jennifer. 2020. *Welfare for Autocrats: How Social Assistance in China Cares for its Rulers*. New York: Oxford University Press.

Pasura, Dominic. 2009. *Zimbabwean Migrants in Britain: An Overview*. Project Report, Network Migration in Europe. Available at: http://eprints.gla.ac.uk/139144/ [accessed 14 June 2021].

Pasura, Dominic. 2010. "Zimbabwe's New Diaspora: Displacement and the Cultural Politics of Survival." In JoAnn McGregor and Ranka Primorac (eds), *Zimbabwean Transnational DiasporaPolitics in Britain*. Oxford: Berghahn Books, 103–21.

Pattie, Charles, Patrick Seyd, and Paul Whiteley. 2004. *Citizenship in Britain: Values, Participation and Democracy*. Cambridge: Cambridge University Press.

Payne, Leigh A. and Gabriel Pereira. 2016. "Corporate Complicity in International Human Rights Violations." *Annual Review of Law and Social Science* 12, 63–84.

Penney, Joe. 2018. "Europe Benefits by Bankrolling an Anti-Migrant Effort. Niger Pays a Price." *The New York Times*, 25 August. Available at: https://tinyurl.com/rc2xn7n [accessed 16 December 2019].

Pepinsky, Thomas. 2007. "Autocracy, Elections and Fiscal Policy in Malaysia." *Studies in Comparative International Development* 42(1/2), 136–63.

Pepinsky, Thomas. 2014. "The Institutional Turn in Comparative Authoritarianism." *British Journal of Political Science* 44(3), 631–53.

Pérez-Armendáriz, Clarisa. 2014. "Cross-Border Discussions and Political Behavior in Migrant-Sending Countries." *Studies in Comparative International Development* 49(1), 67–88.

Pérez-Armendáriz, Clarisa. 2021. "Migrant Transnationalism in Violent Democracies." *Journal of Ethnic and Migration Studies* 47(6), 1,327–48.

Pérez-Armendáriz, Clarisa and David Crow. 2010. "Do Migrants Remit Democracy? International Migration, Political Beliefs and Behavior in Mexico." *Comparative Political Studies* 43(1), 119–48.

Pérez-Armendáriz, Clarisa and Lauren Duquette-Rury. 2021. "The 3 × 1 Program for Migrants and Vigilante Groups in Contemporary Mexico." *Journal of Ethnic and Migration Studies* 47(6), 1,414–33.

Perkins, Richard and Eric Neumayer. 2013. "The Ties That Bind: The Role of Migrants in the Uneven Geography of International Telephone Traffic." *Global Networks* 13(1), 79–100.

Peterson, Brenton D., Sonal S. Pandya, and David Leblang. 2014. "Doctors with Borders: Occupational Licensing as an Implicit Barrier to High Skill Migration." *Public Choice* 160(1/2), 45–63.

Peterson, Timothy M. and James M. Scott. 2018. "The Democracy Aid Calculus: Regimes, Political Opponents, and the Allocation of US Democracy Assistance, 1981–2009." *International Interactions* 44(2), 268–93.

Pevehouse, Jon C. 2005. *Democracy from Above: Regional Organizations and Democratization*. New York: Cambridge University Press.

Pew Research Center. 2017. "Origins and Destinations of European Union Migrants within the EU." *Pew Research Center: Global Attitudes & Trends*, June. Available at: https://tinyurl.com/y7jsdo4y [accessed 5 June 2020].

Pfaelzer, Jean. 2007. *Driven Out: The Forgotten War against Chinese Americans*. New York: Random House.

Pfaff, Steven. 2006. *Exit-Voice Dynamics and the Collapse of East Germany*. Durham: Duke University Press.

Pfutze, Tobias. 2012. "Does Migration Promote Democratization? Evidence from the Mexican Transition." *Journal of Comparative Economics* 40(2), 159–75.

Pfutze, Tobias. 2014. "Clientelism vs. Social Learning: The Electoral Effects of International Migration." *International Studies Quarterly* 58(2), 295–307.

Pinckney, Jonathan C. 2020. *From Dissent to Democracy: The Promise and Perils of Civil Resistance Transitions*. Oxford: Oxford University Press.

Pion-Berlin, David, Diego Esparza, and Kevin Grisham. 2014. "Staying Quartered: Civilian Uprisings and Military Disobedience in the Twenty-First Century." *Comparative Political Studies* 47(2), 230–59.

Pogge, Thomas. 1997. "Migration and Poverty." In Veit Bader (ed.), *Citizenship and Exclusion.* London: Palgrave Macmillan, 12–27.

Pogge, Thomas. 2005. "World Poverty and Human Rights." *Ethics and International Affairs* 19(1), 1–7.

Ponce, Juan, Iliana Olivie, and Mercedes Onofa. 2011. "The Role of International Remittances in Health Outcomes in Ecuador: Prevention and Response to Shocks." *International Migration Review* 45(3), 727–45.

Posso, Alberto. 2012. "Remittances and Aggregate Labor Supply: Evidence from Sixty-Six Developing Nations." *The Developing Economies* 50, 25–39.

Powell, Jonathan M. 2014. "Regime Vulnerability and the Diversionary Threat of Force." *Journal of Conflict Resolution* 58(1), 169–96.

Powell, Jonathan M. and Mwita Chacha. 2016. "Investing in Stability: Economic Interdependence, Coups d'État, and the Capitalist Peace." *Journal of Peace Research* 53(4), 525–38.

Pradhan, Gyan, Mukti Upadhyay, and Kamal Upadhyaya. 2008. "Remittances and Economic Growth in Developing Countries." *The European Journal of Development Research* 20(3), 497–506.

Prichard, Wilson, Alex Cobham, and Andrew Goodall. 2014. "The ICTD Government Revenue Dataset." ICTD Working Paper 19, Available at: https://papers.ssrn.com/sol3/papers.cfm?abstract_id=2496442 [accessed 14 June 2021].

Prichard, Wilson, Paola Salardi, and Paul Segal. 2018. "Taxation, Non-Tax Revenue and Democracy: New Evidence Using New Cross-Country Data." *World Development* 109, 295–312.

Pridham, Geoffrey. 1994. "The International Dimension of Democratisation: Theory, Practice, and Inter-regional Comparisons." In Geoffrey Pridham, Eric Herring, and George Sanford (eds), *Building Democracy? The International Dimension of Democratization in Eastern Europe.* New York: St. Martin's Press, 7–31.

Pritchett, Lant. 1997. "Divergence, Big Time." *Journal of Economic Perspectives* 3(11), 3–17.

Przeworski, Adam. 1991. *Democracy and the Market. Political and Economic Reforms in Eastern Europe and Latin America.* New York: Cambridge University Press.

Quinn, Dennis P. 2002. "Democracy and International Financial Liberalization." Working paper, Georgetown University.

Ratha, Dilip. 2003. "Workers' Remittances: An Important and Stable Source of External Development Finance." In *Global Development Finance 2003.* Washington: World Bank, 157–75.

Ratha, Dilip and William Shaw. 2007. "South–South Migration and Remittances." World Bank Working Paper no. 102.

Ratha, Dilip, Sanket Mohapatra, Çaglar Özden, Sonia Plaza, William Shaw, and Abebe Shimeles. 2011. *Leveraging Migration for Africa. Remittances, Skills and Investments.* Washington: World Bank.

Ratha, Dilip, Supriyo De, Eung Ju Kim, Sonia Plaza, Ganesh Seshan, and Nadege Desiree Yameogo. 2019. "Remittances to Low- and Middle-Income Countries on Track to Reach

$551 Billion in 2019 and $597 Billion by 2021." Washington, DC: World Bank. Available at: https://tinyurl.com/v3x6y2j [accessed 2 March 2020].

Regan, Patrick M. and Richard W. Frank. 2014. "Migrant Remittances and the Onset of Civil War." *Conflict Management and Peace Science* 31(5), 502–20.

Resnick, Danielle and Daniela Casale. 2011. "The Political Participation of Africa's Youth: Turnout, Partisanship, and Protest." Afrobarometer Working Paper no. 136.

Riedl, Rachel Beatty, Dan Slater, Joseph Wong, and Daniel Ziblatt. 2020. "Authoritarian-Led Democratization." *Annual Review of Political Science* 23, 315–32.

Risse, Thomas. 2002. "Transnational Actors and World Politics." In Walter von Carlsnaes Thomas Risse and Beth Simmons (eds), *Handbook of International Relations*. London: Sage, 255–74.

Risse, Thomas and Nelli Babayan. 2015. "Democracy Promotion and the Challenges of Illiberal Regional Powers: Introduction to the Special Issue." *Democratization* 22(3), 381–99.

Rivera, Mauricio and Kristian S. Gleditsch. 2013. "Fresh Carnations or All Thorn, No Rose? Nonviolent Campaigns and Transitions in Autocracies." *Journal of Peace Research* 50(3), 385–400.

Roberto, Rigobon and Dani Rodrik. 2005. "Rule of Law, Democracy, Openness, and Income: Estimating the Interrelationships." *Economics of Transition* 13(3), 533–64.

Roberts, Margaret E. 2018. *Censored: Distraction and Diversion inside China's Great Firewall.* Princeton: Princeton University Press.

Robinson, James A. and Thierry Verdier. 2013. "The Political Economy of Clientelism." *The Scandinavian Journal of Economics* 115(2), 260–91.

Rosenfeld, Bryn. 2017. "Reevaluating the Middle-Class Protest Paradigm: A Case-Control Study of Democratic Protest Coalitions in Russia." *American Political Science Review* 111(4), 637–52.

Rosenfeld, Bryn. 2020. *The Autocratic Middle Class: How State Dependency Reduces the Demand for Democracy.* Princeton: Princeton University Press.

Ross, Michael L. 2001. "Does Oil Hinder Democracy?" *World Politics* 53(3), 325–61.

Ross, Michael L. 2004. "Does Taxation Lead to Representation?" *British Journal of Political Science* 34(2), 229–49.

Ross, Michael L. 2012. *The Oil Curse: How Petroleum Wealth Shapes the Development of Nations.* Princeton: Princeton University Press.

Ross, Michael L., Chad Hazlett, Paasha and Mahdavi. 2017. "Global Progress and Backsliding on Gasoline Taxes and Subsidies." *Nature Energy* 2, art. 16,201. Online first: DOI: 10.1038/nenergy.2016.201.

Roth, Vathana and Luca Tiberti. 2017. "Economic Effects of Migration on the Left-Behind in Cambodia." *The Journal of Development Studies* 53(11), 1,787–805.

Roth, Vathana, Dalis Phann, Vutha Hing, and Sreymom Sum. 2015. "Estimating the Economic Effects of Remittances on the Left-behind in Cambodia." Partnership for Economic Policy, PEP Working Paper 2015–11. Available at: https://papers.ssrn.com/sol3/papers.cfm?abstract_id=3167401 [accessed 14 June 2021].

Rother, Stefan. 2009. "Changed in Migration? Philippine Return Migrants and (Un)Democratic Remittances." *European Journal of East Asian Studies* 8(2), 245–74.

Rudra, Nita. 2005. "Globalization and the Strengthening of Democracy in the Developing World." *American Journal of Political Science* 49(4), 704–30.

Rudra, Nita 2008. *Globalization and the Race to the Bottom in Developing Countries.* Cambridge: Cambridge University Press.

Rueschemeyer, Dietrich, Evelyne H. Stephens, and John D. Stephens. 1992. *Capitalist Development and Democracy.* Chicago: University of Chicago Press.

Ruhs, Martin. 2013. *The Price of Rights: Regulating International Labor Migration.* Princeton: Princeton University Press.

Ruijgrok, Kris. 2017. "From the Web to the Streets: Internet and Protests under Authoritarian Regimes." *Democratization* 24(3), 498–520.

Sachsenröder, Wolfgang. 2018. *Power Broking in the Shade: Party Finances and Money Politics in Southeast Asia.* Singapore: World Scientific.

Safi, Michael. 2019. "Protests Rage Around the World—but What Comes Next?" *The Guardian* October 25. Available at: https://tinyurl.com/yxjdm74k [accessed 12 December 2019].

Saine, Abdoulaye. 2009. *The Paradox of Third-Wave Democratization in Africa: The Gambia under AFPRC-APRC Rule, 1994–2008.* Plymouth: Lexington Books.

Salzbrunn, Monika. 2009. "Glocal Migration and Transnational Politics: The Case of Senegal." Center for Global Studies at George Mason University, Working Paper no. 8.

Sana, Mariano and Chiung-Yin Hu. 2006. "Is International Migration a Substitute for Social Security?" *Well-Being and Social Policy* 2(2), 27–48.

Scarritt, James R., Susan M. McMillan, and Shaheen Mozaffar. 2001. "The Interaction Between Democracy and Ethnopolitical Protest and Rebellion in Africa." *Comparative Political Studies* 34(7), 800–27.

Schedler, Andreas. 2013. *The Politics of Uncertainty: Sustaining and Subverting Electoral Authoritarianism.* Oxford: Oxford University Press.

Schmidt, Jürgen. 2020. "The German Labour Movement, 1830s–1840s: Early Efforts at Political Transnationalism." *Journal of Ethnic and Migration Studies* 46(6), 1,025–39.

Schock, Kurt. 2005. *Unarmed Insurrections: People Power Movements in Nondemocracies.* Minneapolis: University of Minnesota Press.

Schock, Kurt. 2014. "People Power and Political Opportunities: Social Movement Mobilization and Outcomes in the Philippines and Burma." *Social Problems* 46(3), 355–75.

Schrank, Aaron. 2019. "How People in LA Are Helping Elect a Prime Minister In India." *LA-ist,* April. Available at: https://tinyurl.com/yalor2pj [accessed 5 June 2020].

Schrey, Denis, Allan Tran-Sam, and Stefanie Hartwig. 2013. "Parliamentary Elections 2013 and the Development of the Political Parties in Cambodia." KAS International Report 11. Available at: https://www.kas.de/c/document_library/get_file?uuid=1632a800-193a-7745-2475-c52a0d73b04f&groupId=252038 [accessed 14 June 2021].

Schwartzman, Kathleen C. 1998. "Globalization and Democracy." *Annual Review of Sociology* 24(1), 159–81.

Scott, James M. and Carie A. Steele. 2011. "Sponsoring Democracy: The United States and Democracy Aid to the Developing World, 1988–2001." *International Studies Quarterly* 55(1), 47–69.

Sellars, Emily. 2019. "Emigration and Collective Action." *Journal of Politics* 81(4), 1,210–222.

Sen, Amartya. 1999. *Development as Freedom.* Oxford: Oxford University Press.

Shain, Yossi. 1999. *Marketing the American Creed Abroad: Diaspora in the U.S. and Their Homeland*. New York: Cambridge University Press.

Shankar, Soumya. 2019. "India's Liberal Expats Are Modi's Biggest Fans." *Foreign Policy*, 7 May. Available at: https://foreignpolicy.com/2019/05/07/ [accessed 14 June 2021].

Shannon, Megan, Clayton Thyne, Sarah Hayden, and Amanda Dugan. 2015. "The International Community's Reaction to Coups." *Foreign Policy Analysis* 11(4), 363–76.

Shin, Adrian J. 2017. "Tyrants and Migrants: Authoritarian Immigration Policy." *Comparative Political Studies* 50(1), 14–40.

Shirk, Susan L. 2018. "China in Xi's 'New Era': The Return to Personalistic Rule." *Journal of Democracy* 29(2), 22–36.

Siegel, Melissa and Sonja Fransen. 2013. "New Techonologies in Remittance Sending: Opportunities for Mobile Remittances in Africa." *African Journal of Science, Techonology, Innovation and Development* 5(5), 423–38.

Simoni, Valerio and Jeremie Voirol. 2021. "Remittances and Morality: Family Obligations, Development, and the Ethical Demands of Migration." *Journal of Ethnic and Migration Studies* 47(11), 2,516–36.

Sinclair, Thornton. 1938. "The Nazi Party Rally at Nuremberg." *The Public Opinion Quarterly* 2(4), 570–83.

Singer, David A. 2012. "The Family Channel: Migrant Remittances and Government Finance." MIT Working Paper no. 2012–23.

Singer, Peter. 2010. *The Life You Can Save: How to Do Your Part to End World Poverty*. New York: Random House.

Singh, A. Didar and S. Irudaya Rajan. 2015. *Politics of Migration: Indian Emigration in a Globalized World*. New Delhi: Routledge.

Singh, Naunihal. 2014. *Seizing Power: The Strategic Logic of Military Coups*. Baltimore: Johns Hopkins University Press.

Singh, Priyansha and Mohammed Ameen Arimbra. 2019. *Indians in the Gulf: The Other Side of the Story*. Available at: https://tinyurl.com/ybcq2fak. [accessed 5 June 2020].

Slater, Dan. 2010. *Ordering Power: Contentious Politics and Authoritarian Leviathans in Southeast Asia*. New York: Cambridge University Press.

Slater, Dan and Sofia Fenner. 2011. "State Power and Staying Power: Infrastructural Mechanisms and Authoritarian Durability." *Journal of International Affairs* 65(1), 15–29.

Smith, Alastair. 2008. "The Perils of Unearned Income." *Journal of Politics* 70(3), 780–93.

Smith, Benjamin. 2004. "Oil Wealth and Regime Survival in the Developing World: 1960–1999." *American Journal of Political Science* 48(2), 232–46.

Smith, Michael P. and Matt Bakker. 2005. "The Transnational Politics of the Tomato King." *Global Networks* 2(5), 129–46.

Smyth, Jamie and Stephanie Findlay. 2019. "Narendra Modi's BJP Leans on Diaspora to Sway Voters." *Financial Times*, 12 May. Available at: https://www.ft.com/content/0eb2ccae-5b6e-11e9-9dde-7aedca0a081a [accessed 5 June 2020].

Smyth, Regina, Anton Sobolev, and Irina Soboleva. 2013. "A Well-Organized Play: Symbolic Politics and the Effect of the pro-Putin Rallies." *Problems of Post-Communism* 60(2), 24–39.

Sniderman, Paul M. and Louk Hagendoorn. 2007. *When Ways of Life Collide: Multiculturalism and Its Discontents in the Netherlands*. Princeton: Princeton University Press.

Soehl, Thomas and Roger Waldinger. 2010. "Making the Connection: Latino Immigrants and their Cross-Border Ties." *Ethnic and Racial Studies* 33(9), 1,489–510.

Song, Sarah. 2018. *Immigration and Democracy.* New York: Oxford University Press.

Spar, Deborah L. 1998. "The Spotlight and the Bottom Line: How Multinationals Export Human Rights." *Foreign Affairs* 77, 7–12.

Spilimbergo, Antonio. 2009. "Democracy and Foreign Education." *American Economic Review* 99(1), 528–43.

Starr, Harvey. 1991. "Democratic Dominoes: Diffusion Approaches to the Spread of Democracy in the International System." *Journal of Conflict Resolution* 35(2), 356–81.

Stokes, Susan C. 2005. "Perverse Accountability: A Formal Model of Machine Politics with Evidence from Argentina." *American Political Science Review* 99(3), 315–25.

Stokes, Susan C. 2007. "Political Clientelism." In Carles Boix and Susan C. Stokes (eds), *The Oxford Handbook of Comparative Politics.* New York: Oxford University Press, 604–27.

Stokes, Susan C., Thad Dunning, Marcelo Nazareno, Valeria and Brusco. 2013. *Brokers, Voters and Clientelism: The Puzzle of Distributive Politics.* New York: Cambridge University Press.

Svolik, Milan W. 2012. *The Politics of Authoritarian Rule.* New York: Cambridge University Press.

Tannenberg, Marcus. 2017. "The Autocratic Trust Bias: Politically Sensitive Survey Items and Self-Censorship." V-Dem Working Paper no. 2017–49.

Tansey, Oisín. 2016a. *The International Politics of Authoritarian Rule.* Oxford: Oxford University Press.

Tansey, Oisín. 2016b. "The Limits of the 'Democratic Coup' Thesis: International Politics and Post-Coup Authoritarianism." *Journal of Global Security Studies* 1(3), 220–34.

Tansey, Oisín. 2017. "The Fading of the Anti-Coup Norm." *Journal of Democracy* 28(1), 144–56.

Tansey, Oisín. 2018. "Lowest Common Denominator Norm Institutionalization: The Anti-Coup Norm at the United Nations." *Global Governance* 24(2), 287–306.

Tansey, Oisín, Kevin Koehler, and Alexander Schmotz. 2017. "Ties to the Rest: Autocratic Linkages and Regime Survival." *Comparative Political Studies* 50(9), 1,221–54.

Tarrow, Sidney. 2005. *The New Transnational Activism.* New York: Cambridge University Press.

Taundi, Josiah Bob. 2010. *The Pro-Democracy Movement in Zimbabwe (1998–present).* International Center on Nonviolent Conflict. Available at: https://www.nonviolent -conflict.org/wp-content/uploads/2016/02/Zimbabwe-2.pdf [accessed 14 June 2021].

Telegeography. 2020. "Telegeography Report: Executive Summary." Available at: https:// cdn2.hubspot.net/ [accessed 14 June 2021].

Tertytchnaya, Katerina, Catherine E. De Vries, Hector Solaz, and David Doyle. 2018. "When the Money Stops: Fluctuations in Financial Remittances and Incumbent Approval in Central Eastern Europe, the Caucasus and Central Asia." *American Political Science Review* 112(4), 758–74.

*The Economist.* 2011. "Big Oil's Bigger Brothers." *The Economist* 29 October. Available at: https://tinyurl.com/y3u4mpgk [accessed 28 December 2019].

*The Economist.* 2019. "Hikes in the Cost of Petrol are Fuelling Unrest in Iran." *The Economist* 17 November. Available at: https://tinyurl.com/rlhps5r [accessed 18 December 2019].

*The Economist.* 2020a. "Briefing: Ant's Jumbo IPO." *The Economist* 10 October, 19–21.

*The Economist.* 2020b. "Generation Game: Young Africans Want More Democracy." *The Economist* 5 March. Available at: https://tinyurl.com/soog2dj [accessed 8 June 2020].

Thyne, Clayton L. 2010. "Supporter of Stability or Agent of Agitation? The Effect of US Foreign Policy on Coups in Latin America, 1960–99." *Journal of Peace Research* 47(4), 449–61.

Thyne, Clayton L. and Jonathan M. Powell. 2016. "Coup d'État or Coup d'Autocracy? How Coups Impact Democratization, 1950–2008." *Foreign Policy Analysis* 12(2), 192–213.

Tiebout, Charles M. 1956. "A Pure Theory of Local Expenditures." *Journal of Political Economy* 64(5), 416–24.

Tilly, Charles. 2006. *Regimes and Repertoires.* Chicago: University of Chicago Press.

Tolstrup, Jakob. 2013. *Russia vs. the EU: External Actors in Competition for Influence in Post-Soviet States.* Boulder: Lynne Rienner Publishers.

Tsourapas, Gerasimos. 2015. "Why Do States Develop Multi-Tier Emigrant Policies? Evidence from Egypt." *Journal of Ethnic and Migration Studies* 41(13), 2,192–214.

Tsui, Kevin K. 2011. "More Oil, Less Democracy: Evidence from Worldwide Crude Oil Discoveries." *Economic Journal* 121(551), 89–115.

Tucker, Joshua A. 2007. "Enough! Electoral Fraud, Collective Action Problems, and Post-Communist Colored Revolutions." *Perspectives on Politics* 5(3), 535–51.

Tyburski, Michael D. 2014. "Curse or Cure? Migrant Remittances and Corruption." *Journal of Politics* 76(3), 814–24.

Ulfelder, Jay. 2007. "Natural-Resource Wealth and the Survival of Autocracy." *Comparative Political Studies* 40(8), 995–1,018.

Um, Khatharya. 2014. "Cambodia in 2013: The Winds of Change." *Southeast Asian Affairs* 2014(1), 97–116.

Un, Kheang. 2005. "Patronage Politics and Hybrid Democracy: Political Change in Cambodia, 1993–2003." *Asian Perspective* 29(2), 203–30.

UNCTAD. 2019. *World Investment Report 2019: Special Economic Zones.* New York: United Nations.

Unger, Peter K. 1996. *Living High and Letting Die: Our Illusion of Innocence.* New York: Oxford University Press.

United Nations. 2013. *International Migration Policies: Government Views and Priorities.* New York: United Nations, Department of Economic and Social Affairs, Population Division.

United Nations. 2017. *International Migration Report 2017: Highlights.* New York: United Nations, Department of Economic and Social Affairs, Population Division.

United Nations. 2019. *International Migration Stock 2019: Highlights.* New York: United Nations, Department of Economic and Social Affairs, Population Division.

Urdal, Henrik. 2006. "A Clash of Generations? Youth Bulges and Political Violence." *International Studies Quarterly* 50(3), 607–29.

Utarasint, Daungyewa. 2019. "The Deep South." *Contemporary Southeast Asia* 41(2), 207–15.

Van Hear, Nicholas and Robin Cohen. 2017. "Diasporas and Conflict: Distance, Contiguity and Spheres of Engagement." *Oxford Development Studies* 45(2), 171–84.

Vanderhill, Rachel. 2013. *Promoting Authoritarianism Abroad.* Boulder: Lynne Rienner Publishers.

Vari-Lavoisier, Ilka. 2016. "The Economic Side of Social Remittances: How Money and Ideas Circulate between Paris, Dakar, and New York." *Comparative Migration Studies* 4, art. 20: DOI: 10.1186/s40878-016-0039-6.

Varshney, Ashutosh. 2019. "Modi Consolidates Power: Electoral Vibrancy, Mounting Liberal Deficits." *Journal of Democracy* 30(4), 63–77.

Vengroff, Richard and Michael Magala. 2001. "Democratic Reform, Transition and Consolidation: Evidence from Senegal's 2000 Presidential Election." *Journal of Modern African Studies* 39(1), 129–62.

Verba, Sidney, Kay Lehman Schlozman, and Henry E. Brady. 1995. *Voice and Equality: Civic Voluntarism in American Politics*. Cambridge: Harvard University Press.

Vertovec, Steven and Robin Cohen (eds). 1999. *Migration, Diasporas and Transnationalism*. Cheltenham: Edward Elgar.

Victor, David G. 2009. "The Politics of Fossil-Fuel Subsidies." IISD *The Global Studies Initiative*. Available at: https://www.iisd.org/gsi/sites/default/files/politics_ffs.pdf [accessed 14 June 2021].

Villalón, Leonardo A. 1995. *Islamic Society and State Power in Senegal: Disciples and Citizens in Fatick*. Cambridge: Cambridge University Press.

von Soest, Christian. 2015. "Democracy Prevention: The International Collaboration of Authoritarian Regimes." *European Journal of Political Research* 54(4), 623–38.

Waldinger, Roger. 2008. "Between 'Here' and 'There': Immigrant Cross-Border Activities and Loyalties." *International Migration Review* 42(1), 3–29.

Wallace, Jeremy. 2013. "Cities, Redistribution, and Authoritarian Regime Survival." *Journal of Politics* 75(3), 632–45.

Walton, John and Charles Ragin. 1990. "Global and National Sources of Political Protest: Third World Responses to the Debt Crisis." *American Sociological Review* 55(6), 876–90.

Wantchekon, Léonard and Omar García-Ponce. 2017. "Critical Junctures: Independence Movements and Democracy in Africa." Working paper, Princeton University.

Waslin, Michele. 2020. "The Use of Executive Orders and Proclamations to Create Immigration Policy: Trump in Historical Perspective." *Journal on Migration and Human Security* 8(1), 54–67.

Way, Lucan A. and Steven Levitsky. 2006. "The Dynamics of Autocratic Coercion after the Cold War." *Communist and Post-Communist Studies* 39(3), 387–410.

Weidmann, Nils B. and Espen Geelmuyden Rød. 2019. *The Internet and Political Protest in Autocracies*. Oxford: Oxford University Press.

White, Peter B., Dragana Vidovic, Belén González, Kristian S. Gleditsch, and David E. Cunningham. 2015. "Nonviolence as a Weapon of the Resourceful: From Claims to Tactics in Mobilization." *Mobilization* 20(4), 471–91.

Whitehead, Laurence. 1996. "The International Dimensions of Democratization." In Laurence Whitehead (ed.), *The International Dimensions of Democratization*. Oxford: Oxford University Press, 3–25.

Williamson, Jeffrey G. 1998. "Globalization, Labor Markets and Policy Backlash in the Past." *Journal of Economic Perspectives* 12(4), 51–72.

Williamson, John. 1993. "Democracy and the 'Washington Consensus.'" *World Development* 21(8), 1,329–36.

Wimmer, Andreas. 1997. "Who Owns the State? Understanding Ethnic Conflict in Post-Colonial Societies." *Nations and Nationalism* 3(4), 631–66.

World Bank. 2006a. *The Development Impact of Workers' Remittances in Latin America: Main Findings (vol. 1).* Washington: World Bank.

World Bank. 2006b. *The Development Impact of Workers' Remittances in Latin America: Main Findings (vols. 1 & 2).* Washington: World Bank.

World Bank. 2006c. *The Development Impact of Workers' Remittances in Latin America: Main Findings (vol. 2).* Washington: World Bank.

World Bank. 2006d. *Global Economic Prospects: Economic Implications of Remittances and Migration.* Washington: World Bank.

World Bank. 2016. *Migration and Remittances Factbook.* Washington, DC: The World Bank Group.

World Bank. 2017. *Migration and Remittances: Recent Developments and Outlook.* Washington: World Bank.

World Bank. 2019a. *Migration and Remittances: Recent Developments and Outlook.* Washington: World Bank.

World Bank. 2019b. *World Development Indicators.* Washington, DC: World Bank.

World Bank. 2020. *World Development Report 2020: Trading for Development in the Age of Global Value Chains.* Washington: World Bank.

Wright, Joseph. 2008. "Political Competition and Democratic Stability in New Democracies." *British Journal of Political Science* 38(2), 221–45.

Wright, Joseph. 2009. "How Foreign Aid Can Foster Democratization in Authoritarian Regimes." *American Journal of Political Science* 53(3), 552–71.

Wright, Joseph. 2011. "Electoral Spending Cycles in Dictatorships." Unpublished manuscript, Pennsylvania State University.

Wright, Joseph and Daejee Bak. 2016. "Measuring Autocratic Regime Stability." *Research and Politics* 3(1), 1–7.

Wright, Joseph, Erica Frantz, and Barbara Geddes. 2015. "Oil and Autocratic Regime Survival." *British Journal of Political Science* 42(5), 287–306.

Xu, Xu. 2021. "To Repress or To Co-opt? Authoritarian Control in the Age of Digital Surveillance." *American Journal of Political Science* 65(2), 309–25.

Yakouchyk, Katsiaryna. 2019. "Beyond Autocracy Promotion: A Review." *Political Studies Review* 17(2), 147–60.

Yang, Dean and HwaJung Choi. 2007. "Are Remittances Insurance? Evidence from Rainfall Shocks in the Philippines." *The World Bank Economic Review* 21(2), 219–48.

Young, Daniel J. 2009. "Is Clientelism at Work in African Elections? A Study of Voting Behavior in Kenya and Zambia." Afrobarometer Working Paper no. 106.

Young, Lauren E. 2019. "The Psychology of State Repression: Fear and Dissent Decisions in Zimbabwe." *American Political Science Review* 113(1), 140–55.

Youngs, Richard. 2004. "Democracy and the Multinationals." *Democratization* 11(1), 127–47.

Zakaria, Fareed. 2019. "Why Are There So Many Protests across the Globe Right Now?" *The Washington Post* 24 October. Available at: https://tinyurl.com/y4eph9np [accessed 12 December 2019].

Zanker, Francisca and Judith Altrogge. 2019. "The Political Influence of Return: From Diaspora to Libyan Transit Returnees." *International Migration* 57(4), 167–80.

Zeilig, Leo. 2009. "Student Resistance and the Democratic Transition: Student Politics in Senegal 1999–2005." *Social Dynamics* 35(1), 68–93.

Zhunio, Maria Cristina, Sharmila Vishwasrao, and Eric P. Chiang. 2012. "The Influence of Remittances on Education and Health Outcomes: A Cross Country Study." *Applied Economics* 44(35), 4,605–16.

Zunes, Stephen. 1994. "Unarmed Insurrections against Authoritarian Governments in the Third World: A New Kind of Revolution." *Third World Quarterly* 15(3), 403–26.

# INDEX

Note: page number followed by t indicates a table; page number in *italics* indicates a figure.

Africa: middle class in, 127; protests in autocracies in: 109–13, 110t, *111. See also* Sub-Saharan Africa *and specific countries*

Afrobarometer data: for countries with autocratic governments, 205, 207; and remittance surveys, 120, 124, 131, 131t; in swing districts, 157–59; on voter turnout, 153, 155–57

age factors, and total government spending, 82, *83*

Algeria: anti-government protests in, 130; measurement of remittances to, 211; political protests in, 198; and remittances from democracies, 198

Alliance for Patriotic Reorientation and Construction (APRC), 183

Angola, measurement of remittances to, 211

anti-government protests, 100–104, *103*, 130

Armed Conflict Location and Event Data (ACLED), 101

asset protection model, 52–53, 58

Austria, anti-migration in, 2

autocratic regimes: demobilization of supporters in (*see* demobilization of supporters); elite members of, 35–36; and foreign incomes, 13–16, 213; in India, 227–30; and international forces, 35–37; and intra-European migration, 225–26; local support for, 131–35; protests in, 108–30; and remittance funding, 224–30:

welfare spending in, 165; *See also* dictatorship; opposition groups

Baldwin, Richard, 233

Banks' Cross-National Times Series Data, 101

Barrow, Adama, 183

behavior: of individuals, 202–9, 206t; mediation analysis of, 205–7, 206t; remittance effects and, 44, 202–9, 208t; of remittance recipients, 218–19; *See also* protests; turnout; voting

Belarus, political protests in, 30

Belt and Road Initiative, 162

Benin, economic factors in, 232

Bharatiya Janata Party (BJP; Indian People's Party), 227–29

brain drain: in dictatorships, 39; in Guyana, 212; and opposition groups, 98; remittance effects and, 216

Brazil: anti-migration in, 2; demobilization of supporters in, 140

Burkina Faso: anti-government protests in, 130; measurement of remittances to, 211

Cambodia: anti-regime support by migrants from, 52; emigration policies of, 181; gift-giving programs in, 139, 173–75; opposition parties in, 98–99; patronage of supporters in, 137; and remittances from democracies, 198;

Cambodia (*continued*)
surveys of remittances in, 124; voting and protests in, 134, 172–75

Cameroon: government support in swing districts in, 159; surveys of remittances in, 124; voting results in, 134

cash remittances, 203–7

cell phones: in diasporas, 185; and money transfer, 66–67; in remittance surveys, 120

Central and Eastern Europe (CEEU), 225–27

Chad, remittances from autocracies to, 195, 198

China: education and protests in, 48; election frequency in, 136; financial regulation in, 235; foreign policies of, 162, 163; income gaps in, 5; limits on cross-border information in, 234–35; pro-government rallies in, 104; trade vs. migration in, 230–33; turnout in elections in, 144–45

citizenship, and remittance effects in dictatorships, 28–33

civil liberties: and democratization, 222; and opposition party strength, 176–80, *179*; remittance effects and, 92–95

clientelism in dictatorships: and demobilization of supporters, 136–37; and family loyalty, 41–42; and household incomes, 53–54; and political discussions, 206–9; and revenue effects, 72; in Senegal, 171; and substitution effects, 76–77; and voting for ruling party, 142–44; and turnout, 60–62, *62*, and underclasses, 47, 59; weakening of, 214

Clinton, Bill, and trade with China, 231

Cold War order: collapse of, compared to remittance effects, 182; political protests during, 30–31

communication technology, 187–88: emigrants and families connected by, 190, 191–92; virtual presence and telerobotics, 233–35

Communist regimes: and anti-government protests, 97; as destination countries, 193–94; political protests in, 29, 36; pro-government rallies in, 104–5

coups: domestic, 35; military, 29–31, 35

Cuba, remittance tax in, 70

cyber-diasporas, 52

*dahiras*, 74, 170

debit cards, and money transfer, 66

demobilization, 136–61; clientelism and, 149–59; and election of rulers, 138–49, *148*; and poverty, 156–57, *157*; remittance effects and, 149–59; in swing districts, 157–58; and turnout in dictatorships, 144–49, *148*; and vote share of ruling party, 142–44, *143*

democratization: asset protection model of, 52–53; civil society and opposition party strength and, 176–80, *179*; and development, 219; in dictatorships, 42–45, 88–95; and emigration, 11; and foreign funding, 222–23; in The Gambia, 183–85; global forces and, 33–38; in India, 227–30; and neighboring countries, 92; remittance effects and, 162–86, *182*; and remittance inflows, 197–99, *198*; and resource gaps, 164–67; in Senegal, 168–72, *169*; transitions to, 180–183, *182*, 221–24

demographic remittance surveys, 120

diasporas: from Cambodia, 175; conflict-generated, 51–52; from Ethiopia, 52; from The Gambia, 185; and democratization, 190–91; from India, 227–229; and internet communication, 187–88, 191–92; from Senegal, 170–71; from Zimbabwe, 98–99

dictatorships: collapse of, 163; demobilization of support for (*see* demobilization); differences among, 180–81; elite members of, 35–36; leadership turnover in, 45 economic factors: in China, 231–32; in dictatorships, 34; in sub-Saharan Africa, 232

Ecuador, effects of remittances to, 74–75

education levels, and protests in autocracies, 48, 50

Egypt: clientelism and voting in, 47; remittances during elections in, 52

elections: in autocracies, 221; effects of remittances on, 178–79; and economic factors, 231–33; frequency of, 137; in India, 227–29; and government spending, 82, 83; monitoring of, 34; turnout factors in, 144–49, 148

elite, in dictatorships, 35–36

El Salvador, voting in, 51

emigration: ethics of, 216–17; from The Gambia, 184–85; and incumbent rulers, 224–25; from India, 227–29

employment, in remittance surveys, 120

Eritrea, election frequency in, 136

error-correction model (ECM), 79

ethics of migration policies, 214–21; and emigration, 216–17; and immigration, 217–21

Ethiopia: diaspora from, 52; remittance tax in, 70; turnout in elections in, 147

European Union (EU): as destination, 196; migration policies in, 4; populist parties in, 225–226

exit, voice, and loyalty (EVL) framework: and brain drain, 9–10, 98; and demobilization of supporters, 138; and dictatorships, 38–43; and labor migration, 226; and remittance effects, 45–56, 98

factor-price equalization, 121

foreign investment: and autocracy, 13–16, 14; and family income, 41; and oil revenues, 69; vs. remittances, 8, 223

Forum on China-Africa Cooperation, 163

Frente Farabundo Marti de Liberacion Nacional (FMLN), 51

fuel subsidies: and remittance effects, 85–88; and substitution effects, 75

FUNCINPEC, in Cambodia, 172–73

Gabon: voting results data for, 134, 135; turnout in elections in, 145–147

Gambia, The: anti-government protests in, 130; democratic transition in, 183–85; measurement of remittances to, 211; voting and remittances in, 51

geography, and remittance effects, 122

Germany: democratization in, 190; pro-government rallies in, 104

Ghana, political protests in, 29

gift-giving programs, in Cambodia, 139, 173–75

Global Burden of Disease Health Financing Collaborator Network, 84

global forces and democratization, 33–38: emigration, 9–13; foreign income and autocracy, 13–16, 14; migration vs. trade and investments, 230–33; political changes, 7–18, 233–36; remittance effects, 18–23, 19, 213. See also democratization; dictatorships

globalization. See global forces and democratization

Global North, roboticization of production in, 234

Global South: remittance effects in, 130, 163, 164, 213; socio-economic development in, 215; technology changes in, 234

Global System for Mobile Communications (GSMA), 67

government support: and substitution theory, 74; in swing districts, 157–59, 160

Guyana, brain drain in, 212

Haiti: measurement of remittances to, 211; migration from, 199; remittances from democracies to, 198

healthcare in dictatorships: foreign aid and, 70; government spending on, 83–85; and substitution effects, 73–75

Hungary: anti-migration sentiment in, 2, 3; populist leaders in, 226
Hun Sen, 172, 176

immigration: and democracy, 221–24; ethics of, 217–21
income: and clientelism, 54; and protests, 58; and voting turnout, 61, 64
incumbent rulers: in India, 227–30; intra-European migration and, 225–26; and remittances, 224–30
India: Bharatiya Janata Party (BJP), 227–29; India Development Relief Fund (IDRF), 228, 229; remittances and democracy in, 227–30
information technology, 234–35
infrastructure: and clientelism, 54; and substitution of government revenue, 74
International Centre for Tax and Development (ICTD), 78
International Organization for Migration, 188
international organizations: non-governmental organizations, 27–28, 34–37; and tax revenue in developing countries, 78–79
internet communication, 187–88, 191–92
Iran, petrol subsidies to, 85
Ireland, 121
Italy, anti-migration sentiments in, 2,3
Ivory Coast, measurement of remittances to, 211

Jammeh, Yahya, 183–85
Jordan, remittances during elections in, 52

Kazakhstan, measurement of remittances to, 211
Kenya, political protests in, 29
Khmer Rouge, 172

labor: high-skilled workers, 212–13; migration programs for, 218–20
Laos, measurement of remittances to, 211

Latin America, 203
Lesotho, 199
Libya: election frequency in, 136; measurement of remittances to, 211; migration policies of, 4
loyalty: in dictatorships, 38–42; and oil revenues to state, 69; and opposition party strength, 176–80, 179; and political dissent, 20–21; in swing districts, 157–58

Madrid, Senegalese associations in, 170
Malaysia: gift-giving programs in, 139, 140; political protests in, 29–30; voter patronage in, 137
marabouts, 168–70
Mass Mobilization in Autocracies Database (MMAD), 105–8
Mauritania, measurement of remittances to, 211
Mexico: demobilization of supporters in, 138, 140, 142; democracy in, 46; inflow of remittances to, 195; political discussions in, 203; political protests in, 29; and remittances from democracies, 54, 198; substitution of government revenue in, 74; voter patronage in, 137
middle classes: and asset protection, 53, 59; and remittance effects, 126–28
Middle East and North Africa (MENA), 67
migrants: and anti-immigrant politics, 2–4; and destination countries, 196–97; and emigration from autocratic rule, 12, 18–23; and ethics of immigration policies, 216–21; funding of opposition by (see opposition groups); in Global South, 17–18; and globalization and political change, 7–18; international destinations of, 188; intra-European, 225–26; money transfers by, 12–13; as percentage of world population, 1; remittance surveys of, 120–21; restriction of, 196; socialization of, 189–91; Temporary Migrant Programs (TMP), 219–220

military: in autocracies, 221; coups by, 29–31, 35; and demobilization of supporters, 140; government spending on, 81, 83–85; revenue effect of, 72–73; and substitution effects, 74

Mobi, Narenda, 227

mobilization: in autocracies, 47; and political interests, 49; pro-government, 104–108, *107*; resource theory of, 56–58

MoneyGram, 66

money transfer: from migrants, 12–13; and supporter demobilization, 137; technology of, 66–67

Morocco, remittances to, 195, 198

Movement for Democratic Change (MDC), 98–99

Mozambique: measurement of remittances to, 211; political discussions in, 203; voting results in, 134

Namibia: measurement of remittances to, 210; and remittances from democracies, 198; voting results in, 134

National Iranian Oil Company, 68

Nicaragua, political protests in, 29

Niger, anti-migration sentiments in, 4

Nigeria, remittance recipients in, 196

Non-Resident Gujarati Foundation (NRG), 228

nongovernmental organizations (NGO): and dictatorships, 37; foreign funding of, 222–223; and oil revenues, 69, 70

North Korea: election frequency in, 136; pro-government rallies in, 104

Norway, 191

oil and gas: remittance effects on, 85–88, 163, 164; revenues from, 67–68, 72–75; and substitution spending, 75

opposition groups: anti-government, 100–104, *103*; in autocracies, 108–30; in Cambodia, 173; and civil society groups, 176–80, *179*; in dictatorships, 51; and global protests, 100–108; 110t, *111*; and

poverty, 126–30, *129*; pro-government, 104–8, *107*, 131–35, 131t; remittance funding of, 97–135; in Senegal, 170–71; surveys of, 115–19, *116*,     124–26, 125t, 132–35132,135

Orbán, Viktor, 3

partisanship, and political remittances, 154

patronage: in autocracies, 164–67; in Cambodia, 173–74; and demobilization of supporters, 139; in dictatorships, 42–45

petrol subsidies. *See* oil and gas

Philippines, Documentary Stamp Tax in, 70

Poland, populist leaders in, 226

political rights and behavior: remittance effects on, 92–96, 214

polling stations, 146

population size, and government spending, 79

Portugal, remittance funding of opposition in, 97

poverty: and clientelistic networks, 141, 151–52; and the middle class, 127–28, *129*; and political preferences, 56–64; in remittance surveys, 120; and voting, 59–62, *62*

propaganda, 104

protests: anti-government, 100–104, *103*; clientelism and, 113–19; in dictatorships, 29–30, 48; in India, 227; methods of, 108–30, 110t, *111*; and opposition party strength, 176–80, *179*; political factors in, 22–23, 57–59; 202–9, 208t; poverty factors in, 108–9; pro-government, 104–8, *107*; remittances and, 99–108, *103*; and voting turnout, 61–63, *62*

religion, and demobilization of supporters, 142

remittances: and anti-incumbent politics, 224–230; in cash, 203–7; clientelism and, 119, 149–59; and demobilization of supporters, 136–61; and democracy, 195–202, *198*, *215*, 221–24, 227–30; and

remittances (*continued*)
  destination regimes, 191–95; and dictatorships, 79–88, *80,83*; and election of rulers, 138–49; and ethics of migration policies, 215–21; and funding of opposition, 97–135,*103,107,111*; to The Gambia, 184–85; and globalization, 230–36; and government revenue and spending, 79–88, *80, 83*; measurement by origin of, 209–11; and petrol subsidies, 85–88; and poverty, 156–57, *157*; and protests, 108–30, 110t, *111*; and repression of civil liberties, 88–95, *91, 94*; social vs. financial, 11, 187–211, 206t; sponsors of, 116–18; surveys of, 115–16, *116*; in swing districts, 157–58; taxation of, 79–80, *80*, 141–42; vs. trade and investments, 230–33; and voting turnout, 144–49, *148*; World Bank data on, 101
repression: in dictatorships, 42–45, 88–95, remittance effects and, 90–92, *91*; revenue effects and, 72–73
resource theory of mobilization, 56–58
Russia: foreign policies of, 162, 163; democratization in, 191; measurement of remittances to, 211; remittance recipients in, 196
Rwanda: measurement of remittances to, 211; turnout in elections in, 145

Salvini, Matteo, 3
Saudi Arabia: election frequency in, 136; foreign policies of, 162
Saudi Aramco, 68
Schengen Agreement, 225
Senegal: Muslim brotherhoods in, 168; *ndigal* practice in, 168–170; protests in, 51, 52, 55, 168–172, *169*; substitution of government revenue in, 74; voter patronage in, 137. *See also* dahiras; marabouts
Senegalese associations, 170
Serbia, political protests in, 30
Singapore, gift-giving programs in, 139
Social Conflict in Africa Data (SCAD), 101

South Africa: measurement of remittances to, 210; migration from, 198
Soviet Union, collapse of, 31
Spain, anti-migration sentiments in, 3
spending, government: and civil liberties and political rights, 92–95, *94*; on health and military, 83–85; petrol subsidies, 85–88; and repression, 88–95, *91*; and substitution effect, 73–77
Sub-Saharan Africa: demobilization of supporters in, 138, 152; democratic transitions in, 183; dictatorships in, 29, 36; economic liberalization in, 232
Sudan: political protests in, 29; remittances from autocracies to, 198
surveys: demobilization of supporters, 149–50; electoral support, 134–35; external validity, 134–35, *135*; falsification of votes, 150; geographical factors, 153–56, *155*; government sponsors, 123–24, 132–33; non-response, 132–33, *132*; political discussions, 203–5; remittance and protests, 119–24, *123*
Sustainable Development Agenda of United Nations, 67
Sweden: anti-migration sentiments in, 3; and factor-price equalization, 121
swing districts: political preference and turnout in, 157–58; and political remittances, 154–56, *157*; poverty levels in, 156–57, *157*
Syria, measurement of remittances to, 211

Taiwan, political protests in, 29
Tajikistan, remittances from democracies to, 198
Tanzania: gift-giving programs in, 140; government support in swing districts in, 159; measurement of remittances to, 211; and remittance surveys, 124; voter patronage in, 137; voting results in, 134
taxation: in dictatorships, 44, 50; and government spending, 79; and political

brain drain, 216–17; of remittances, 77–78, 141–42

technology: communication, 187–88, 191–92, 233–36; and dictatorships, 32–33; effect of Covid-19 on, 234; income gaps and, 5–6

telerobotics, 233–34

Temporary Migrant Programs (TMP), 219–20

Thailand: demobilization of supporters in, 140; measurement of remittances to, 210; migration patterns from, 198

Togo: government support in swing districts in, 159; measurement of remittances to, 211; and surveys of remittance, 124; voting results, 134

trade vs. migration, 230–233

transborders, political discussions of, 204, 207

Trump, Donald, 2–4

Tunisia, 52

Turkey, remittances during elections in, 52

turnout, electoral: in Cambodia, 174; and demobilization of supporters, 144–49, 148; geographical factors in, 153–56, 155; non-response by individuals in, 150; and political discussion, 202–9, 208t; in swing districts, 157–58; and vote buying, 60–62, 62

Uganda: foreign aid to, 70; government support in swing districts in, 159; measurement of remittances to, 211; and surveys of remittance, 124

United Nations: and digital money transfer, 67; and remittance transfers, 236; Sustainable Development Goals, 6; Transitional Authority in Cambodia, 172

United States, and remittance recipients, 196

Uzbekistan, oil revenues in, 69

Vajpayee, Atal Bihari, 227

value-added tax (VAT), 73, 80

Varieties of Democracy Projects, 90, 93, 94, 178

Venezuela: measurement of remittances to, 211; oil revenues in, 68; political protests in, 29; remittance tax in, 70

Vietnam: emigration policies in, 181; remittance tax in, 70; turnout in elections in, 144

voice and loyalty: and clientelism, 49–55; and political dissent, 20–21; See also exit, voice, and loyalty (EVL)

von der Leyer, Ursula, 4

voting: and clientelism, 54–56; and electoral support, 134–35; falsification of, 150; and political discussion, 202–9, 206t; political preferences and, 22–23, 59–62, 62; and turnout in elections, 144–145, 148

Wade, Abdoulaye, 167, 171–72

welfare spending: and petrol subsidies, 87; substitution of, 76–77

Western Union, 66

World Bank: health and military spending data from, 84; remittance data from, 70–71, 101; and remittance transfers, 236; as source of foreign income, 15–16, 68

World Trade Organization (WTO), and China, 231

Xi Jinping, 231

Yemen: inflow of remittances to, 195; measurement of remittances to, 211; remittance effects in, 54; remittances from autocracies to, 198

Zimbabwe: clientelism and voting in, 47; measurement of remittances to, 211

## A NOTE ON THE TYPE

This book has been composed in Arno, an Old-style serif typeface in the classic Venetian tradition, designed by Robert Slimbach at Adobe.